"Are Economists Basically Immoral?"

and Other Essays on
Economics, Ethics, and Religion
by Paul Heyne

Paul Heyne

"Are Economists Basically Immoral?"

and Other Essays on
Economics, Ethics, and Religion
by Paul Heyne

EDITED AND WITH AN INTRODUCTION BY

Geoffrey Brennan and A. M. C. Waterman

LIBERTY FUND · INDIANAPOLIS

This book is published by Liberty Fund, Inc., a foundation established to encourage study of the ideal of a society of free and responsible individuals.

The cuneiform inscription that serves as our logo and as the design motif for our endpapers is the earliest-known written appearance of the word "freedom" (*amagi*), or "liberty." It is taken from a clay document written about 2300 B.C. in the Sumerian city-state of Lagash.

C 10 9 8 7 6 5 4 3 2 1
P 10 9 8 7 6 5 4 3 2 1

Library of Congress Cataloging-in-Publication Data

Heyne, Paul T.
    Are economists basically immoral?: and other essays on economics, ethics, and religion / by Paul Heyne; edited and with an introduction by Geoffrey Brennan and A.M.C. Waterman.
        p.   cm.
    Includes bibliographical references and index.
    ISBN 978-0-86597-712-9 (hardcover: alk. paper)—ISBN 978-0-86597-713-6 (pbk.: alk. paper)   1. Economics—Moral and ethical aspects.   2. Economics—Religious aspects.   3. Economics.   I. Brennan, Geoffrey, 1944–   II. Waterman, Anthony Michael C.   III. Title.
    HB72 .H49   2008
    174—dc22

                                                                2008009188

Liberty Fund, Inc.
8335 Allison Pointe Trail, Suite 300
Indianapolis, Indiana 46250–1684

Contents

Introduction

SHORTLY BEFORE he died in 2000, Paul Heyne wrote that he had "wandered into economics in the 1950s as a divinity student interested in social ethics." Over the course of his life, he "gradually became an economist with an interest in ethics rather than an ethicist with an interest in economics." As he put it:

> I started out wondering why economists arrived at so many immoral conclusions and gradually discovered both that social systems were far more complex than I had supposed and that my notions of morality were much too simple.

Paul Heyne was unusual in many ways that do him much credit. Perhaps the most eccentric of his virtues—eccentric at any rate in a professional scholar—was an ability to see that he was wrong, and a willingness to change his mind. As a Lutheran ordinand in the mid-1950s, it had seemed to him perfectly obvious that private property and market exchange are contrary to the laws of God. He had become "radicalized" through a chance encounter and "began spouting anti-capitalist rhetoric at the seminary."[1] But he had the grace and the intellectual humility to listen to "older and wiser heads" who urged him to "study economics before proposing godly reforms of the system."[2] In odd hours during his last years at Concordia

---

1. Paul Heyne, letter to David Brat, 31 July 1998.
2. Ibid.

Seminary in St. Louis, he "picked up the equivalent of an undergraduate major in economics at Washington University," and then "took another year to acquire an M.A. in economics." [3] By this time or soon after, Heyne had fairly gotten his teeth into the intractable problem that gives this book its title: *Are economists basically immoral?* And for the rest of his life he never ceased to shake and worry it, with richly varied but almost always fruitful results. Virtually all of his thinking, teaching, and writing arose out of the deep need he felt, as a faithful believer and an honest man, to make sense of the equally valid but seemingly incompatible claims of Christian ethics and economic science.

For this reason, it is difficult to appreciate Paul's writings fully without situating them in an account of his life, and without connecting the solid intellectual core of his thinking—sometimes camouflaged by its sparkling diversity—with his own distinctive sense of vocation. That is our chief purpose in this introduction. But we hope that the exercise will also help explain our reasons for choosing these among his many writings, and why we believe it especially appropriate that they should now appear under the aegis of Liberty Fund.

I. Life

Paul Theodore Heyne was born in St. Louis, Missouri, on 2 November 1931, and was brought up in a Lutheran family of German ancestry. His father was a pastor in the Lutheran Church–Missouri Synod (LCMS). After pre-seminary training at St. Paul's Junior College and Berkeley, Paul enrolled in Concordia Seminary, the principal theological college of the LCMS.

This Protestant denomination was founded in 1847 by Saxon immigrants "seeking freedom from religious rationalism in Germany." [4] It remains out of communion with most other Lutheran bodies in the United States, maintains that the pope is the antichrist, that women cannot be ordained, and that homosexuality is sinful. It grounds such decidedly conservative doctrines in the supposed inerrancy of the Protestant Bible:

3. Ibid.

4. S. Nafzger, "An Introduction to the Lutheran Church" (St. Louis, Mo.: Concordia Publishing House, 1994).

We reject the doctrine which under the name of science has gained wide popularity in the Church of our day that Holy Scripture is not in all its parts the Word of God, but in part the Word of God and in part the word of man and hence does, or at least, might contain error. We reject this erroneous doctrine as horrible and blasphemous . . .[5]

During the later 1950s and 1960s, however, Concordia Seminary had begun to acquire a reputation in LCMS for theological liberalism; only after a schism in 1974, during which about half of its faculty and student body walked out to protest an official attempt to enforce strict obedience, did it again become the denominational guardian of rigorous Lutheran orthodoxy.

Relatively sheltered, therefore, from the most intransigent repudiation of liberal sensibilities, Paul studied at Concordia those arts subjects deemed a suitable preparation for divinity and received a bachelor of arts in 1953. He remained a further three years in the seminary program, receiving a master's of divinity in 1956.

The radicalism that Heyne describes as developing in his later seminary years was not merely political. Indeed, the "anti-capitalist rhetoric" that he "spouted" may well have awakened a sympathetic response in many a fundamentalist bosom. Far more disturbing to the authorities, perhaps, was his unseemly desire to ask questions about religion. His widow reports that during his last year at Concordia, Paul initiated and led a discussion group that debated such matters as the historicity of Adam and Eve and the literal truth of the virgin birth of Christ. As a result, he was arraigned and tried by the seminary authorities for heresy. However, he won his case on what he later described as a "technicality"—perhaps the friendly intervention of some liberal faculty members—and was duly allowed to graduate.[6] However, Paul did not seek holy orders at this time, perhaps because the LCMS requires of its ministers their *ex anime* assent to the ancient Lutheran formularies.

Meanwhile, he had already begun those very different inquiries for which we now chiefly remember him. During 1955–56 he attended classes

---

5. Available at www.lcms.org/pages/internal.asp?Nav=563.
6. Juliana Heyne, letter to H. Geoffrey Brennan, October 2005.

in economics at Washington University in St. Louis, obtained credit, and was accepted into the M.A. program, which he completed the following year. At that stage he seems to have realized—here too perhaps with the assistance of "older and wiser heads"—that he was not well suited to be a pastor in the LCMS, and that his talents and inclinations pointed in a more academic direction, though still within the Lutheran Church broadly considered. As he put it at the end of his life,

> My plan was to enroll in the University of Chicago Divinity School (then a part of the Federated Theological Faculty), decorate myself with a Ph.D. in Ethics and Society, and then go and teach ethics at a seminary somewhere.[7]

He moved to Chicago, entered the Divinity School, and supported himself by lecturing in economics at Valparaiso University, which was conveniently located at the southwestern end of Lake Michigan and within easy reach of the University of Chicago. By 1963, having completed his doctorate in social ethics, he had been promoted to the rank of associate professor with tenure in the Valparaiso Economics Department, a position he held for two further years. Though founded by Methodists in 1859, the school had been purchased in 1925 by the Lutheran University Association and now advertises the "Lutheran heritage of scholarship, freedom and faith." During this period, Paul became friendly with a senior cleric at Valparaiso who was also pastor to a rural congregation. This colleague induced Paul and a number of other junior academics to be ordained in the Lutheran ministry, ostensibly as assistants in his congregation but actually to function as chaplains in the University Chapel. Valparaiso University, it would seem, valued "freedom" more highly than did the LCMS. During these same years Heyne supplemented his income by taking visiting lectureships in economics at other universities: Indiana University–Calumet; Roosevelt University; and Concordia College–River Forest.

In 1965, Heyne wrote his first book, *The World of Economics,* in the Christian Encounters series then produced by Concordia Publishing House, the publishing arm of LCMS. He declined subsequently to list this publication

---

7. Paul Heyne to Brat, 31 July 1998.

in any extant curriculum vitae, and alluded to it in private correspondence as *The Christian Encounters the World of Economics.*[8] In that same year, he left Valparaiso University "for family reasons" and became visiting associate professor in business and society for 1965–66 at the University of Illinois–Urbana-Champaign. In 1966 he moved to Dallas, Texas, as associate professor of economics at Southern Methodist University, with responsibilities not only in economics but also as a leading member of the newly established interdisciplinary undergraduate humanities program in the University College. From 1968 to 1972 he was coordinator of the freshman liberal studies program, the Nature of Man. By this stage, Paul was clearly identifiable as a professional economist, though one with unusually broad intellectual interests. The transition from would-be pastor to academic was seemingly complete.

The years during which Paul Heyne came to intellectual maturity, from the early 1950s to the early 1970s, were times of growing moral and political turmoil in the United States. His early years in seminary coincided with Senator Joseph McCarthy's sustained and bitter persecution of all who might be suspected of ever having been communist, which began early in February 1950 and was only finally discredited in March 1954. Heyne left St. Louis and began his doctoral studies in Chicago just as the campaign to end racial discrimination against blacks began at Little Rock, Arkansas, in September 1957. Paul's father, who ministered to a black LCMS congregation in St. Louis, joined Martin Luther King's historic march from Selma to Montgomery in March 1965. The local chapter of the Ku Klux Klan planted a cross on the Heyne family's front lawn. Paul's years in Chicago were increasingly clouded by the Vietnam War. In 1961 the December White Paper appeared which moved government policy toward more direct military intervention; a substantial and highly controversial military build-up took place in 1964 and 1965; and on 15 October 1965, shortly after Heyne had left Valparaiso to take up his visiting position at the University of Illinois, draft cards were being publicly burned for the first time by disaffected students.

As Heyne moved to Southern Methodist University in the fall of 1966, protest against the war was mounting against the background of an inter-

---

8. Paul Heyne, letter to A. M. C. Waterman, 11 March 1981.

national revolution in youth culture. The confluence of a "soft" cultural revolution of sex, drugs, blue jeans, and pop music, created by unprecedented affluence of the young and a concomitant rejection of ancient disciplines, with a "hard" political revolutionary movement that aimed to "smash the system," was an explosive mix. Marxism suddenly appeared or reappeared in universities after decades of contemptuous neglect, and other, originally unrelated protest movements such as the Campaign for Nuclear Disarmament and women's liberation were able to ride for a while on the popular tide.

In this climate all Americans seemed compelled to take sides. But "taking sides" was something Paul steadfastly refused to do. His warm heart constrained him to sympathize with the good and the honorable on both sides of the great national divide. His cool head obliged him to weigh and criticize unsound reasoning and dishonest use of facts by radical and conservative alike.

It may not always have seemed like this to his less intimate colleagues. Though the study of economics had by now cured him of Marxism,

> I...gave it undeserved allegiance in the 1960s; so I am not chastising others for sins of which I'm guiltless. My own problem, I think, was that I wanted to avoid being accused of any kind of McCarthyism, wanted to be openminded and even "radical," and wanted to concede as much as possible to "the other side."[9]

Paul was therefore zealous in resisting all attempts by the university authorities to limit freedom of discussion, the more so as he viewed his Liberal Studies program as precisely the proper locus of debate on all fundamental questions of morals and politics. He invited the eminent Marxist economist Paul Sweezy to speak to his classes, and argued with him late into the night about Castro, Ho Chi Minh, and Mao Tse Tung. Heyne later acknowledged that Sweezy convinced him "to rethink his views about Mao for a time."[10] Much as he disagreed with the notorious Timothy Leary, apostle of the drug culture and declared by President Nixon to be "the most dangerous

---

9. Paul Heyne, letter to A. M. C. Waterman, 30 July 1997.
10. Juliana Heyne to Brennan, October 2005.

man in America," Paul fought and won a battle with the administration to allow Leary to speak on campus. When members of Students for a Democratic Society came to proselytize SMU, they would sometimes stay with the Heynes. "I recall one especially intense visit in 1968," his widow says, when Paul and Mark Rudd (who later led a student rebellion at Columbia University) engaged in a disputation

> that seemed to go on for days. They were debating, among other things, whether or not the proletariat would rise up. Paul maintained the proletariat didn't want a revolution, but rather wanted another car in the garage. He used to say, facetiously of course, that he'd convinced Mark Rudd that the American working class wouldn't rise up and that's why Rudd (& others) despaired of non-violent revolution and formed Weatherman to effect violent revolution. And Paul wasn't entirely kidding when he said that.[11]

It is hardly surprising, in the climate of that time, that Paul's friendly relations with so many controversial figures should have caused some fluttering in the somewhat old-fashioned bosoms of the authorities of Southern Methodist University. Ultimately, "lack of support at the highest administrative levels" led Paul in 1972 to resign from his position as coordinator of the Nature of Man program, then compulsory for all freshmen in arts and sciences. The resignation caused "a great uproar on campus," and a colleague, William Torbert (now of Boston College), distributed a paper throughout the university titled "Is Paul Heyne a Good Man?" This paper purported to provide an objective assessment of Paul's "assets and faults in quite bracingly clear language," and its author now reports that "what struck him most was Paul's willingness to have such a question discussed so publicly."[12]

Meanwhile, Heyne continued to wear his other hat as an economist. As associate professor of economics, he taught both undergraduate and graduate students, and "maintained a place among the leading dozen or so teachers in the University" during his decade at SMU.[13] His still useful

11. Ibid.
12. Ibid.
13. Harley, letter to Douglass North, 17 February 1976.

book *Private Keepers of the Public Interest* appeared during his second year, and the first edition of his most successful work, *The Economic Way of Thinking,* was published in 1973. The former was dedicated to his wife Juliana, "his most friendly and helpful critic." During his last years at SMU he collaborated with Thomas Johnson in a more conventional (and much larger) textbook, *Toward Economic Understanding,* published in December 1976 and immediately divided into two halves: *Toward Understanding Macroeconomics,* and *Towards Understanding Microeconomics;* Heyne was responsible for the latter. In 1973 Heyne was made a professor, "in spite of the fact that some of [his] colleagues were less enthusiastic as a result of the fact that Paul [had] little interest in writing for professional journals."[14] Shortly after this, a new department head was appointed, and supported by some of these "less enthusiastic" colleagues quickly declared his determination to seek "increased national prominence" for the department by encouraging publication in refereed journals. Paul had never concealed his contempt for the academic rituals of publication and "career progress" and, since both Paul and the new head had "strong personalities, it was inevitable that they would clash."[15] It was conceded by a sympathetic contemporary at that time that Paul had a few "rough edges." At last, Paul resigned "the comforts of rank and tenure" in the spring of 1975, quitted or was extruded from the economics department, and spent his final year at SMU in the University College, teaching once again for his beloved Liberal Studies program.[16]

When Paul Heyne resigned from SMU in 1975, he had no place to go in September 1976. In what seems to have been the last flowering of his youthful idealism, he and his wife proposed to move to Seattle and "strike out on their own" in a communitarian "social experiment."[17] He was then forty-five and his wife eight years younger. They had five children.

Fortunately for all, romantic zeal was tempered by economic calculation. Heyne wrote to Douglass North, then chairman of the Department of Economics at the University of Washington, offering his services as an instructor on a one-year appointment with option for renewal.[18] North

14. J. Carter Murphy, letter to Douglass North, 24 February 1976.
15. Ibid.
16. Paul Heyne, letter to Douglass North, 18 September 1975.
17. Murphy to North, 24 February 1976.
18. Paul Heyne to North, 18 September 1975.

liked Paul's letter, knew and admired the Heyne "little principles book," and believed that his own department was "loaded with scholars, very few of whom are qualified in my view to teach introductory economics."[19] North had little difficulty in getting the support of his colleagues and the approval of his dean for the appointment. So Paul became lecturer in economics initially for the academic year 1976–77. Paul never sought or received tenure, but the appointment was renewed by unanimous vote of his colleagues in each of the more than twenty years until his death. He was made senior lecturer in 1989. With his usual drollery Paul liked to say—in what passed for a curriculum vitae in later years—that North hired him "because he liked my approach to economics, and so I have somewhat presumptuously taken his subsequent receipt of a Nobel Prize as an endorsement of my own work."

As an unintended and wholly benign consequence of his "courageous, almost foolhardy" resignation from Southern Methodist University,[20] Paul now entered the most tranquil and productive period of his life, which ended only with his death on 9 April 2000 after a very short and unexpected struggle with cancer. As he put it to a friend,

> the University of Washington turned out to be one of my most spectacular pieces of good fortune . . . comfortably, profitably and happily housed . . . writing lots of papers on one aspect or other of the tension between ethics and economics.[21]

Over this period, Heyne gradually became internationally famous as an outstanding and innovative teacher of economics. *The Economic Way of Thinking* went through nine editions in his lifetime and was translated into Russian, Czech, Romanian, Hungarian, Bulgarian, Albanian, Korean, and Spanish; its offshoot, *Microeconomics,* was first published in 1988. He was in continual demand as a speaker not only in the United States, but also and notably in Eastern Europe. Between 1980 and 1999, he was extensively involved in Liberty Fund conferences, twenty-one as director or discussion leader. He spent "a lot of time and energy enjoying 'community ser-

19. Douglass North, letter to Paul Heyne, 23 September 1975.
20. James Earley, letter to North, 17 February 1976.
21. Paul Heyne, letter to Paul Trescott, 22 September 1992.

vice' activities."[22] Paul and his family lived in a large, old-fashioned house about twenty-five minutes from the university by bicycle. He became an Episcopalian.

This was the Paul Heyne now remembered by his friends, colleagues, and former students. All but two of the twenty-six papers reprinted in this collection were written during these Seattle years.

II. Thought

Eight years before his death, Heyne listed his "strong convictions" in a letter to an old friend:

Lecturing is a poor way to teach;

economists spend far too much time on the theory of optimizing and too little on the prerequisites, forms and consequences of exchange;

less than 1% of what is published by academics in the social sciences and the humanities has any value and 90% of it would have been rejected by any editor with a modicum of intelligence and a concern for the public interest and would thus not even have been allowed to compete for attention and survival;

theology has absolutely nothing to contribute to the discussion of public policy issues;

there are "natural" or non-arbitrary norms for the conduct of human behavior, but they must be learned from the study of actual human perceptions, judgments and interactions;

people should pay to drive their cars into and through cities;

trains are fun to ride but are no solution to problems of urban congestion;

parents should be given vouchers to spend at any school they choose for their children, public or private, and the principals of the public schools should be assigned full authority and responsibility;

environmentalism has become a dogmatic, fundamentalist, persecuting religion that will keep us from ameliorating our environmental problems;

22. Paul Heyne to Waterman, 11 March 1981.

urban neighborhoods should be privatized in any and every way possible;

drugs should be legalized with the stipulation that no one has a right to use recreational drugs and impose costs on other people;

markets alienate people but also provide the only way to secure freedom and prosperity in modern societies.[23]

Paul had come a long way, it would seem, from the naïve, "anti-capitalist rhetoric" of his seminary days. Yet his years at Concordia laid the foundation of much of his thinking forty years later. Heyne's grounding in the humanities was more thorough than usual for American arts graduates even then, far more so than for those aiming at a career in economics. Whilst still a student himself he was teaching Latin to others; he had a working knowledge of Greek and Hebrew; his wide reading in philosophy and in classical and modern literature began in those Concordia years; his lucid and elegant prose was refined in homiletic exposition. As a result, he was completely at home in the Liberal Studies program at SMU as few other economists could have been. Speculation about the nature of man was part of the air he breathed as a seminarian.

The opportunity cost of all this was a lack of mathematics, which Paul seems never to have studied in later years when he had both the time and the incentive. Although he took economics courses to the master's level in St. Louis, it was still possible to do so in the early 1950s with no formal mathematics whatsoever. Yet this was precisely the period in which high theory was becoming almost exclusively mathematical, and in which Paul Samuelson's world-famous "introductory analysis" disguised the use of difference equations and differential calculus with ingenious diagrams. To the end of his days, Heyne resisted the suggestion that many analytical problems in economics are best formulated mathematically. This attitude influenced his view of the scope and nature of economic science, and probably accounts in part for his contempt for those numerous publications by his colleagues that ought to have been rejected by editors with "any concern for the public interest." It may also explain both his preference for

---

23. Paul Heyne to Trescott, 22 September 1992. His widow believes that Paul had modified his position on some of these matters by the end of his life.

a "catallactic" rather than an "economizing" account of economic theory, and his willingness to invest time and energy in the history of economic thought, especially that of Adam Smith.

Even more important, the years at Concordia made Heyne completely inward with Christian theology. Like economics, theology is best understood to be a method of thinking rather than a body of knowledge. Though the doctrines taught at Concordia were archaic and relentlessly unfashionable, deep scholarship, scrupulous honesty, and intellectual rigor (admittedly within the prevailing LCMS assumptions) were required of all. Heyne was almost certainly better trained in theological thinking than he would have been at many a more liberal seminary. At any rate, despite his brush with authority, he retained contact with Concordia at least until 1970, when he published an essay in *Seminar,* a forum for exchange of ideas among members of the Concordia Seminary community; and he remained a Lutheran, though no longer of Missouri Synod, until the move to Seattle.

Most important of all, Paul Heyne had clearly identified the central intellectual concern of his life before he left St. Louis in 1956. Christian scripture and church doctrine would seem to require all individuals to take moral responsibility for the human consequences of their "economic" transactions: producing and consuming, buying and selling, hiring and firing, saving and investing. But economists have inherited from Adam Smith the presumption that many (perhaps most) consequences are unintended and can never be known in advance; and that by acting purposefully and seeking only to further their own interest, individuals may do more good to their neighbors than they would have if motivated entirely by moral considerations. Christians who find economic theory convincing are therefore forced to confront Heyne's question: "Are economists basically immoral?" Though Heyne first conceived the problem in a specifically Christian context, he later came to realize that the question is relevant for anyone who takes seriously any moral obligation to act for the welfare of other people.

Few economists have addressed the relation between economic ethics and Christian doctrine as thoroughly as Frank Knight, who argued powerfully in many works that "a specifically Christian ethic only addresses the personal relations between individuals, whereas maxims for a genuinely social ethic must take the form of impersonal rules and that Christian theology can therefore make no contribution to normative social theory."[24] Heyne was already aware of Knight's objections before leaving St. Louis. Therefore, as he reported near the end of his life, "at Chicago I focused on the theological and philosophical presuppositions of economics. My goal was to refute Frank Knight. I lost. His writings (he was retired but still around while I was there) have probably been the most powerful influence on my views as an economist."[25] Heyne's doctoral thesis at Chicago, *The Presuppositions of Economic Thought: A Study in the Philosophical and Theological Sources of Economic Controversy,* which he never published or drew attention to in any way, would seem to be the source of many of his later essays both on methodology and on the futility of Christian "social teaching."

The influence of Frank Knight on Paul's thinking went much deeper than his "views as an economist." In important respects, Knight served as a model. An essay of Heyne's published in 1994, not included in this collection, contains a description of Knight that reads like a self-portrait:

> Knight was determined to see all sides of the phenomena he studied, to point out the limitations of the argument he himself accepted, to build on no foundations without also undermining them, to draw no strong conclusions without acknowledging the compelling force of the exactly opposite conclusion. . . . His scorn for those who believed that "Science" commands the highway to "Truth" was as sharp his dislike of those who wanted to impose a "revealed" truth.[26]

Knight had famously rejected the standard analytical assumption that tastes or wants are "given," and had argued that what most people want is "*better* wants." In Knight's view, the most important task of the social scientist is "to promote the free discussion of values, a process that forms the essence of democracy and lies at the heart of a liberal society."[27]

24. Paul Heyne, "If the Trumpet Does Not Sound a Clear Call," in *Religion and Economics: Normative Social Theory,* ed. J. M. Dean and A. M. C. Waterman (Dordrecht: Kluwer, 1999), p. 150.

25. Paul Heyne to Brat, 31 July 1998.

26. Paul Heyne, "Review of the Evidence," in *Economics and Religion: Are They Distinct?,* ed. G. Brennan and A. M. C. Waterman (Dordrecht: Kluwer, 1994), p. 219.

27. Ibid., pp. 219–20.

Whether consciously or unconsciously internalized, Knight's un-settling ideas combined with Heyne's love of humane letters learned at Concordia, with Paul's un-Knightian belief in the importance of sound theology, and with his professionally eccentric, antimathematical view of economic theory to produce the unique and highly flavored Heyne intel-lectual style. Part of that style includes the view that, in the humanities and the social sciences, the criteria of "scientific" knowledge are at best merely provisional and at worst illusory, and that the elaborate rituals of academic credentialism—grant applications, peer review, professional journals, promotion and tenure—are neither respectable nor socially use-ful. Since "the free discussion of values . . . lies at the heart of a liberal soci-ety," universities ought to promote this above all else (and not least when passions run high). The most important duty of an academic is to teach young men and women to discuss "values." Scholarship is vital to this: "re-search" is not. Since (as his own experiences at Concordia had taught him) the imposition of "revealed" truth is as dangerous in religion as exagger-ated epistemological claims are in science, official and in particular "estab-lished" religion is likely to do more harm than good. Just as the economic problems of society "require for their solution a certain amount of earth-bound realism"[28] and because Christians can have no monopoly on such realism, there can be no "uniquely Christian perspective" on economic policy. For "if our contribution is not of value, what merit can there be in its uniqueness? And if it is of value, what besides arrogance should prompt us to label it unique?"[29]

Paul Heyne once described himself as "a Lutheran by training, an Epis-copalian by choice, and a Mennonite by instinct."[30] He "joined the Episco-pal Church in 1976, finding a spiritual home in the Anglican emphasis on reason, tradition, and liturgy, and *its relative lack of interest in doctrine.*"[31] What he called his Mennonite "instinct" refers to a deep distrust of hier-

28. Paul Heyne, *The World of Economics,* (St. Louis, Mo.: Concordia Publishing House, 1965), pp. 84–85.

29. Paul Heyne, "Focus: Christians and Economic Thinking," *Seminar* (Concordia Seminary Student Publications, St. Louis, Mo.), December 1970: 12.

30. Paul Heyne to Brat, 31 July 1998.

31. Funeral brochure, 15 April 2000; our italics.

archical authority in church and state that Paul may have derived as much from Frank Knight as from Anabaptist theology. Paul professed to regard Constantine's official adoption of the Christian religion as a disaster, and regretted the "establishment" aspects of Anglican culture. Perhaps there was always something of the rebel and the outsider in Paul's temperament. Certainly the circumstances at Southern Methodist University in the 1960s and early 1970s lent greater prominence to these characteristics than the more peaceful climate of his years in Seattle.

Christian faith and economic science remained in creative tension for the whole of Paul Heyne's professional life. However, there was at least one fundamental respect in which he viewed the two through exactly the same lens, and this similarity may be a key to unlock his deliberately unsystematic and heterogeneous thought. Each is a "way"; neither is a destination. *Economics is a way of thinking.* Too much sophisticated technique may become an end in itself and divert our attention from the real world. *Christianity is a way of life.* Too much "interest in doctrine" can divide us from one another and divert our attention from faith, hope, and charity. To engage in either "way" is to join with others who are already embarked on a journey of exploration that no one expects to end during his or her own life.

III. Writing

For a man who so often disparaged publication as an activity, Paul Heyne wrote a great deal in the thirty-six years between his University of Chicago doctoral dissertation of 1963 and his last paper, written for the Hoover Institution in 1999.

Out of sixty-four papers found in Heyne's office at the University of Washington and sorted by Andrew Rutten while at Liberty Fund, thirty-four had been published: in academic journals such as *Research in Law and Economics* and *Forum for Social Economics;* in more popular periodicals such as *Religion and Liberty, This World, Chronicle of Higher Education,* and *Financial Analysts Journal;* as pamphlets and booklets published by such bodies as the Cato Institute and the Intercollegiate Studies Institute, including the substantial *The Promise of Community* of which he was very proud; or in books edited by others. To these we must add, in addition to Heyne's doctoral dissertation, his early book for Concordia Press,[32] the four books published during his years at Southern Methodist University,[33] and his last microeconomics textbook,[34] published after the move to Seattle.

The provenance of Heyne's thirty extant unpublished papers is not always easy to identify. Of those where this is clear, eight are the texts of public lectures delivered at various universities in North America, five are papers read at conferences of the Southern Economic Association and other professional bodies, and five were commissioned for conferences organized by Liberty Fund. Liberty Fund records indicate that Heyne was an author at nine conferences between 1980 and 1999. Two of his symposium papers were published as chapters in books. Therefore at least one— and possibly more—have been lost.

We may also note various other extant writings not classified by Rutten: Heyne's 1970 publication in *Seminar* mentioned above; and in 1993 alone, two articles in the *Fortune Encyclopedia of Economics,* a long review essay on Daly and Cobb[35] for the *Critical Review,* and book reviews in *Journal of Economic Literature* and *Journal of the History of Economic Thought.* Photocopies of eleven other book reviews from 1975 to 1999 are among the "reviews and shorter pieces" collected but not classified by Rutten. Doubtless there were other papers in earlier and later years that their author lost and forgot about, or did not bother to advertise to his friends. In sum, this is a substantial output, especially for an academic who spent most of his professional time and energy teaching undergraduates, and who devoted many working hours in later years to revising his best-known books.

Why bother to republish any of this material? Paul Heyne's most influential book is still in print, brought up to date by other authors and now in its eleventh edition.[36] His other economics books are still in use and readily

---

32. *The World of Economics* (St. Louis: Concordia, 1965).

33. *Private Keepers of the Public Interest* (New York: McGraw Hill, 1968); *The Economic Way of Thinking* (Chicago: Science Research Associates, 1973); *Toward Understanding Macroeconomics* (Chicago: Science Research Associates, 1976); *Toward Understanding Microeconomics* (Chicago: Science Research Associates, 1976).

34. *Microeconomics* (Chicago: Science Research Associates, 1988).

35. Herman E. Daly and John B. Cobb Jr., *For the Common Good* (Boston: Beacon Press, 1989).

36. Heyne, Peter J. Boettke, and David L. Prychitko, *The Economic Way of Thinking* (Upper Saddle River, N. J.: Prentice Hall, 2005).

available in libraries. Some of his more substantial essays were published in well-known journals. Their author cared so little for much of the rest that he either neglected to publish them or failed to record the periodicals in which they appeared.

The justification for the current collection gradually came to us as possible editors when we read and re-read the University of Washington papers and all other Heyne material we had access to. That justification became clearer as we discovered things Paul had never bothered to tell us of his intellectual development from 1953 to 1976. For though he was an intimate friend of each of us, he much preferred to debate the latest (or perennial) issues we disagreed upon than to talk or write about himself. Paul Heyne, we now see, was a man with a prophetic mission—something he naturally conceived as a calling. This vocation was not to be a Lutheran pastor, or a working economist, or even just a university teacher—though he sometimes spoke as though the last were the case. It was, rather, to explain to a society ignorant of the principles of economics, and sentimentally attached to a half-remembered Christian ethic of interpersonal relations, that the seemingly immoral prescriptions of economists are often the best way to achieve ethical goals that all would approve.

Are economists basically immoral? When they consider the question at all, most decent, right-minded people still instinctively think so. Paul Heyne believed otherwise, and devoted his life to helping others to acknowledge and understand the arguments that he held to be conclusive. This is a high calling, not only in Eastern Europe where for some years he was an apostle of the economic way of thinking, but also in his own country. Paul had a capacity to pursue it in ways that were exceptionally engaging and compellingly presented, in his writing no less than in other contexts. For these reasons, a selection of those papers that most effectively capture his message should be placed in as many hands as possible.

In making our selection, we began by eliminating book reviews, printed works of one or two pages in little-known publications, and short, unpublished typescripts of unknown provenance. Next we eliminated all essays based on arguments more fully worked out or better expressed elsewhere. Because of the occasional character of much of Paul's writing, there is considerable overlap of theme and subject matter. We think we have been able to bring our collection down to the twenty-six printed here, roughly one-third of the University of Washington material, without missing too much.

The first eleven of the papers, grouped in the first three parts of the book, have to do directly with Paul's lifelong concern with ethics and theology, and the relations between these and economics. Part 4 contains two scholarly essays of a historical character, the second commissioned for a Liberty Fund symposium directed by the Fraser Institute in 1982 at which we and Paul met together as a trio for the first time. Parts 5 and 6 contain six essays on teaching, the first being Paul's introductory lecture at Southern Methodist University in September 1968 on "The Nature of Man" which, with the possible exception of an undated essay in part 3, affords our earliest glimpse of the author in action. Because defining "economics" is crucial to any genuine discussion of economics and ethics, methodology was always important to Paul, and we print three mainly methodological essays in part 7. The last part illustrates Paul's approach to the relation of economics and ethics by printing four of his many essays on specific policy issues.

We think it especially fitting that this book is to appear under the imprint of Liberty Fund. For one thing, four of the essays in the collection (chapters 4, 9, 11, 13, 21) were first written for Liberty Fund conferences between 1981 and 1993. But there are other, more fundamental reasons. If there be any such person, Paul Heyne was the quintessential Liberty Fund man. In the last two decades of his life, he attended on average each year more than four Liberty Fund colloquia, symposia, or seminars, many as director or discussion leader. He was invited to his first Liberty Fund conference in March 1965; one of the participants in this event was Liberty Fund's founder, Pierre Goodrich. Paul believed passionately in "the ideal of a society of free and responsible individuals" and agreed strongly with Goodrich "that education in a free society requires a dialogue centered in the great ideas of civilization." Like Goodrich, "he saw learning as an ongoing process of discovery." Few perhaps have realized more fully than Paul Heyne "that the best way to promote the ideal of a society of free and responsible individuals is through full and open discussion." [37]

___

37. All quotations in this paragraph are taken from the Liberty Fund brochure and are drawn from Pierre Goodrich's original memorandum of understanding.

In the formulation and execution of this project we have incurred a number of debts: to Emilio Pacheco of Liberty Fund; to the Liberty Fund publications staff, and most particularly Laura Goetz; to Andy Rutten, whose initial efforts in tracing the Heyne papers were truly indispensable; to Paul's widow, Juliana Heyne, for providing historical background that might otherwise have been lost; and to those of Paul's former colleagues and friends who have given permission to reproduce excerpts from their correspondence.

Paul was a remarkable man. We think these essays show something of that remarkableness. We feel honored to have had a small part in bringing them to the attention of a wider public.

GEOFFREY BRENNAN
A. M. C. WATERMAN

PART I

Economics and Ethics

CHAPTER I

Are Economists Basically Immoral?

WHENEVER MY WIFE and I have economists and their spouses over for dinner, I try to keep the conversation away from politics, because otherwise it almost always ends up in a somewhat rancorous dispute, not about candidates or policies, but about the democratic political process itself. The division is always the same: all the economists insist that voters have no incentive to cast an informed ballot, while the non-economists protest that this is a cynical and immoral view of the world.

As another example, I recently gave my students a newspaper article that was headlined "Food Aid from West Falls Prey to Corruption." It began with this line: "Western food aid to former Soviet Republics is being syphoned off to the black market or falling into the hands of corrupt local authorities." I asked my students to tell me in writing what difference this makes and why donor nations should be concerned that their food is being stolen. I found that some of the students were appalled at my claim that stolen food was more likely to get to hungry people than food that had not been stolen. I hastened to add, I said, that I do not approve of theft. But the damage was done; the students were very upset. It was wrong to argue that thieves are usually more effective in getting food to hungry people than Red Cross officials are. But thieves have a more effective incentive: no sale, no profit.

Reprinted from *Policy* 9 (Autumn 1993): 33–36, by permission of The Centre for Independent Studies (www.cis.org.au).

What do you think of the following statement?: "One in every seven health-care dollars spent each year in the US is on the last six months of someone's life; this is not an efficient way to allocate resources." You will have lots of company if you think that it is immoral to discuss the efficiency of spending money to save lives. But economists not only discuss such questions; they try to get other people to take their discussions seriously. How much is too much to save a life? Is that an immoral question?

Lawrence Summers, the chief economist of the World Bank, got himself in serious trouble last December when he sent a memo to some bank colleagues arguing that polluting activities ought to be shifted from developed to less developed countries. He argued that the demand for a clean environment has a very high income elasticity: which means that people become keener on it as their incomes rise. He said that wealthier people are ordinarily willing to sacrifice more for aesthetically pleasing environments than are poor people. Moreover—and I suspect this is what really got him into trouble—he claimed that the health effects of pollution are less in a poor country than in a rich country because the forgone earnings of people whose health is adversely affected by pollution are so much lower in poor countries, because of both lower incomes and shorter life expectancies. Someone leaked that memorandum to an environmental group and a hail of criticism descended on the World Bank and Lawrence Summers. Summers protested that his statements were designed as a "sardonic counterpoint, an effort to sharpen the analysis." Summers is a Harvard PhD and a nephew of not one but two Nobel Laureates in economics, Kenneth Arrow and Paul Samuelson. He was too faithful an economist to retreat completely, and he insisted that it was a legitimate question whether environmental standards should be the same worldwide.

Risk and Choice

These are the kinds of incidents that make me raise my question: are economists basically immoral? In order to clarify the issue I want to use the case of International Conglomerate (IC), a hypothetical corporation that produces "gizmoes" (I made them up too). Gizmoes are very useful devices that make people comfortable, happy and healthy. A profitable market exists for gizmoes if gizmoes can be produced at a low enough cost, and the key to cost is workers' safety. IC cannot produce gizmoes profitably in Australia because it can't obtain competent employees without paying very high wages because Australian workers demand high wages as compensation for the high risk to life and limb inherent in the production of gizmoes. But IC can produce gizmoes profitably in Malaysia, where employees are willing to accept the risk of working in a gizmo factory for relatively low wages. Is IC behaving immorally when it opens a gizmo factory in Malaysia?

As a baptized and confirmed economist I would say that if the Malaysian workers know what the risks are, then IC is not behaving unfairly to anyone. It is providing gizmoes to people who value them, providing profits to the shareholders of IC, and providing income to the Malaysian workers; everyone wins, or at least everyone with the right to be consulted. No one is exploited or treated unjustly. My question is: Why do so many people, at least in my country and I trust in yours too, believe otherwise? Why would so many people insist that IC is behaving unjustly in a case like that? When you ask them (and I have done a lot of asking), they say something like this: "Well, opening a plant in Malaysia amounts to saying that the lives of Malaysians are worth less than the lives of Australians: that is immoral."

Now there are all kinds of risky jobs. Certain kinds of construction work are risky; fishing in the Gulf of Alaska is very risky. I've got friends who were injured and killed there. Racing hydro-planes is risky, guiding climbers up the Himalayan mountains is risky. I would not work at any of these, but other people do; and is anyone asserting that their lives are less valuable than mine? Less valuable to whom? What this seems to mean is that some people are more willing than others to accept certain kinds of risk. And for all sorts of reasons; perhaps because they're highly skilled and they think that the risk to themselves is low; possibly because they have, as Adam Smith put it, an absurd presumption in their own good fortune. Perhaps because they enjoy challenge and risk. Or perhaps because they are so poor that they prefer the small risk of an industrial accident to the certainty of poverty.

Aha, says the critic, that's the problem. The Malaysian workers accept these dangerous jobs only because they have such poor alternative opportunities. IC is taking advantage of their poverty, of the scarcity of good jobs in Malaysia, of the underdeveloped state of the Malaysian economy.

The weakness in this response is that all of us regularly in our exchange transactions take advantage of the limited opportunities available to others. A couple of weeks ago I hired a man to fix my front porch at what some people would say is an outrageous price; but I took advantage of the fact that no one else was willing to hire him for an even more outrageous price that week. What the critic is really saying is that sometimes people's opportunities are so poor that we should not—not what? That's the question: not what? Not offer them somewhat better opportunities? What are the options for IC in this case? Should IC not produce gizmoes at all? That won't help the poor Malaysian workers; it would leave them worse off as well as depriving eager consumers of the gizmoes they so dearly love. The Malaysian worker who takes a job in the risky gizmo factory increases his life expectancy. He will eat better and get better health care as a result.

Some people would say that IC should just not produce gizmoes in Malaysia. If Australians or other rich westerners want gizmoes then they should shoulder the risks inherent in gizmo production and not put the risk on people in other countries. But the trouble with this is that since the gizmo consumers in Australia are likely to be different people from the gizmo producers, the argument has little moral force.

No doubt IC should adopt safe ways to produce gizmoes. The trouble is that any productive process can always be made safer but only at some cost. In my hypothetical example, the cost of improved safety conditions is too high to make safe gizmo production profitable. Then the question rises: How safe is "safe enough"? Airline travel could always be made safer if we required planes to taxi from one city to another. But travel would become less safe because people would drive their cars, which is far more risky.

The US Federal Aviation Administration is thinking about requiring that all children under two years old have their own seats so that they can be strapped in. That might save one life every ten years, but we might kill about ten babies every year as mummy and daddy drive to see grandma instead of taking the plane.

Intentions vs. Consequences

The critics of International Conglomerate in my hypothetical case are calling for different decisions because they assume a different world from the one in which we live. They are assuming a social system that's completely known and completely controllable. And that's a very common practice in public discussions of social policy. The widespread moral suspicion, if not outright disapproval, of economists and economic analysis is rooted, I believe, in the fact that economists specialize in the analysis of social systems that no one controls and that produce results that no one intended. Moreover, economists don't merely analyze such systems; they applaud them. Now you might wonder what's morally dubious about a social system that no one controls and that produces outcomes no one intended. What many people find dubious about such systems was memorably expressed by Adam Smith in his famous passage on the invisible hand in *The Wealth of Nations*. Those who participate in such systems, Smith said, promote the public interest most effectively by pursuing their own interest. Most people seem to believe that is just not the moral way to promote the public interest. Morality has to do with intentions more than with results; so the person who tried to run you down with his car but missed is morally more culpable than the person who actually ran you down but while trying to get to church.

Now it's true that morality does have to do fundamentally with intentions. Most of us assess the morality of other people by judging or attempting to judge their intentions and their motives. That's how we learn what it means to be moral. We were praised or blamed when we were young not for what we did but for what we tried to do. Our intentions reveal our character, and moral training is a matter of nurturing the right motivations. But the fact remains that we live in social systems that, while they emerge from human intentions, nonetheless produce results that no one intended. Market systems (which is what I am talking about) simply would not work if the results had to be foreseen and intended. They are directed and coordinated not by achieving agreement on the goals to be pursued, but by achieving agreement on the rules of the game and then letting people exchange as their interests dictate.

Face-to-Face vs. Commercial Society

It seems clear to me that we all of us live simultaneously in two kinds of societies, each with its own quite distinct morality. One is the face-to-face society, like the family, in which we can and should directly pursue one another's welfare. But we also live in large, necessarily impersonal societies in which we cooperate to our mutual advantage with thousands, even millions, of people whom we usually do not even see, but whose welfare we promote most effectively by diligently pursuing our own welfare. We live predominantly in what Adam Smith called a "commercial society." When the division of labor, he wrote earlier in *The Wealth of Nations,* has thoroughly extended itself through society, then everyone lives by exchanging; everyone becomes, he says, in some measure a merchant and the society grows to be what is properly called a commercial society.

Economists have acquired their bad reputation largely by defending commercial society. Commercial society simply does not function in accordance with the moral principles that most people learned in their youth and now take for granted as the only possible principles of morality. In many people's judgment that makes commercial society and its defenders morally objectionable. Now, I think most of these critics are deeply confused. In a family, or another face-to-face society, the members know one another well. In these situations people can reasonably be expected to take the other person's specific interests and values into account. But in a large society this is impossible. If I tried to apply in a class of 50 or even 25 students the principles of justice that I try to use in my own family, such as "from each according to their ability, to each according to their need," I would end up behaving not justly but arbitrarily. And therefore unjustly. I should not be expected to distribute grades to my students on the basis of need. The economist Kenneth Boulding once formulated the issue I'm asking you to consider by contrasting what he called "exchange systems" with "integrative systems." Integrative systems work through a meeting of minds, through a convergence of images, values and aspirations. Participation in integrative social systems can be deeply satisfying, and I think some participation in integrative systems is essential to human health and happiness. But it is a serious mistake to use the features of integrative systems to pass moral judgment on exchange systems.

Here's an example of such a mistake. It's from an essay by the nineteenth-century British art critic John Ruskin, who criticized economists even more harshly than he criticized bad architecture and bad painting. "Employers," Ruskin said, "should treat employees the way they would treat their own sons" (he didn't say "daughters" because he didn't contemplate women working). Does that strike you as a worthy ideal? Even if a hopeless ideal, people might say it's a worthy ideal, something we should strive for. But I want you to think again. It is a *monstrous* ideal. The proper term for it is "paternalism": or, as my wife tells me, "parentalism," a much better word. Parentalism is a non-sexist word for what we used to call paternalism; it really captures the idea, which is behaving like a parent. Parentalism degrades its victims and corrupts its perpetrators. I do not want the Chancellor of my university to treat me like a child, not even like his own child; he is in reality not my father and should not behave toward me as if he were. Parentalism is appropriate at most in actual parents who know their children intimately, who love them as much as, if not more than, they love themselves, and who recognize that their children have a unique claim on their resources. In those cases parentalism is appropriate. When those conditions are not met, then parentalism is degrading and corrupting. Employers should treat their employees like human beings, of course, with decency and common courtesy. But beyond that they should treat them as people who have something of value to offer the firm for which they will therefore have to be paid. This is not only efficient; it is also less unfair than the parentalist alternative. It is more worthy of both the employer and the employee.

The employer/employee relationship is properly part of the exchange system in which people are equals and do things for one another. Our hankering to personalize our relationships is a romantic revolt against dominant features of the modern world. It's the kind of yearning that if carried through would have us abandon such coldly impersonal social mechanisms as traffic lights in favor of an integrated system in which the motorists who meet at each intersection form an encounter group to decide who most needs to go through the intersection first. This romantic yearning to make the family the norm for every kind of social interaction is fueled by another misunderstanding, the mistaken notion that commercial society and economic theory presuppose and endorse selfish behavior. But the economic theory that explains commercial society assumes only that people pursue their own interests. This is often inaccurately stated as the assumption that people are selfish. But people who pursue their own interests are behaving selfishly only if their interests are selfish.

The economist merely assumes that people pursue those projects that interest them, whether it's bringing medicine to Ukraine, selling cocaine in Los Angeles or lecturing at the Centre for Independent Studies, and that they redirect their efforts in response to any changes in the anticipated costs and benefits of doing so. In other words, if I think you'll smile at me, I'll talk a little longer.

Interests and Incentives

I sometimes wish economists would pay a bit more attention to the nature of the interests that people pursue. We often sound confident that all the interests that people pursue are good ones; but they're not. Be that as it may, the economist does assume that people pursue their own interests; and the question is, what follows from that? That is still the key question. That's the question that Adam Smith posed. Under what circumstances will the pursuit of self-interest by the various members of society produce something that can reasonably be called the public interest? That is still the question for economists and for the rest of society. And economists answer that question without assuming a benevolent despot. It is characteristic of the economic way of thinking to ask what incentives are producing the present situation that we don't like. What incentives would produce something better and how might we get from here to there, given the fact that we are here with our present incentive structure? Now that's a very laid-back way to approach the world. The good economist is often perceived as immoral because he is suspicious of what Adam Smith called the "man of system" who in his own conceit supposes that the members of a great society can be moved about as easily as the hand moves the pieces on a chessboard.

I shall conclude with two recent newspaper items. One is a short news item reporting that Mother Teresa was about to appeal to prevent the execution of a convicted California murderer. I don't know whether she did appeal or not, but the newspaper said that she was going to call the Governor and say that this man should be forgiven because that is what Jesus would have done. Now I don't want to get into the issue of capital punishment; I just want to point out that if Mother Teresa made that argument she was mixing different moralities. I choose Mother Teresa because

I can't think of a person for whom I have more respect; she is a far better person than I am. But forgiveness is appropriate only in face-to-face relations or for God. The criminal-justice system of the State of California is not God nor is it running a face-to-face society. A judge who forgives a convicted criminal is not a candidate for sainthood but for impeachment. The morality of large social spheres is simply different from the morality of face-to-face systems. Arguments against capital punishment must take those differences into account, and so must our arguments for revised economic policies.

The other news item reports a recent call for a US$10-billion expansion of government food programs to end hunger in America. According to this article, adequate nutrition is a basic human right. Someone was quoted as saying "Hunger is an injustice." I want you to think about that for a moment, because I am now going to seem immoral. I say the spokesman is confused. Hunger may be an evil. (How about fasting, an ancient and venerable religious tradition?) But it is not an injustice, because no one intends the hunger of other people. I can imagine someone intending to starve someone to death; that would be an injustice. But hunger is usually the product of a lot of interrelated choices, some of which may entail unjust acts but most of which probably do not.

If you were concerned about adequate nutrition for everyone then you would achieve your goal not by labeling it a basic human right but by changing the whole web of incentives that people face. It is an economic problem much more than it is a moral problem. Economists acquire their reputations for immorality by making statements like that; but I think it is our vocation to make such statements and I think I would be faithless to my vocation and therefore immoral if I said anything else.

CHAPTER 2

Economics and Ethics: The Problem of Dialogue

Is ECONOMICS a science or an ideology? Does it provide trustworthy descriptions and reliable predictions? Or are the descriptions and predictions of economists distorted by ideological presuppositions and commitments?

From Confidence to Confusion

As recently as fifteen years ago it would have been difficult to assemble a session on those questions at a professional economics meeting in this country. There were almost no Marxist economists in academic positions in the United States to press the argument that orthodox economics is bourgeois apologetics.[1] And the "institutionalists," who had vigorously attacked the philosophical and political biases of mainstream American economics a generation earlier,[2] were by 1960 mostly intimidated, converted, compromised, or quarantined.[3] Most economists simply accepted without serious question the position expressed in 1953 by Milton Friedman, that

Reprinted from *Belief and Ethics,* ed. W. Schroeder and G. Winter (Chicago: Center for the Scientific Study of Religion, 1978), 183–98, by permission of Mrs. Juliana Heyne.

1. See Martin Bronfenbrenner's "Notes on Marxian Economics in the United States," *American Economic Review* (December 1964), pp. 1019–26, the subsequent exchange with Horace B. Davis, *American Economic Review* (September 1965), pp. 861–64, and Bronfenbrenner's insightful survey "The Vicissitudes of Marxian Economics," *History of Political Economy* (Fall 1970), pp. 205–24.

2. Their best-known manifesto was *The Trend of Economics,* edited by Rexford Tugwell and published in 1924.

3. A good sense of the situation two decades ago can be obtained from Kenneth Boulding, "A New Look at Institutionalism," with comments by discussants, *American*

"economics can be, and in part is, a positive science" and that "positive economics is in principle independent of any particular ethical position or normative judgments."[4]

The complacent consensus has been loudly shattered over the last decade. Those economists who remain convinced that economics is a purely positive science have found it increasingly difficult to ignore the charge that the theoretical corpus of their discipline is in large part an elaborate justification of capitalist society.[5] Formation of the Union for Radical Political Economics;[6] the selection by the American Economic Association of a president notorious for maintaining that economics is "a system of belief" and his subsequent presidential address castigating the profession for its blindness, biases, and sterility;[7] the revival of a militant institutionalist movement organized in the Association for Evolutionary Economics;[8] articles and reviews attacking "neoclassical economics" appearing regularly in official publications of the American Economic Association[9]—the evidence is abundant that what was until recently a settled truth within the profession is today a very doubtful dogma indeed. Even the more deter-

Economic Review (May 1957), pp. 1–27; also Fritz Karl Mann, "Institutionalism and American Economic Theory: A Case of Interpenetration," *Kyklos* (July 1960), pp. 307–23.

4. The quotations are from Friedman's influential essay on "The Methodology of Positive Economics," published in his *Essays in Positive Economics* (Chicago: University of Chicago Press, 1953), pp. 3, 4. Friedman's essay triggered an extensive discussion, but the discussion revolved almost exclusively about his claim that the proper test of a theory was the conformity of its predictions to observation rather than the realism of its assumptions. The premise with which he began, that there can be and is a positive science of economics independent of any particular ethical position or normative judgments, went largely unchallenged.

5. The charge that the analytical tools employed by the majority of economists are marred by a fundamental bias in favor of *laissez faire* has been made most often and most vociferously by Joan Robinson, who enjoyed the forum of a Richard T. Ely Lecture for "The Second Crisis of Economic Theory," *American Economic Review* (May 1972), pp. 1–10.

6. The Minutes of the Annual Business Meeting of the American Economic Association in December, 1970, record one impact of URPE upon the larger profession: *American Economic Review* (May 1970), pp. 487–89. See also Martin Bronfenbrenner, "Radical Economics in America: A 1970 Survey," *Journal of Economic Literature* (September 1970), pp. 747–66.

7. John Kenneth Galbraith, "Economics as a System of Belief," *American Economic Review* (May 1970), pp. 469–78; "Power and the Useful Economist," *American Economic Review* (March 1973), pp. 1–11.

8. The Association publishes the *Journal of Economic Issues*. The issues of December 1975, and March 1976, will adequately illustrate the militance of the institutionalist renaissance.

9. See the *Journal of Economic Literature* and the annual issue of the *American Economic Review* which publishes the Association's Papers and Proceedings.

mined defenders of the positive-normative distinction now admit that the line is extraordinarily difficult to draw.[10]

It would appear that Gunnar Myrdal, after many years of swimming "against the stream" (the title of a recent collection of his essays),[11] is now riding triumphantly on the flood. When in the 1920's he was composing his monograph on *The Political Element in the Development of Economic Theory,* Myrdal believed that it was possible to purge all political, ideological, or other normative elements from economic theory and thereby to construct a purely positive science of economics. But he soon afterward repudiated that position, calling it "naive empiricism." Over the last forty years Myrdal has persistently criticized the implicit and explicit belief of economists "in the existence of a body of scientific knowledge acquired independently of all valuations." He put the criticism succinctly in his Preface to the English edition of *The Political Element:*

> Facts do not organize themselves into concepts and theories just by being looked at; indeed, except within the framework of concepts and theories, there are no scientific facts but only chaos. There is an inescapable *a priori* element in all scientific work. Questions must be asked before answers can be given. The questions are an expression of our interest in the world, they are at bottom valuations. Valuations are thus necessarily involved already at the stage when we observe facts and carry on theoretical analysis, and not only at the stage when we draw political inferences from facts and valuations.[12]

Myrdal's argument, elaborated subsequent to the 1930's in books, essays, introductions, and appendices, was never seriously challenged. Nonetheless, economists continued to uphold and employ the positive-normative

10. Friedman's rethinking of his position is discussed in the Introduction, "Why Economists Disagree," to his collection of essays, *Dollars and Deficits* (Englewood Cliffs, New Jersey: Prentice-Hall, Inc., 1968), pp. 1–16.

11. Gunnar Myrdal, *Against the Stream: Critical Essays on Economics* (New York, New York: Pantheon, 1973).

12. Gunnar Myrdal, *The Political Element in the Development of Economic Theory,* trans. Paul Streeten (London: Routledge & Kegan Paul, 1953), p. vii. Paul Streeten assembled Myrdal's scattered writings between 1933 and 1957 on the role of values in social science and wrote a lengthy introduction for the volume *Values in Social Theory* (London: Routledge & Kegan Paul, 1958). The most succinct statement of Myrdal's essential position is his note on facts and valuations in Appendix 2 of *An American Dilemma,* reprinted in *Value in Social Theory,* pp. 119–64.

distinction in methodological essays, textbook introductions, and *obiter dicta* until the 1960's, when the tide of opinion underwent a rapid reversal. Thomas Kuhn's *Structure of Scientific Revolutions*,[13] assisted by a changing political climate, accomplished quickly what Myrdal's patient arguments had failed to do: convince a substantial number of economists that the science of economics is inescapably grounded upon non-scientific commitments. The new word with which to refute the defenders of a purely positive science became "paradigm." Despite its considerable ambiguity— one careful reader has distinguished at least twenty-one different senses in which Kuhn employed that word[14]—the concept of a paradigm became for some a philosopher's stone that could transform any and every alleged science into a mere systematic elaboration of particular biases. Whether or not Kuhn intended this interpretation,[15] and whether or not those who invoke his authority have actually read him, the entire context within which the positive-normative distinction was used, defended, or criticized by economists did change drastically toward the end of the 1960's.

The resulting situation is unsatisfactory from any responsible point of view. Many economists continue to affirm the possibility of a positive science of economics, continue to assure their students and one another that economists possess or can create a purely scientific, purely descriptive, value-free, logical-empirical system of thought and knowledge, and continue to condemn as unscientific any attempt to derive economic generalizations with the explicit aid of value judgments. Such a rigid adherence to an untenable position severely restricts dialogue and inquiry[16] and transforms suspicion into conviction for many who are beginning to wonder whether economics is not more ideology than science.[17]

13. Thomas S. Kuhn, *The Structure of Scientific Revolutions* (2d ed., enlarged; Chicago, Illinois: University of Chicago Press, c. 1962, 1970).

14. Margaret Masterman, "The Nature of a Paradigm," in Imre Lakatos and Alan Musgrave (eds.), *Criticism and the Growth of Knowledge* (Cambridge: At the University Press, 1970), pp. 61–65.

15. Kuhn's two contributions to *Criticism and the Growth of Knowledge* pass up numerous opportunities to dissociate himself from this position. See "Logic of Discovery or Psychology of Research," *op. cit.*, pp. 1–23, and "Reflections on My Critics," pp. 231–78.

16. A recent and particularly glaring example of an effort to restrict inquiry with the aid of this distinction may be found in Richard A. Posner, "Economic Justice and the Economist," *The Public Interest* (Fall 1973), pp. 109–19.

17. In an extended review of Assar Lindbeck's *The Political Economy of the New Left: An Outsider's View* (New York, New York: Harper and Row, 1971), Bruce McFarlane impa-

At the same time we find economists and jubilant critics of economics who, in the words of Robert Solow, "seem to have rushed from the claim that no social science can be value-free to the conclusion that therefore anything goes,"[18] or who—the words are again Solow's—"have corrupted Thomas Kuhn's notion of a scientific paradigm, which they treat as a mere license for loose thinking."[19]

The Fatal Distinction

Where can dialogue begin? Surely it could begin with a universal agreement to abandon the positive-normative distinction. It is philosophically untenable, and all attempts to use it lead to question-begging procedures that stop discussion and impede the growth of knowledge. Myrdal's basic argument, that values enter inevitably into the construction of any scientific generalization, has never been refuted because it is irrefutable. The analysis applies to every science, not just to the social sciences, as has been amply demonstrated by such distinguished and diverse students of the history and philosophy of science as E. A. Burtt,[20] R. G. Collingwood,[21]Alfred North Whitehead,[22] Michael Polanyi,[23] and now Thomas Kuhn. The citation of names is hardly an argument; but the horse is too dead for flogging. It is *not* possible, not even "in principle" (that strange phrase economists invoke when they do not know how to do what they nonetheless believe

tiently complains that Lindbeck assumes "objective research" is possible and "ignores what Thomas Kuhn has taught us about the nature of discovery in social sciences, to say nothing of Myrdal who not only maintains that research in the social sciences *is* subjective and based on political values, but especially singles out economics." *The Review of Radical Political Economics* (Summer, 1972), p. 88.

18. Robert M. Solow, "Science and Ideology in Economics," *The Public Interest* (Fall 1970), p. 101.

19. Robert M. Solow, "Discussion," *American Economic Review* (May 1971), p. 63.

20. E. A. Burtt, *The Metaphysical Foundations of Modern Science* (rev. ed.; Garden City, New York: Doubleday, c. 1932, 1954).

21. R. G. Collingwood, *The Idea of Nature* (New York, New York: Oxford University Press, c. 1945, 1960).

22. Alfred North Whitehead, *Science and the Modern World* (New York, New York: The Free Press, c. 1925, 1967); *Modes of Thought* (New York, New York: The Free Press, c. 1938, 1968).

23. Michael Polanyi, *Personal Knowledge: Towards a Post-Critical Philosophy* (rev. ed.; New York, New York: Harper and Row, c. 1958, 1964).

can somehow be done) to construct a science of economics that is "independent of any particular ethical position or normative judgments." [24]

But the next constructive step is not so easy to discern. Myrdal has maintained that economists have an obligation to reveal their presuppositions as fully as possible so that readers can more easily assess the significance and limitations of any piece of analysis or description. There is an obvious deficiency in this procedure, however, that makes it at least as likely to mislead further as to reveal more fully. And Myrdal's own "confessions" demonstrate the danger. They tend to tire the reader well before they succeed in adequately exposing the crucial presuppositions. Myrdal probably exaggerates the effectiveness of introspection and assigns insufficient importance to the role of *criticism by others* in detecting the preconceptions that shape our knowledge. The widespread neglect for so long of Myrdal's diagnosis may be grounded in large part in economists' dissatisfaction with his prescription: the constant explication of underlying value judgments. Lionel Robbins, for example, has complained of "the minute search for implicit value judgments, which . . . has even become something of a heresy hunt—and, like most heresy hunts, something of a bore." [25] Those who are in general agreement with Myrdal's analyses may find his prefaces instructive; but those who consider his analyses inadequate or misleading will most likely find the same flaws in his presentation of the value framework underlying the analysis.

Robbins' objection suggests another reason why most economists have not responded to Myrdal's epistemological diagnosis. They believe that the value judgments which enter inevitably into scientific inquiry are trivial or ones which all serious inquirers hold in common. But if that claim was ever defensible, it is no longer. The fact is that the guiding preconceptions which have shaped the development of economic theory *are* being disputed today, and disputed in quite specific and concrete ways. Economists are accused of doing economics on the basis of analytical preconceptions that cause them to count as solutions what their critics perceive as

24. Whether or not we choose to designate these preconceptions as value judgments is less important than that we recognize the fact of pre-analytic commitments in scientific inquiry.

25. Lionel Robbins, *Politics and Economics* (New York, New York: St. Martin's Press, 1963), p. 6.

problems and that prevent them from even seeing certain social relationships as in any sense problematic. If someone were to suggest, for example, that college professors ought to do their own typing and a portion of the janitorial work in their own classrooms and offices, most economists would invoke the principle of comparative advantage in defense of present procedures. That is not an illegitimate response, but it is certainly a limited response. The principle of comparative advantage is at best a clumsy tool for dealing with the social meaning of work or the alienation that accompanies specialization and the hierarchical organization of labor, and at worst it is a tool of thought that conceals these problems altogether.

This is hardly a trivial or peripheral objection. The principle of comparative advantage is at the very center of price theory, which is surely the closest thing to a ruling paradigm in contemporary economic science. It is the pursuit of comparative advantage that makes demand curves slope downward to the right and that establishes opportunity costs, thereby giving supply curves their tendency to slope upward to the right. The crucial concept of efficiency is defined in economics in terms of comparative advantage, and it is the pursuit of comparative advantage that establishes prices which are indicators of social scarcity, that induces efficient decisions, and that gives meaning to the concept of equilibrium in price theory. The comparative advantage concept provides a theoretical orientation that is neither trivial in importance nor universally accepted by those who think systematically about social interaction. One may legitimately ask: Can economists defend the significant theoretical decision to view social reality through the prism of relative price theory and the principle of comparative advantage?

One reply is to say simply that it works; that it yields good predictions or that it explains what we want to understand. But that begs important questions. What are we trying to predict or explain? Which aspects of social reality are brought into prominence by our analytical procedures and which aspects are submerged or even distorted? Why this and not that?[26]

26. The issue is not simply between radical and conservative points of view, of course. The various social sciences employ differing analytical frameworks, with the consequence that one group of scientists may see as a solution what another group takes as its problem. This point is clearly argued and illustrated in Mancur Olson, Jr., "Economics, Sociology, and the Best of All Possible Worlds," *The Public Interest* (Summer 1968), pp. 96–118. Albert Hirschman has perceptively explored some consequences of the alternative frameworks

Economists and other practicing scientists easily become impatient with questions of this sort and are tempted to reply that each scientist, including the critic, has the right to study whatever interests him in whatever way he chooses. But such an individualistic, *laissez faire* conception of science is unrealistic. The separate sciences are not collections of individuals who do as they please; they are professional communities with definite intellectual standards and substantial power to enforce those standards. They exercise this power by granting or withholding membership in the community, the rewards of income and recognition, and opportunities to influence society through the dissemination of research results. The theoretical decisions of scientists have coercive power.[27] Moreover, knowledge is always power, and absolute power corrupts absolutely.

The Criterion of Science

The determination of some economists to find and enforce unambiguous criteria for genuinely scientific work arises in fact from their recognition of the social power of science. Genuine science leads to the progressive accumulation of warranted knowledge while other modes of inquiry do not—or at least do so less surely and effectively. And knowledge is useful, not least in the social sciences, where the inevitable conflicts engendered by opposition of interests are so often exacerbated by disagreement over matters of fact. A purely scientific, purely descriptive, value-free, logical-empirical science of economics could be immensely useful as an impartial conciliator of social conflict.[28]

---

brought by economists and political scientists to the study of social systems in *Exit, Voice, and Loyalty* (Cambridge: Harvard University Press, 1970).

27. This is one of the themes running through Kuhn's *Structure of Scientific Revolutions*. He has stated that if he were writing the book again he would begin by discussing the community structure of science. Kuhn, "Reflections on My Critics," p. 252 and also pp. 237–41. The creative and disciplinary role played by the community in every science has been ably described by John Ziman in *Public Knowledge: An Essay Concerning the Social Dimension of Science* (Cambridge: At the University Press, 1969). Further implications of the fact that most sciences are now integral parts of the industrial and political structure are pointed out in Jerome R. Ravetz, *Scientific Knowledge and Its Social Problems* (New York, New York: Oxford University Press, 1971).

28. This is the argument used by Friedman to support the sharp separation of positive from normative economics in "The Methodology of Positive Economics," *op. cit.*, pp. 3–7.

The Holy Grail is *objectivity*. The activities, institutions, and achievements of science rest upon the presupposition of an objective universe, a reality external to each observer that is what it is irrespective of the opinions people entertain about it; truth, in other words, is "beyond human authority." [29] This conviction or article of faith has given rise in turn to the concept of "objective truth." But if by "truth" we mean correct statements about reality, the phrase "objective truth" is confusing. [30] Statements, propositions, or judgments are made and held by subjects and are therefore always subjective. It might be argued that they are "objective" insofar as reality confirms them. But as soon as we speak less metaphorically we realize that it is always other subjects and never objects that confirm or disconfirm a judgment. Hypotheses in biology concerning pigeons are confirmed by biologists, not by pigeons; and hypotheses in economics concerning business cycles are confirmed by economists, not by business cycles.

There is consequently no way to establish the validity of a proposition in economic science except by persuading other economists. To persuade anyone, it is necessary to begin with what he is willing to grant and to reply to the objections he raises. *This is the method of science.* Science is not a purely logical procedure whereby true judgments are inexorably extracted from objective reality by automata called scientists. Science is a social activity, an activity of a community, and the cardinal rule of scientific procedure is: Submit your conclusions without reservation to the critical examination of others. [31] Scientific knowledge grows by testing; but it is scientists who do the testing, not "objective reality."

29. The quotation is from Karl Popper, who has consistently criticized both the notion of an authoritative source for knowledge and the absolute relativism which is its polar opposite. See especially Popper, *Conjectures and Refutations: The Growth of Scientific Knowledge* (New York, New York: Harper and Row, 1965), pp. 29–30.

30. The concept of "objective knowledge" is legitimate if it means knowledge that has been objectified by being expressed in language or some other external form. It is then *public* knowledge. Ziman finds a unifying principle for all of science in the quest for "public and *consensible*" knowledge. *Public Knowledge,* p. 11 and *passim.* If I understand him correctly, this is also what Popper has in mind in *Objective Knowledge: An Evolutionary Approach* (Oxford: At the Clarendon Press, 1972).

31. "It is important to guard against the illusion that there can exist in any science methodological rules the mere adoption of which will hasten its progress, although it is true that certain methodological dogmas . . . may certainly retard the progress of science.

It is true, of course, that scientists are not at liberty to accept or reject scientific conjectures on arbitrary or irrelevant grounds. But it is the scientific community that finally decides what is arbitrary or irrelevant. Within the confines of what Kuhn calls "normal science,"[32] such decisions are often made with little reflection and typically without controversy. But they are relatively simple decisions only because and insofar as members of the scientific community have no serious doubts about the adequacy of their ruling paradigm.

The danger lies in the circularity of this system of community control. One must step outside a paradigm in order to examine realities that the paradigm overlooks or distorts, but work done outside the paradigm is not accepted as scientific. *Extra ecclesiam nulla veritas.* Scientists tend to reject with indignation the very possibility that someone doing competent scientific work might be excluded from influential journals or positions because he adheres to unpopular values. But such a rejection misconceives the problem. The values at issue are ones that affect the content and presumptive quality of scientific work. The problem has even arisen in the natural sciences;[33] it is clearly far more serious in a discipline like economics where the very perception of problems to be studied depends so fundamentally upon conceptions of what human beings and human societies ought to be or can become.

Unfortunately, the view that value judgments cannot be fruitfully discussed because they are allegedly mere statements of subjective preference has acquired wide currency within the economics profession. Some economists may be insisting upon the possibility of a purely positive science because they have accepted the odd notion that "men can ultimately only fight"[34] when their value judgments conflict, that the issue is then

---

All one can do is to argue critically about scientific problems." K. Klappholz and J. Agassi, "Methodological Prescriptions in Economics," *Economica* (February 1959), p. 74.

32. "Normal science" means research firmly based upon one or more past scientific achievements, achievements that some particular scientific community acknowledges for a time as supplying the foundation for its further practice." Kuhn, *The Structure of Scientific Revolutions,* p. 10.

33. Instructive case studies from the natural sciences may be found in Polanyi's *Personal Knowledge.* The problem is one of implicit beliefs rather than any kind of bad faith. See also Kuhn, *The Structure of Scientific Revolutions,* especially pp. 77–90, 110–34.

34. Friedman, "The Methodology of Positive Economics," p. 5.

reduced to one of "thy blood or mine."[35] But it is sheer dogmatism to deny the possibility that one's choice of a theoretical orientation may have been significantly affected by prior judgments concerning such matters as the value of freedom versus equality, the relative importance of individual opportunity and social harmony, the merits of democracy versus some kind of aristocracy, the risks and the possible gains from conservative and from radical approaches to social reform, or the nature of man and the meaning of the good life.[36] And obscurantism is added to dogmatism by the strange insistence that such disagreements can never be resolved through discussion.[37] The soft side of the positive-normative distinction is the implicit encouragement that it gives to ethical solipsism. Everyone agrees that political or value judgments must be added to positive economics in order to obtain policy recommendations. The positive-normative distinction implies that these judgments are essentially arbitrary, mere matters of personal preference that cannot be tested or revised through rational discourse.[38]

35. Lionel Robbins, *An Essay on the Nature and Significance of Economic Science* (2d ed.; London: Macmillan, 1935), p. 150.

36. An excellent stimulus for economists willing to reflect on these questions has recently been rescued from the relative obscurity of its initial publication and reprinted as the leading essay in Edmund S. Phelps (ed.), *Economic Justice* (Baltimore, Maryland: Penguin, 1973): See W. S. Vickrey, "An Exchange of Questions between Economics and Philosophy," pp. 35–62. This extraordinary essay was originally published in the first volume of the old Federal Council of Churches series on Ethics and Economic Life, *Goals of Economic Life*, edited by A. Dudley Ward (New York, New York: Harper and Brothers, 1953), pp. 148–77.

37. Why do so many social scientists dogmatically assume that criticism of conflicting judgments (inevitably?) produces consensus in one area but is altogether useless in another? For philosophically informed discussions of this issue by economists, see Sidney S. Alexander, "Human Values and Economist's Values," in Sidney Hook (ed.), *Human Values and Economic Policy* (New York, New York: New York University Press, 1967), pp. 101–16, and Amartya K. Sen, *Collective Choice and Social Welfare* (San Francisco, California: Holden-Day, 1970), pp. 56–64.

38. "We must certainly hold fast to the idea of a neutral science of economics.... To have recognized in this connection the distinction between positive and normative judgments is one of the achievements of thought since Adam Smith and the Physiocrats; and nothing but confusion could come from any attempt to slur it over. But the idea that there can be constructed a system of prescriptions which results more or less inevitably from the results of positive analysis can involve scarcely less of a confusion: any theory of economic policy must depend partly on conceptions and valuations which are imported from outside." Robbins, *Politics and Economics*, p. 19. But if value judgments are arbitrary statements of subjective preference and also an inescapable part of any policy recommen-

The preceding argument is a modest one. Economists should stop talking about positive and normative economics and speak instead simply about the science of economics. Economics is a science because knowledge about economic phenomena has long been systematically cultivated and continues to be cultivated by a recognized community of inquirers who read, build upon, and criticize one another's work. No more is required. Science neither rests upon nor discovers indubitable truths. The theories and generalizations of economic science are conjectures; but they are warranted conjectures because and insofar as they have withstood attempts at critical refutation. Such a conception of science clearly implies that scientists are not entitled to withhold *any* of their conjectures from criticism, and that the disciplinary boundaries within which they will inevitably work must be regarded as potential sources of error as well as guides to the discovery of truth.

Furthermore, economists ought to re-examine their thinking on the whole subject of value judgments. They enter inevitably into scientific work. Their critical examination can sometimes contribute at least as much to the development of warranted knowledge as can the further refinement of data or the logical improvement of formal models. Economists will, of course, shy away from such a challenge if they continue to maintain that value judgments are nothing but statements of subjective preference. But this is itself a dogma that flies in the face of the undeniable fact that people do hold at least some value judgments to be interpersonally valid, that they do offer evidence and reasons to support their value judgments, and that rational discussion often does lead to consensus among people who began by holding (or supposing that they held) conflicting ethical or political positions.

Radicals and Neoclassicals

How does contemporary American economics fare when we apply this criterion, openness to criticism, to determine whether it is scientific or ideological? Contrary to what most outside observers currently seem to be-

---

dation, then are not all policy recommendations finally arbitrary? And what then is the value for policy of a positive science?

lieve, it satisfies the criterion remarkably well. Despite formal adherence to the positive-normative dichotomy, with all its potential for begging questions and deflecting fundamental criticism, the economics profession over the past decade has encouraged the publication of radical criticism, has paid attention to it, and has publicly responded to it. This is not enough, of course, for those critics who define as ideological any position incompatible with their own or who distinguish science from ideology by looking at conclusions rather than procedures. And it will never be admitted by those who, whether from ignorance or malice, persist in caricaturing or flatly misrepresenting what economists are currently doing.[39]

The *Journal of Economic Literature,* an official publication of the American Economic Association, has repeatedly opened its pages in recent years to critics of "establishment" works and ways. The Association's other journal, the *American Economic Review,* has also published, usually in the annual Papers and Proceedings volume, numerous criticisms of orthodox economics. Other prestigious "establishment" journals, such as the *Quarterly Journal of Economics* and the *Journal of Political Economy,* have offered articles, reviews, and symposia in which general and specific criticisms were forcefully presented. The accusation of official indifference or conspiratorial silence in the face of radical criticism simply cannot be sustained by anyone who pays attention to what economists have actually been doing in the last decade.

On the contrary, it is the critics who have tended to substitute dogma for dialogue by failing to modify their criticisms in the light of the responses that have been given to their arguments. Kuhn's concept of scientific paradigms has become in some radical circles a justification for refusing to listen to those who do not begin with the correct presuppositions. The distinguished Marxist economist Paul Sweezy, commenting on Assar Lindbeck's *The Political Economy of the New Left: An Outsider's View,* complained that Lindbeck "has no empathy for the radical position" so that "I,

---

39. As long as the market for tirades is so much better than the market for balanced, judicious assessments, the intelligent lay public will continue to derive most of its notions about economics from books like Robert Lekachman's *Economists at Bay: Why the Experts Will Never Solve Your Problems* (New York, New York: McGraw-Hill, 1975). The reasons for this harsh judgment may be found in a review of the book in *Worldview* (September 1976), pp. 53–54.

as a radical, find it as irrelevant and boring as most neoclassical economics."[40] Lindbeck's responses was testy:

> If the impossibility of intellectual communication between different groups of social scientists is accepted, these groups belong in (different) divinity schools rather than in social science faculties of universities.[41]

Empathy is essential, of course, to genuine dialogue, but consensus is the goal of dialogue, not its precondition. While passion neither can nor should be excluded from scientific discussion, it does not entail or excuse abusive and *ad hominem* argument. And it surely does not justify a refusal to pay attention to what opponents are actually saying and doing.

Anyone who follows the professional literature and also reads the complaints leveled against it must wonder occasionally about the good faith of the critics. The charge is constantly made, for example, that economists ignore questions of income distribution and that this is an "untouchable" topic. Did the critics perhaps overlook the publication of two comprehensive books on income distribution by two well-known economists in 1971?[42] Or the pair of review articles on these books featured in the *Journal*

40. "Symposium: Economics of the New Left," *Quarterly Journal of Economics* (November 1972), p. 659. Lindbeck's book, first published in 1971, has been reprinted in an expanded version that contains the contributions to this symposium plus additional reviews of the book and a further rejoinder by Lindbeck (New York, New York: Harper and Row, 1977). The book itself, its reception by economists, and now its republication along with vigorous radical criticism of the book (including a long and hostile review article from *The Review of Radical Political Economics*) are continuing evidence of establishment economists' willingness to confront controversy and honor dissenting views.

41. *Ibid.*, p. 668. The Ethics and Society Department in the University of Chicago Divinity School would surely want to object to Lindbeck's choice of a home for solipsists. If divinity schools are to be sanctuaries for those who wish to work without criticism within closed systems of thought, their faculties are no more entitled to a place in the university than are fundamentalist social scientists. For at least as long as Alvin Pitcher has been quartered in Swift Hall, students in the Divinity School have been urged to criticize fundamentalism of every type, religious or scientific, not to give it a comfortable home. This note offers a good opportunity to thank Al Pitcher for pushing me along the road of dialogue almost twenty years ago and for continuing efforts in the recent past to prevent my straying in the company of economists too far from the straight path.

42. Martin Bronfenbrenner, *Income Distribution Theory* (Chicago, Illinois: Aldine-Atherton, 1971) and Jan Pen, *Income Distribution: Facts, Theories, Policies* (New York, New York: Praeger, 1971).

of Economic Literature?[43] Or the Richard T. Ely Lecture to the 1974 meeting of the American Economic Association?[44] Or the research and arguments associated with the names of Lester Thurow,[45] A. Michael Spence,[46] or Doeringer and Piore?[47] The income distribution studies of Thurow, Spence, and Doeringer-Piore are specifically mentioned here because they have significant non-conservative implications and have attracted considerable attention among economists and others interested in public policy.

The Neoclassical Perspective

Fortunately, an alternative hypothesis to that of bad faith can be constructed. And as we sketch it out we begin to discover the nature of the gulf that currently divides Marxists from so-called neoclassical economists. The radical critics of orthodox economics are reluctant to concede that any research undertaken within the framework of neoclassical theory could constitute genuine investigation of real problems. Not even the radical implications of Thurow's work or of Spence's can redeem research that employs the perspective of marginal productivity theory. Marginal productivity theory is allegedly circular, empty, incoherent, and consequently nothing more than apologetics for capitalism.[48] But marginal productivity

43. C. E. Ferguson and Edward J. Nell, "Two Books on the Theory of Income Distribution: A Review Article," *Journal of Economic Literature* (June 1972), pp. 437–53. These are actually two separate review articles. Ferguson was a neoclassical stalwart (he died before his review could be published). Nell writes from a neo-Marxist perspective.

44. Alice M. Rivlin, "Income Distribution—Can Economists Help?" *American Economic Review* (May 1975), pp. 1–15.

45. Arguments developed by Thurow against the notion of effective wage competition are summarized in his *Generating Inequality: Mechanisms of Distribution in the U.S. Economy* (New York, New York: Basic Books, 1975).

46. Major presuppositions of the "human capital" approach to research on income distribution are sharply questioned in A. Michael Spence, *Market Signaling Informational Transfer in Hiring and Related Screening Processes* (Cambridge: Harvard University Press, 1974).

47. The authors' theory of dual labor markets is presented in Peter B. Doeringer and Michael J. Piore, *Internal Labor Markets and Manpower Analysis* (Lexington, Mass.: Heath, 1971).

48. A surprising number of Marxists and other radicals who know nothing else about the professional literature of contemporary economics have heard about the Cambridge Capital Controversy and its alleged result: demolition of the marginal productivity

theory is essentially nothing but the neoclassical or orthodox perspective applied to questions of resource pricing and allocation. It is the fundamental perspective of that broader theory to which radical critics are really objecting.

The neoclassical perspective is a way of thinking about social phenomena that conceives society as composed entirely of individuals whose conscious actions aim at maximizing expected utility. People choose continuously among perceived options, weighing the expected benefits and costs of each decision and electing those actions through which they expect to secure for themselves the largest net advantage attainable. Monetary prices are an important set of data for decision makers because they provide a common denominator through which the relative advantage of innumerable options can be precisely compared. The decisions people make entail offers and bids which ultimately establish these prices by moving them toward market clearing values.

Neither selfishness, materialism, nor obsession with money is assumed. The maximization of expected utility can lead to anything from self-sacrifice to self-aggrandizement; the self whose interests are pursued is not prescribed in the neoclassical perspective. Moreover, the notion that economizing is peculiarly directed toward "material" wealth is probably a careless inference from the correct observation that neoclassical economics is centrally concerned with exchange and consequently directs most of its attention to goods that are augmentable and transferable. The substantial role played by monetary costs and monetary transactions in economists' analysis and research is simply a consequence of the fact that the institution of money enormously facilitates exchange.

Why is this perspective so offensive to most radical critics of economics?[49]

---

theory. But the Cambridge Controversy only showed that marginal productivity theory could not produce a consistent and coherent theory of the aggregative distribution of income between workers and capitalists. The claim that it *could* perform this task was never central to neoclassical theory. No adequate account of the Cambridge Controversy will be easy reading. For good summaries by economists with opposite sympathies, see G. C. Harcourt, "Some Cambridge Controversies in the Theory of Capital," *Journal of Economic Literature* (June 1969), pp. 369–405, and Mark Blaug, *The Cambridge Revolution: Success or Failure* (London: Institute of Economic Affairs, 1975).

49. But not to all! Some Marxist economists have maintained that neoclassical theory will be an indispensable tool also in a socialist society because it can handle more effec-

To begin with, it assigns fundamental importance to the actual preferences of individuals. Every sensible economist knows that the wants of individuals are the product of socialization and that people's socialization sometimes serves them badly. But neoclassical economists place a heavy burden of proof upon anyone (Galbraith, Nader, Marcuse, or the Federal Communications Commission) who claims to *know* that what individuals want is not in their best interest.[50] Wants expressed in the market are at very least the beginning point for all evaluative judgments.

Secondly, the neoclassical perspective assumes that each party to a voluntary exchange gains from that exchange; otherwise it would not occur. This is not the same as assuming a complete harmony of interests in society, as radical critics repeatedly claim. But voluntary exchange is the focus of attention and voluntary exchange is a method of inducing others to cooperate by *adding to* their range of opportunities rather than subtracting from them. Market interaction secures social cooperation, in short, through persuasion rather than coercion; and orthodox economic theory has developed over the last two centuries largely in an effort to explicate the coordinative potential in voluntary exchange. It must be noted at the same time that this preoccupation of economists with exchange relationships has produced a vast literature on "market failure" in which the limitations of market arrangements have been minutely explored. Orthodox economists have paid far more attention to the deficiencies of market arrangements than advocates of socialism have paid to the deficiencies of central planning.

This is closely related to a third major difference in approach. The neoclassical perspective views power as an insecure possession, because the advantages that power confers upon its possessor will tend to attract additional bids and offers that will undermine the power base. It is misleading to claim, as radicals do persistently, that orthodox economists ignore the

tively than Marxist theory problems of efficient planning. See for example the classic statement of Oskar Lange, "Marxian Economics and Modern Economic Theory," reprinted from *The Review of Economic Studies* (June 1935) in David Horowitz, ed., *Marx and Modern Economics* (New York, New York: Monthly Review Press, 1968), pp. 68–87.

50. For evidence that neoclassical theory can be used effectively to criticize the outcome of "consumer sovereignty," see Staffan Burenstam Linder, *The Harried Leisure Class* (New York, New York: Columbia University Press, 1970) and Tibor Scitovsky, *The Joyless Economy* (New York, New York: Oxford University Press, 1976).

problem of power. Ownership of resources is clearly recognized as power, and resource control coupled with the ability to exclude competitors is a constant object of study by neoclassical economists. It is ironic that the critics so rarely see the blindness toward the problem of power implicit in their own stated preference for a usually unspecified "social control" of resources. And it is an empirical question, on which neoclassical theory sheds important light, whether particular private individuals or organizations in any society actually possess excessive power through disproportionate resource ownership.

It is, furthermore, a critical difference between orthodox and Marxist economics that the former views competition as occurring between parties *on the same side* of the market. Thus employers compete against employers, employees against employees. This point of view is hostile toward notions of "the power of the capitalist class" or "the solidarity of the working class." But these alternative conceptions so central to Marxist social analysis have not fared nearly as well as the neoclassical approach in explaining and predicting observed events. The radical contention that orthodox economists deliberately conceal the class basis of the distribution of income ought to be, but largely is not, supported by arguments and evidence showing that a class-oriented analysis can better explain actual changes over time in patterns of income distribution.[51]

Finally, neoclassical economics, by focusing on the efficient allocation of resources, implicitly asserts that the task of assigning resources to their most advantageous use is a task of great importance and complexity. This follows from the almost incalculable variety of presumably legitimate wants that individuals have and from the infinitely varied ways in which resources can be combined. Marxist economists deny the fundamental importance or difficulty of the allocative task and assert that efficient coordination is a relatively simple problem. They do this by claiming that people's real wants are fairly simple and uniform and that the appropriate ways of combining resources for production are largely known data of

51. There would seem to be no *a priori* reason to assume that any single theory will best explain both the British and the American economies. The relative preference of British economists for a class-based theory of income distribution may in part reflect the persistence of the class distinctions that were so obvious in David Ricardo's time (the time of Jane Austen).

technology. If the Marxists are correct, markets are a dispensable social institution and central planning will encounter no major information problems. If the neoclassical perspective is more nearly correct, the problem of information may not be solvable except through decentralized decision-making and market coordination.[52]

Conclusion

The thesis of this entire essay has been that the enemy is dogmatism, and the requirements of brevity have at the end led to a manner of statement which is unfortunately dogmatic in tone if not in intent. But perhaps these insufficiently qualified interpretations of the principal radical-orthodox disagreements will serve to focus attention on the depth of the divisions that give rise today to controversies over theory. Debates about marginal productivity theory are symptoms of divergent visions. It could not be wholly a waste of scientific energy for economists to explore, through critical but empathetic dialogue, the conflicting conceptions of human nature and society that the West and, increasingly, the entire world has inherited from the Enlightenment. We might begin, for example, with the French Revolution and ask to what extent liberty presupposes fraternity and the circumstances under which equality is the enemy and the circumstances under which it is the precondition of defensible liberty and genuine fraternity. But that is clearly a task too large to begin here.

52. The classic statement of the problem is still the essay of F. A. Hayek, "The Use of Knowledge in Society," *American Economic Review* (September 1945), pp. 519–30.

CHAPTER 3

Income and Ethics in the Market System

AMONG THOSE who lecture or write about economics and ethics, the market system generally has a dubious reputation. That reputation rises and falls in response to historical events and the shifting discontents of civilization. But even in those times when ethicists are speaking well of capitalism or the market system, they usually do so with faint damns rather than genuine praise. They may grant that it works, that it gets people fed, clothed and housed. They may even be willing to concede that alternatives cannot be made to work nearly as well—at least not yet. But they will attribute this, more often than not, to something like the compatibility of capitalism with human greed, which isn't a very inspiring recommendation from a moral point of view.

A New Look at an Old Complaint
Why is this? What is the basic moral flaw, or supposed moral flaw, in the market economy? Why have so many eminent and respectable moral thinkers looked upon capitalism and pronounced it an unfortunate necessity at best? I want to argue this evening that the condemnation rests largely upon a set of interrelated misunderstandings. But these are not, I also want to maintain, the misunderstandings of which people in the

Unpublished typescript of lecture at Montana State University in Bozeman, Montana, 20 October 1982. Reprinted by permission of Mrs. Juliana Heyne.

business community usually complain when they set out to defend the profit system against its critics. The misunderstandings run deeper than the customary rejoinders recognize, which is why the arguments in defense of capitalism rarely silence the critics or even slow them down.

Of course, my arguments aren't likely to change many minds, either. When it comes to this issue, those who care are quite certain of their views, and they listen to talks such as this one more in order to grade the speaker's position than to reexamine their own. Or else they know in advance where the speaker stands and have only come out in order to hear once again that old-time religion that so comforts the heart. They want to nod approvingly while the speaker flails the greed and materialism of the corporate sector or, on the other side, flails the ignorance and self-righteousness of those who flail the greed and materialism of the corporate sector.

This is not a complaint. The topic before us has been treated so often that everyone's entitled to assume that nothing new is likely to be said. Nonetheless, I mean to try. The issues are extremely important both for the way in which we organize our political life and for the way in which we think about ourselves and our society. Alfred North Whitehead was profoundly correct when he contended, more than half a century ago, that a great society was a society whose principal members thought greatly of their functions. In a society dominated as ours is by the business mind, it is essential that business and economic activity be seen, at least by those who participate in it, as a worthy vocation. Is that possible? The answer will depend in large part on our moral assessment of the free-market economy.

Standards for Assessment

What should we consider when we want to assess the morality of a social system? Two criteria immediately suggest themselves: the criteria of justice and efficiency. Social systems must obviously be just or fair if they are to be ethically acceptable. But they also have to be efficient in the sense that they enable us to accomplish our purposes. Is anything more required? In particular, do we also want to take account of intentions, of motives, as we ordinarily do when we pass ethical judgment on the actions of individuals?

Motives and Consequences

We all recognize the importance of distinguishing between motives and consequences in judging people's behavior. If I knock you over accidentally, I may be a clumsy lout, but I'm not an evil person. If I *try* to knock you over, however, with no provocation, I'm a malicious person even if I miss you completely. The law agrees. Attempted murder is a more serious crime, with more severe penalties, than involuntary homicide. Should this distinction also be applied to social systems?

The temptation to personify non-persons is sometimes irresistible. We curse chairs over which we stumble and we blame the weather when it upsets our plans. Of course, we also realize that these are irrational responses, signs of our own frustration rather than of any genuine intentions on the part of chairs or the weather. But what about social systems and institutions? They aren't impersonal objects, and we know that motives do matter within social systems. Since they seem to have intentions as well as consequences, we are disposed to judge them, as we judge individual persons, by what they are aiming at as well as by what they finally achieve.

And so Adam Smith's famous statement about the invisible hand leaves many of us feeling ambivalent at best. Even if he was correct, and there really is some kind of invisible-hand process that extracts the public interest from everyone's pursuit of purely private gain, wouldn't it be better if people aimed at the public good directly? Doesn't it count against a social system, at least from an ethical standpoint, that the motives which make it work are selfish, even if it should be the case that the ultimate consequences are completely satisfactory from a moral perspective?

But this whole line of argument is fundamentally mistaken. Social systems, including the market economy, have no intentions at all, and to suppose that the motives or intentions of those who participate in the system are the motives and intentions of the system itself is a confusion of thought that can lead us seriously astray. It is an especially dangerous confusion when we start to ask about the justice of social systems. Moreover, self-interest is not the same as selfishness, and the narrow pursuit of private purposes has no necessary connection with greed, materialism, or a lack of concern for others.

Those are strong statements. Can I persuade you that they may all be true?

A Roundabout Route

The position for which I want to contend can best be understood if we approach it indirectly, by reflecting on a social system with which we're all familiar but which doesn't arouse the belligerent convictions that so often infuse the discussion of economic systems. It's a social system that serves us remarkably well and that has often served me effectively when I wanted to get people reflecting on the basic nature of social systems. It's the system we use to move about on our urban streets.

This *is* a social system. From Boston to Bucharest to Bozeman, people would not be able to get from home to work and back again without the system of social coordination that we casually refer to as the traffic system. Have you ever thought about how it works?

Radical Individualism

It's a radically individualist system, to begin with. Drivers sit in their own vehicles, cut off from any communication with the other drivers who surround them, pass them, meet them, and cross their path. There are citizens-band radios, of course, but it's my impression that drivers use them to communicate with people who aren't close by and whom they don't expect to encounter. I've seen no evidence that drivers use citizens-band radios to work out problems of potential conflict on the freeways, during the rush hour, or generally while driving in urban areas.

On the contrary, drivers formulate their plans quite independently, with no knowledge of the plans that have been or will be made by others whom they're going to encounter. Each of us decides what time to leave for work and what route to take, and we do so without even consulting anyone else. The choice of both ends and means is made by individual drivers who characteristically don't have the slightest inkling of what others are going to do. There is certainly no grand plan, no overarching design constructed by the Department of Commuting to make sure that you and I aren't planning to occupy the identical road space at the same time. (The urban traffic system, in short, is *not* like the air traffic control system.)

Individualism, Selfishness, and Concentration

Now one could correctly say of this system, as Adam Smith said about investors in his day: Each person intends only his own gain. But is that selfish? Is it selfish of me, while driving, to focus exclusively on getting to my chosen destination as quickly as is consistent with my personal well-being? Is it selfish of me to ignore completely, not even to think about, the welfare of other drivers? If in fact I start to wonder where other drivers are going and whether their missions might be more urgent than mine, I'm beginning to daydream, and I become to that extent a greater menace not only to my own welfare but also to the welfare of other drivers in my immediate environment. An important insight emerges from this: Responsible, ethical behavior will often require an exclusive preoccupation with the technical task at hand. Driving in traffic is an example that we will all concede. So is the act of performing surgical operations; surgeons don't operate on close friends or relatives, because the personal relationship could easily introduce considerations irrelevant to the task at hand and inimical to success.

Might this also be true of most activity in the market? We'll return to that question.

Morality or Muddle?

Meanwhile, let's note in the traffic situation what harm is likely to be done by people who decide to insert "morality" into their decisions. What will a driver accomplish if he refrains from advancing when the light turns green, perhaps because he's running early and suspects that some in the cross-traffic are running late? He will almost certainly not persuade the cross-traffic to go on red; he will delay people behind him, who could well be on much more urgent missions than his own; and he will increase the likelihood of an accident by introducing substantial new uncertainties into the calculations of drivers who are observing and trying to anticipate his erratic behavior. And, of course, if everyone decided to be "unselfish" in this manner, traffic would come to a halt, as drivers regularly got out of their vehicles to discuss the relative urgency of their current goals and to insist that the welfare of others be advanced before their own.

Is this also generally true of ordinary market activity, that it would come to a halt, at enormous cost to all participants, if they were all to act consistently on the principle of advancing the welfare of the most needy or the most worthy—rather than focusing on the accomplishment of their own personal goals? To that question, too, we'll want to return.

The Rules of the Game

I have not mentioned a very important aspect of traffic systems: They are *not* systems of complete anarchy. There are definite rules of the game that must be obeyed by participants if the system is to work. Drive to the right, stop for red lights, stay close to the legal speed limit, and, above all, do not touch the cars around you. We even have rules for suspending the rules: Everyone stops and yields to vehicles with sirens and flashing lights, and uniformed police officers may trump *all* the rules.

Clarity and Stability

In the case of a social system for moving traffic, the rules are often arbitrary. Drive to the right. Why not to the left? Stop on red. Why not on green instead? What the rules stipulate is often unimportant. What matters, in addition to the rules' being mutually consistent, is that they be clear to all and stable over time. We have to know exactly what the rules are. Recall the panic that you must have felt at some time in your life when you found yourself heading in the wrong direction on a one-way street, or trapped in the exit lane on a freeway when you wanted to go through, because the relevant rule hadn't become clear to you in time. This is why uniform rules are so desirable. Imagine the confusion if drivers had to keep remembering whether they were in a town that drove on the left or on the right, that required drivers to stop on red or on green, or that did or did not permit right-hand turns against a red light.

Stability over time also promotes the clarity that is so essential for traffic rules, but in addition, it reduces the costs of adjusting to changes in the rules. It doesn't much matter that people drive on opposite sides of the road in England and France, but it does matter that it's the left side in England and the right side in France, because those are the rules to which other rules and practices have adjusted over time. The most obvious example is the placement of the driver's seat in cars made respectively for British and French operation. One reason England doesn't conform on this matter to the way that most of the world drives is simply the cost of readjustment.

All this is quite obvious and non-controversial. Is it equally true—it is certainly less obvious and more controversial—with respect to economic systems in general? Does it matter greatly what the rules of the game are, as long as they are clear and stable? In addition, of course, the rules must be obeyed. That's all true, I shall argue, in economic systems as well as in traffic systems.

Parallel Definitions

Let me now try to summarize in one sentence the social system for moving traffic with which we are all familiar. It is a system in which individuals pursue their own interests on the basis of the situation they perceive, obeying a few clear and stable rules of the game.

And let me follow that up with an equally brief definition of capitalism, or a free-market economy. It is also a social system in which individuals pursue their own interests on the basis of the situation they perceive, obeying a few clear and stable rules of the game.

Looking at the Consequences

What emerges from the traffic system? Some fatal accidents. More damaged fenders. A certain amount of anxiety. Occasional incidents of personal nastiness. But if those were the principal consequences of the system's operation, none of us would participate. The fact is that we do play the game, and we do so voluntarily, because we expect to be better off by playing than by not playing. We venture into traffic every day, and we regularly get back home in satisfactory condition. The system works. Judged by its consequences, it's a success. I don't doubt that improvements will be made in the system in the future as they're discovered and we learn how to implement them. But the system works astonishingly well as it is right now, with all its warts; and no one really knows how to design a better system for enabling people who live in dense population clusters to move about quickly, freely, safely, comfortably, and inexpensively.

Social Cooperation as Mutual Accommodation

One of the elements that make it work is the mechanism of mutual accommodation that it embodies. This mechanism becomes especially important and visible in large cities during the rush hours. Have you ever wondered—we too seldom ask such absurdly instructive questions—why it never happens that everyone using the freeway chooses to drive in the same lane? Just too unlikely, you might think. But isn't it also most unlikely that each of the four alternative lanes on a freeway will be chosen by precisely twenty-five percent of the drivers? And yet that's roughly what happens every day, morning and evening. A coincidence too improbable to be believed—until we notice how and why it happens.

A lane carrying fewer than one-fourth of the traffic will move more quickly; that advantage will be noticed by a few drivers traveling in adjacent lanes; they will respond by changing lanes. As they do so, they slow down the lane which they enter and accelerate the lane which they left. Through this continuous process of marginal adjustments, initiated by individual drivers responding to the perceived advantages to themselves of changing lanes, the traffic is continuously adjusted to keep each lane moving at approximately the same speed. And thereby the sum of the time traveled by all of the commuters together is minimized.

Each participant intends only his own gain, as Adam Smith put it.

> But he is in this, as in many other cases, led by an invisible hand to promote an end which was no part of his intention. Nor is it always the worse for the society that it was no part of it. By pursuing his own interest he frequently promotes that of the society more effectually than when he really intends to promote it.

In a market economy, the changing net advantages that participants perceive are communicated not by different lane speeds but primarily by changing relative prices. When suppliers and demanders aren't accommodating each other very well, relative prices start to move. The prices that rise relative to other prices induce suppliers to offer more and demanders to ask for less. The prices that decline encourage demanders and discourage suppliers. These responses begin to close the gaps that had opened up between what producers were offering and what users were requesting, which in turn checks the relative price movements that had induced the mutually accommodating responses. Changing money prices serve both as information and as incentive in that remarkable system of social cooperation that we call *a market economy*.

The Limited Relevance of Productivity

It's not enough, however, that the market system be efficient and productive. Productivity and efficiency are in fact far less important in our time and society than they were in the Europe of Adam Smith. In the eighteenth century, a decline in national wealth (or what we today call gross national product) meant actual destitution for masses of people, including the possibility of starvation. Adam Smith's emphasis upon economic growth was a sensible and humane emphasis in his time, grounded as it was in his desire that the great majority of the people, whose labor fed, clothed, and housed the whole society, should "be themselves tolerably well fed, cloathed and lodged."

During a recession such as we're now experiencing, one may have to argue a bit for the position that additions to GNP aren't very important. The issue is complicated by the fact that the costs of a recession are so unevenly distributed; most of the costs fall upon a small percentage of the total population. But even the unemployed in our society don't face the prospect of genuine destitution. For Americans, an economic reverse entails principally the frustration of expectations. We fail to obtain what we had hoped to obtain and counted on obtaining. We make our plans in the expectation that we'll be receiving no less than some minimum amount of income; and when those expectations aren't fulfilled, we're compelled to revise our plans, our life patterns, and sometimes even our conception of our own worth.

Income, Expectations, and Injustice

I am not trying to minimize these costs of economic failure. Social expectations are vitally important. We look to one another for assistance and cooperation in obtaining not just the goods that money will buy, but also the more fundamental goods (more fundamental, at least, in an affluent society) of justice and respect. When our income expectations are frustrated, most of us feel the cost primarily in the ultimate frustration of expectations with regard to our personal worth. If at the same time we believe that we were morally entitled to the fulfillment of those expectations, we will conclude that an injustice has been perpetrated against us. And we will begin to look for changes in the legal-political order that might correct the injustice we think we have suffered.

It is in this area that we find the deepest and most genuine moral dilemmas of the market system. Complaints about selfishness and materialism are altogether wide of the mark. Ethical thinkers who object to capitalism on the grounds that it is based on or even that it encourages selfishness or materialism only prove, to me at least, that they have not paid close attention to the system they claim to be criticizing.

Selfishness: A False Indictment

There is nothing peculiarly selfish about the behavior of participants in a free-market system. Whether we judge that behavior by its consequences or by its presumed intentions, there is simply no basis for a general verdict of "selfish." The primary consequence of people's participation in the market system is a continuous expansion of cooperative endeavor, mutual accommodation, and valued goods. That's certainly not a selfish outcome.

But it's the intentions, not the outcomes, against which most critics want to level the charge of selfishness. At this point I appeal to the traffic analogy. Surely no one would want to argue that drivers are selfishly motivated when they concentrate exclusively on using the means available to achieve their own personal objectives. Drivers *cannot* take any effective account of what others want, and any attempt to do so will make others worse off rather than better off. A narrow obsession with their own welfare, if you want to call it that, is what distinguishes the best drivers. But I think we could more accurately call it a dedication to the task at hand.

The Complexities of Motivation

There is, after all, nothing inherently selfish about trying to reach one's destination as quickly and safely as possible. Doesn't it matter crucially what that destination is and why one has chosen to go there? A driver could be taking children to school, going to work as a hospital volunteer, heading for an illicit rendezvous, meeting a friend to rob a bank, driving to church, or heading to a lecture on the ethics of the market system. Even that information wouldn't be enough to tell us whether the driver's intentions were selfish. *Why* is he going to that lecture? To find arguments with which to intimidate his friends? To get out of his turn at doing the dishes? To nourish his soul? To pick up some easy academic credit?

We are much too ready to impugn people's motives, including even our own at times. Participants in the market system are human beings, with all the variety of motivation and intention that this entails. People don't do many things for simple reasons, much less for simply selfish reasons. Insofar as the claim that capitalism relies on, rewards, or encourages selfish behavior can be given any clear meaning, I maintain that the claim is false. Whatever plausibility that claim might have—and public opinion polls show that it unfortunately has a great deal—stems largely from the fallacious identification of focused responsibility with selfishness. This confusion is compounded by the fact that responsibility is monitored in a market system primarily through the comparison of values expressed in monetary terms. And we have great difficulty breaking free from the notion that there is something inherently immoral about trying to maximize monetary magnitudes.

Monetary Values, Greed, and Morality

An almost perfect example of the confusions to which I'm referring was provided by a recent *Wall Street Journal* article on inner-city churches that have been selling their property to developers. The background facts are simple. Many old church buildings sit on pieces of real estate that would have enormous value in residential or business uses. The congregations are typically small, because most members have long since moved away. Moreover, the buildings, being old, are frequently expensive to maintain. The pressure on churches to sell their property in such situations is easy to understand.

But the article reports some interesting comments. A Seventh-Day Adventist congregation in Manhattan found that it couldn't afford to maintain a building that it had purchased two years earlier from a synagogue for $400,000. When the members decided to sell, the first offer was for $800,000—twice what they had paid. As additional offers came in at progressively higher figures, the church decided to take sealed bids, in order—I quote the language of a member on the church's sale committee—"to avoid a bidding war." *War?* What an inappropriate and yet revealing choice of words!

The article gets even more interesting. A Manhattan pastor was interviewed, one who obviously doesn't want to see old churches torn down. I quote his comment directly from the *Journal* article: "'I don't give a damn what others think,' he says. 'It's a perversion that property is more important than beauty.'" An extraordinary statement! Property cannot be more important than beauty for the same reason that mountains cannot be more important than beauty: the categories aren't comparable. What the indignant pastor must mean is that the aesthetic values to be realized from preserving old churches are more important than whatever alternative values are promoted through sale of such property. That's a claim that can be discussed. Of course, it will be hard to discuss it with someone who doesn't give a damn what others think because he has decided that any opposing view is based on a love of property and is therefore a perversion. Arrogance of that sort is much easier for people who have somehow convinced themselves that it's immoral or materialistic or greedy to allocate scarce resources in accord with monetary bids. Such people very rarely ask what the alternative method of allocation might be, and so they don't discover, as they almost surely would if they thought more carefully, that alternative systems would have far less tolerable consequences.

Who Is Being Selfish?

The *Journal* article quotes two other Manhattan critics of property sales by inner-city churches, neither one, incidentally, a member of the congregation whose decisions they've opposed. One is a woman who lives near a Christian Science church that was put up for sale and who questioned the motives of the members. "I wonder if they need the money," she is quoted as saying, "or if it's all just a matter of greed." Another woman, who chairs a community organization on Manhattan's Upper West Side, credits her organization with saving a number of churches from what she calls the "demolition squads" of condominium developers. This was done by persuading the New York City Landmarks Preservation Commission to designate the buildings as historical landmarks, sometimes over the objections of the congregations that owned them and wanted to sell. In defending this tactic she argued that many such sales are "a matter of greed."

The confusion that permeates the whole area of economics and ethics is vividly revealed in the willingness of so many people to accept such arguments uncritically. It is not greedy for the members of a congregation to sell their church building to the highest bidder. The Seventh-Day Adventist congregation eventually sold its property for $2.4 million in cash, from which it then established a scholarship fund and made donations to other churches. On its face I would call that far less greedy than the behavior of the woman who wanted to preserve a church building because it contributed to the attractiveness of the neighborhood in which she lives. The critic, not the church members, is the one who seems to be setting her own personal welfare ahead of the welfare of others, by claiming new rights for herself even though this violates the well-established rights of many others. I'm not really sure what greed is, especially not in people other than myself, but the statements and behavior of the Manhattan church critics seem far more selfish to me than the actions of the congregations whose alleged greed they're criticizing.

An Impersonal System

In that system of social interaction that we call a market economy, decision makers focus their attention on changing money prices. Their motives in doing so are infinitely varied and complex, and no more likely to be selfish or otherwise morally objectionable than the motives of people at a church picnic or a university lecture. The principal consequence of their behavior is ongoing mutual accommodation among millions of people who do not even know of one another's existence, but who are nonetheless dependent upon one another for the basic necessities of life as well as the innumerable luxuries to which we have become accustomed.

We have indeed become accustomed to the near-miraculous benefits of social cooperation through the mechanism of money prices; we expect them as our due. We have, however, not learned to accept the social system without which these benefits would be impossible. We feel an inner disquiet and are morally suspicious of a social system that works so *impersonally*.

The Root of Our Moral Discontent?

Isn't that, when all is said and done, the deepest root of our chronic moral dissatisfaction with capitalism or the market system? We use such words as greedy, selfish, and materialistic; we complain about the excessive importance of money or property values; but what we are really objecting to is a system that works so impersonally. We don't *want* people to be fed, clothed, and lodged through the operation of an impersonal system, because persons are too important. We aren't satisfied with a system in which the public good isn't aimed at directly, but only emerges as an unintended consequence of much more limited objectives, because such a system seems somehow to violate our profound moral conviction that nothing is more valuable than individual persons, and that each person ought to be treated as a unique end, never as a means to some further end.

These moral convictions also underlie, I suggest, our misgivings about the justice of capitalism. Income and the other goods produced by the social system ought to be distributed among individuals, we believe, in accord with what they deserve as unique persons. The market system clearly does not satisfy that test. The benefits people receive in a market system derive from a complex interplay of mostly impersonal decisions, and the results are a varied and unpredictable product of effort and luck.

The Critical Problem of Information

The problem with this whole way of thinking, however, is that we cannot have the benefits of a market system unless we're willing to accept its impersonal features. The remarkable productive achievements of the market system are the result of its ability to gather vast amounts of detailed, continually changing information and to disseminate it quickly to precisely those persons who want it. That won't happen unless people respond in their actions to the signals that prices emit and those prices are in turn allowed to respond to people's actions. The impersonality of the market system that so much disturbs us is an essential feature of that system. We cannot have the benefits of a market system if we are at the same time determined to prevent that system from operating in an impersonal manner. An economic system that successfully coordinates the efforts of millions of people will *necessarily* work like an urban traffic system: Individuals will pursue their own goals, obeying general rules of the game, in response to the net advantages they perceive in their immediate environment, and adjusting those net advantages in the process so that they more adequately accommodate the diverse wants and abilities of the participants.

It's important to notice that what I have just asserted about large economic systems is true of *all* large economic systems, not just of so-called capitalist systems. Socialist systems don't escape this limitation. The abolition of private property doesn't abolish the information problems that all economic systems must solve if they are to be efficient and productive. It only changes the rules of the game. Moreover, it changes them so that they become less clear and certain and less stable over time.

Justice in Large Societies

The consequences, as so much twentieth-century history now demonstrates, include low levels of productivity and notorious inefficiencies. But that's not all. Clear and stable rules are also a prerequisite of fairness in any large society. What many advocates of economic justice fail to recognize is that, in a large society, the one indispensable condition for justice is the existence and enforcement of impartial rules. How large is large? No precise numerical answer can be given. Justice requires impartial rules in any society so large that tasks and benefits cannot be fairly allocated on the basis of the principle: from each according to ability, to each according to need and merit. That's the principle we use in families. It works effectively and fairly in families, for the most part, because the people involved are few enough and close enough to care for each other in a personal way. In societies significantly larger than families, the members simply cannot know enough to assign tasks and benefits on the basis of personal circumstances and still do it fairly.

The problem is knowledge; it is not simply goodwill. Goodwill by itself will not enable us to determine one another's abilities, needs, or merit in a society as large as two hundred people, much less one of two hundred million people. Any attempt to do so is bound to produce arbitrary and hence unfair results.

The Spurious Conflict Between Efficiency and Justice

Justice and efficiency, it turns out, are not conflicting objectives between which we must choose. They are complementary. If we have failed to see that justice and efficiency in a large society both presuppose clear and stable rules of the game, it is probably because we have not yet seen the fundamental impossibility of securing justice in a large society in any other way. I am not making any sort of case for laissez-faire or even for a smaller government role in the economic system. I am rather insisting that to whatever extent government controls the use of resources and the distribution of income, it ought to do so by promulgating and enforcing clear and stable rules. That leaves a great deal of room for government assistance to less fortunate members of society. What it excludes are vague and uncertain rules, which permit and encourage bureaucratic self-seeking, tyranny, and other political injustices, while making it more difficult for members of the society to plan effectively. I am far from arguing that government has no place in the economy. I am rather insisting that, on economic and ethical grounds, in the interest of both justice and efficiency, government must establish clear and stable laws.

The Pursuit of Community

Our persistent yearning for a more personal society does not have to be denied or suppressed. But it must find its expression where it is appropriate, where people can actually relate to one another on the basis of the "family principle." That can't possibly be at the level of national politics or even state politics; the scale is far too large. The illusion that government can extract just outcomes from the economic system, outcomes consistent with our notions of what individuals deserve as unique persons, prevents us from insisting that government promote justice in the one way it can do so: by clarifying, stabilizing, and enforcing impartial laws. Our vain pursuit of a chimerical justice produces not only inefficiency but also more injustice. On top of that, our obsession with government solutions to social problems prevents us from finding and acting upon our genuine opportunities to nurture personal relationships and community.

Conclusion

Let me summarize briefly. Most ethical criticism of the market system reflects confusion and misunderstanding. Moreover, it does positive harm, because it fosters political interventions that produce not only inefficiency but also injustice. It is the injustice that troubles me most. A nation without justice, St. Augustine observed, is no more than a robber band. The productivity of our economic system has given us a lot of room to practice inefficiency and folly. We have far less room to practice injustice. The tragic irony is that so many of the "best people" among us are today undermining the foundations of social justice in the name of ethics.

PART 2

Economics and Theology

CHAPTER 4

Can *Homo Economicus* Be Christian?

CAN HOMO ECONOMICUS be Christian? The answer will depend both on how we understand *Homo economicus* and on what it means to be Christian. The first issue is surprisingly elusive and the second one highly controversial. Fortunately, this paper was commissioned to facilitate discussion, not to settle the matter.

The question before us is an important one. It is important because *Homo economicus* allegedly dominates capitalist societies, or market economies, or what I prefer to call, following Adam Smith's suggestion, commercial societies. Christian critiques of commercial society, as well as other critiques based on moral considerations, have regularly focused on *Homo economicus,* and have often used his dominating presence to condemn such societies. Those Christians who understand how commercial societies actually work must decide how much weight should be assigned to these frequent and often impassioned criticisms, and should learn to challenge them effectively where they are misguided or ill-informed.

I. *Homo Economicus* Among the Economists

Who is *Homo economicus*? Is he a mere theoretical construct, no more than an analytical fiction, a heuristic device existing only in the models of

Unpublished typescript prepared for a Liberty Fund conference, "Christianity, Economics, and Liberty," in Alexandria, Virginia, 16–19 January 1992. Reprinted by permission of Mrs. Juliana Heyne.

economists? If so, he can hardly be Christian. Or is he in fact a flesh-and-blood person, capable (perhaps only after a conversion experience) of dwelling in the Kingdom of God?

The First Methodologists

Economists never have achieved a consensus on this rather fundamental issue. When John Stuart Mill began to reflect on the nature of the new science of political economy that had grown up in England in the early nineteenth century, he concluded that it

> does not treat of the whole of man's nature as modified by the social state, nor of the whole conduct of man in society. It is concerned with him solely as a being who desires to possess wealth, and who is capable of judging of the comparative efficacy of means for obtaining that end. It predicts only such of the phenomena of the social state as take place in consequence of the pursuit of wealth. It makes entire abstraction of every other human motive; except those which may be regarded as perpetually antagonizing principles to the desire of wealth, namely, aversion to labour, and desire of the present enjoyment of costly indulgences.[1]

Then he added this caution:

> Not that any political economist was ever so absurd as to suppose that mankind are really thus constituted, but because this is the mode in which science must necessarily proceed. When an effect depends upon a concurrence of causes, those causes must be studied one at a time.... With respect to those parts of human conduct of which wealth is not even the principal object, to those Political Economy does not pretend that its conclusions are applicable. But there are also certain departments of human affairs, in which the acquisition of wealth is the main and acknowledged end. It is only of these that Political Economy takes notice. The manner in which it necessarily proceeds is that of treating

1. John Stuart Mill, "On the Definition of Political Economy; and on the Method of Investigation Proper to It," written in 1831, first published in 1836. Reprinted in *Collected Works of John Stuart Mill,* vol. IV (Toronto: University of Toronto Press, 1967), p. 321.

the main and acknowledged end as if it were the sole end; which, of all hypotheses equally simple, is the nearest to the truth.[2]

For Mill, then, *Homo economicus* was an analytical fiction. And the discipline that employed this fiction did not pretend to explain all areas of human conduct.

Mill's distinguished contemporary Nassau Senior saw the matter very differently. He asserted that the science of political economy was grounded on the true proposition "[t]hat every man desires to obtain additional Wealth with as little sacrifice as possible."[3] Here is how Senior interprets that proposition:

> In stating that every man desires to obtain additional wealth with as little sacrifice as possible, we must not be supposed to mean that everybody, or indeed anybody, wishes for an indefinite quantity of every thing; still less as stating that wealth, though the universal, either is, or ought to be, the principal object of human desire. What we mean is, that no person feels his whole wants to be adequately supplied; that every person has some unsatisfied desires which he believes that additional wealth would gratify.[4]

Those unsatisfied desires, moreover, are as varied as human character.

> Some may wish for power, others for distinction, and others for leisure; some require bodily and others mental amusement; some are anxious to produce important advantage to the public; and there are few, perhaps there are none, who, if it could be done by a wish, would not benefit their acquaintances and friends.[5]

The only object universally desired, according to Senior, was money, because money is "abstract wealth," something whose possessor

---

2. *Ibid.*, p. 322.
3. Nassau Senior, *An Outline of the Science of Political Economy,* first published in 1836 (New York: Augustus M. Kelley, 1965), p. 26.
4. *Ibid.*, p. 27.
5. *Ibid.*

may satisfy at will his ambition, or vanity, or indolence, his public spirit or his private benevolence; may multiply the means of obtaining bodily pleasure, or of avoiding bodily evil, or the still more expensive amusements of the mind.[6]

No area of human conduct lies outside the domain of political economy as Senior understands it. And Senior's *Homo economicus* is a full-fledged human being. Senior considered Mill's argument, in fact, and explicitly rejected it. "It appears to me," he wrote,

> that if we substitute for Mr. Mill's hypothesis, that wealth and costly enjoyment are the *only* objects of human desire, the statement that they are universal and constant objects of desire, that they are desired by all men and at all times, we shall have laid an equally firm founda-tion for our subsequent reasonings, and have put a truth in the place of an arbitrary assumption.[7]

Perhaps the reason that Mill makes *Homo economicus* a mere analytical fiction is his exaggerated conception of David Ricardo's role and influence in political economy. James Mill had put his eldest son through an intensive course on Ricardo's *Principles* when he was only 13 years of age, and John Stuart seems never to have recovered fully from the experience. All his life he held an exaggerated notion of the merits and influence of Ricardo, who was notorious for deriving his conclusions in political economy from as-sumptions that were manifestly not true. As Ricardo once put it in a letter to his friend Malthus: "I imagined strong cases."[8]

Contemporary Methodology

Do contemporary economists follow Mill or Senior at this point? Do they believe that people really behave, for the most part, as their models

6. *Ibid.*

7. Nassau Senior, *Four Introductory Lectures on Political Economy,* first published in 1852. Reprinted in Nassau Senior, *Selected Writings on Economics* (New York: Augustus M. Kelley, 1966), p. 62.

8. David Ricardo, *Works and Correspondence,* edited by Piero Sraffa with the collabora-tion of M. H. Dobb, vol. VIII, p. 184. The letter is dated May 4, 1820.

assume? Or do they regard *Homo economicus* as no more than a construct useful for analytical purposes? The safest answer is that they generally don't think about it very carefully.

Among the most widely-cited recent examinations of the *Homo economicus* assumption is Amartya K. Sen's 1977 essay on "Rational Fools." Sen maintains that a poll of economists of different schools on the status of the rational choice assumption that many of them employ would reveal

the coexistence of beliefs (i) that the rational behavior theory is unfalsifiable, (ii) that it is falsifiable and so far unfalsified, and (iii) that it is falsifiable and indeed patently false.[9]

When the American Economic Association launched *The Journal of Economic Perspectives* in the Summer of 1987, it promised a regular feature titled "Anomalies." An anomaly was defined as an empirical result that is hard to reconcile with the fundamental paradigm of economics. The feature's statement of that paradigm contained an implicit definition of the *Homo economicus* who is supposed to inhabit the models of contemporary economists:

Economics is distinguished from other social sciences by the belief that most (all?) behavior can be explained by assuming that agents have stable, well-defined preferences and make rational choices consistent with those preferences in markets that (eventually) clear.[10]

This is very similar to Gary Becker's well-known and forcefully defended summary of "the economic approach to human behavior":

The combined assumptions of maximizing behavior, market equilibrium, and stable preferences, used relentlessly and unflinchingly, form the heart of the economic approach as I see it.[11]

9. Amartya K. Sen, "Rational Fools: A Critique of the Behavioral Foundations of Economic Theory," *Philosophy and Public Affairs* (Summer 1977), p. 325.

10. See almost any issue between vol. 1, no. 1 (Summer 1987) and vol. 5, no. 1 (Winter 1991).

11. Gary Becker, *The Economic Approach to Human Behavior* (Chicago: University of Chicago Press, 1976), p. 5.

What would a person have to do to demonstrate that he was *not* a *Homo economicus* by these definitions? I'm not at all sure. Behave capriciously? Prefer one thing today and another tomorrow? Choose without deliberating? Even these behaviors can be reconciled with the rational choice assumption, of course. People's preferences change; people have a taste for variety; there is a marginal utility of not bothering about marginal utility. It doesn't take a whole lot of ingenuity to come up with a rationalization to account for almost any anomalous behavior. Gary Becker adopts the assumption of stable preferences to avoid turning the assumption into a tautology with no refutable implications. If I read him correctly, he is coming down on Mill's side. He does economics *as if* people's preferences were stable in order to see what testable implications can be obtained. The Chicago methodology asserts that the realism of the assumptions is irrelevant—in some limited way that has never been completely clear to me.

I tried to get a clearer sense of what an official journal of the American Economic Association regards as the nature of *Homo economicus* by examining the content of the Anomalies feature from its initial appearance in the Summer of 1987 to its last regular appearance in the issue of Winter 1991 (after which date it was scheduled for only "occasional" publication).

Most of these columns treated anomalies that were related to the market-clearing rather than the *Homo economicus* part of the fundamental assumption. In the Summer 1988 issue, however, the feature editor and his co-author made this assertion: "Much economic analysis—and virtually all game theory—starts with the assumption that people are both rational and selfish."[12] The column then went on to demonstrate that the predictions derived from "the assumption of rational selfishness" are frequently refuted. The authors of the column seemed to be saying that most economists believe their assumption of selfish rationality accurately describes actual human nature, that the evidence refutes this belief, and that economists therefore ought to revise their beliefs to conform more closely to the available evidence.[13] They take Senior's position insofar as they want economics to be grounded in a true proposition regarding human nature.

The article in the succeeding issue dealt with the role of fairness considerations in economists' analyses. Rational behavior is defined by some

12. Robyn M. Dawes and Richard H. Thaler, "Anomalies: Cooperation," *Journal of Economic Perspectives*, vol. 2, no. 3 (Summer 1988), p. 187.
13. *Ibid.*, pp. 188–96.

of the economists cited in the article as behavior directed exclusively at increasing *monetary* wealth, so that evidence that people's utility functions contain non-monetary arguments becomes "anomalous." The discovery in particular that people hold strong notions of fairness and are willing at times to sacrifice monetary wealth in order to uphold or enforce those standards is regarded as information that will surprise most members of the economics profession. Apparently the profession is wrong again in what it assumes about human nature.[14]

The article in the Spring 1990 issue dealt with preference reversals and was even more critical of accepted practice. The concluding commentary quoted David Grether and Charles Plott:

Taken at face value the data [showing preference reversals] are simply inconsistent with preference theory and have broad implications about research priorities within economics. The inconsistency is deeper than the mere lack of transitivity or even stochastic transitivity. It suggests that no optimization principles of any sort lie behind the simplest of human choices and that the uniformities in human choice behavior which lie behind market behavior may result from principles which are of a completely different sort from those generally accepted.[15]

Column editor Richard Thaler brought in two of his favorite co-authors, Daniel Kahneman and Jack Knetsch, to complete this line of attack on the *Homo economicus* assumption in the last regular appearance of the Anomalies column, in the issue of Winter 1991. The article showed that the basic notion of a stable preference order had to be abandoned or thoroughly revised in the light of all the evidence that people have strong biases in favor of the status quo and that preferences are neither symmetrical nor reversible.[16]

14. Richard H. Thaler, "Anomalies: The Ultimatum Game," *Journal of Economic Perspectives*, vol. 2, no. 4 (Fall 1988), pp. 195–206.

15. Amos Tversky and Richard H. Thaler, "Anomalies: Preference Reversals," *Journal of Economic Perspectives*, vol. 4, no. 2 (Spring 1990), p. 209. The Grether and Plott article appeared in *American Economic Review*, vol. 69 (September 1979), pp. 623–38.

16. Daniel Kahneman, Jack L. Knetsch, and Richard H. Thaler, "Anomalies: The Endowment Effect, Loss Aversion, and Status Quo Bias," *Journal of Economic Perspectives*, vol. 5, no. 1 (Winter 1991), pp. 193–206.

Homo Economicus Redivivus?

The *Homo economicus* that gradually expired in the Anomalies columns of *The Journal of Economic Perspectives* was a rather bloodless creature from the beginning, one well suited, perhaps, for a leading role in the purely formal dramas much preferred by contemporary economic theorists, but not someone likely either to animate an economic system or to give ethical offense. In the midst of all this, a more interesting and challenging portrait of *Homo economicus* appeared in *Passions Within Reason,* an influential book published in 1988 by Robert H. Frank, professor of economics at Cornell University.[17] Frank had introduced his ideas to the economics profession in a widely-discussed article printed in the September 1987 issue of *The American Economic Review:* "If *Homo Economicus* Could Choose His Own Utility Function, Would He Want One with a Conscience?"[18]

The opening paragraphs of the article are worth quoting, both for the summary view that they provide of Frank's work and for the confusion that they reveal about the basic nature of *Homo economicus* as understood by Frank.

> The rational choice model takes tastes as given, and assumes that people pursue self-interest. The model performs well much of the time, yet apparent contradictions abound. Travelers on interstate highways leave tips for waitresses they will never see again. Participants in bloody family feuds seek revenge even at ruinous cost to themselves. People walk away from profitable transactions whose terms they believe to be "unfair." The British spend vast sums to defend the desolate Falklands, even though they have little empire left against which to deter future aggression. In these and countless other ways, people do not seem to be maximizing utility functions of the usual sort.
>
> In this paper, I investigate the familiar theme that seemingly irrational behavior can sometimes be explained without departing from the utility-maximization framework.... Instead of treating taste as a

17. Robert H. Frank, *Passions Within Reason: The Strategic Role of the Emotions* (New York: W. W. Norton and Company, 1988).

18. Robert H. Frank, "If *Homo economicus* Could Choose His Own Utility Function, Would He Want One with a Conscience?" *American Economic Review,* vol. 77, no. 4 (September 1987), pp. 593–604.

datum, I retreat a step and ask, "What kind of tastes would maximize the attainment of selfish objectives?" This is essentially the behavioral biologist's approach. It treats tastes not as ends in themselves, but as means for attaining important material objectives.[19]

The casual assumptions in these paragraphs are their most interesting feature. Leaving a tip for a waitress whom we will never see again is, on its face, irrational behavior, not utility-maximizing behavior. Rational, utility-maximizing behavior would maximize the attainment of selfish objectives, which are all material objectives. The same assumptions run throughout the book. Self-interest is identified with selfishness, selfish interests are assumed to be material interests, and concern for justice or fairness is regarded as irrational. The chapter on "Fairness" (Chapter 9) is particularly revealing. "The self-esteem of professional economists," Frank says at the beginning of the chapter,

> derives in no small measure from their belief that they are the most hardheaded of social scientists. In their explanations of human behavior, only self-interested motives will do.... Material costs and benefits reign supreme.... The rationalists complain that fairness is a hopelessly vague notion.[20]

Frank wants to retain the self-interest model, the assumption that people are selfish, the claim that selfishness is rational, and the notion that people respond to material incentives. He proposes to deal with the many anomalies that this model encounters by assuming that people find it in their (selfish, material) interest to be known as persons with certain kinds of emotional commitments. If I am known as one who cares deeply about fairness, people will be less likely to try to cheat me, because they will fear that I might irrationally accept costs far beyond any benefits I might anticipate in order to punish their behavior. If I am known as one in thrall to such irrational emotions as love, others will be more willing to commit resources to the cultivation of mutually profitable relationships with me.

19. *Ibid.*, p. 593.
20. Frank, *Passions Within Reason*, pp. 163–64.

Since the best way to acquire a reputation for having these emotions is actually to have them, it is in people's narrow, selfish, rational, material interest to take on these emotions and to live accordingly.[21]

Many of the most eminent and sophisticated theorists in the economics profession make no effort to distinguish between self-interest and selfishness or between rational behavior and greedy behavior. In an essay written several years ago for *The Public Interest,* Frank Hahn asserted that Adam Smith was the first who realized the need to explain why millions of "greedy, self-seeking individuals" pursuing their ends with little control by government did not produce anarchy.[22] Kenneth Arrow and Hahn, in the preface to their textbook on general equilibrium theory, equate "motivated by self-interest" with "motivated by individual greed."[23] This is an extraordinary state of affairs in a discipline descended from Adam Smith. Robert Frank goes so far as to claim that his theory is recovering the tradition advanced by Smith in *The Theory of Moral Sentiments.* Yet Frank himself has not begun to understand Smith's theory of human nature. Smith distinguishes clearly between self-interest and selfishness and explicitly insisted, against Bernard Mandeville, that self-love could be a virtuous motive of action. Nonetheless Frank writes:

> And in a passage that could easily have been lifted from Adam Smith, a prominent book on equity in personal relationships begins by saying that "Man is selfish. Individuals will try to maximise their outcomes." Psychologist Daniel Goleman nicely summarizes the continuing trend: "In recent years, the mainstream of psychological research has looked at love almost as if it were a business transaction, a matter of profit and loss."[24]

That is *not* Adam Smith's theory.

21. *Ibid., passim,* but especially pp. 163–64.

22. Frank Hahn, "General Equilibrium Theory," *The Public Interest,* special issue (1980), p. 123.

23. Kenneth J. Arrow and F. H. Hahn, *General Competitive Analysis* (San Francisco: Holden-Day, 1971).

24. Frank, *Passions Within Reason,* p. 186.

Critics of the Economists' Model

With the defenders of *Homo economicus* doing such a poor job of identifying him, the critics are free to accuse him of just about anything. A recent book that has had considerable influence among those who write on economics and religion is *For the Common Good: Redirecting the Economy Toward Community, the Environment, and a Sustainable Future* by Herman E. Daly and John B. Cobb, Jr., an economist and a theologian. Daly and Cobb lay the blame for many of the attitudes and policies that have, in their judgment, subverted community and destroyed the natural environment, at the door of economic theory. And one of that theory's principal deficiencies, as they see it, is the conception of *Homo economicus* that underlies it. What is that conception? According to Daly and Cobb, *Homo economicus* has insatiable wants, is indifferent to his relative position in society, cares not a whit for the welfare of other people except in the rare case where he has affected their welfare through a gift, is completely uninterested in fairness, and refuses to make any value judgments. This *Homo economicus* is an abstraction, of course, not a real person. But according to Daly and Cobb, economists have forgotten the dimensions of human nature from which they have abstracted, and have then used the distorted anthropology adopted for "analytical convenience" to construct disastrous policy conclusions.[25]

It strikes me as preposterous to suppose that our contemporary environmental problems and the absence of effective community in our society are consequences of the methods, much less the methodology, of professional economists. Daly and Cobb's strictures only demonstrate that economists take little care to clarify their working assumptions. I conclude that we will do best to abandon the abstractions of economic theory, to follow Nassau Senior's counsel, and to look for *Homo economicus* in the world of real people.

Adam Smith's Anthropology

When we do so, we probably ought to go back to Adam Smith, the man who started it all.

25. Herman E. Daly and John B. Cobb, Jr., *For the Common Good: Redirecting the Economy Toward Community, the Environment, and a Sustainable Future* (Boston: Beacon Press, 1989), pp. 85–96, 159–60.

Smith's published writings and lectures reveal a carefully-constructed, coherent, and—at least in intention—realistic anthropology. Smith does not assume for analytical purposes that people behave in some way other than the way he thinks they actually do behave. Moreover, he does not believe that they are consistently greedy or selfish, that they are interested exclusively or even primarily in material goods, that they pay no attention to justice or fairness in their decisions, or that they make rational choices consistent with a set of stable, well-defined preferences.

In the first place, it isn't selfishness but self-love that motivates people in the Smithian world. While self-love or self-interest is certainly capable of producing selfish behavior, it need not do so. Self-interested behavior is morally neutral, embracing acts of laudable generosity as well as acts of despicable greed. In the Smithian world, people strive to further the projects in which they are interested. Whether those projects are commendable or contemptible is a matter for investigation. To condemn self-interested behavior, as Smith uses the concept, amounts to condemning purposive behavior.[26]

Smith goes further and tells us what the general project is that most people are in fact interested in most of the time. They want above all else to *better their condition*. The desire to better our condition, Smith says, "comes with us from the womb, and never leaves us till we go into the grave." It is "uniform, constant, and uninterrupted," so that "there is scarce perhaps a single instant in which any man is so perfectly and completely satisfied with his situation, as to be without any wish of alteration or improvement of any kind."[27]

Does this mean that people want above all else to increase their monetary wealth or income? "An augmentation of fortune is the means... the most vulgar and obvious,"[28] Smith writes, by which to better one's con-

---

26. "How selfish soever man may be supposed," Smith says in beginning *The Theory of Moral Sentiments,* thus leading many who have read no farther to conclude falsely that Smith presupposed universal selfishness. Adam Smith, *The Theory of Moral Sentiments,* first published in 1759 (Indianapolis: Liberty Fund, 1982), p. 9. For a clear statement of the distinction Smith made between selfishness and self-love, see *op. cit.,* p. 309.

27. The *locus classicus* is book II, chapter III in *The Wealth of Nations.* Adam Smith, *An Inquiry into the Nature and Causes of the Wealth of Nations,* first published in 1776 (Indianapolis: Liberty Fund, 1981), pp. 330–49.

28. *Ibid.,* pp. 341–42.

dition, and thus the means that most people usually choose to employ. Consequently, most members of all societies work diligently and attempt both to save some portion of their income and to invest those savings prudently. Note, however, that augmentation of fortune is a *means* toward the bettering of our condition. Wealth without limit is not the goal of life.

What *is* the goal? It is ultimately enhanced standing in the opinions of those whose opinions matter to us. Our ultimate concern, according to Smith, is for our reputation. It is true that this concern will often lead to mere vanity; but it can also express itself as a love of true glory, or even, among the best of us or in the best moments of any of us, as a love of virtue. Vanity prompts us to appear praiseworthy even when we are not. The love of true glory, however, prompts us toward behavior that genuinely merits praise. Moreover, people generally learn that the easiest way to *seem* praiseworthy is to *be* praiseworthy, so that mere vanity will tend "naturally, or even necessarily," to use one of Smith's favorite locutions, to lead to the pursuit of true glory.

And those who love virtue will do what is praiseworthy even if, because of the ignorance or misunderstanding of other people, they expect it to bring them unmerited condemnation. The opinion that matters to those who love virtue is the opinion of "the impartial spectator," the individual's conscience or "the man within the breast" who judges the person's actions with a full knowledge of motives as well as consequences and who always judges impartially.[29]

A clear implication of all this, but one that I have never seen explicitly noted, is that self-respect is for many people a primary objective in self-interested behavior. A large portion of the "anomalies" to which Frank and other students of the self-interest model have called attention disappear the moment we recognize that it is in many people's clear self-interest to behave in ways that will allow them to retain their self-respect. Do we need any more than this to explain why people regularly leave tips for waiters whom they never expect to see again?

The frequent claim that Smith thought all would be for the best in society if individuals were left free to pursue their own interests ignores the important qualification that he laid down. When Smith argued that

---

29. Smith, *The Theory of Moral Sentiments*, pp. 50, 309–11.

everyone should be "left perfectly free to pursue his own interest his own way," it was only on the important condition that "he does not violate the laws of justice."[30] *The Wealth of Nations* is peppered with condemnations of those who perpetrate injustice by violating the rights of others. The "invisible hand" will not extract the public good from the pursuit of private advantage when private advantage is pursued by means of unjust laws and regulations. Legislation is unjust, in Smith's view, when it promotes the interests of one group of citizens by imposing unequal restraints on the actions of other groups.

> To hurt in any degree the interest of any one order of citizens for no other purpose but to promote that of some other, is evidently contrary to that justice and equality of treatment which the sovereign owes to all the different orders of his subjects.[31]

As for the claim that Smith thought people were always calculating costs and benefits, always worrying about how to extract from available means the greatest quantity of satisfaction—this is another caricature. Smith was quite proud, in fact, of what he thought was his own original insight, that people often come to value the means more than the ends that the means were originally intended to promote. People often pursue power and riches throughout their lives at great personal cost, he insisted, despite the fact that these really do very little to ward off anxiety, fear, sorrow, diseases, danger, or death. "They keep off the summer shower, not the winter storm." The pleasures of wealth and greatness nonetheless "strike the imagination as something grand and beautiful and noble, of which the attainment is well worth all the toil and anxiety which we are so apt to bestow upon it." Moreover, this delusion, this confounding of means and ends, is what "rouses and keeps in continual motion the industry of mankind." It is not "the lore of nicely-calculated less or more,"

---

30. Smith, *The Wealth of Nations*, p. 687.

31. *Ibid.*, p. 654. Since I have never seen a listing of the passages in *The Wealth of Nations* from which a reader can extract Smith's views on the nature of justice and injustice, I'll supply one here. The first number refers to the page, the second to the section paragraph: 43, 10; 138, 12; 145, 27; 157, 59; 174, 32; 326, 100; 448, 32; 530, 16; 539, 39; 561, 15; 582, 44; 588, 59; 610, 53–54; 626, 80; 654, 30; 687, 51; 722, 25; 815, 3; 827, 7; 898, 64; 910, 7; 932, 64.

rejected by Wordsworth in the name of Heaven, that is responsible for the growth of national wealth—at least not according to Adam Smith. It is rather an almost irrational fascination with *means* that impels human beings "to cultivate the ground, to build houses, to found cities and commonwealths, and to invent and improve all the sciences and arts, which ennoble and embellish human life." [32]

Perhaps this would be the proper occasion to add that Smith never thought of himself as laying the foundations for a new science of economic systems. He did not recognize the existence of any "economic" system that could be distinguished from the total social system and that was governed by laws of its own. Economic goods, economic motives, economic problems, economic factors—these are all anachronisms when we use them to discuss social thought prior to the nineteenth century. Smith does not speak of economic goods but of "necessaries and conveniences." He knows nothing of economic motives, though he does know about desires to enhance our reputations, to augment our fortunes, to avoid irksome labor, to obtain present ease and enjoyment, to advance complex projects, to domineer over others, and to enjoy the merited respect of our fellows.

There was nothing narrow about the social analysis of Adam Smith. This probably makes his anthropology useless for those who want to do economics in the manner of Ricardo or of the general equilibrium theorists in our own day, who have transformed the Ricardian *tendency* to reason deductively from abstract premises into a *methodological principle*. But Smith remains an instructive guide for those who want to construct an economics that is relevant to public policy decisions. He also provides, it seems to me, an effective first response to those who despise commercial society for the human characters that it requires or produces. *Homo economicus* as Smith conceives him is completely capable of being a moral and public-spirited person.

Philip Wicksteed on Homo Economicus

The most careful and complete articulation of a realistic anthropology for economists is probably the one provided at great length, perhaps at

32. Smith, *The Theory of Moral Sentiments*, pp. 179–87.

excessive length, by Philip Wicksteed in *The Common Sense of Political Economy*.[33] It has the special virtue of having appeared *after* the reformulation of economic theory at the end of the nineteenth century that produced the fundamental structure of that theory as it exists today. If Wicksteed had been a little less prolix, he might have been more widely read. And if he were more widely known, it is certain that much less nonsense would be uttered today about *Homo economicus*.

Wicksteed devotes attention to the *two* important aspects of economic man's behavior: the economizing aspect and the exchange aspect. The first paragraph of the Introduction to *The Common Sense* spells out the economizing aspect:

> In the ordinary course of our lives we constantly consider how our time, our energy, or our money shall be spent. That is to say, we decide between alternative applications of our resources of every kind, and endeavour to administer them to the best advantage in securing the accomplishment of our purposes or the humouring of our inclinations. It is the purpose of this book to evolve a consistent system of Political Economy from a careful study and analysis of the principles on which we actually conduct this current administration of resources.[34]

Wicksteed's subsequent descriptions of the economizing process, invariably illuminating and frequently delightful, leave room for every kind of behavior in which human beings are known to engage. He does not, for example, use the principle of sunk costs to rule out behavior that would violate that principle. Here is a sample of what he says:

> [T]he value of what we have does not depend on the value of what we have relinquished or endured in order to get it. If there is a coincidence, as in a wisely conducted life there will be, it is because the value that we foresee a thing will have determines what we will encounter or forego in order to get it.... We do not always like to face this fact ... and accordingly we sometimes try to believe that a thing is useful or

33. Philip H. Wicksteed, *The Common Sense of Political Economy*, first published in 1910 (London: Routledge and Kegan Paul Limited, 1933).

34. *Ibid.*, vol. 1, p. 1.

ornamental because we have given a high price for it, or valuable because we have taken trouble to get it....

There is no doubt a strong tendency in many minds to economize a stock which was bought at a high price, even if it could be replaced at a low one, and perhaps a still stronger tendency to deal prodigally with a stock purchased at a low price, although it will have to be replaced at a high one. But this secondary reaction is recognized as irrational when we deliberately consider it.[35]

Here is Wicksteed applying marginal principles to the spiritual life:

In a story of South America, after the war, we are told of a planter who, when warned by his wife in the middle of his prayers that the enemy was at the gate, concluded his devotions with a few brief and earnest petitions, and then set about defending himself. Had he been a formalist those final petitions would never have been uttered at all; but under the circumstances the impulse to prayer, though sincere and urgent, became rapidly less imperative and exacting relatively to the urgency of taking steps for defence, as the successive moments passed.... [A]n entirely devout and sincere person may find himself in the dilemma of having either to curtail (or omit) family prayers or to hurry a guest over his breakfast and perhaps run him uncomfortably close for his train. If he shortens, but does not omit, the prayers, it shows that he attaches declining significance to his devotions as minute is added to minute. And in this we shall see nothing ludicrous, as soon as we give up the cant of the absolute in a world in which all things are relative.[36]

Will money buy happiness?

All the things that we so often say "cannot be had for money" we might with equal truth say cannot be had or enjoyed without it. Friendship cannot be had for money, but how often do the things that money commands enable us to form and develop our friendships! Domestic peace

35. *Ibid.*, pp. 93–94.
36. *Ibid.*, pp. 79–80.

and happiness cannot be had for money, but Dickens's Dr. Marigold was of opinion that many a couple live peaceably and happily together in a house, who would make straight for the divorce court if they lived in a van.[37]

Are human desires insatiable?

Indeed, just as it is easy to have so many houses that we have no home, so in general there is a point at which the command of exchangeable things may cease to support and begin to oppress, or feed upon, our store of ultimately desired experiences.[38]

Are people motivated solely by the desire to possess wealth?

Now since we have already seen that no ultimate object of desire can ever be the direct subject of exchange at all, we perceive at once that to regard the "economic" man (as he is often called) as actuated solely by the desire to possess wealth is to think of him as only desiring to collect tools and never desiring to do or to make anything with them.[39]

Unlike many contemporary economic theorists who seem unable to move beyond the maximizing concept, Wicksteed also saw clearly that there is much more to the science of economics than the "psychology of choice, or the principles which regulate our selection among alternatives." [40] The economizing aspect of economic life came to be emphasized only after the reformulation of economic theory that occurred in the last quarter of the nineteenth century. With Adam Smith the focus was on exchange. Indeed, Richard Whately protested in his 1831 lectures at Oxford University that the science of political economy might better have been called *catallactics,* or the science of exchanges, from the Greek word for exchange.[41]

37. *Ibid.,* p. 153.
38. *Ibid.,* p. 156.
39. *Ibid.,* p. 163.
40. *Ibid.,* p. 40.
41. Richard Whately, *Introductory Lectures on Political Economy,* delivered in 1831, 2d ed. (New York: Augustus M. Kelley, 1966), pp. 4–10.

Adam Smith had cited the division of labor as the principal cause of increasing national wealth. The division of labor, of course, requires exchange. Once the division of labor has extended itself throughout the society, then everyone lives by exchanging. Everyone "becomes in some measure a merchant," Smith said, "and the society itself grows to be what is properly a commercial society."[42] The task Smith set for himself, especially in Book I of *The Wealth of Nations,* was to explain how such a commercial society is coordinated through the spontaneous formation and continual readjustment of relative money prices.

Here is Wicksteed's description of "commercial society":

Thus, by teaching Greek to men who can neither make shoes nor drive an engine, I can get myself shod and carried by men who have no wish to be taught Greek. It might be a valuable exercise for any one who is "earning his living" to attempt to go through a few hours or even a few minutes of his daily life and consider all the exchangeable things which he requires as they pass, and the net-work of cooperation, extending all over the globe, by which the clothes he puts on, the food he eats, the book containing the poems or expounding the science that he is studying, or the pen, ink, and paper with which he writes a letter, a poem, or an appeal, have been placed at his service, by persons for the direct furtherance of whose purposes in life he has not exercised any one of his faculties or powers. Such an attempt would help us to realise the vast system of organized co-operation between persons who have no knowledge of each other's existence, no concern in each other's affairs, and no direct power of furthering each other's purposes, by which the most ordinary processes of life are carried on. By the organisation of industrial society we can secure the co-operation of countless individuals of whom we know nothing, in directing the resources of the world towards objects in which they have no interest. And the nexus that thus unites and organises us is the business nexus—that is to say, a system of exchanges, conducted for the most part in terms of a medium that enables us to transform what we have into what we want at two removes.[43]

42. Smith, *The Wealth of Nations,* p. 37.
43. Wicksteed, *op. cit.,* p. 140.

Wicksteed devotes a long chapter entirely to "Business and the Economic Nexus," in the course of which he manages to discuss and dispel most of the misunderstandings that have animated so many moral critics of commercial society. He is particularly good on the topic of egoism and altruism in "the system of 'economic relations,'" defined as

> that system which enables me to throw in at some point of the circle of exchange the powers and possessions I directly command, and draw out other possessions and the command of other powers whether at the same point or at some other.[44]

The economic relation is entered into, Wicksteed points out, "at the prompting of the whole range of human purposes and impulses, and rests in no exclusive or specific way on an egoistic or self-regarding basis."[45]

> [W]hen Paul of Tarsus abode with Aquila and Priscilla in Corinth and wrought with them at his craft of tent-making we shall hardly say that he was inspired by egoistic motives. It is, indeed, likely enough that he was not inspired by any conscious desire to further the purposes (pastoral, military, or what not) of the men for whom he was making or mending tents, but it is very certain that he was impelled to practise his craft by his desire not to be a burden to the Churches, and that his economic life was to his mind absolutely integral to his evangelising mission.[46]

The economic relation, Wicksteed argues, liberates people

from the limitations imposed by the nature of their own direct resources. And this liberation comes about by the very act that brings a corresponding liberation to those with whom they deal. "It is twice bless'd. It blesseth him that gives and him that takes." Surely the study of such a relation needs no apology, and there seems to be no

44. *Ibid.*, p. 167.
45. *Ibid.*, p. 169.
46. *Ibid.*, pp. 170–71.

room to bring against it the charge of being intrinsically sordid and degrading.[47]

Why is this charge so frequently made? Wicksteed returns to "the example of the apostolic tent-maker" to show "the ground on which this stubborn prejudice rests." Although Paul was not thinking of his own advantage when he was making tents, neither was he thinking of the advantage of those whose wants he was supplying.[48] In fact, says Wicksteed, this is the essence of a purely economic transaction.

> If you and I are conducting a transaction which on my side is purely economic, I am furthering your purposes, partly or wholly for my own sake, perhaps entirely for the sake of others, but certainly not for your sake. What makes it an economic transaction is that I am not considering you except as a link in the chain, or considering your desires except as the means by which I may gratify those of someone else—not necessarily myself. The economic relation does not exclude from my mind every one but me, it potentially includes every one but you. You it does indeed exclude. . . .[49]

Wicksteed summarizes the matter succinctly: "The specific characteristic of an economic relation is not its 'egoism' but its 'non-tuism.' "[50]

The temptation to quote Wicksteed at length on this whole topic is irresistible:

> A man's purposes may, of course, be selfish, but however unselfish they are he requires the co-operation of others who are not interested, or who are inadequately interested in them, in order to accomplish them. We enter into business relations with others, not because our purposes are selfish, but because those with whom we deal are relatively

---

47. *Ibid.,* p. 173.
48. *Ibid.*
49. *Ibid.,* p. 174.
50. *Ibid.,* p. 180.

indifferent to them, but are (like us) keenly interested in purposes of their own, to which we in our turn are relatively indifferent.[51]

A bit later he notes:

[I]t may be true enough that, as a rule, the average man of business is not likely to be thinking of any "others" at all in the act of bargaining, but even so the term "egoism" is misapplied, for neither is he thinking of himself! He is thinking of the matter in hand, the bargain or the transaction, much as a man thinks of the next move in a game of chess or of how to unravel the construction of a sentence in the Greek text he is reading.... It would be absurd to call a man selfish for protecting his king in a game of chess, or to say that he was actuated by purely egoistic motives in so doing.... If you want to know whether he is selfish or unselfish you must consider the whole organisation of his life.[52]

To those who would argue that, since every person should be the object of our direct interest and benevolence, the economic relation is fundamentally amoral or even immoral, Wicksteed replies that the position cannot be seriously maintained. "The limitation of our powers would prevent our taking an equally active interest in every one's affairs."[53]

While defending economic relations against the unthinking charges of moralistic critics, Wicksteed rejects the "school of cheerful optimism ... based upon the creed that if every man pursues his own interests in an enlightened manner we shall get the best of possible results."[54] He is not a defender of laissez faire.

The enlightened student of political economy and of society will take care to assume nothing as to the economic forces except the constant pressure which they bring to bear upon men's action and their absolute moral and social indifference. He will see that it is our business in every instance to endeavor to yoke these forces, where we can, to

51. *Ibid.*, p. 179.
52. *Ibid.*, pp. 180–81.
53. *Ibid.*, p. 182.
54. *Ibid.*, p. 191.

social work, and to restrain them, where we can, from social devasta-
tion; never to ignore them, never to trust them without examination;
and no more to take it as axiomatic that they will work for social good,
if left alone, than we should take it for granted that lightning will invariably strike things that are "better felled." [55]

In the judgment of Philip Wicksteed, economist, theologian, scholar,
and probably the most careful and thorough writer ever to examine the
character of *Homo economicus,* there is nothing in his makeup to keep him
from being a public-spirited and thoroughly moral citizen.

II. *Homo Economicus* Among the Christians

It may be the case that Christians make excellent citizens. The First Letter
of Peter urges Christians to

> maintain good conduct among the Gentiles, so that … they may see
> your good works and glorify God on the day of visitation. Be subject
> for the Lord's sake to every human institution…. For it is God's will
> that by doing right you should put to silence the ignorance of foolish
> men. Live as free men, yet without using your freedom as a pretext
> for evil; but live as servants of God. Honor all men. Love the brother-
> hood. Fear God. Honor the emperor. (I Peter 2:12–17)[56]

But it does not follow that behaving like a good citizen is the same as behaving like a Christian. *Homo economicus* as described by Adam Smith and
Philip Wicksteed can be a thoroughly moral and public-spirited citizen.
It remains to be asked whether he can also be a Christian. And there are
good reasons to ask.

Homo Economicus and the Message of the Gospels

The New Testament is a socially more radical document than well-
established churchmen have usually been willing to admit. The changes in

---

55. *Ibid.,* pp. 191–92.
56. The translation used is the Revised Standard Version.

language between the Beatitudes in Luke and the Beatitudes in Matthew are especially revealing. "Blessed are you poor" becomes "Blessed are the poor in spirit"; "Blessed are you that hunger now" becomes "Blessed are those who hunger and thirst for righteousness" (Matthew 5:3, 6; Luke 6:20–21). And the "Woes" that follow the "Blesseds" in Luke's Gospel—woes to the rich, to those who are well-fed, to those who are currently laughing—don't appear at all in Matthew's version (Luke 6:24–26). One senses the hand of a conservative editor eager to adapt the extreme demands of the original message to the realities of social life.

There are at least two powerful tensions between the message of the New Testament and the character of *Homo economicus*, corresponding to each of the two aspects of economic man's behavior pointed out by Wicksteed: the economizing aspect and the exchange aspect.

Various passages in Matthew 6 (also presented in Luke 12) well express the tension between the calculating, prudential attitude of *Homo economicus* and the Gospel imperative:

Do not lay up for yourselves treasures on earth.... For where your treasure is, there will your heart be also. (Matthew 6:19, 21)

[D]o not be anxious about your life, what you shall eat or what you shall drink.... Look at the birds of the air: they neither sow nor reap nor gather into barns, and yet your heavenly Father feeds them. (Matthew 6:25–26)

And why are you anxious about clothing? Consider the lilies of the field, how they grow; they neither toil nor spin; yet I tell you, even Solomon in all his glory was not arrayed like one of these. But if God so clothes the grass of the field, which today is alive and tomorrow is thrown into the oven, will he not much more clothe you, O men of little faith? (Matthew 6:28–29)

Mark and Luke both recount the story of the poor widow whom Jesus commended for contributing to the temple treasury "everything she had, her whole living" (Mark 12:41–44; Luke 21:1–4). Would not *Homo economicus* have to regard such behavior as imprudent at best and probably recklessly irresponsible? Wouldn't he also be critical of the members of the Jerusalem church who, in their enthusiasm, "sold their possessions and goods and distributed them to all, as any had need" (Acts 2:45)? Yet Jesus does say, "Sell your possessions and give alms" (Luke 12:33). And all three of the Synoptic Gospels tell the story of the man who decided not to be a disciple when Jesus counseled him to sell all his possessions and give the proceeds to the poor (Matthew 19:16–22; Mark 10:17–22; Luke 18:18–23).

The Gospels advocate a trusting dependence on God that coexists uneasily with the desire of *Homo economicus* to make adequate provision for his own future. The determination to provide for oneself reveals a lack of faith, a lack of faith that in turn prevents people from practicing the mutual concern that will characterize the Kingdom of God. Luke presents this theme most clearly.

Consider the message of the forerunner, recounted by Luke as an introduction to Jesus' ministry. When the multitudes who came out to the wilderness to be baptized by John asked him, "What then shall we do?" John replied: "He who has two coats, let him share with him who has none; and he who has food, let him do likewise" (Luke 3:7–11).

Jesus' first recorded sermon, in the synagogue of Nazareth, took as its text the words of Isaiah:

> The Spirit of the Lord is upon me, because he has anointed me to preach good news to the poor. He has sent me to proclaim release to the captives and recovering of sight to the blind, to set at liberty those who are oppressed, to proclaim the acceptable year of the Lord.

When he closed the book from which he had been reading, Jesus said: "Today this Scripture has been fulfilled in your hearing" (Luke 4:16–21).

Most scholars interpret this as a proclamation of the Jubilee Year, in which slaves are to be liberated, land returned to the families that have lost it through foreclosure, and all debts forgiven. The good news that God's reign is being established is a message for the *people* of God, who are called to acknowledge the arrival of God's kingdom by beginning to care for one another as God had intended they should do. Forgiving the debts of the poor is a part of that, a part important enough to be incorporated into the prayer that Jesus taught his disciples.

The ethos of the New Testament is radically communitarian. This has always posed problems for Christian thinkers who believe that Christian ethics must be "realistic," capable of being practiced without disastrous consequences for the social order. One solution has been to bracket as "counsels of perfection" or "ideals" applicable only "eschatologically" all those New Testament injunctions that require us to give to everyone who asks, to repay evil with good, or to put the welfare of others ahead of our own. Another solution, but one that rarely obtains a serious hearing, is to assert that the *agape* commanded by the New Testament extends only to those in the household of faith,[57] a community which people can choose to join, from which they can choose to exclude themselves, and from which they can be excluded (excommunicated) when their behavior reveals that they have in effect excommunicated themselves. The most common solution, however, is to invoke the ideals selectively, where it seems that they can be put into practice without overly disruptive consequences, and to ignore them the rest of the time. This is what usually happens among those who condemn as un-Christian the "non-tuistic" behavior of market participants.

"And as you wish that men would do to you, do so to them" (Luke 6:31; also Matthew 7:12). If that is indeed, as Jesus says in Matthew, "the law and the prophets," it does seem that a commercial society is fundamentally incompatible with Biblical ethics. It also appears, however, that "the law and the prophets" never contemplated the evolution of commercial society, a society in which the division of labor has proceeded so far that almost all social interactions are between people who don't even know one another. Any serious attempt to make the Golden Rule a guiding principle for the actual conduct of our everyday life would require, as a precondition, a thoroughgoing reorganization of society into small villages with no significant interaction among the villages.

Aristotle, one of the first serious thinkers to reject a society that featured extensive exchange among its participants, wanted something like that.[58] Those today who might think they would prefer a society reorganized in

57. For a cogent presentation of this position, see Gerhard Lohfink, *Jesus and Community*, translated by John P. Galvin from *Wie hat Jesus Gemeinde gewollt?*, published in 1982 (Philadelphia: Fortress Press, 1984).

58. See Thomas J. Lewis, "Acquisition and Anxiety: Aristotle's Case Against the Market," *Canadian Journal of Economics*, vol. XI, no. 1 (February 1978), pp. 69–90.

this much simpler way have almost surely not thought about what this would entail. We would have to give up not just our air-polluting automobiles and leaf-blowers, but also our books, recorded music, antibiotics, modern dentistry, and, without doubt, a large portion of the earth's people, who simply could not survive in a world that had sacrificed all the products of an extensive division of labor.

Christian Critics of Homo Economicus and Commercial Society

My goal in the preceding section has been to point out the tensions that I think exist between the character of *Homo economicus* and the ethos of the New Testament. I do not believe, however, that these tensions are the chief cause of the hostility toward *Homo economicus* and commercial society that one finds in so many Christian thinkers. I think that hostility, while perhaps nurtured to some extent by these tensions, is rooted in two misunderstandings that I would now like to explore.

Robert Bellah provides a convenient case study for examining the first of the misunderstandings. Bellah and the same colleagues with whom he wrote *Habits of the Heart* have recently produced another book, this one titled *The Good Society. The Christian Century* published an excerpt from the book in its issue of September 18–25, 1991, titled "Taming the Savage Market." [59]

Why do they call the market *savage?* The only reason I could find in the excerpt is that the French (at least according to Bellah *et al.*) speak of American capitalism as *"le capitalisme sauvage."* With all respect to whatever perceptions inspired the French critics whom Bellah quotes, savagery is not and cannot be the source of the specific ills that he blames upon the market. For the complaint of Bellah *et al.* is that Americans are increasingly finding the market *more attractive* than other institutions as the provider of the goods they want. Attractiveness is very different from savagery.

In an article written for the *New Oxford Review,* Bellah complains about "the colonization of personal and social life" by the market, and refers to

---

59. Robert N. Bellah, Richard Madsen, William M. Sullivan, Ann Swidler, and Steven M. Tipton, "Taming the Savage Market," *The Christian Century* (September 18–25, 1991), pp. 844–49.

this as "market totalitarianism." [60] What does he have in mind? Let's see what he mentions.

There is a new McDonald's on Pushkin Square in Moscow. A recent poll showed that the one thing affluent Americans said they could not live without was their microwave oven. An increasing number of Americans never have a meal together. The members of a church in the San Francisco Bay area can donate to the church for 90 days and then get their money back if they think they made a mistake or did not receive a blessing. Most students are in college today to acquire money, not knowledge. There are also a number of complaints included in a quotation from Robert Heilbroner: the movement of more women into the labor force and the rise of prepared foods, laundry services, home entertainment, and the pharmaceutical industry. [61]

In all these cases, the problem, insofar as there is one, has been created by the attractiveness of the opportunities that the market provides, not by the market's savagery. What worries Bellah and his colleagues is that people are not cultivating families, neighborhoods, churches, and other face-to-face institutions because they find that they can obtain the services they want at lower cost through the market. It may be rhetorically effective to call this the savagery of the market and to refer to colonization and market totalitarianism; but it is sloppy thinking. The problem, as Albert Hirschman perceptively pointed out over 20 years ago, is that when people are offered a choice between "exit" and "voice" as ways of inducing other people and institutions to serve their purposes, their private benefit-cost analysis regularly finds "exit" more attractive. It's easier to go somewhere else than to stay and fight about it. [62]

The exit option is the market option, as ordinarily understood: We patronize the grocery store of our choice rather than requesting representation on the board of directors of our neighborhood grocery store. An unintended consequence is that we develop no personal attachments or loyalties toward the institutions that serve us. While that might be com-

60. Robert N. Bellah, "The Triumph of Capitalism—or the Rise of Market Totalitarianism?" *New Oxford Review* (March 1991), pp. 8–15.

61. *Ibid.*, pp. 10–11.

62. Albert O. Hirschman, *Exit, Voice, and Loyalty: Responses to Decline in Firms, Organizations, and States* (Cambridge, Mass.: Harvard University Press, 1970).

pletely acceptable in the case of grocery stores, the unintended consequences can become cumulatively disastrous when we use the exit option in our neighborhood, church, school, and even our family. The voice option nurtures loyalty, fidelity, deeper attachments, personal relationships.

It also generates problems, of course, such as tyranny, domestic abuse, personal harassment, and unhealthy dependencies. But no commercial society can succeed or even endure without support from those face-to-face institutions in which individuals are socialized and values are nurtured. Insofar as commercial society, by the very attractiveness of the opportunities it creates, undermines the smaller, face-to-face institutions within it, commercial society may be digging its own grave. Bellah and his colleagues, along with many other moral critics of commercial society, have allowed their hatred of this society to obscure their understanding of it. The saddest part of it all is that many people who read *The Good Society* will accept its fulminations as a legitimate critique of *Homo economicus* and commercial society. I am heartened by the number of reviewers, especially in periodicals that one would expect to be sympathetic to the book, who have already called attention to the superficiality of its analysis.[63]

Moral critics of commercial society have often failed to see that the effectiveness of commercial society, whether for good or ill, is largely a product of its *persuasive* character. Commerce is fundamentally a persuasive, not a coercive activity. It functions by offering people additional opportunities rather than by threatening to deprive them of opportunities—which is the essential distinction between a persuasive and a coercive institution. It is the *sweetness* of *Homo economicus* (*per suavitatem* = through sweetness) that makes him effective. Those who fail to see this will never produce an adequate diagnosis of the ills to which commercial society is in fact prone, much less a suitable prescription for the cure of those ills.

The second misunderstanding that produces so much hostility toward commercial society is found with distressing regularity in the social encyclicals of the Roman Catholic Church. It takes the form of the assumption that some vantage point exists above the fray, a vantage point from which, once it is attained, all social ills can be corrected. Since that van-

63. See for example Glenn Tinder, "An Innocent Proposal," in *The Christian Century* (October 2, 1991), pp. 885–88, and the first part of "Disunited States" by Alan Ryan in *The New Republic* (November 4, 1991), pp. 28–30.

tage point exists, we have a moral obligation to ascend its height and set the social world in proper order. Consider the following excerpt from *Centesimus Annus:*

> A given culture reveals its overall understanding of life through the choices it makes in production and consumption. It is here that *the phenomenon of consumerism* arises. In singling out new needs and new means to meet them, one must be guided by a comprehensive picture of man which respects all the dimensions of his being and which subordinates his material and instinctive dimensions to his interior and spiritual ones. If, on the contrary, a direct appeal is made to his instincts—while ignoring in various ways the reality of the person as intelligent and free—then *consumer attitudes and life-styles* can be created which are objectively improper and often damaging to his physical and spiritual health. Of itself, an economic system does not possess criteria for correctly distinguishing new and higher forms of satisfying human needs from artificial new needs which hinder the formation of a mature personality. *Thus a great deal of educational and cultural work* is urgently needed, including the education of consumers in the responsible use of their power of choice, the formation of a strong sense of responsibility among producers and among people in the mass media in particular, as well as the necessary intervention by public authorities.[64]

Questions come tumbling out. Who is the "one" who must be guided? Are business decision makers supposed to assess the overall cultural and spiritual effects of every new product they are thinking about introducing? If so, who assigned them such an awesome responsibility? Is there not something arrogant about taking this responsibility upon oneself?

What does it mean that an economic system "of itself" does not possess criteria for correctly making the distinction that the encyclical insists upon? Doesn't an economic system include the ideas and values of its participants? If the people who participate in an economic system are not in possession of these criteria, who is?

---

64. *On the Hundredth Anniversary of Rerum Novarum: Centesimus Annus* (Washington: United States Catholic Conference, 1991), p. 71. Emphasis in original.

Who is supposed to do all the educational and cultural work that is so urgently needed? Who is competent to educate consumers, producers, and the mass media? Who can be *trusted* with the task?

Does the last phrase perhaps imply an answer? Is government in command of the vantage point from which the overall truth can be discerned and all the proper measures put in place? Or is it only governments obedient to bishops?

A review by John Paul II of *Rerum Novarum,* whose 100th anniversary *Centesimus Annus* commemorates, reminds us that Leo XIII assigned some very large responsibilities to government. It must assure workers a just wage, defined as a wage sufficient to support the worker along with his wife and family and to allow for some saving; preserve Sunday as a day of rest; exercise a special care and concern for the weak and defenseless; and watch over "the common good" to ensure that every sector of social life, including the economic one, both contributes to the common good and respects the rightful autonomy of every other sector.[65] *Centesimus Annus* enlarges these responsibilities to include protection of the environment, stabilization of aggregate levels of economic activity, regulation of monopolies, and state production when the private sector is "not equal to the task at hand."[66]

The extraordinary assumption running through all this is that the state is *always* "equal to the task at hand." Recently decolonized states will sometimes lack "a class of competent professional people capable of running the State apparatus in an honest and just way";[67] but this is apparently never a problem in advanced societies.

Why do the social encyclicals (and so many denominational pronouncements on the economy) assume so casually and uncritically that the government always promotes the public interest? I would locate the answer in a failing that is characteristic of all intellectuals and not just of specifically religious thinkers. They believe—it is a matter of vocational commitment—that ideas and ideals matter. But they are unwilling to undertake, or at least reluctant to contemplate, the long and arduous task of acting on this conviction in the only way that is consistent with liberal and

---

65. *Ibid.,* chapter I, "Characteristics of *Rerum Novarum,*" pp. 8–24.
66. *Ibid.,* pp. 78, 93–94.
67. *Ibid.,* p. 41.

democratic principles.[68] "Government" provides the shortcut they need. The myth of the benevolent despot satisfies the vanity of the "man of system," who "seems to imagine that he can arrange the different members of a great society with as much ease as the hand arranges the different pieces upon a chess-board." The *Homo economicus* assumption reminds him of the uncomfortable fact that "in the great chess-board of human society, every single piece has a principle of motion of its own."[69]

Adam Smith recognized, perhaps with occasional lapses, that the desire of individuals to better their condition would be found among government officials as often as among merchants and manufacturers—and also, it might be added, among members of the clergy at all levels.[70] In his social analysis, there is no position above the fray. Even the philosophers who write about social problems are themselves participants in the drama they are trying to describe.

I think that two of the characteristics of *Homo economicus* most offensive to religious critics are his limited knowledge and his partial interests. The existence of those characteristics implies that we cannot count on economic man, either singly or in concert, always to intend, much less always to achieve, the public interest.

But what follows from this? We can certainly work to expand the knowledge and broaden the interests of *Homo economicus*. But when we do so, we ought to be fully aware that we are working to expand one another's knowledge and to broaden one another's interests. For we are all instances of *Homo economicus*. Impartiality and omniscience have not been granted to any of us, not even to government officials and bishops. We are only human. And the same is true, I think, of *Homo economicus*. When properly understood, he is merely human.

Can *Homo economicus* be Christian? It's always a possibility.

---

68. There is a chronic tendency for writers in the older Roman Catholic tradition to caricature liberalism in order to avoid dealing with it. For a recent example, see Francis Canavan, "The Popes and the Economy," *First Things*, no. 16 (October 1991), pp. 35–41.

69. The quotations are from Smith, *The Theory of Moral Sentiments*, pp. 233–34.

70. Smith, *The Wealth of Nations*, pp. 788–814.

CHAPTER 5

Economic Scientists and Skeptical Theologians

How FAR should theologians trust economists? That is the question to be pursued but never quite caught in the essay that follows.

As economic issues have taken on a greater perceived importance in public life, theologians have become increasingly eager to discuss them.[1] In doing so, they inevitably rely in part on the work of economists. By carefully selecting the economists whom they consult, however, theologians become their own economists to a very large extent. What criteria are they using to pick and choose? How are the theologians deciding which economists to trust?[2]

Theology and Mathematics

"One suspects sometimes," the economist Kenneth Boulding observed more than thirty years ago, in a debate with the theologian Reinhold Niebuhr, "that there are only two rational sciences, theology and mathematics, and that all differences arise from the first and agreements from

Unpublished typescript, reprinted by permission of Mrs. Juliana Heyne.

1. For a widely publicized recent example, see Bishops' Pastoral on *Catholic Social Teaching and the U.S. Economy,* released on November 11, 1984, and second draft, released October 7, 1985.

2. For example, why was Charles K. Wilber, co-author of a recent book titled *An Inquiry into the Poverty of Economics* (University of Notre Dame Press, 1983), the only professional economist among the consultants to the Ad Hoc Committee on Catholic Social Teaching and the U.S. Economy?

the second."[3] A substantial number of economists today would give a hearty second to the thrust of Boulding's comment.

Many contemporary economists see their discipline as a branch of mathematics, in the enlarged sense intended by Boulding. They believe that the systematic, logical procedures of science are gradually producing a body of reliable knowledge about economic processes that deserves public acceptance. They also believe that the introduction of theological considerations, again in Boulding's enlarged sense of the term, into the discussion of economic policies is more likely to confuse than to advance the cause of understanding and consensus. Milton Friedman spoke for many contemporary economists when he wrote:

> I venture the judgment...that currently in the Western world, and especially in the United States, differences about economic policy among disinterested citizens derive predominantly from different predictions about the economic consequences of taking action—differences that in principle can be eliminated by the progress of positive [i.e., scientific] economics—rather than from fundamental differences in basic values, differences about which men can ultimately only fight.[4]

Friedman did not mean to say that values cannot be rationally discussed, since he has himself often argued on behalf of particular values. It is *"fundamental* differences in *basic* values" about which Friedman says we can *"ultimately* only fight" if we disagree. Since we always seem to be able to find further arguments to support any values we're defending, we may never reach the point at which fighting is our only remaining recourse. Nonetheless Friedman and Boulding are advancing a significant claim, which we might state as follows: Debates about economic policy are likely to proceed more satisfactorily if they focus on "the economic consequences of taking action," or the causal connections that the science of economics can establish, than if they wander off into theological issues or questions of basic values.

3. Kenneth E. Boulding, *The Organizational Revolution: A Study in the Ethics of Economic Organization* (Harper, 1953), p. 245.

4. Milton Friedman, "The Methodology of Positive Economics," in *Essays in Positive Economics* (University of Chicago Press, 1953), p. 5.

Science and Ideology

Boulding and Friedman both published the comments quoted in 1953, a decade before Thomas Kuhn published *The Structure of Scientific Revolutions.*[5] Kuhn's influential account of the role that paradigms play in the practice of any science raises serious questions about the sharp distinction between "theology" and "mathematics." Widespread acceptance of Kuhn's analysis has made it much more difficult for economists to ignore or dismiss charges of ideological distortion at the root of their work. The objectivity and value neutrality of properly conducted economic inquiry has had to be defended in recent years against the claim, coming from many directions, that economics is an ideology as much as it is a science. And theologians, upon being told that they are ignorant of economic science, can now more effectively reply that economists are in turn unaware of the hidden "theology" undergirding their scientific claims.[6]

Whether economics is a science, an ideology, or something of both, this much is clear: the conclusions that economists reach in the course of their inquiries must be believed if they are to be acted upon. And since economists are seldom kings, even the most solidly-established conclusions of economic science will have to be accepted by a large number of non-economists if they are to have any effect on public policy. People will have to be *persuaded* that what economists say they know is both true and relevant to the issues at hand.

When it comes to persuading theologians, mainstream economists operate under a severe handicap. By "mainstream" I mean those economists who believe that price theory, now often called microeconomic theory, is a powerful aid toward understanding the social interactions that we refer to as "economic activity." The handicap under which mainstream economists labor in their efforts to persuade theologians is the basic hostility of the theologians toward what they take to be the micro-economist's presuppositions. What seems initially plausible and, in some cases, al-

---

5. Thomas Kuhn, *The Structure of Scientific Revolutions* (University of Chicago Press, 1962).

6. Theologian J. Philip Wogaman, for example, has tried to describe the ideology that he thinks informs each of the principal schools to be found in contemporary economics, and then to criticize the economics by assessing the ideology. See J. Philip Wogaman, *The Great Economic Debate: An Ethical Analysis* (Westminster Press, 1977).

most undeniable to the mainstream economist will frequently strike the theologian as either immoral or absurd and possibly both. As a result, theologians tend to support or construct their positions on economic issues by consulting primarily economists who reject price theory or make little use of it.

The Influence of Adam Smith

Adam Smith is at the root of the problem. It is his conception of the way that economic systems work which modern theologians find objectionable when they encounter it in the analyses of contemporary economists. Smith taught that economic systems are coordinated by the pursuit of self-interest, and that they actually function more satisfactorily when participants aim at their own advantage than when they intend to pursue the public interest. Government direction of economic activity is neither necessary nor desirable, according to Smith, and it is seldom successful when it tries to divert resources away from the applications to which their owners prefer to put them.

Theologians object to the individualism and selfishness that seem to be assumed and endorsed in the Smithian approach. They are not willing to grant that social systems can be effectively and satisfactorily coordinated by the interplay of self-interested actions. They believe that a morally acceptable social system must offer a larger role for altruism, benevolence, and public-regarding actions. The Smithian system is condemned in their eyes by its rejection, as unnecessary and even counterproductive, of conscious efforts to promote the public interest. "It is not from the benevolence of the butcher, the brewer, or the baker, that we expect our dinner," Smith writes, "but from their regard to their own interest."[7] And again: "I have never known much good done by those who affected to trade for the public good."[8] The statesman, moreover, who would attempt to tell private people how they ought to use their resources, would be assuming

7. Adam Smith, *An Inquiry into the Nature and Causes of the Wealth of Nations*, book I, chapter II, pp. 26–27 in the Glasgow Edition of the Works and Correspondence of Adam Smith (Oxford University Press, 1976; Liberty Fund, 1981).

8. *Ibid.*, book IV, chapter II, p. 456.

an unnecessary and dangerous authority, Smith says, and one "which would nowhere be so dangerous as in the hands of a man who had folly and presumption enough to fancy himself fit to exercise it."[9] All this is a scandal to the modal theologian of today.

The Smithian perspective nonetheless lives vigorously in the work of mainstream economic theorists. It is sometimes suggested that Adam Smith is alive and well only at such outposts as the University of Chicago. It would be more accurate to say that Smith lives almost anywhere that economists congregate. The exception would be those circles in which microeconomic theory is deliberately denigrated, or where economists are in conscious rebellion against the mainstream tradition. Unfortunately, many of Smith's supporters help to perpetuate an erroneous notion of the Smithian vision.[10] Their misrepresentations may have contributed to the rejection of both the Smithian view of society and the insights of economic theory into social processes. A re-examination of Smith's actual doctrines might therefore go some distance toward overcoming the difficulties that economists currently experience in their efforts to communicate with theologians and other cultured despisers of economic theory.

The Smithian Perspective

In the first place, it isn't selfishness but self-love that motivates people in the Smithian world. While self-love or self-interest is certainly capable of producing selfish behavior, it need not do so. Self-interested behavior is

9. *Ibid.*

10. Economists who intend no particular criticism of Smith persist in stating that his analysis presupposes universal selfishness, an inaccurate assertion that rouses immediate moral objections among many people. For example, the eminent British theorist Frank Hahn, in writing a layperson's account of general equilibrium theory in economics, begins with Adam Smith. He says that Smith tried to explain how order rather than chaos emerged from the actions of "millions of *greedy,* self-seeking individuals." Frank Hahn, "General Equilibrium Theory," *The Public Interest* (Special Issue, 1980), p. 123. A new book by an economist appraising the market system asserts on the second page: "Adam Smith claimed that nothing more than *selfishness* is necessary for society to achieve optimal social outcomes." Andrew Schotter, *Free Market Economics: A Critical Appraisal* (St. Martin's Press, 1985), p. 2. Emphasis added in both quotations.

morally neutral, embracing as it does acts of laudable generosity as well as despicable greed. In the Smithian world, people aim consistently at the accomplishment of their own purposes.[11] Whether those purposes are commendable or contemptible will vary from person to person and case to case. To condemn self-interested behavior, as Smith uses the concept, amounts to condemning purposive behavior. All purposive or "rational" behavior is self-interested; the moral quality of that behavior depends largely upon what purposes people find it in their interest to pursue.

Adam Smith believed that most people wanted above everything else to "better their condition." The desire to better our condition, Smith says, "comes with us from the womb, and never leaves us till we go into the grave." It is "uniform, constant, and uninterrupted," so that "there is scarce perhaps a single instant in which any man is so perfectly and completely satisfied with his situation, as to be without any wish of alteration or improvement of any kind." Moreover: "An augmentation of fortune is the means ... the most vulgar and obvious" by which to better one's condition, and so the means that most people choose to employ. Consequently, most members of all classes in society work diligently and attempt to save and prudently invest some of the income that their efforts produce. This dominant behavior on the part of the members of society promotes the division of labor and hence an expansion in the per capita production of the "necessaries and conveniences" of life.[12]

The desire to better our condition thus advances the welfare of others, and especially of the large majority, the laboring classes, who through this process come to be more adequately fed, clothed, and lodged.[13] But the nagging question remains, is not this urge to better our condition, whatever its effects, excessively individualistic in intention and therefore in moral quality?

---

11. F. A. Hayek recommends this way of characterizing the Smithian actor, and points out that freedom to pursue one's own purposes is as important to the altruist as it is to the egotist. Friedrich A. Hayek, *Law, Legislation and Liberty*, volume I: *Rules and Order* (University of Chicago Press, 1973), pp. 55–56.

12. The quotations are all from Adam Smith, *op. cit.*, book II, chapter III. The core of Smith's argument is presented in pp. 337–46.

13. Smith differed from many of his contemporaries in the great importance he assigned to "improvement in the circumstances of the lower ranks of the people." *Ibid.*, book I, chapter VIII, p. 96.

From Vanity to Virtue

It is not, at least not in Smith's view. It is fundamentally a social urge, to begin with, because its final object is enhanced standing in the opinions of those whose opinions matter to us. Our ultimate concern, in short, is with status. It is true that this concern will often be no more than vanity; but it can also express itself as a love of true glory, or even, among the best of us, as a love of virtue. Vanity prompts us to appear praiseworthy even when we are not. The love of true glory, however, prompts us toward behavior that genuinely merits praise. And those who love virtue will do what is praiseworthy even if, because of the ignorance or misunderstanding of other people, they expect it to bring them unmerited condemnation. The opinion that matters to those who love virtue is the opinion of "the impartial spectator." There would not seem to be anything inordinately individualistic or selfish in this view of human nature and social action.[14]

The claim that Adam Smith defended a society based on "unrestrained individualism" is wholly misleading. In any society, the freedom and power to act is always restrained by the freedom and power that others have. The issue is never whether individuals should be unrestrained, but rather what restraints ought to operate. A respect for justice is one restraint. When Smith argued that everyone should be "left perfectly free to pursue his own interest his own way," it was only on the important condition that "he does not violate the laws of justice." [15]

The Significance of Justice

The Wealth of Nations is peppered with condemnations of those who perpetrate injustice by violating the rights of others. Most of these indignant outbursts are directed against businessmen—"merchants and manufacturers"—who use their knowledge and influence to secure inequitable legislation. Legislation is unjust, in Smith's view, when it promotes

14. This summary of Smith's views is based primarily on arguments presented in *The Theory of Moral Sentiments,* especially part I, section III, chapter II and part VII, section II, chapter IV. See pp. 50–58 and 306–14 in the Glasgow Edition (Oxford University Press, 1976; Liberty Fund, 1982).

15. Adam Smith, *An Inquiry into the Nature and Causes of the Wealth of Nations,* book IV, chapter IX, p. 687.

the interests of one group of citizens by imposing unequal restraints on
the actions of other groups. "To hurt in any degree the interest of any one
order of citizens," Smith says, "for no other purpose but to promote that
of some other, is evidently contrary to that justice and equality of treatment which the sovereign owes to all the different orders of his subjects." [16]
The "invisible hand" will *not* extract the public good from the pursuit of
private advantage when private advantage is pursued by means of unjust
laws and regulations. The Smithian system is fundamentally misunderstood by anyone who ignores the role Smith assigns to "the laws of justice" in shaping legislation and restraining self-interested behavior.

Contemporary economists in the mainstream tradition are generally
much less interested than Adam Smith was in questions of justice. It is
nonetheless the case that supply curves and demand curves, the basic all-
purpose tools in the economist's analytical kit, presuppose an extensive
consensus on rights and obligations.[17] This consensus is usually taken for
granted in expositions and applications of economic theory, and attention
is focused on people's responses to changing relative prices. The essential
background of stable, agreed-upon values is simply regarded as given. It
is easy to lose sight of what we take for granted; but it would be a serious
error to claim that conceptions of fairness make no important difference
to the way an economic system functions.

From Moral Philosophy to Economic Science

It did not take long, however, for Adam Smith's successors to filter out
the explicit ethical and political concerns that mark *The Wealth of Nations*.
Within fifty years from the time of his death in 1790, the moral philosophy
of Adam Smith had been thoroughly transformed into the science of political economy.[18] Such typical Smithian terms as "generally," "I believe,"

16. *Ibid.*, book IV, chapter VIII, p. 654.
17. A vast and instructive literature on the importance to economic processes of
clearly-defined rights and obligations has grown up in the past quarter century. The seminal article is Ronald H. Coase, "The Problem of Social Cost," *Journal of Law and Economics*,
Vol. III (October 1960): 1–44.
18. In France and England, writers could refer without explanation to "the science of
political economy" by 1803 or 1804. For instances, see J. B. Say, *Traité d'économie politique*
(1803), J. C. L. Simonde de Sismondi, *De la richesse commerciale: Ou, principes d'économie
politique* (1803), and James Maitland, Lord Lauderdale, *An Inquiry into the Nature and Origin
of Public Wealth* (1804).

"it seems," and "perhaps" disappeared in favor of sharply etched postulates, principles, and laws. Adam Smith reasons with the reader; his successors, the political economists of the nineteenth century, are more eager to enunciate the truths that science has discovered.

Adam Smith, it is interesting to note, never thought of himself as laying the foundations for a new science of economic systems. He never even recognized the existence of any "economic" system that could be distinguished from the total social system in order to discern the laws governing its operation.[19] Economic goods, economic motives, economic problems, economic factors—these are all anachronisms when we use them to interpret social thought prior to the nineteenth century. Smith does not speak of economic goods, but of "necessaries and conveniences." He knows nothing of "economic motives," though he does recognize such desires as those to better our condition, to augment our fortune, to advance complex projects, or to domineer over others. His book is not about economic factors and economic growth, but an inquiry into the nature and causes of the wealth of nations.

Whether or not economics today can properly be called a science, it is certainly a *specialty*. It was not a specialty in Adam Smith's way of thinking. It became a specialty, with practitioners who claimed for themselves a superior knowledge, at the beginning of the nineteenth century. And in the last quarter of the nineteenth century, economics was academicized, acquiring its own professors and an accepted place in the structure of universities. The inevitable consequence was accelerating esotericism: economics grew steadily more technical, and its research results became ever more inaccessible to the non-specialist, except through faith.

That brings us back to the question with which this essay began: Why should theologians (or anyone else) have faith in economists?

The Problem of Credibility

This question has bothered economists almost since their specialty was born. Convinced that their *gnosis* includes vital truths, knowing that

---

19. Thus Karl Polanyi properly (but not consistently) exempts Adam Smith from much of the indictment he levels against the classical political economists for transforming Aristotle's *zoon politikon* into *Homo economicus*. See *Primitive, Archaic and Modern Economies: Essays of Karl Polanyi*, edited by George Dalton (Doubleday Anchor, 1968), pp. 127–29.

these truths have to be accepted by persons in power if they are to affect public policy, and aware of all the interests and prejudices eager to refute their doctrines, economists have frequently worked at enhancing their credibility.

The strategies have varied. Some have opted for rigorous deductions from undeniable axioms in order to construct irrefutable conclusions. Ricardo and his friend James Mill took this approach early in the nineteenth century,[20] and Ludwig von Mises used it in the twentieth century.[21] Though the preference of economists today for rigor over relevance is primarily a response to professional pressures, it has roots in the desire to construct arguments that produce inescapable conclusions. It doesn't succeed as a strategy for authenticating economists' results for the simple reason that non-specialists, being in no position to appreciate a rigorous argument, cannot be demolished by one.

In recent years a substantial number of economists have employed a "testable implications" doctrine to secure credibility for their views amid the clash of opposed opinions. According to this doctrine, competing claims can be judged by extracting their implications and comparing these implications with what we actually observe.[22] This is certainly a commendable scientific procedure. But it rarely succeeds in settling policy disagreements, because there is always enough uncertainty and ambiguity in the application of the procedures to justify continued skepticism on the part of those who find the results unpalatable.[23]

Our question remains unanswered. When can theologians have confidence in economists? How are non-specialists to determine which, if any, of the contending claims that economists put forward are sufficiently well established to warrant acceptance?

20. T. W. Hutchison, "James Mill and Ricardian Economics: A Methodological Revolution?" in Hutchison, *On Revolutions and Progress in Economic Knowledge* (Cambridge University Press, 1978).

21. See the methodological discussions at the beginning of Ludwig von Mises, *Human Action: A Treatise on Economics* (Yale University Press, 1949).

22. The definitive exposition of the doctrine is the essay by Milton Friedman cited in note 4 above. Though identified particularly with the "Chicago School," the doctrine has had a wide influence on economists' methodological pronouncements.

23. The deficiencies of the doctrine have often been pointed out, but seldom more concisely and cogently than by Ronald H. Coase in his lecture *How Should Economists Choose?* (American Enterprise Institute, 1982).

The Concern for Policy

The question would appear to be most urgent for those who want to affect legislation or otherwise change the course of public policy. Shall we deregulate taxicabs in our cities? Remove price controls on natural gas? Bring the unemployment rate down below four percent? Impose restrictions on imports in order to reduce the international trade deficit? Put the Federal Reserve under tighter political control? Adopt an industrial policy in imitation of (or in defense against) the Japanese? What is the actual status of the social security system, and what should we do about it? How should health care costs be contained? What ought we to do about the "feminization of poverty"? Should we legislate equal pay for work of "comparable worth" as we legislated "equal pay for equal work"? What would be the probable consequences of various tax reform proposals?

Probable consequences—those are what we would like to learn about, and what the science of economics should be able to predict. "Different predictions about the economic consequences of taking action" are, according to Milton Friedman, the basic cause of disagreements about economic policy *and also* differences that economic science is capable of resolving—at least in principle. But can it do so in fact? The evidence that it can is extremely weak.

There are a handful of public policy issues where one might argue that economists' predictions determined the outcome. The progressive deregulation of commercial airlines in the United States and the abolition of the Civil Aeronautics Board at the beginning of 1985 would be a prime exhibit. But even in this case one could also make a good argument for the essential irrelevance of economists' predictions to the outcome, and the importance of fortuitous political factors. A decision that is based on scientific analysis ought to be firmer and less easily reversible than this decision would seem to be. (While the CAB has been abolished, most of its powers are latent in the hands of still-existing agencies, such as the FAA and the Department of Transportation.) In the city of Seattle, economic analysis led a few years ago to the deregulation of taxicabs. The cabs have recently been extensively re-regulated, against the nearly unanimous advice of economists.

There is a sizable set of policy issues on which something close to consensus exists among economists, but without any noticeable effect on policy outcomes. Farm price supports, rent controls, and legal restrictions on speculators of various sorts are regularly discussed in economics textbooks, because they are such clear examples of policies that fail to produce the consequences used to justify them—*and* because the policies conveniently remain in place, thereby illustrating both the applicability of economic analysis and the inability of that analysis to affect policy.

Who Cares What Economists Say?

Perhaps we should alter our original question. *What difference does it make* whether theologians trust economists, or what criteria theologians use to choose the economists on whom they rely? If it only matters because theologians want to affect policy outcomes, then it wouldn't seem to matter much at all. Public policies don't depend to any noticeable extent on the predictions that economists make about the consequences of taking action, or, for that matter, on the policy manifestos that theologians compose after consulting the economists of their choice. Public policies in a democracy grow out of a complex process of interaction among many people's interests and values, a process that no one really controls and which even the most powerful political figures in the society can usually affect only marginally.

It isn't that the opinions of economists don't matter. They obviously matter to those in business and government who seek economists' advice and pay for it, in the hope that economists can tell them things they want to know. Economists' opinions also matter to their peers, because economics is played by the rules of the game of science, which call for specialized research within a fairly well-defined framework plus evaluation of the results by other members of the specialty. But if the opinions of economists shape the course of public policy, they would appear to do so only in a very slow and indirect way, and not at all in a way that could arouse legitimate fears of technocracy.

Much of the concern that one encounters today about economists as potential technocrats is a hangover from the 1960s, when economists were claiming to have discovered the secret of uninterrupted economic growth with perpetual high employment and no serious inflation. Those were the days in which many economists saw themselves as philosopher-kings, or at least as philosophers who had the ear of kings. The actual record of the U.S. economy with respect to growth, employment, and price stability since the 1960s would be grounds for an anti-technocrat revolt if economists actually possessed even a fraction of the influence they claimed to have.

The Primacy of Politics

The partially-comforting truth is that politicians only heed economists when doing so is likely to serve the politicians' interests. It matters very little whether our elected officials find Keynesian or monetarist theories more convincing; whatever their theoretical convictions, the actions they actually take will be aimed at the next election. This is not said in any spirit of contempt for politicians, who are constrained by the system in which they find themselves. That system is one in which politicians cannot survive except by paying attention to the interests of those who are paying informed attention to the politicians' decisions.

There is a "logic of collective action" that constrains the political process in a democracy, and it does not seem to produce a defensible version of the public interest from the welter of self-interested decisions that people make.[24] That is one major reason why the analyses of economists have so little effect on policy. It is also a cogent reason for doubting that the inadequacies of the economic system can be corrected by the political system.

The Problem of Credulity

Why, then, should theologians trust *politicians*? Perhaps they don't. They do, however, reveal a quite remarkable degree of confidence in "government." One could easily compile a long list of statements by theologians, issued steadily over the past century and more, in which the deficiencies of the "economic" system are presented as conclusive arguments for government action. Is it by definition or by divine ordination that government always promotes the common good? Theologians have often ridiculed the "faith" of mainstream economists in the "invisible hand," largely ig-

---

24. The classic text is Mancur Olson, *The Logic of Collective Action* (Harvard University Press, 1965).

noring the actual analysis in which economists have specified the process by which, the circumstances under which, and the extent to which the pursuit of private interest promotes an efficient allocation of resources. By what process, one wonders, do these theologians suppose that government officials are constrained to promote a just assignment of tasks and benefits?

One of the principal criteria which theologians seem to use in selecting the economists to whom they will listen is the degree to which the economist exalts political processes over "economic" ones. If there is a persuasive rationale for this preference, it is never spelled out. The moral preference of many theologians for community over individualism seems to predispose them to favor "government" over "business," without much regard for the ways in which governments and businesses actually perform.

The manifest failures of twentieth-century governments to produce results commensurate with their rhetoric has had an astonishingly small effect on theological ethics and church pronouncements. Even the murderous tyrannies that have been constructed in our century by governments acting in the name of noble ideals seem to be regarded by leading church officials more as aberrations that will be corrected next time than as evidence of some fatal flaw in the social vision of those who want a further politicization of contemporary social life.

Social Visions

It takes more than evidence to refute an ideology, and contemporary theologians who write about economic issues are almost always in the grip of a recognizable ideology. Since that word has so many pejorative connotations, however, let's substitute "social vision," and say that contemporary theological pronouncements on economics tend to reflect a particular social vision, one that is favorably disposed toward "government" and suspicious of "business."

The pot is not trying here to lecture the kettle on its blackness. The policy-relevant work that economists do also reflects a particular social vision or ideology. Because economists generally want to be mathematicians rather than theologians (in Boulding's sense), they are usually less willing or able to recognize ideological elements in their own work. A definite social vision does nonetheless inform economic theorizing and its empirical applications. Among mainstream economists, that vision is still in large part the social vision of Adam Smith, in which "society" is the product of many people's intentions but not of anyone's design.

None of us can reflect intelligibly upon the social order without the aid of such an informing vision, a set of preconceptions that pose the questions we will ask and that answer the questions we haven't thought to ask. Mathematics, we might say, will always have its theological foundations. Moreover, the way in which economists influence the formation of social policy is primarily through their elaboration of a vision that proves attractive and compelling, rather than through their specific research output. Economists read and respond to "mathematical" studies; but citizens consult the "theology" which they find these studies expressing or supporting.

It is difficult to evaluate and discuss competing social visions. That is why it sometimes seems that "theology" is the source of all our differences and that we could come to agreement if only we resolved to focus exclusively on "mathematical" issues. But this is an illusion. Our "mathematical" discussions progress only insofar as they take place within a common, accepted "theological" framework. Absent this consensus, our progress will be largely toward mutual incomprehension.

Toward Choosing a Social Vision

A compelling social vision will be one that both explains and inspires. It will be able to account satisfactorily for the flow of events; but it will also give adequate weight to the values that emerge from those events. The Marxian vision survives and often prospers among theologians, despite its well-known explanatory and predictive failures, largely because it seems to give such vigorous support to the values that they cherish. The considerable explanatory power of the Smithian vision, by contrast, is generally not recognized among theologians, largely because they don't give it a sympathetic hearing. They are prejudiced because of the support which it seems to offer to individualism, selfishness, and materialism—not a highly respected trio in most theological circles.

The Smithian vision deserves a more attentive hearing. The units of analysis in Adam Smith's social vision are individuals; but the object of

understanding is the cooperation that occurs among them. Self-love is assumed; but so is respect for the laws of justice. The Smithian vision tells
us how the supply of "vendible" goods increases in a society; but it also explains the social origins and effects of government, churches, universities,
and vocational associations. Human projects, great and humble, are acknowledged and honored in the Smithian vision; but the dangers of pride,
pretension, and hypocrisy are also kept in mind, and their manifestations
are exposed. The Smithian vision allows for extensive and fundamental
social changes over time; but these changes are explained as the product
of evolution within a stable framework, and are not assumed to require
revolutions more likely to produce disruption than progress.

Most important of all, perhaps, for any dialogue between economists
and theologians is that *no one is in control* in the Smithian vision. Everyone chooses, but all choices are constrained by the freedom and power
to choose that others retain and exercise. There is no superior class with
a special destiny, no elite ordained to guide the course of history, no secret *gnosis* to which the uninitiated must bow. In the Smithian vision, no
human can prescribe the outcome.

Why is that vision generally so unattractive to theologians in our day?
If it could be made more compelling and attractive, at least relative to the
available alternatives, perhaps theologians would be willing to trust economists more than they currently do.

CHAPTER 6

Christian Theological Perspectives on the Economy

I

THE MOST INTERESTING FACT about Christian theological perspectives on economic systems is how many conflicting ones there are.[1]

I do not know why this fact disturbs so few of those theologians who continue to draft or endorse new church pronouncements on the economy. If they believe that truth is most likely to emerge from contention among many conflicting viewpoints, they ought to be concerned that so little dialogue actually occurs among those who come to flatly contradictory conclusions about the implications of the Christian faith for the ordering of economic life. Perhaps they think that the task of theological ethics is to raise consciousness, and that the mere process of producing a church pronouncement justifies itself by generating concern. The trouble

Reprinted from *This World* 20 (Winter 1988): 26–39, by permission of the publisher and Mrs. Juliana Heyne.

1. A single illustration may be more effective than an attempt at documentation. Between January 1983 and October 1985, four vastly different visions of the economic order were published, all by committees of eminent Roman Catholics in North America: The Episcopal Commission for Social Affairs of the Canadian Conference of Catholic Bishops, *Ethical Reflections on the Economic Crisis* (Ottawa, January 5, 1983); Lay Commission on Catholic Social Teaching and the U.S. Economy, *Toward the Future* (New York, 1984); U.S. Bishops Ad Hoc Committee on Catholic Social Teaching and the U.S. Economy, *First Draft: Pastoral Letter* (Washington, D.C., 1984); and from the same committee, *Second Draft: Pastoral Letter* (Washington, D.C., 1985). The differences between the two drafts of the U.S. bishops' pastoral are quite striking. Between the ethical reflections of the Canadian bishops and those of the U.S. lay committee that drafted *Toward the Future*, so great a gulf is fixed that none can pass.

with such a rationale is that it undermines its own objective by implying that theological pronouncements are not serious intellectual statements.

It is hard to account for the apparent equanimity with which so many contradictory positions, all claiming to express the Christian vision, are met by those who claim to take the Christian faith seriously. It is easier, I think, to explain how this Tower of Babel arose and why it flourishes. The confusion of tongues reflects a profound uncertainty in our culture about the status and meaning of ethical judgments.

Ethical Judgments and Moral Visions

When we put forward ethical judgments regarding the economy, most of us believe that we are making statements about the world to which our judgments apply: about the actions of the people who participate in it and the situations of those who are affected by it. We do not believe that we are merely saying something about our own inner feelings in the guise of a statement about the external world. We may agree, in the spirit of tolerance and humility, that we are only offering "our own opinion" when we claim, for example, that "current levels of unemployment are morally unacceptable"; but we mean by this that we could be wrong, not that we are merely reporting how we feel when we contemplate a 7 or a 10 percent unemployment rate.

What exactly is it, however, about which we might be wrong? Suppose we wanted to test the statement just quoted, from the second draft of the Roman Catholic bishops' pastoral letter on the U.S. economy, that "current levels of unemployment are morally unacceptable."[2] How could we do it? To what would one have to point, what arguments would one have to muster, to persuade the bishops that they are in fact quite wrong, and that current levels of unemployment are in reality altogether acceptable from a moral point of view? I do not believe that the bishops or any of the other commissions and task forces that have recently presented statements of the Christian perspective on economic life could give a satisfactory answer to that question. By this I mean that they could not give an answer that would satisfy themselves, one that they would be willing to articulate and defend.

2. *Second Draft: Pastoral Letter,* para. 142.

The pastoral letter of the U.S. Catholic bishops contains a long chapter on "The Christian Vision of Economic Life." It is in fact a hodgepodge of citations from the Bible, papal encyclicals, and other church documents, mixed with ringing assertions about dignity and justice that could only be questioned by someone who wanted to know exactly what they mean, sprinkled periodically with claims that I cannot believe the bishops intend to be taken seriously, all held together by little but a continuously earnest tone.[3] The tedious length of the chapter serves to conceal these failings from all but the most patient and persistent reader. I am sure that most of those who actually tried to read the letter skimmed quickly through the rhetoric of Chapter II in order to reach Chapter III, where they could find out what the bishops actually wanted done about unemployment, poverty, farm prices, and international economic relations.[4]

The bishops set themselves an impossible task when they decided to construct a "moral vision" that could be used to make ethical judgments about the economy. Their vision had to be Christian, of course, and more specifically Roman Catholic, or the bishops would have had no warrant for issuing their letter. But they also wanted to enter into "a dialogue with those in a pluralistic society who, while not sharing our religious vision or heritage, voice a common concern for human dignity and human free- dom."[5] Their "Christian vision" consequently had to express "universal moral principles."[6]

---

3. This description is harsh; but I think it is accurate. The text overwhelms the reader with citations from authorities—three Biblical references, for example, to buttress the claim that God is the creator of heaven and earth (para. 37), and no fewer than six books, cited in their entirety, without specific page references, to support the contention that "[i]n Luke Jesus lives as a poor man, and like the prophets takes the side of the poor, and warns of the dangers of wealth" (para. 56). Statements with no clear meaning abound, such as: "Basic justice demands the establishment of minimum levels of participation in the life of the human community for all persons" (para. 81). A good example of an asser- tion the bishops surely cannot intend seriously is that not only individuals but also the nation should make an "option for the poor," so that "justice for all" requires "privileged claims" for some, namely, "those who are marginalized" (para. 89).

4. I have discussed the pastoral letters on the economy with many people since the appearance of the first draft. Some strongly favored the pastoral, some were staunchly opposed. But I have spoken with only one person who admits to having read any of the drafts all the way through.

5. *Second Draft: Pastoral Letter*, para. 34.

6. *Ibid.*, para. 133.

No such vision can be constructed, least of all in the last quarter of the twentieth century. The idea of a single Christian vision on the economic order is troublesome enough. Will it be Thomist, Lutheran, Calvinist, Anabaptist, or Anglican? Which of H. Richard Niebuhr's models for relating Christ and culture will it choose? When these questions are settled, the really serious difficulties begin. Will the universal moral principles be those of John Rawls, Robert Nozick, or Alan Gewirth? Or will they be the principles of those who say there are no universal principles, either because moral principles reflect social relationships grounded in modes of production, or because moral principles are given by each community's history, or because moral principles are in the last analysis mere statements of personal preference?

The serious question is not whether a committee of theologians can articulate a Christian vision of economic life that is also capable of commanding the assent of all those who profess to value human freedom and dignity. They obviously cannot.[7] The question is rather why so many Christians persist in believing that this *can* be done.

Yearning for Christendom

It is probably because they believe that it *ought* to be done. The Christian faith makes claims about a God who created heaven and earth, all things visible and invisible. It says that this God intervened in human history in the person of one Jesus of Nazareth. It asserts that this Jesus is now Lord and that all things are eventually to become subject to him. Does it not follow inevitably that there exist moral principles that are peculiarly Christian and yet sufficiently universal that they can be used to order social structures in contemporary societies? And if they exist, is it not the obligation of faithful Christians to discover them, articulate them, and secure their acceptance?

An affirmative answer will be automatic only for someone who as-

---

7. For a carefully reasoned criticism of attempts to construct a Christian ethics that is grounded in universal moral principles, see Stanley Hauerwas, *The Peaceable Kingdom* (Notre Dame, 1983), pp. 1–2, 12–13, 17–18, 22–23. Hauerwas has written what he himself called a "broadside attack" on the methodology of all such documents: "Work as Co-Creation: A Remarkably Bad Idea," *This World* (Fall 1982), pp. 89–102.

sumes that *Christus dominus* implies *Christendom,* so that the Lordship of Christ entails the legislation of New Testament principles—suitably modified, of course, so that they can be accepted by "those in a pluralistic society who, while not sharing our religious vision or heritage, voice a common concern for human dignity and human freedom." In an age when professed Christians were numerous, this fallacious identification of Christianity with Christendom produced political oppression. In our age it produces vacuous political pronouncements.[8]

The pronouncements of church commissions and moral theologians on the economic order are not merely useless; they probably do actual harm. They encourage posturing and oversimplification and thereby tend to polarize political discourse. Who is going to listen attentively and accept instruction from a group that begins by positing its own moral superiority?[9] Such claims may be essential to Christendom, but they coexist uneasily with Christianity.

8. A large part of the problem is that the political pronouncements of ecclesiastical groups usually have to be written by committees, and committees inevitably blur the issues they discuss. Any useful attempt to integrate religious conviction and economic understanding will be written by an individual, not a commission. But even such an excellent and still useful study as Denys Munby's *Christianity and Economic Problems* (London, 1956) moves on a very high level of abstraction when it tries to articulate theological-ethical foundations. Munby wants to set out "certain principles which . . . would probably be accepted by most Christians" that are "the true principles of human nature in society, which form the basis of a Christian approach to social problems." *Op. cit.,* p. 33. But the principles he explicates, dealing with "Man and the Material World," "Man and Nature," "Man and Property," "Human Societies," and "The State," yield no clear implications. They are vague, sensible, and not peculiarly Christian. In a revealing last paragraph to the chapter on "Christian Ethics and Human Society," Munby writes: "The social principles are general, their application is unsure, they provide no certain guide to a changing world. But they are not entirely useless. And if we can sum them up in any way, it is in the phrase, 'People matter'. . . and matter . . . because God made them and saved them." *Op. cit.,* p. 39. But "People matter" is a mere slogan that no one will deny and that leaves every disputed issue as open as it was before; and the reason given for why they matter makes the assertion religious, but adds nothing to its implications for understanding or ordering economic life.

9. How could this be avoided, even by people determined to avoid it, when the group has no basis for asking to be heard *except* an alleged superiority of moral insight? And those who draft such documents don't always make an effort to avoid it. The second paragraph of the U.S. Catholic bishops' pastoral letter says: "We approach this task as pastors and teachers of the gospel. . . . The ministry of the Church has given it firsthand knowledge of the hopes and struggles of many groups and classes of people, both in this country and throughout the world." There is much more with this tone.

II

Most of the religious or theological statements on economic life produced these days, especially those published by so-called "mainline" church organizations, reveal a fundamental hostility toward or at least deep suspicion of "capitalist" institutions and policies. I want to argue in this section that the hostility and suspicion are even more radical than the authors of these statements realize. They are actually rejecting *the economy*.

We use the term "the economy" in everyday conversation with little doubt that we know what we mean and that we're going to be understood correctly. But economists who have thought carefully about the subject matter of their discipline, about just what it is that economists do, are aware that "the economy" is an extraordinarily elusive concept. Alfred Marshall's famous definition of economics, in the introductory chapter of his *Principles of Economics*, reveals the problem.

Economies: Material Goods or Monetary Transactions?

Marshall says that economics "examines that part of individual and social action which is most closely connected with the attainment and with the use of the material requisites of well being." [10] In reality economics ignores the vast majority of individual and social actions that affect "the material requisites of well being," treating them as outside its concern. Moreover, neither "material requisites" nor "well being" turns out to have an essential connection to what economists study. How did we come to accept the odd notion that "the economy" produces the *material* requisites of well being? Anyone today who maintains that "the economy" has some special relation to "material goods" is almost certainly identifying "material goods" with whatever "the economy" produces. The Oxford English Dictionary illustrates the confusion when it defines "economic man" as "a convenient abstraction used by some economists for one who manages his private income and expenditure strictly and consistently in accordance with his own *material* interests" (emphasis added). [11] This is simply wrong: *Homo economicus* has no particular attachment to *material* goods.

The identification of "economic" with "material" might have made

10. Alfred Marshall, *Principles of Economics*, ninth (variorum) edition (New York, 1961), p. 1.

11. A *Supplement to the Oxford English Dictionary*, vol. I (Oxford, 1972), p. 905.

some sense in a society where daily work was predominantly directed toward the provision of food, clothing, and shelter; but it makes no sense in contemporary societies like the United States. What Marx and Engels called "the production and reproduction of life," or what we call "making a living," probably has more to do today with desires for entertainment and social status than with materially grounded or physiological desires.[12] The question remains therefore: What do we really have in mind when we talk about "the economy"?

We move much closer to capturing what actually seems to be meant by "the economy" when we focus on the description of economics that Marshall put forward in the second chapter of his *Principles*. There he informs us that economics concerns itself chiefly with those activities that are directed by the desire for money, where the force of people's motives can be approximately measured by the amount of money they will be willing to give up to obtain a satisfaction, or the sum they will insist upon as a condition for supplying a service.[13] This is much more accurate. There is obviously a close connection between the use of money and what we ordinarily think of as "the economy." "The economy" appears to be the set of social interactions in which transactions are typically carried out through the use of money. Social behavior becomes "economic activity," part of "the economy," when money becomes the dominant medium of social exchange.

The Emergence of Economies

The idea of "the economy" as a distinguishable sector of society is a remarkably recent notion. It is part discovery, part invention, but in either case a concept that was generally unknown prior to the nineteenth century.[14]

---

12. Donald Snygg, "The Psychological Basis of Human Values," in A. Dudley Ward, ed., *Goals of Economic Life* (New York, 1953), pp. 335–64. This is one of fifteen essays in the first volume of the series on ethics and economic life produced by a study committee established after World War II by the Federal Council of Churches. I cite the essay here because it perceptively undercuts a great deal of casual commentary on "economic man," and also to remind readers that valuable thinking about religion, ethics, and economics was done long prior to the current surge of church pronouncements.

13. Marshall, *op. cit.*, pp. 14–15.

14. Among the major discoverers were Bernard Mandeville, Richard Cantillon, A. R. J. Turgot, and a number of participants in the Scottish Enlightenment, including David Hume, Adam Ferguson, and, of course Adam Smith.

I can find no evidence in his writings that Adam Smith, for example, recognized an economy or economic order or economic system within the societies whose workings he described. Smith discerned regularities within the flux of social interactions, regularities that could to some extent be systematized and used to predict the consequences of particular policies or to explain the evolution of certain institutions. He also saw that these regularities would lead, under appropriate conditions, to the continuous expansion of a nation's wealth, the "necessaries and conveniences" available to its population. But he never discerned an "economy," a distinct sector or segment of society on which one might have a special moral or religious perspective.[15]

What eventually gave rise to the concept of "the economy" was the eighteenth-century discovery that order can emerge from the interplay of human purposes without the benefit of any controlling design or consensus. This was first discovered in a sphere where it could be most readily observed and understood: the interactions of merchants and others who exchanged with the aid of money. The social "mechanism" by means of which these activities were coordinated became, in the nineteenth century, the subject matter of a special "science," the science of political economy, which enunciated the "laws" regulating "the economy." "The economy" then came to mean that sphere which these "laws" controlled.

I suggest that when we speak of "the economy," we mean that abstraction from the total social system in which the self-interested activities of individuals are coordinated through the continuous comparison of quan-

---

15. I have found no clear instance prior to 1803 of a writer's using the term "political economy" to refer to the science which contemporary economics continues and with whose founding Adam Smith is identified. In the writings of Smith and every other eighteenth-century English or French writer with whom I am familiar, "political economy" means what its etymology suggests: the art or science of managing the political household. The term shifts its meaning suddenly and decisively at the beginning of the nineteenth century, with the discovery that an *oikonomia* did not necessarily require an *oikonomos*, and might even function more effectively without one. The one place in *The Wealth of Nations* where Smith may be using the term "political economy" in its nineteenth-century sense is in his discussion of the Physiocrats, where he refers to it as a "very important science." But elsewhere in the same discussion he also uses the term in a way that clearly makes it refer to the art or science of governing the state. Adam Smith, *An Inquiry into the Nature and Causes of the Wealth of Nations* (Indianapolis, 1981). Compare the uses of the term on pp. 678 and 679, which *may* convey the later sense, with his reference on p. 675 to "a political economy . . . both partial and oppressive," which is clearly the eighteenth-century sense.

tified value magnitudes attached to the products of these activities. Stated more simply, "the economy" is the *concept* (!) of a social system tied together by the processes of supply and demand, with money prices usually providing the common denominator for evaluations by the transactors—the suppliers and demanders. In "the economy," everything of interest has a money price.

Two points should be noted. When "everything has a (money) price," everything becomes a substitute for anything else; and this makes coordination of activities much easier than it would otherwise be. But by making everything a substitute for anything else, the system also abstracts from the personal characteristics of participating individuals, except insofar as those personal characteristics affect the monetary value of their products.

Moral Criticism of "the Economy"

Some of the common moral criticisms that have been directed against the operation of such a social system reflect misunderstanding. There is nothing inherently selfish about such a system. Self-interested actions are not necessarily selfish actions. People are simply pursuing their own projects. And a system that coordinates the initially incompatible projects of diverse individuals should be applauded, not condemned as selfish.[16] It is also a mistake to speak of the processes of supply and demand that bring about this coordination as "unbridled" or "unrestrained," for they never are. Self-interested actions within "the economy" are regulated by the prevailing laws and the accepted morality of the society, as well as by the alternatives that other actors offer.

There is, however, one important moral criticism that can legitimately be raised against "the economy": its de-personalization of social relations. As Thomas Carlyle complained and as Marx and Engels indignantly reminded readers of *The Communist Manifesto*, the system established the "cash nexus" as the controlling relation between people.[17] To

16. I have discussed the misunderstandings that arise between economists and theologians around this issue, with special reference to Adam Smith's views, in Paul Heyne, *Economic Scientists and Skeptical Theologians*, Occasional Report No. 1, Economic Education for Clergy, Inc. (Washington, D.C., 1985), pp. 3–6.

17. Carlyle complained that cash payment had become the sole nexus of man to man in *Chartism* (Boston, 1840), pp. 58, 61. Marx and Engels refer to "the cash nexus" in the first section of *The Communist Manifesto* (1848).

the extent that this is a vice, "the economy" is a vicious social system; for de-personalized transactions are the essential characteristic of "the economy." Economic criteria, which is to say, the criteria appropriate to the functioning of "the economy," are abandoned whenever decision makers substitute "personalized" criteria for monetary advantage.

I am not making any kind of recommendation here, but only pointing something out. It is silly to say, as some have done, that business decision makers *ought* to pay attention exclusively to monetary magnitudes or the anticipated return on investment. Such an attitude would be impossible even if it were desirable. Remember that "the economy" is an abstraction and that it exists wherever and to the extent that exchanged goods are valued predominantly for the sake of their contribution to the magnitude of monetary values. To argue that people should be treated "as individuals, not as commodities," amounts to arguing that *particular transactions* ought to be withdrawn from "the economy." Conversely, to argue that profitability should be the criterion for managerial decisions in business corporations, rather than some alternative conception of "social responsibility," is to argue that social transactions *in a particular area* ought to be governed by the principles of "the economy." Such arguments must be settled by inquiry and good judgment.

I have said nothing up to this point about capitalism versus socialism. The silence is significant. Because I do not call myself a socialist, I am reluctant to foist any definition upon those who do. But it seems to me that the fundamental arguments on behalf of socialism are always arguments for limiting the scope of "the economy." Marx described capitalism as a system based on "commodity relations," and looked forward to its displacement by some other kind of system. The only alternative I can imagine is a society based on *personal* relations. That isn't what Marx had in mind, of course, since that describes the kind of society displaced by capitalism in the progressive movement of history. But history has yet to reveal any third option.[18] We seem to be stuck with the choice between interacting on the basis of personal criteria and interacting on the basis of

---

18. Denys Munby quotes the "cash nexus" passage from *The Communist Manifesto* and then comments: "Christians have usually cheered the Marxists at this point. But might we not turn this upside down and assert that it is precisely the glory of modern society to free men from the crushing burden of these so-called 'idyllic relations,' and to limit the

impersonal criteria, and our only choice is how to mix these two modes of social cooperation.

What Are We After?

Moral theologians are strongly disposed to condemn commodity relations as morally inferior to personal relations. They should notice, when they do so, that demonetizing social relationships is not sufficient to re-personalize them; demonetization may only succeed in making social transactions less effectively cooperative and more productive of frustration and resentment.

When money prices, rather than concern for each other as persons, coordinate social transactions, social cooperation becomes possible on a far more extensive scale. Those who would like to force all social transactions into the personal mode do not realize how much of what they now take for granted would become wholly impossible in the world of their ideals. Some might argue that it would be a better world today if "the economy" had not developed to the extent that it has over the past two centuries, so that people by and large still produced food, clothing, and shelter to satisfy their own wants and the wants of those whom they know personally. I think that such a judgment reflects either ignorance or arrogance and most likely some combination of both. In any event, we cannot abolish the past two centuries or the human populations and social achievements that these centuries have brought forth, and I do not believe that any of the moral critics of "the economy" genuinely want such an outcome. They are probably assuming that we can somehow render "the economy" morally acceptable without destroying it or giving up anything of human importance that it has created for us. I would hope that this is so. But I am certain that it cannot be done along the lines suggested by so many contemporary moral and religious critics of "the economy."[19]

I do not know all that Christian love requires. But if it should require

---

impositions of men on each other to 'callous cash payment'?" Denys Munby, *The Idea of a Secular Society and Its Significance for Christians* (London, 1963), pp. 23–24.

19. F. A. Hayek constructed the arguments of the second volume of *Law, Legislation and Liberty* in large part as a response to just such religiously-based objections to "the discipline of abstract rules." F. A. Hayek, *Law, Legislation and Liberty.* vol. II: *The Mirage of Social Justice* (Chicago, 1976), pp. xi–xii, 135–36.

that we cooperate, through an extensive division of labor, in producing for one another food, clothing, shelter, medical care, prayer books, kneeling cushions, and other such material goods—then love requires that we interact extensively with one another on the basis of impersonal, monetary criteria. If we were all god-like, both in knowledge and impartial benevolence, we could do directly and personally for one another all that love requires. It is irresponsible, however, to argue on behalf of a moral vision that denies our humanity by insisting that we be gods. Until we have transcended the human condition, we had better learn to cherish "the economy" and to nurture the conditions that are prerequisites for its successful functioning.

III

Economists have not been very successful in countering the moral high-mindedness that leads so many contemporary religious leaders to repudiate essential features of the economic order. A large part of the reason is that the theologians and church officials who take the lead in articulating allegedly Christian visions of economic life do not trust economists. They think economists suffer from an ideological bias that makes them ultimately unreliable.

Positive-Normative: The Fateful Distinction

A distressingly large number of economists contribute substantially to this suspicion and mistrust through their endorsement and deployment of the positive-normative distinction. They have repeatedly insisted, in situations where theologians were listening, that economics offers a body of morally neutral social knowledge to which theologians must defer because it is *science*. It is ironic that economists accompany this claim to possess a body of authoritative knowledge with professions of great modesty. "We know nothing," they say, "about values and norms. These are for others to determine. We are merely humble artisans, experts on nothing except the *facts*."

It is hard to imagine a more effective procedure for alienating theologians—or anyone else of sense. As economists know perfectly well, "facts" have a prestige in our society that "values" do not possess; and the claim to be a "mere" custodian of the facts is the economist's own form of moral superiority or arrogant humility. In reality, as everyone else realizes, economists have not created a body of knowledge that is independent of all political or ethical values. Our "facts" are not "data"; they are "made," not "given."[20] So-called factual or scientific judgments are formulated on the basis of particular preconceptions and addressed to others who appropriate them on the basis of their own preconceptions.[21] Economic theory is a set of special spectacles through which economists filter experience in order to manufacture facts. If economists cannot see that they are wearing such spectacles, or cannot recognize any of the ways in which political and ethical values have ground the lenses, they had better at least recognize that many others have noticed. Moral theologians have definitely noticed.[22]

The positive-normative distinction took deep root in the economics profession because economists have been frustrated, almost from the birth of their discipline, by the frequency with which their views are repudiated as mere political prejudice. Economists seem to have thought that they could secure acceptance for their presentation of the facts if they surrendered all claims to be able to deduce policy proposals from those facts.[23]

20. I use the etymology for dramatic effect, not to prove a point. I have no idea whether the history of the English words would support my argument.

21. Donald McCloskey has done much in the last few years to make this approach more acceptable, or at least more familiar, in the economics profession. McCloskey, "The Rhetoric of Economics," *Journal of Economic Literature* (June 1983), pp. 481–517. The argument is more fully presented in the author's book with the same title (Madison, Wisc., 1985). For some evidence on the degree of its acceptance, see the review of two recent books of readings on the methodology of economics by Arjo Klamer in *Economics and Philosophy* (October 1985), pp. 342–49. These arguments are in part a recovery of important work done in the 1940s and 1950s by Michael Polanyi and incorporated in his *Personal Knowledge* (Chicago, 1958).

22. J. Philip Wogaman, *The Great Economic Debate: An Ethical Analysis* (Philadelphia, 1977). In this book, widely used in the United States, I am told, in seminary courses on economics and ethics, Wogaman exposes what he sees as the ideological foundations of the major schools of economic analysis. It isn't particularly relevant that his outsider's understanding of economics leads him to set up straw men. The point is that he has helped convince moral theologians who deal with economists that economists have a hidden ethical-political agenda.

23. The basic history is recounted with his usual scholarly care by T. W. Hutchison in *"Positive" Economics and Policy Objectives* (Cambridge, Mass., 1964), pp. 13–50.

The strategy did not work, for reasons which are not hard to appreciate. Economists obviously did and do have policy preferences, and no one who wanted to oppose those preferences was going to begin by conceding the economists' version of the relevant facts.

This untenable and rhetorically ineffective distinction acquired new vitality from certain developments in twentieth-century philosophy. G. E. Moore's doctrine of the "naturalistic fallacy," the misinterpretation of Hume that yielded the dogma of the is-ought disjunction, and the various projects for achieving a definitive methodology of science all helped give new life to a distinction that many economists badly wanted to make. When these philosophical movements disintegrated under more careful criticism, economists conveniently failed to notice. As Sidney Alexander succinctly put the matter, "the economist's calendar of philosophy lies open to the year 1936";[24] and it tells them all that they need to know in order to feel comfortable and confident about inserting the positive-normative distinction into the first chapter of their textbooks and the opening or closing paragraphs of their articles.[25]

One unfortunate consequence of this, as I have suggested, is that it has aggravated the mistrust of moral theologians and similarly disposed critics of economics. By claiming that their analysis is independent of all ethical or political judgments, economists have succeeded only in convincing opponents that they are naive, philistine, and possibly even dishonest. That hardly helps when economists take it upon themselves to persuade theologians that their moral critique of market relations is confused and untenable.

The Fear of Value Judgments

While economists' claims of dominion over the realm of fact have generally not been accepted outside their own circle, their claim to know nothing at all about values has been accepted much too readily. The strange

24. Sidney S. Alexander, "Human Values and Economists' Values," in Sidney Hook, ed., *Human Values and Economic Policy* (New York, 1967), p. 102.

25. Any economists who want to invoke the is-ought dichotomy to support their use of the positive-normative distinction should at least read Stuart Hampshire, "Fallacies in Moral Philosophy," *Mind* (October 1949), pp. 466–82, and Alasdair MacIntyre, "Hume on 'Is' and 'Ought,'" *The Philosophical Review* (1959), pp. 451–68.

notion that economic analysis has nothing to say about the justice or equity of any economic system is in part, I suspect, the illogical corollary of the view that it speaks authoritatively about efficiency.[26] But it also reflects something of the deep confusion that I mentioned earlier about the meaning of ethical judgments.

Economists cannot admit that they might be able to say something about the justice of the phenomena they study because they can't imagine what the subject matter of such a statement might be. Although most economists, like almost everyone else, regularly use moral language to approve or condemn, they are reluctant to do so in their professional work. Professional work should be confined to scientific judgments, judgments that can be defended or attacked as true or false because they make statements about reality, statements that others can compare with reality to refute or confirm. What is the reality, however, to which ethical judgments refer?

I suggested earlier that the authors of theological pronouncements on economic life, who cannot avoid the necessity of making moral judgments, construct vague, convoluted, and incoherent patchworks of slogan and quotation to conceal from themselves and others that they do not know (literally) *what* they are talking about. Economists, facing no imperative to make moral judgments, stay out of that swamp. An unfortunate result is that they surrender the area to those who know far less about it.

A major part of the fear that keeps economists from discussing the morality of economic phenomena stems from the conviction, which they seem to share with most moral theologians, that a valid ethical judgment has to be deduced from "universal moral principles." But that isn't so, as we discover if we pay attention to our actual practices when engaged in serious moral discussion. When I am discussing reforms in the law of tort liability over coffee with a friend or colleague, I use the language of morality without embarrassment. "It is *unfair*," I say, "to impose punitive damages on a producer who could not reasonably have been expected to know the

26. That it does not in fact speak authoritatively about efficiency has been demonstrated many times in recent years by legal scholars seeking to contain the imperialistic advances of economics into law. One of the best demonstrations is by an economist: Mario J. Rizzo, "The Mirage of Efficiency," *Hostra Law Review* (Spring 1980), pp. 641–58. The basic criticism is that efficiency is a ratio of valuations and that valuations presuppose rights to value and hence an existing set of property rights.

adverse consequences that followed the use of his product." I do not worry
whether the concept of fairness that I am implicitly using can be derived
from some universally accepted moral principle. I am concerned only that
my concept of fairness be accepted by the person to whom I am speaking.
If it is, I proceed to show how and why particular practices offend against
that concept. If I discover it is not accepted, I try to find out why it isn't, and
I probe for some similar or perhaps deeper concept of fairness that *will* be
accepted by the person with whom I'm speaking, while still managing to
express my own ordered judgments about fundamental fairness.[27]

What is the source of this disabling lust for universal moral principles?
Why are economists so unwilling to make a public judgment until they
have attained a god-like perspective? Is there a connection between their
timidity in this area and their naive arrogance about "positive" economics? Do they suppose that their "positive science" *does* flow from "universal
principles"? Is this all part of the pattern which includes the profession's
extraordinary devotion to formal theory and rigorous argument, even
where it precludes any possibility of a contribution to public discourse?

The second section of this paper ended with a criticism of those moral
theologians who despise market transactions because they want human
beings to display a god-like omniscience and impartiality. This section
concludes with a criticism of economists who, by a quite different route,
have come to a remarkably similar conclusion: that human beings have no
real authority to speak until they have transcended the human condition.

IV

I want to return in this last section to the question of a Christian perspective on the economy. I shall assume the argument of section II and omit

---

27. Economists seem usually to assume that an ethical judgment about economic
phenomena can only be a judgment about *states of affairs*. It rarely occurs to them that
most of our moral judgments, when we are engaged in serious moral discussions, refer to
processes. When economists use their analytical tools and skills to elaborate the processes
through which particular situations emerge or that evolve out of particular situations,
they regularly generate material that lends itself quite readily to evaluation by reference
to the accepted moral criteria of those to whom the economists are speaking. See Paul
Heyne, "Between Sterility and Dogmatism: The Morality of the Market and the Task of
the Economics Teacher," *Journal of Private Enterprise* (Fall 1986), pp. 14–19.

the quotation marks. The economy will be understood here as the whole set of impersonal, price-coordinated transactions in which the members of a society engage.

The New Testament Perspective

Any perspective held by a Christian could properly be called a Christian perspective. I am now searching, however, for a stronger sense of the term. If this strong sense is to mean more than any perspective at all that has been maintained and argued for by a substantial number of persons calling themselves Christians, then I think we must let the New Testament record be normative. A Christian perspective on the economy, in this strong sense, would be the perspective revealed in the New Testament writings.

It follows at once that there is no Christian perspective on the economy for the same reason that there is no Christian perspective on organ transplants. The issue simply was not contemplated in the first century of the Common Era, because the economy had not yet been discovered. What we do find in the New Testament is an extraordinary disregard for almost everything in which economists are interested.

Consider the account of the church in Jerusalem immediately after Pentecost, where the nature of the first Christian community is vividly sketched in a few brief sentences:

> They met constantly to hear the apostles teach, and to share the common life, to break bread, and to pray. A sense of awe was everywhere, and many marvels and signs were brought about through the apostles. All whose faith had drawn them together held everything in common: they would sell their property and possessions and make a general distribution as the need of each required. With one mind they kept up their daily attendance at the temple, and, breaking bread in private houses, shared their meals with unaffected joy, as they praised God and enjoyed the favour of the whole people. And day by day the Lord added to their number those whom he was saving.[28]

28. Acts 2:42–47. The translation is that of the New English Bible.

The perspective described in these passages is one of joyful spontaneity. It is the opposite of the calculating, consequence-oriented perspective that we associate with *Homo economicus.* Not only do these people hold all their possessions in common, with no regard for the distinction between mine and thine; they also refuse to be concerned for the future. They liquidate their assets so that they can readily provide for anyone in need.

The reaction of the Jerusalem church to the Pentecost event appears to have been a courageous and faithful response to the proclamation of Jesus as recorded in the synoptic gospels: Take no thought for tomorrow; give to everyone who asks; do not pass judgment. Those who correctly hear what Jesus is proclaiming will be reckless of consequences in their social dealings. The underlying theme is the need to trust in God rather than possessions. It is easier for a camel to pass through the eye of a needle than for a rich person to enter the coming kingdom, because wealth tempts its owners to place their confidence and trust in their own possessions and thus to cling to what they have rather than share it with others. Those who are anxious about food and clothing do not understand what is required for life.

This is surely not advice for the operation of any economy. It would be odd, then, if this attitude of recklessness toward personal possessions were accompanied by a concern for the reform of social systems. No such concern can in fact be found in the New Testament. All three synoptic gospels record the question directed to Jesus about the payment of taxes and his response: Hand over to Caesar the things of Caesar, and to God the things of God.[29] The Greek word *apodote,* translated *render* in the King James Version, conveys a sense of putting something away by surrendering control.

The Apostle Paul restates Jesus' radical teaching of love toward one's enemies in the 12th chapter of his letter to the Romans. Never repay evil with evil or seek revenge, he urges his readers. In the last verse of the chapter he writes: "Do not be conquered by evil, but conquer evil with good." Chapter 13 then opens with the exhortation: "Let each person subordinate himself to the officers of the government." Because government officials are God's agents, the faithful should hand over (*apodote*) what is owed to

29. Matthew 19:23–26; Mark 10:23–27; Luke 18:24–27.

such officials: obedience, respect, and taxes. Beyond this the only obligation that the faithful ought to owe is the obligation to love one another.

We encounter the same message in the other classical New Testament
source for a doctrine of government, the First Letter of Peter: "Subordinate yourselves to every human institution for the sake of the Lord." The
emperor and his deputies are specifically mentioned. And Christians who
happen to be house slaves are commanded to be obedient and respectful
to their masters, even when those masters are perverse or unfair.[30] Subor-
dination of self to the ruling authorities is enjoined also in Titus 3:1. The
Greek word in Romans, I Peter, and Titus is *upotasso,* which means *to place
oneself under,* not merely *to obey.* The attitude of the Christian toward social
institutions is to be one of dutiful acceptance and wholehearted service.

Christianity and the Ethos of Liberalism

It is quite true, of course, that the Roman empire was not a democracy
and that the early Christians were in no position to influence the political
institutions of their day. But it does not follow that the New Testament
would have spoken in a wholly different manner had it been addressed
to the members of a democratic society. To suppose that Peter and Paul
would have sounded like Thomas Jefferson in an appropriate historical
context is to make the very debatable assumption that the New Testament ethos is compatible with the democratic ethos. The New Testament
ethos is no doubt compatible with a variety of governance mechanisms
often associated with democracy, such as majority rule. But it is another
question whether a successful democracy could ever have developed in a
society most of whose members were committed to the ethics of the New
Testament.

Those who profess allegiance today to both Christianity and democracy are eager to believe in their compatibility; but the historical record
is not very supportive. Many centuries passed before democratic political institutions established themselves in any Christian nation, and then
only after the Renaissance, the Reformation, and the Enlightenment had
undermined the unity and authority of "Christian" culture. I suspect that

30. Compare I Peter 2:11–3:17 with Romans 12:1–13:10.

the historical roots of democracy are to be found less in the teachings of the New Testament than in actual opposition to certain church doctrines and associated political practices. It may well be that the church doctrines against which "liberal" political thought was rebelling had distorted and even reversed the "political" teachings of the New Testament. But even if this is granted, we are a long way from establishing the fundamental compatibility of New Testament ethics and the liberal ethos that has undergirded durable democratic political institutions where they have arisen in the Western World.[31]

If the ethos of the New Testament is indifferent toward democracy, it is positively unfriendly, I think, toward the values, attitudes, and characteristic practices of "capitalism." Is that sufficient to condemn capitalism for any one committed to the message of the New Testament? I don't think so. I believe that "capitalism" is simply a pejorative synonym for "economy," and that capitalism consequently cannot be rejected without simultaneously repudiating the basis of contemporary life. Christians who want to reject capitalism ought to know what else they are rejecting at the same time: the coordination of complex cooperative activities in the only way they can be coordinated. The cost would not be just the loss of some luxuries; it would be famine, disease, and a new dark age as the communities of science, literature, and art disintegrated right along with the institutions that provide our "necessaries and conveniences."

State and Community

"Every state," Aristotle says at the beginning of his *Politics*, "is a community of some kind, and every community is established with a view to some good." That statement appeals strongly to moral theologians in our time, who tend to believe that the state should control or at least set

---

31. Frank Knight is one thinker who has argued strenuously for the essential incompatibility of the Christian and the liberal-democratic ethos. His most complete statement of the case is in Frank H. Knight and Thornton Merriam, *The Economic Order and Religion* (Westport, Connecticut, 1979; original publication in 1945). Richard John Neuhaus offers a very different sort of argument in *Christianity and Democracy* (Washington, D.C., 1981). For another position by a Christian that contrasts sharply with Neuhaus, see John Howard Yoder, "The Christian Case for Democracy," in Yoder, *The Priestly Kingdom* (Notre Dame, 1984), pp. 151–71.

bounds for the economy, that community ought to take precedence over the individual, and that a nation should be united in the pursuit of common goods. But the modern state is no *polis;* it cannot be a community (*koinonia*) of the kind that Aristotle contemplated; and the only goods that it can pursue justly and effectively will necessarily be highly general and abstract.

I am persuaded that the modern state does very well indeed if it simply manages to become a community of law, and to pursue the vision of impartiality before the law for each of its members. If it can do this at all adequately, many other communities will develop and thrive within it. If the modern state, urged on perhaps by religious visions, attempts to be a *polis,* it will not succeed. But it will both undermine and crush many of its citizens' projects in the attempt.

One such project for which I am concerned is the radical *koinonia* of Christianity. That *koinonia* does not seem to prosper in ages of Christendom. I don't find anything surprising about that, or about persistent efforts to re-create Christendom in the name of Christianity. Until I am shown otherwise, however, I will continue to maintain that these efforts reflect both a misunderstanding of the New Testament and an ignorance of economics.

CHAPTER 7

Controlling Stories: On the Mutual Influence of Religious Narratives and Economic Explanations

IF THE FOUNDATIONALISTS in economics and the fundamentalists in religion are correct, this paper investigates illegitimate forms of influence. Because I am neither a foundationalist nor a fundamentalist, I did not set out to condemn either kind of influence. I shall nonetheless conclude at the end that the patterns of influence we can observe have generally not been salutary for either religion or economics.

Foundationalists and Fundamentalists

Foundationalists in economics are people who believe that economic science can and should consist of clear and unambiguous axioms and hypotheses that jointly generate implications that can be checked against equally clear and unambiguous observations. Foundationalists revere the positive-normative distinction, and maintain that a science of economics can be constructed that is uncontaminated by policy preferences or any other kind of normative judgment and, it goes without saying, is impervious to influences emanating from religious belief.

Religious fundamentalists are equally interested in secure and solid foundations. They ground their religious beliefs and practices upon a few

Unpublished typescript of paper presented to the Southern Economic Association session on "The Influence of Religion on Economics (and Vice Versa)," 18 November 1990. Reprinted by permission of Mrs. Juliana Heyne.

fundamentals that they take to be sufficiently clear, unambiguous, and certain that they cannot be affected by the discoveries of any science or other form of inquiry.

I reject both foundationalism and fundamentalism. I believe that we do not fully know what it is we know, why we believe it to be true, where we obtained our knowledge, or everything that this knowledge implies.[1]

Storytellers in Economics and Religion

Both economists and theologians attempt to persuade, and they usually do so most effectively by telling stories.

The traditional storyteller begins, "Once upon a time...." The persuasive economist begins, "Let's assume that...." Economists tell stories about demand curves that slope downward to the right, about the process of capitalizing expected values, about the exploitation of comparative advantage, about exchanges based on attention to marginal values, about persons pursuing the projects that interest them in accordance with the accepted rules of the game and paying attention to the net advantages of alternative means as reflected largely in the price tags attached to those means and generated by the totality of social transactions. They tell all these stories with the intention of persuading others that an orderly and cooperative pattern lies beneath the seeming chaos and conflict of observed social transactions, and that discernment of this pattern enables one to predict the general consequences of contemplated policies.

The claim that Christians tell stories is more familiar. (And I am going to confine my attention, for reasons of both interest and competence, to *Christianity* and economics.) I shall not deal with the question, "Are they *mere* stories," because I don't think *mere* should be used in this context to modify *stories*. As a non-fundamentalist, I do not believe that religious

---

1. Michael Polanyi's *Personal Knowledge* (Chicago: University of Chicago Press, 1958) contains most of what I would want to say if asked to spell out my epistemological position. For a fuller understanding of the epistemology that informs this paper, or a clearer target for those who want to shoot down my arguments, consult the varied writings on the rhetoric of economics of Donald McCloskey, whose positions I almost always find insightful and persuasive. His basic book is *The Rhetoric of Economics* (Madison, Wis.: University of Wisconsin Press, 1985).

faith amounts to the acceptance of certain facts as scientific history or that faith is created and nurtured by empirical or logical demonstrations. To put my position simply and only a little bit misleadingly: Religious faith is born and grows in those who find certain stories increasingly compelling.

The Question and an Approach

Are the stories that economists tell when they are doing economics ever influenced in important ways by the stories these same economists rehearse when they are engaged in religious practices? Are the religious narratives that economists hear and repeat ever modified by the stories they are accustomed to telling in their work as economists?

My views on all this are apparently idiosyncratic. Let me try to spell out the main conclusions in advance. It is generally admitted without much argument that conclusions about economic *policy* are affected by religious beliefs, because policy conclusions require value judgments and religious beliefs generate value judgments. I think it would be a good idea to admit less and argue more, for the nature of this influence is far from clear. It seems to me that Milton Friedman was quite correct when he hypothesized (in his influential essay on "The Methodology of Positive Economics") that disagreements about economic policy are more often rooted in disagreements about how economic systems function than in conflicting value judgments. If this is the case, how, by what process, do religious narratives influence economic policy judgments? I shall argue that religious narratives affect economic policy preferences indirectly, through their influence on conceptions of how economic systems function. In other words, people use their theology to choose the economics to which they will subscribe.

The great danger in an inquiry of this kind is that it can easily degenerate into a debunking and name-calling operation, in which opinions with which one disagrees are "shown" to be dishonest in the sense that they were not derived from the sources alleged by the author, but from concealed and less authoritative sources. Charges are made that theological positions have been taken on the basis of an economic analysis, and that judgments about the operation of contemporary economic systems have been proffered on the basis of documents that do not address the issues because they were written centuries ago. One way to reduce this danger is to discuss writers whom one genuinely respects.

A Case Study

Herbert Schlossberg is a careful and competent student of economics and theology with whose writings I find myself in substantial agreement. He therefore provides an excellent illustration and test case for the thesis I shall advance.

Schlossberg argues that an economic science informed by un-Biblical or anti-Christian presuppositions will be unrealistic in its analysis and misleading in its prescriptions. In a discussion of "The Imperatives of Economic Development" he writes:

> Christians will be able to act more constructively in this area only as we think in a way that is true to our own traditions and cease accepting uncritically ideas on development advanced by experts who disagree with the fundamentals of the Christian faith. Expertise is almost always mixed with value judgments based on worldviews. The experts give us information and recommendations produced not only by scientific investigation, but also by the beliefs of the investigators and by those who interpret their findings. Even if we use this information well, we may come to the wrong conclusions, because the "facts" on which we are relying may be dependent on false ideologies.[2]

I completely agree that expertise comes mixed with value judgments based on worldviews. But is it true that Christians should for this reason look more critically upon the economic analyses of experts who disagree with fundamentals of the Christian faith? Let us see how Schlossberg implements his own recommendation.

In two earlier chapters of the book from which I took the passage quoted above, Schlossberg examined the views on economic development

2. In *Freedom, Justice, and Hope: Toward a Strategy for the Poor and Oppressed,* ed. Marvin Olasky (1988), p. 99.

of Gunnar Myrdal and Peter Bauer. In the chapter on Myrdal, he emphasizes the philosophical and ethical presuppositions which, by Myrdal's
ready admission, inform his work in economics. And he writes at the end
of the chapter:

> Rooted in assumptions that depart from the Biblical underpinnings of
> our civilization, Myrdal's ideas carry over the moral fervor but none
> of the understandings that are necessary for bringing healthy vibrant
> economies into existence.[3]

But Schlossberg also presents criticisms of Myrdal's work that would
be regarded as highly relevant by any secular economist. He argues that
Myrdal ignores important evidence, makes insufficient use of the analytical tools of economics, and contradicts himself. Which of these sets of
criticism—the theological or the scientific—provides the most cogent reasons for a Christian to reject Myrdal's analysis of economic development
and nondevelopment?

Schlossberg's own answer emerges implicitly in his evaluation of Peter
Bauer's work. After a strongly positive review of Bauer's contributions to
the study of economic development (in contrast with the sharply negative
review of Myrdal's work), Schlossberg concludes as follows:

> A major reason for the difference [between Myrdal and Bauer] is that
> Bauer insists that the economic data have to be taken seriously, refus-
> ing to burden them with ideological baggage. As we would expect,
> his work is much less value-laden than Myrdal's, but he does provide
> clues that tell us something of his values. He is critical, for example,
> of the single-minded pursuit of increased income. Per capita income is
> reduced by both births and medicines, but people like to have children
> and would prefer to have them remain alive. Bauer is not unhappy that
> children are valued, and he does not believe it justifiable for planners
> to violate religious and ethical convictions in order to raise income.
> But Bauer stops short of specifying what the values that inform policy

3. *Ibid.*, pp. 62–63.

ought to be. That leaves the reader uncertain as to his foundational assumptions. In a world of economists who often substitute ideology for evidence, from what source does Bauer's empirical orientation derive? We do not know. Nor can we easily determine the philosophical filters through which the raw data are filtered.[4]

We do not know Bauer's "foundational assumptions"! Why then does Schlossberg accept Bauer's economic analysis and its policy implications? I submit that it is because he finds Bauer to be a *good economist.* Bauer respects the data and makes extensive and able use of the tools of economics. He also rejects such notions as that an increase in per capita GNP is desirable even if brought about by a high rate of infant mortality. But so would many other economists, and probably without any assist from specifically Christian or Biblical values. It is characteristic of economists to ground "welfare" in the choices of individuals. A very conventional and thoroughly non-Christian (not anti-Christian) argument asserts that if parents invest resources in trying to prevent the death of a child, they thereby reveal that the satisfactions obtained from the child exceed in value the satisfactions they will lose through a reduced per-capita income for the family. Their real income consequently declines when the child dies. A fixation on per-capita GNP as the relevant measure of welfare in a society is as much an indicator of mindlessness as of anti-Christian or un-Biblical values.

How Clear Are the Foundations?

A serious problem for anyone who asserts that economics ought to be based on Biblical or Christian "foundational assumptions" is the difficulty in determining just what these assumptions are. In what follows I have extracted from Schlossberg's chapter on "Imperatives for Economic Development" four of the assumptions that he specifically mentions as relevant to understanding economic development, and have added my own critical observations.

1. *The earth was created by a just and loving God, so that its resources are*

4. *Ibid.,* p. 98.

not going to "run out" before their Creator intends. Schlossberg employs this assumption to oppose highly alarmist claims of an impending ecological crisis. But one could concede this assumption and go on to ask whether anyone knows the Creator's timetable. Is this assumption a prescription for good stewardship, which Schlossberg takes it to be? Why could it not just as well be used as a proscription against *any kind* of planning for the future? Jesus does say, after all, that we are to "take no thought for tomorrow" but to trust God's providence. I grew up in a denomination that once condemned life insurance as an un-Christian reliance on one's own resources for the contingencies of the future. I am not persuaded that this stance was contrary to the New Testament.

2. *God created us in His image, but this image is marred by sin.* This assertion can be made to imply almost anything, depending on whether the person using it chooses to stress the image or the marring. Schlossberg uses it to reject certain forms of historical determinism in favor of personal autonomy and the power to choose. Moreover, he views markets as an instrument used by people to make their choices more effective. However, one could also deduce from this theological assumption, as some have indeed done, fundamental limitations on human freedom and a consequent necessity for extensive government regulation of the economy. Moreover, if the market is seen as limiting people's freedom to choose (by curtailing their power, which is in fact one of the consequences of open markets), an emphasis on human freedom could prompt, at least among those with a poor understanding of how markets work, a decided "theological" hostility toward them.[5]

3. *The Biblical message on economics is that we reap the consequences of what we sow.* But is that not a very partial presentation of the Biblical message on the matter of reaping and sowing? Doesn't the Bible also say that God sends rain on the just and the unjust? Does the doctrine of grace have no implications whatsoever for the Christian's understanding of the economic system? Doesn't the doctrine that we reap what we have sown encourage the proud belief that we can justify ourselves by our achievements?

---

5. As seems to have occurred in *Economic Justice for All* (1986), the Roman Catholic Bishops' analysis of the U.S. economy. See, for example, paragraph 96.

4. *Work, an orientation to the future, investment, saving and the control of consumption are essential ingredients in a healthy economic system and specified in the Bible as requirements for those who are to be faithful to God.* In each case I would want to ask, *How much* is required? Work can be an idol, and for many people it is. The net thrust of the New Testament seems to me to be more toward a high rate than a low rate of time discount. The exhortation *not* to lay up treasure on earth where moth and rust corrupt should raise at least a few questions for dedicated investors. And the New Testament admonitions to be recklessly generous could well be used to modify substantially the saving directive that Schlossberg finds in the Bible. The rate of economic growth will almost certainly increase in a society where these imperatives begin to operate. But I am not convinced that they are altogether Christian or Biblical imperatives.

On the Irrelevance of Assumptions

What do "foundational assumptions" mean, after all? I find myself increasingly attracted in an unexpected way to Milton Friedman's old "irrelevance of the assumptions" argument. Whatever its deficiencies, it contained an important insight: A lot of different structures can be built on any given set of foundations, and foundations inadequate for some purposes may be more than adequate for others.

For example, I do not accept some of the fundamental assumptions of F. A. Hayek. Nonetheless I find his analysis of markets and "spontaneous orders" passing almost every test to which I can put it: coherent, consistent with the evidence, applicable to a vast range of circumstances, predictive, explanatory, generative of new insights. On the other hand, the fundamental assumptions of Ronald Sider agree substantially with my own. The religious narratives he tells are by and large the narratives that I also recount. Nonetheless I reject his basic social analysis because it fares poorly on the tests that Hayek's analysis passes so spectacularly.

The evidence shows, I think, that theological assumptions almost never carry implications for the economy that are sufficiently clear to resolve issues in controversy. The "clear implications" are discerned only by those who have already reached these conclusions by other means. In the case of those economist-theologians who are today insisting that Christianity lends moral support to capitalism, I maintain that they discovered the virtues of capitalism through the study of economics, and that the theological support they find in the Bible is in fact a product of their economic analysis.

This is almost as true of those who use the Bible to condemn capitalism and endorse socialism. I say *almost* because I believe that it is easier to turn an impartial and uncommitted person who is also ignorant of economics into a defender of socialism on the basis of the New Testament than into a defender of capitalism. I disagree strongly with those critics who claim that liberation theology owes everything to Marx and nothing to the New Testament. The conception of the church that informs the writings of most liberation theologians is deeply grounded in New Testament narratives.

At the same time I find totally unpersuasive the attempts of liberation theologians to deduce recommendations for the reorganization of secular economic systems from these theological insights. The New Testament contains no advice for the reform of the Roman Empire or contemporary economic systems. It is concerned for the life together of those who acknowledge Jesus as Lord, and its message to the outside world is an invitation to join that company. Law is in the realm of coercion. While the New Testament does not condemn coercion—it even refers to those who "bear the sword" as God's own agents—its narratives certainly suggest that Christians will not be interested in exercising dominion over others.

Influence and Resistance

If I were asked to explain why so many Christian thinkers continue to prefer socialism to capitalism, I would say that their religious beliefs have led them to read anti-market economics too much and too uncritically and pro-market economics too little and too unsympathetically. The fundamental flaw in all the successive versions of the U.S. Catholic bishops' so-called pastoral letter on the economy[6] was its utter neglect of the pricing system.

6. National Conference of Catholic Bishops, Ad Hoc Committee on Catholic Social Teaching and the U.S. Economy, *Pastoral Letter on Catholic Social Teaching and the U.S. Economy, November 11, 1984,* 1st draft (Washington, D.C.: United States Catholic Conference, 1984).

The authors of the letter had obviously not given any sustained thought to the coordinating functions of the price system in a modern economy characterized by extensive division of labor and continuous change. Why? Because economics of this sort provides no grist to their mill. Since there were plenty of economists not especially interested in microeconomics, they felt no obligation to study those who were. One of the great advantages possessed by those who enter a discussion without knowing its context is that they can employ weak arguments with a clear conscience.

A partial understanding of economics can in turn influence one's way of interpreting religious narratives. This explains, for example, the regularity with which theologians on the left read "poor" and "oppressed" as synonyms. Their understanding of the way in which economic systems operate tends to attribute both wealth and poverty to oppressive acts and institutions.

I would offer a similar analysis if asked to explain the relationship between the economics and the theology of those who take positions in economics with which I agree. Michael Novak is a particularly instructive case, because in the early 1970s he was "converted" to a new set of economic stories. Did he undergo a roughly simultaneous religious conversion? The religious narratives that inform his 1969 book *A Theology for Radical Politics*[7] are very different, it seems to me, from the religious narratives contributing to the "theology of the liberal society" that Novak sets forth in his 1986 book on liberation theology, *Will It Liberate?*[8] What was cause and what was effect? Did new religious insights produce a new appreciation of democratic capitalism? Or did a new appreciation of democratic capitalism produce new religious insights? My reading of Novak pushes me strongly toward the latter hypothesis. The new economics is clear, concrete, and buttressed by examples. The new theology is vague, abstract, and filled with ambiguities.

7. New York: Herder and Herder.
8. New York: Paulist Press.

A Confessional Interlude

Perhaps I am making the mistake of assuming that everyone else thinks as I do. I know that I have over my many years of learning and teaching economics developed numerous clear and concrete convictions about how economic systems work in practice and what can and, more importantly, cannot be done to improve their performance. And I have a library of detailed stories that I regularly tell to students in my efforts to persuade them to view social transactions through the economist's spectacles. It is very hard indeed for any new religious insights to topple this structure of interlocking secular beliefs. Any religious insights that seem to challenge these beliefs will in the process find themselves challenged. And they will probably be reformulated so that they are not inconsistent with those secular beliefs that I find myself unable to deny. I am like a Christian biologist whose thought has been so thoroughly penetrated by the theory of evolution that he simply cannot read the book of Genesis in a way that rules this theory out.

My theological thinking has been deeply influenced over the last decade or so by the writings of John Howard Yoder. Under his influence I have learned to read the New Testament in a different way, and I have modified the stories I tell about God's saving work in history, about community, and about mutual obligation. How has all of this affected my economics? That is a question I have frequently asked myself.

As I reflect on the evolution of my social analysis or "social science thinking" since I first encountered Yoder, it seems to me that the economic stories I tell have simply been far too persuasive (to me) to be altered by the religious narratives I now find compelling. The implications of these religious narratives for my economic understanding are vague and ambiguous, too uncertain to alter the clear implications of my economic stories. If Yoder has influenced my social analysis at all, it has been by pushing me further in directions I was already inclined to go. Thus the pacifist stance to which Yoder's narratives bear witness supports the preference for uncoerced exchange that is rooted in my economics. Yoder's animus toward all-encompassing systems that lead Christians to prefer intellectual consistency to a lived-out faithfulness nurtures the hostility toward general equilibrium analysis and macroeconomic fine-tuning that I have developed through my work as an economist. Yoder's way of doing theology has even helped to persuade me that Donald McCloskey's way of doing economics is sound.

I do not want to blame any of this on John Howard Yoder or build any sort of case for my economics on Yoder's theology or any other theology. I have offered a report of influences that is intended as a confession—an instructive confession, I hope—not as an argument.

A Few Concluding Thoughts

Theological economists and economic theologians are much too ready, it seems to me, to declare that God is interested in this or that social project. I can't help but wonder how they came to know God's interests and why those alleged interests so closely resemble the interests of the theologian making the claim.

Most of us have a strong desire to "get it all together." The academic mind in particular deplores incoherence and inconsistency, and I think this is a useful trait. We also love to be correct, however, to win arguments, to rise triumphant over those who disagree with us. And so we often welcome support wherever we find it. We also go looking for it sometimes in places where it should not be sought. An economist ought to ignore any and all support for his economic analyses that comes from people who are not competent in the field. The ethos of science declares firmly that truth is not established by indiscriminate headcounting, but by consensus among those who are entitled to hold opinions because they can *uphold* those opinions. An economist who quotes a theologian's views on, let us say, the importance of human work in the Creator's plans *as a way of supporting his own views on the feasibility of fine-tuning* is out of bounds.

Theology, at least as it is commonly practiced today, is much less methodologically restrictive than economics. The theologian whose avowed concern is "the whole of God's creation" may even reject the very idea of disciplinary trespassing. A few caveats can nonetheless be registered. Invoking the name of God in support of one's position on controverted public policy issues has the effect of polarizing discourse. The claim that I am correct because my position is morally superior pollutes public discourse by turning discussions into arguments and arguments into fights. In the community of believers, pushing controversial public policy positions on the basis of dubious theological arguments has the effect of excommunicating all those who have been persuaded by an alternative analysis.

Religious stories and economic stories will continue to influence one another. That cannot be prevented. But it does not have to be encouraged.

PART 3

Economics, Theology, and Justice

CHAPTER 8

Justice, Natural Law, and Reformation Theology

THE "CRISIS IN LAW" is almost axiomatic today. The apparent impotence of positivistic conceptions of law in the face of the totalitarianisms of our generation has brought fresh urgency to discussions of natural law. There is general agreement that ancient or classical conceptions of natural law cannot simply be summoned back to life in the twentieth century. But theologians and, with increasing frequency, jurists are insisting that some way must be found to deal with the "lawlessness of law," to recover a "natural rule of justice," to establish a criterion of legality which "everywhere has the same force and does not exist by people's thinking this or that."[1]

Unpublished typescript, provenance unknown, reprinted by permission of Mrs. Juliana Heyne.

1. *Nicomachean Ethics*, V, 7. Representative of the literature are the following: Gustaf Aulen, *Church, Law and Society* (1948); A. R. Vidler and W. A. Whitehouse, eds., *Natural Law: A Christian Reconsideration* (1946); Arthur L. Harding, ed., *Religion, Morality and Law* (1956); Heinz-Horst Schrey *et al.*, *The Biblical Doctrine of Justice and Law* (1955); Nathaniel Michlem, *Law and the Laws* (1952); articles in the *Journal of Religion*, April 1945, April 1946, and July 1946, on various aspects of natural law; an issue of *The Christian Scholar*, September 1957, devoted to theology and jurisprudence and including articles by Wilber Katz, William Stringfellow, and Samuel Enoch Stumpf; an article by Jacques Ellul continuing the discussion in the June 1959 *Christian Scholar*; Richard V. Carpenter, "The problem of value judgments as norms of law," 7, *Journal of Legal Education*, 163ff.; much of Karl Barth's shorter post-war writings, included in *Against the Stream* (1954); and, of course, a voluminous literature from the pen of Emil Brunner, including *Justice and the Social Order* (1945), *Christianity and Civilization* (2 vols., 1948–49), *etc.*

Wilber G. Katz, Professor of Law in the University of Chicago Law School, has been an influential figure in the continuing conversations of theologians and jurists. He asks:

> What is it that the Christian lawyer asks of the theologian? He is seeking primarily for help in dealing articulately with a widely held legal-ethical philosophy which he senses is inconsistent with Christianity. This is the philosophy of legal positivism (which attempts to insulate law from morals) and ethical relativism (which reduces morals to a matter of personal opinion and cultural history). The lawyer Christian rejects this position; he knows that law is not merely a means by which the powerful impose their wills upon the remainder of the community. He insists that criticism of rules of law is not merely expression of subjective preference....
>
> But the Christian lawyer runs into difficulty when he looks for satisfactory terms in which to declare his belief in the moral foundations of the law, when he seeks for the meaning of objectivity in legal criticism and for criteria in terms of which law may be criticized.[2]

In what terms can the Christian lawyer declare his belief in the moral foundations of the law? That is the principal question. But let us be clear about the question: Why should he want to?

And the answer is that the Christian lawyer believes right and wrong are not merely conventional, that they are in some sense rooted in the nature of things, that certain acts would be wrong though no law condemned them, and that laws themselves are capable of being illegal or, to avoid the apparent contradiction, unjust.

Thus the Christian lawyer asks for the standard of justice. He finds himself driven toward the conception of a law beyond the law, a higher law by which positive law may be judged.

Here, then, is the question with which this paper begins: Does Reformation theology have any answer for the jurist who asks for the standard of justice? In stating the question thus we do not intend to be bound

---

2. Wilber G. Katz, "Law, Christianity, and the University," *Christian Scholar* (September 1957), pp. 164–65.

by the specific declarations of the sixteenth-century reformers. But we do declare our theological starting point: the principle of justification by grace through faith, as understood in the Lutheran Reformation.

Lutheran theology has historically been guided—some would say obsessed—in its theological method by the distinction between law and Gospel. The Formula of Concord declares:

Nachdem der Unterscheid des Gesetzes und Evangelii ein besonder herrlich Licht ist, welches darzu dienet, dasz Gottes Wort recht geteilet und der heiligen Propheten und Apostel Schriften eigentlich erkläret und verstanden: ist mit besondern Fleisz über denselben zu halten, damit diese zwo Lehren nicht miteinander vermischet, oder aus Evangelio ein Gesetz gemacht, dardurch der Verdienst Christi verdunkelt. . . .[3]

God has two distinct ways of dealing with men, through the law and through the Gospel: this is the methodological presupposition. This schematization of God's activity is in turn the basis for the doctrine of the two realms. The Christian is alleged to live in two kingdoms, one characterized by law, the other by grace.[4] The kingdom which God rules by law is the kingdom of this world, the kingdom to which all men belong by virtue of their creation. But God also rules by the Gospel, in the kingdom not of this world, the kingdom to which only the Christian belongs and that by virtue of his redemption.

The inference drawn from this schematization of God's activity is that the Christian lives by two different sets of lights, under two sets of imperatives, with two largely independent concerns. In the kingdom of law he pursues the goals of order, minimization of conflict, reasonable equity, and the preservation of physical life by preservation of the necessary conditions of life. This is justice. In the kingdom of the Gospel, however, mere justice gives way to the life of love. The Christian does not resist evil, forgives all, and is prepared to sacrifice his life or to risk the loss of the conditions of life.

---

3. *Konkordienformel, Solida Declaratio*, V, *Die Bekenntnisschriften der Evangelisch-Lutherischen Kirche.*

4. See, for example, Werner Elert, *The Christian Ethos* (1949, translated 1957), with its major divisions, "Ethos under Law" and "Ethos under Grace."

Emil Brunner, though not a Lutheran, is the best-known of contemporary theologians employing this approach. It informs somewhat the fragmentary *Ethics* of Dietrich Bonhoeffer, though we would hold he has definitely emancipated himself from the system. And it dominates the ethical treatises of Lutherans generally.[5]

These two realms are not, of course, to be thought of as separate and unrelated. They are always united in the person of the individual Christian. And rather than being an attempt to keep the world at arm's length, this is a view designed to hold civilization and Church together— without permitting either to interfere with the proper autonomy of the other. It is the view which H. Richard Niebuhr ably describes under the heading "Christ and Culture in Paradox."

For Luther there was simply no way to gain knowledge of statecraft from the Gospel; nor was it necessary to do so, since another source of such knowledge was available. Similarly, there was no way to extract the spirit of service, humility, and confident hopefulness from political principles. These areas had to be distinguished sharply, for the failure to do so would lead to a perversion of both. If rules for the political community are drawn from the Gospel, we are in danger not only of destroying the political community, but also of confusing the Gospel with human efforts, of substituting human self-righteousness for the righteousness of God, and thereby making the Gospel void and without effect.

> Christ deals with the fundamental problems of the moral life; he cleanses the springs of action; he creates and recreates the ultimate community in which all action takes place. But by the same token he does not directly govern the external actions or construct the immediate community in which man carries on his work.[6]

This is the point to be emphasized: For Luther the rules to be followed in political life were independent of Christian or of church law.

But to say this is to seem to say too much. For Luther did not contend

---

5. The work by Elert is perhaps the clearest example.
6. H. Richard Niebuhr, *Christ and Culture* (c. 1951), p. 174 (Harper Torchbook).

that the State was free to do as it pleased, that there was no higher law by which positive law could be judged. The law of the State was to be judged, not by the Gospel, but by the law of nature.

In recognizing the existence of a natural law all the reformers, with the possible exception of Zwingli, simply preserved continuity with the Middle Ages. The natural law is not a conclusion but an assumption of their thought. There is, according to Luther, a law of nature "inhering in the conscience," "naturally and indelibly impressed upon the mind of man." Even if God had never given the Decalog, Luther asserts, the mind of man would naturally have the knowledge that God is to be worshipped and our neighbor loved. Though Luther's view of reason was more pessimistic than that of Aquinas, so that he was less confident of man's ability truly to perceive the law of nature and to act upon it, he was nevertheless not willing to give up the assumption that all men had some knowledge of the natural law sufficient to provide a basis for human law.[7]

The Lutheran Confessions echo this view, speaking of "das natürliche Gesetz... in aller Menschen Herzen angeboren und geschrieben ist," of "das Gesetz Gottes ihnen in das Herze geschrieben, und dem ersten Menschen gleich nach seiner Erschaffung auch ein Gesetz gegeben darmach er sich verhalten sollte," and again of marriage as a "creatio seu ordinatio divina in homine" which is "ius naturale," for which reason "sapienter et recte dixerunt iuris-consulti coniunctionem maris et feminae esse iuris naturalis."[8]

As Lutheran theology began to systematize its differences with Rome and Scholastic theology, the concept of natural law gradually gave way to that of the orders of creation. Brunner defines them as

> those existing facts of human corporate life which lie at the root of all historical life as unalterable presuppositions, which, although their historical forms may vary, are unalterable in their fundamental

---

7. John T. McNeill, "Natural Law in the Teaching of the Reformers," *Journal of Religion* (July 1946), pp. 168–72.

8. The quotations from *Die Bekenntnisschriften* are respectively from *Apologie*, IV; *Konkordienformel, Solida Declaratio*, VI; and *Apologie*, XXIII. In the first quotation cited the Latin version differs from the German.

structure, and, at the same time, relate and unite men to one another in a definite way.[9]

Werner Elert speaks of "forms of existence" which "represent God-given realities. This structuralization of society does not create order, it is order."[10]

Much of Continental theology has continued, consequently, to discuss justice under the doctrine of Creation. Emil Brunner's *Justice and the Social Order* is probably the best-known example of this theological approach, illustrated also by his *The Divine Imperative* and the two-volume work on *Christianity and Civilization*. Brunner is not willing to concede to the positivists that there is no "law above the law." Nor will he grant that justice, the criterion of positive law, can be known only by the regenerate. Justice is the demand of God as Creator, and it therefore sets standards for all human action, also in the secular state.

The doctrine of *Schöpfungsordunungen* is thus an obvious Protestant (more specifically Lutheran) counterpart to the Roman Catholic use of natural law. It would seem to differ only in the theological insight which it seeks to preserve: the distinction between law and Gospel and the doctrine of justification by grace through faith which that distinction is meant in turn to preserve. By placing their natural law teaching in the context of God's twofold activity, as Creator and Redeemer, and thus developing an explicit or implicit doctrine of the two kingdoms, Lutheran theologians have meant to provide a social ethics without diminishing the radical tension between law and grace.

This paper in its effort toward the construction of a social ethics also wishes to preserve the tension between law and grace, insofar as the preservation of that tension is essential to the explication of the fundamental and determinative article of belief: justification by grace through faith. We are not convinced, however, that the doctrine of the two kingdoms is necessary to this end, nor that it succeeds in accomplishing today the purpose for which it was evolved, nor that it is even true to its own controlling and shaping insight.

---

9. *The Divine Imperative* (1932), p. 210.
10. Elert, *op. cit.*, p. 18.

Let us return to the concept of justice, a concept which we obviously hold to be fundamental for social ethics. Now no discussion of Reformation theology and justice can possibly ignore the Biblical message of the "righteousness of God." It was Luther's gradually clearer appreciation of the nature of God's righteousness, referred to in both Old and New Testament, which eventually led to what is sometimes called the rediscovery of the Gospel. This is history that does not require retelling. Nonetheless, it is customary for Lutheran theologians to discuss the problem of justice without mentioning the Old Testament *tsedeqah* or the New Testament *dikaiosune*.

English usage distinguishes by a terminological convention the *dikaiosune* (or *tsedeqah*) of God and the *dikaiosune* (or *tsedeqah*) of men. Such a distinction via terminology, between the *righteousness* of God and the *justice* of men, may be rooted in a more basic distinction. But it may also serve to conceal a deeper unity. We have chosen to translate *dikaiosune, tsedeqah,* and their variant forms along with the German *Gerechtigkeit* and its variants with the single word justice. We feel this aids rather than retards understanding.

We would begin, then, by asking the question: What light is thrown by the Biblical message as a whole on the problem of law and justice?

The Third Ecumenical Study of the World Council of Churches states that

> the Christian integrity of the Biblical teaching about law and justice can only be appreciated and safeguarded provided we acknowledge from the outset that the Bible's first word to us concerns God's justice which actively secures justice for men by the justification wrought in Christ.[11]

The value of starting at this point may certainly be questioned. But it must be remembered that we are concerned to relate Reformation theology to a problem of contemporary society. We may finish constructing the bridge and then find that the actual *terminus ad quem* is not the one we had intended. We may find that the bridge is too shaky to support more than a

11. Heinz-Horst Schrey, Hans Hermann Walz, and W. A. Whitehouse, *The Biblical Doctrine of Justice and Law* (1955), pp. 41–42.

minimum of traffic, and then only adventuresome travelers at that. But at least we shall not find, at the conclusion of our task, that in attempting to build a bridge from here to there, we didn't even start here. The *terminus a quo* is Reformation theology and, therefore, the Biblical description of God's justice.

> Justice, as the Bible speaks of it, is not best conceived as a quality of some persons or of some action taken in isolation, but rather as a personal contribution made within a concrete relationship. It is directed towards maintaining the security and the right of the parties involved, and toward rectifying the relationship where it has been damaged or broken. The relationship which is always in view when the Bible speaks of God's justice is a covenant which he has made with human partners; a covenant by which he committed himself to establish mankind in an existence which secures the honor of both parties. This existence is a life for man in community with God and with his fellow-men which rests on the basis of self-giving love.[12]

The New Testament is especially clear that man's status over against God and over against his fellow man has been re-created and secured against assault by God's intervention, the justice of God.

The Ecumenical Study from which we have been quoting concludes:

> There is a divine answer to man's craving and man's quest for justice. There is the justice of God. But this justice of God is active in his works and ways. It has a strangely "historical" character. It is expressed in particular acts of salvation which are indeed the very foundation of all history. It cannot be reduced to some abstract quality inherent in these acts, nor to some hidden mystery which these acts suggest. It is justice clothed in action and vested in power. All that enters into human experience under the names of law and justice stands related to it.... This conviction is one with which faith must wrestle, not only in theory but also in practice.[13]

12. *Ibid.*, p. 51.
13. *Ibid.*, p. 185.

It seems to me that this account necessitates a considerable departure from the two kingdoms doctrine. For it abandons the assumption traditional within Lutheranism (and much of Protestantism) that the basis for justice in human life is to be found by exclusive reference to the first article of the Creed. It abandons the notion of *Schöpfungsordungen* in order to treat the Christian concern for justice within the context of the Christian life, as a concern vitally related to God's redemptive activity. While it undoubtedly runs the risk—this would probably be the orthodox Lutheran objection—of confusing law and Gospel, and therefore *eo ipso* of obscuring the cardinal principle of justification by grace through faith, it does have considerable merits even within the theological circle which it appears to threaten.

These may be detailed briefly. First of all, it strikes at the roots of the ethical schizophrenia which seems to characterize much of Lutheranism. It was indeed no part of Luther's intention that his followers should live in two worlds, in one of which their faith was totally irrelevant. But this is what seems to happen. To fulfill one's vocation in love has come to mean simply to fulfill one's vocation, that is, to do whatever is normally done by persons stationed similarly. The alternative here suggested at least recreates tension where the doctrine of the two kingdoms had the effect of alleviating all tension.

Secondly, this view, however skimpy the guidelines which it eventually provides, at least does not suggest that the Christian has no peculiar direction in his political life. At minimum it allows room for such a notion as the Christianizing of the law or the re-structuring of society in accord with Christian ideals. These remain elusive and treacherous slogans, but the doctrine of the two kingdoms simply left the ordering of society exclusively to those, Christian or non-Christian, who happened to possess the best scientific information. Again, this outcome was not part of Luther's intention.

Thirdly, the proposed view seems to take seriously the faith of the Reformation itself. We confess ourselves at a loss to explain the readiness of orthodox Lutheranism to limit and circumscribe so sharply its own controlling insight: the conviction that there is ultimately no justice save the justice of God. God's justice has been deemed adequate to rectify the broken relationships of individual men. It has somehow not been deemed adequate to the needs of a community of men (in spite of the Old Testament witness). This emasculation of the controlling idea has gone so far as to deny the ability of God to justify entire classes of actions which Christians might feel compelled to take as they sought, in one of Luther's favorite expressions, to "let faith be active in love."

Finally, the doctrine of the two kingdoms compelled the development of a theory of natural law, one which took the specific form of the doctrine of created orders. Lutheranism does not seem ever to have asked whether this doctrine could itself be an integral part of Reformation theology. The answer seems to me to be a clear "no," though a somewhat unusual kind of "no." But in trying to show why this is so, we must examine the whole question of natural law and its relation to Christian theology.

Assuming as we do that the doctrine of created orders is just a special form of natural law teaching, we may ask: Is the Christian committed to some version of natural law theory?

What kind of evidence can be adduced in favor? Amos Wilder has called attention to "natural law equivalents in the teaching of Jesus." He finds Jesus accepting common ground with pagan ethics and the ethics of the Old Testament. He finds him making appeal to or recognizing an existing "natural" goodness in his hearers, or voicing a protest against its absence. Jesus' appeal, Wilder offers in conclusion, is "to the moral discernment of men" in his teaching. It is allegedly because the soul of man is *naturaliter Christianum* that natural law can prepare him for the ethic of the kingdom.[14]

Wilder argues persuasively, but he only establishes that Jesus was an effective teacher who took advantage of existing moral valuations to present his own teaching.

The classical conception of natural law, a universal standard of justice binding on all men and discernible by unaided reason, was early accepted by the Church. Romans 2:14, 15 was the *sedes doctrinae* which permitted natural law to become "a normal part of the mental furniture of Christendom." It was, of course, accorded extensive treatment in medieval theology. And, as has already been pointed out, the sixteenth-century reformers made no

---

14. Amos Wilder, "Equivalents of Natural Law in the Teaching of Jesus," *Journal of Religion* (April 1946), pp. 130–35.

break with medieval theology at this point. They were not only willing, they were anxious to retain the notion of a universal standard of right and wrong, binding in the absence as well as the presence of revelation.[15] Thus the concept comes to us hallowed by long usage.

The argument from antiquity will not be dismissed lightly by anyone skeptical of the opinion that darkness reigned until now, but light came in this generation. We hope to show later, however, that antiquity is no argument in this case.

It must be noted that the decline of natural law in Protestant theology cannot be attributed to any mere theological tendency. The concept gradually came to seem untenable, irrelevant, or perhaps even unnecessary and embarrassing under the hammering of legal positivists. Protestant theology developed in the late nineteenth century in an intellectual climate captivated by the distinction between matters of fact and matters of value. It became the mark of contemporary wisdom to admit that no list of descriptive statements, however long, was sufficient to permit the legitimate deduction of a single value proposition. What *is* simply does not tell us anything of what *ought to be*. A philosophical argument which had been waged for centuries was finally settled in the Age of Science by popular vote.

The general thrust of twentieth-century philosophy has been to make the distinction between is and ought even more clear, the gulf more impassable, and any notions of natural law, as a consequence, increasingly untenable.

This is the point in history at which Protestantism has chosen to reaffirm the doctrine of natural law. In doing so it joins the small corps of Lutherans who have been affirming it all along, in disguised form, of course, with little enthusiasm, and to a somewhat captive audience. The reason for this renaissance is clear. The dramatic events of recent history, especially the rise of Nazism and of totalitarianism, have convinced many that, however difficult the task, some way must be found to recover the achievements of natural law. Civilization is threatened by legal positivism and ethical relativism.

It must be conceded by anyone who has inspected the literature of

15. McNeil, *op. cit., passim.*

the past fifteen or twenty years that the efforts at effecting a renaissance have not been very successful. Theologians have spoken of the doctrine of creation, of the image of God in man, of the Eternal Logos and human reason—but none of these attempts has been satisfactory, for they all derive from theological premises. Grant a different theology (or no theology at all) and the argument collapses. If the term natural law is not a mere playing with words, the Christian must be able to discuss the moral foundations of the law in terms which non-Christian jurists can also appropriate.

Now if it were to be established that this *cannot* be done, then much of the current theological interest in natural law would evaporate. It is precisely our contention that it cannot be done, that there is no possible way to provide a more than positivistic theory for modern law, and that the joint efforts of theologians and jurists to do so rests upon a mistake. Let us see if this is not so.

We begin with a formulation of the question: Is there a foundation for law which can provide us with objective criteria for determining the justice or injustice of positive legal enactments?

What is asserted in this question? First, that the existence of such a foundation has not yet been established. There is no presently known way of discovering, to the satisfaction of both religious and non-religious jurists, such criteria.

Second, and most important, the question implicitly asserts a definition of "objective." Objective criteria are those to which assent must be given, which make differences in opinion, if not impossible, at least rather odd. A man may assert that the sun goes around the earth. But we all agree on how to deal with such a person. We first learn whether he means to be serious. If we find that he does, we call his attention to the observations and experiments of scientists, especially astronomers. If he nonetheless persists in his opinion, or if he fails to see that the observations and experiments have definite bearing on his opinion, we scratch our heads and give up. He won't accept objective evidence.

A convinced Roman Catholic may shake his head at a Protestant's inability to "see" the natural immorality of contraceptive devices. He may think the Protestant morally obtuse. But he will not think him "odd" in the way we would almost all regard the twentieth-century Ptolemaicist as "odd." The Roman Catholic does not accuse the Protestant of refusing to accept "objective evidence." And this is in fact what we mean by the existence or non-existence of objective criteria. We are not content that we have located truly objective criteria until we can feel perfectly easy about ignoring as "peculiar" anyone who finds these criteria simply irrelevant.

It should not be necessary to go into metaphysics to gain acceptance for the proposition that the meaning of "objective criteria" will vary with culture, both in time and space; or, in other words, that the meaning of objective evidence is not everywhere or at all times the same. Anyone reading the first book of Plato's *Republic* must be struck by this fact in the dialogue between Socrates and Thrasymachus. Arguments are concluded on grounds which we today find anything but conclusive. The arguments are only conclusive, of course, if the metaphysical presuppositions of the disputants are accepted. The vague sense of discomfort which we feel at Socrates' tactics is an objection to his metaphysics, not to his debating technique. Socrates (or Plato) *could* only have established his argument within a certain framework of presuppositions.

Now the simple, undeniable fact is that most of us in the second half of the twentieth century do not share the metaphysics of Plato, nor of Aristotle, Thomas, Luther, Calvin, or the eighteenth-century philosophers in quest of the heavenly city. Yet we persist in asking questions which can only be answered within a metaphysics which these men held but we do not. We ask for the moral foundations of law, moral foundations which can be expressed in purely natural terms. But the question as asked has no meaning. It is logically absurd. It is like a blind man's asking for a visual criterion of color.

Perhaps our age is metaphysically naive. Perhaps our metaphysics is intolerable to any man of broad discernment. To call for metaphysical reconstruction in such a case might be a hopeless plea, but it would not be self-contradictory. To ask, however, for an objective standard for positive law consistent with the metaphysics of our day is to ask for something inherently impossible.

It is impossible for Protestantism to reaffirm the theory of natural law at this point in history.[16]

---

16. The writer wishes to acknowledge at this point the crucial jog to his thinking provided by S. I. Hayakawa, "The Great Books Idolatry and Kindred Delusions," *ETC* XVII, 2, pp. 133–48. For the benefit of the suspicious, indebtedness to contemporary "Oxford philosophy" is also freely admitted. Cf. especially Stephen Toulmin, *Reason in Ethics* (1950) and R. M. Hare, *The Language of Morals* (1952). Obfuscations are original. While the use

There is great reluctance in many circles to accept this conclusion. Hands are wrung in dismay. Is there then really no difference between right and wrong? Were Hitler's laws to achieve racial purity no more or less just than American laws forbidding sibling marriage? Is the definition of justice merely that which has been enacted into law? Is morality nothing but a matter of subjective preference?

These are the kinds of questions which the natural law devotees persist in asking. And because they cannot stop asking these questions, they do not stop searching for the natural law. Therefore, we cannot expect the search to cease until the absurdity of the questions has been recognized. We cannot (a) grant the assumption that normative propositions cannot be deduced from objective data, and then (b) prove on the basis of objective data that one ought not to persecute Jews.

But is this cause for despair? The Christian who is tempted to flirt with natural law ought to be aware of history. The Greeks found slavery in accord with natural law. So did the American South before the Civil War. And Martin Bormann, head of the Nazi party organization in 1942, wrote:

> We National Socialists set before ourselves the aim of living ... by the light of nature: that is to say, by the law of life. The more closely we recognize and obey the laws of nature and of life, the more we observe them, by so much the more do we express the will of the Almighty.[17]

James Luther Adams, in an instructive article written near the beginning of the current renaissance efforts, called attention to the tremendous ambiguity which natural law has always displayed. The conception has frequently been invoked in support of directly opposing contentions. After pointing to the varied history of the word "nature" and to the almost equally varied history of the word "law," Adams comments: "The possi-

---

in these pages of the word *metaphysics* does not correspond to that of R. G. Collingwood, being more akin to the customary somewhat loose usage of the term, Collingwood's *Essay on Metaphysics* (1940) has supplied much of the framework of these pages.

17. Quoted by William Stringfellow, "The Christian Lawyer as a Churchman," *The Christian Scholar* (September 1957), p. 232, footnote.

bilities of confusion are legion; and—it should be added—all these possibilities would seem to have been realized." [18]

Suppose for a moment that we secure a general metaphysical conversion which enables everyone to grant the premise of a genuine ontological status for Laws of Nature. Now how do we go about acquiring knowledge of these laws? Well, reason tells us that good is to be chosen, evil to be avoided. So far so good. That dictum would seem to be logically entailed by the very concept of natural law. The proposition is purely analytic. Reason has indeed told us. But just what things are good and which evil? How does reason go about putting flesh on the barebones of "choose good, avoid evil"?

Many would prefer to proceed by the *a priori* method, positing some kind of correspondence between the Eternal Reason which created the universe and the reason of man. But the *apriorists* have never been very successful in locating a body of natural laws which can actually be applied to positive law. At the crucial moment they generally abandon the postulated correspondence between the minds of Creator and creature and lean on some kind of revelation. We have no objection to revelation. But revealed law is not natural law.

The *a posteriori* method has yielded better results, if by better we mean more intelligible. But again it turns out that the laws discovered, the laws in this case which are found among all societies everywhere and at all times, furnish no practical guidance. The effort to move from this kind of comparative jurisprudence to the evaluation of existing laws has almost always involved a theological leap of some sort. To repeat: theological leaps are not forbidden. But where they occur, law is not *natural*.

Combining the two methods, perhaps in the manner of Aquinas or Hugo Grotius, has also not proved to be a satisfactory mode of procedure. We simply do not get any clear, generally agreed-upon, practical content.

Gerhard O. W. Mueller has probably summed up the case for most students of contemporary jurisprudence in his "answer of a positivist." Why insist, he finally asks, "that morality and with it positive law have some

---

18. James Luther Adams, "The Law of Nature: Some General Considerations," *Journal of Religion* (April 1945), p. 92.

immutable substantive ingredient—in the light of all the history that shows us the contrary?"[19]

Are we implying, then, that the Church must stand mute in the face of legal lawlessness? I doubt that this follows from what has been said. The proclamation of the justice of God is itself more than silence. But let's turn the question around and ask whether the Church, relying on natural law, has historically had much to say (that was relevant) in the face of legal lawlessness. History seems to indicate that the Church might as well have kept its peace completely.

Why mourn the loss of a useless weapon? A formal burial of natural law is not, after all, an execution. The burial is only an act of charity when the patient is already dead.

But there may even be positive gains which would accrue from such a burial. Injustice, stubbornly defended, is bad enough. Injustice defended in the name of God's Eternal Law becomes intolerable. In an age such as ours, where conflicting ideologies threaten to tear humanity apart and consign us all to a new barbarism, ought the Church to add further ideological faggots to the fire? Did Luther make a contribution to the cause of justice when he invoked the natural law and called on the princes to butcher the peasants? Did Calvin advance the cause of justice when he approved, as in agreement with natural law, the burning of Servetus? The Inquisition, let us remember, was carried on in the name of natural law. And today the Roman Catholic Church opposes some forms of totalitarianism, supports other forms, and creates its own ecclesiastical totalitarianism—all in the name of the law of nature.

In 1948 Emil Brunner consulted the law of nature and then addressed an open letter to Karl Barth, urging him to condemn Communism as he had once condemned Nazi-ism. It is difficult to find fault with Barth's reply, from its opening "You do not understand" to its concluding reminder that there are times to speak and times to keep silent. The Church's obligation, Barth answered, does not lie in fulfilling the law of nature, but in obedience to its living Lord. The Church for that reason never thinks, speaks, or acts "on principle." It rather judges spiritually and by individual

---

19. Mueller, "The Problem of Value Judgments as Norms of Law: The Answer of a Positivist," 7 *Journal of Legal Education* 571.

case, judging each new event afresh. Whereas Nazi-ism in the 1930's had posed an insidious temptation, was a "spell with power to overwhelm our souls," who in the Western world is tempted by Communism and needs to be warned away? It is not the duty of the Church, Barth comments tartly, to give theological backing to what every citizen can read in his daily paper or learn from President Truman and the Pope. If the Church witnessed against Communism, "whom would it teach, enlighten, rouse, set on the right path, comfort and lead to repentance and a new way of life?" The question is obviously rhetorical. No, Barth insists, for "when the Church witnesses it moves in fear and trembling, not with the stream but against it."[20]

We seem to learn little from history. Each assured pronouncement delivered from the Olympian heights of natural law turns out eventually to be a product of time-bound man's time-bound estimate of his own nature, generously mingled, more often than not, with extensive rationalization of his current behavior. Yet we persist in believing that our next effort to read off the content of the natural law will penetrate to the true essence of things. Christians should learn to evaluate positivism more highly than they have been accustomed to do. Positivism represents an ideological suspension of judgment, a refusal to overcome the plurality of values in public life by any kind of value monism or imposed value hierarchy. A church which proclaims the justice of God and of God alone ought to be able to make some common cause with a secular movement so keenly aware of man's propensity to define justice in terms of his self-interest, given half a chance.

But if Christians continue to maintain that the idea of natural law is somehow a Christian one, let us finally ask for its Christian credentials. How is it related to the heart of the Christian faith? It must be related, if it is to be baptized, in some way more vital and dynamic than the Thomistic architectonic way or the neo-Lutheran compartmentalized way. That way has not yet been suggested. We doubt that there is any.

Once natural law is abandoned, of course, the traditional method of both Catholicism and Lutheranism for dealing with social ethics becomes impossible. Catholicism may be able to hang on: it has the metaphysics

20. Barth, *Against the Stream* (1954), pp. 114–16.

which natural law requires. But Catholicism runs the risk of irrelevance if the official metaphysics and the actual metaphysics of the faithful do not agree. Lutheranism, however, possessing no metaphysics of its own, has no choice but to abandon the doctrine of the two kingdoms and to work out once again, on the basis of the theology (rather than the metaphysics) of the Reformation, its answer to the question of justice in human society.

The direction in which we feel this reconstruction must move has already been indicated. Justice must ultimately be defined as the justice of God who was in Christ, reconciling man to God and man to himself. Whether such a beginning will be able eventually to provide much more than largely formal directives cannot now be predicted. But this is not necessarily an argument against the approach suggested. Even the formal relevance of the historic Lutheran social ethics can be doubted. We are not willing to despair at the outset of an effort toward reconstruction which takes seriously the central theme of the Reformation: the justice of God. And we believe it can be done—*pia sententia*—without prejudice to "the proper distinction between law and Gospel."

CHAPTER 9

The Concept of Economic Justice in Religious Discussion

Identifying the Problem

WHAT IS *economic justice?* The concept is clearly a central concern for those who believe that the salvation and the righteousness of which the Bible speaks are social and not merely individual.[1] Nonetheless, the concepts of economic justice commonly employed or assumed in theological essays and denominational statements do not seem to have been thought through with any care. A critical reader might wonder if those who use the phrase know themselves what they mean by it, and whether they could really intend what they seem to be asserting.

Justice is notoriously hard to define in any way that goes much beyond platitude and still commands wide assent. That probably explains, at least in part, why most people who use the term do so without defining it. They assume (or hope) that others will understand the word as they do. But by excusing themselves from the necessity of stating clearly what they mean, advocates of justice often fail to discover that what they are proposing has no defensible meaning at all.

Reprinted from *Morality of the Market: Religious and Economic Perspectives,* ed. W. Block, G. Brennan, and K. Elzinga (Vancouver: The Fraser Institute, 1985), by permission of The Fraser Institute. First draft presented at a Liberty Fund/Fraser Institute conference, directed by Walter Block, Paul Heyne, and A. M. C. Waterman on "The Morality of the Market" in Vancouver, British Columbia, 9–11 August 1982.

1. If the Hebrew words *yeshuah* and *tsedeq* and the Greek words *soteria* and *dikaiosune* are translated as "deliverance" and "justice," the individualistic connotations of "salvation" and "righteousness" are diminished.

The problem of talking clearly and sensibly about justice diminishes considerably, however, when we shift our focus and talk about *injustice*. "Injustice wears the trousers," as J. R. Lucas has put it.

> [I]t is when *injustice* is in danger of being done that we become agitated.... And therefore we should follow the example of Aristotle, and adopt a negative approach, discovering what justice is by considering on what occasions we protest at injustice or unfairness.[2]

What, then, do writers in the biblical tradition have in mind when they protest against economic injustice?

Unequal Money Incomes

They most commonly seem to be pointing to an objectionable *inequality of money incomes*. Since no one is willing to argue that *all* inequality is unjust, the question immediately arises: When and why is inequality of income unjust? When the question is seriously pursued, it proves extraordinarily difficult to answer satisfactorily.

A basic but generally neglected difficulty stems from the fact that inequality of current money income is not a reliable indicator of inequality in the power to acquire valued goods. There are many reasons for this. One important example is provided by the case of Americans over sixty-five. While their money incomes tend to be low, they often own capital goods (home, automobile, furniture, a lifetime's accumulation of household tools) and special entitlements (reduced fares, tax exemptions, Medicare benefits) that make their money income a very poor gauge of their real income.

The situation of older persons raises the more general question of age. Since earnings typically change with age, it will always be misleading to compare the incomes of different groups without taking explicit account

---

2. J. R. Lucas, *On Justice* (1980), p. 4. I am indebted to James Buchanan for urging me to read this book. The "negative" character of justice is a central point in F. A. Hayek's *Law, Legislation and Liberty,* where he also traces the long intellectual history of the insight that we can best approach an understanding of justice through our ability to recognize its absence. See especially *op. cit.,* vol. II (1976), pp. 35–48, 162–64. My indebtedness to Hayek in this essay will be obvious to anyone familiar with his more recent work.

of their ages. The average income of U.S. families in which the principal earner is 45 to 54 is about twice the average of income of families in which the principal earner is under 25.[3] This is obviously an inequality, but it is not an injustice. On the contrary, it would be unjust to allow a medical student to qualify for welfare assistance, on the grounds of low current income, rather than having to borrow against expected future income.

Choices and Incomes

Family size and composition also affect both money income and the welfare significance of that income. Other things being equal, people's incomes decline when they separate or divorce, or when they choose to live alone rather than with relatives. Inequalities resulting from such decisions are not injustices unless we believe that people have a right to make these decisions without experiencing any income change as a consequence.

People make many other decisions that cause their incomes to differ in ways that few who thought about it carefully would want to call unjust. Some families have a single earner, others have two adult members pursuing careers. Some people work a forty-hour week or less, while others seek overtime, moonlight, or take up a trade or profession that enables or requires them to work twice as long and hard as their neighbors work. Some devote their resources predominantly to current consumption, while others opt more heavily for investment activities: schooling, training, or the purchase of assets that will yield larger future returns. Some simply manage their resources more carefully than others. Everyone does not have an equal opportunity to make such choices, of course; but it is surely not unjust to let these choices have some effect on people's incomes. A quite substantial inequality of money incomes would seem to be compatible with even highly egalitarian concepts of economic justice.

But why do we focus so exclusively on money incomes and the goods that money will buy directly? Our society also displays a highly unequal distribution of power, prestige, challenging and satisfying work opportu-

3. Here are the mean incomes of families in the U.S. in 1978, by age of what the Census Bureau now calls the "householder": 14–24 years, $12,570; 25–34 years, $18,205; 35–44 years, $22,575; 45–54 years, $25,363; 55–64 years, $22,408; over 65 years, $13,754. Per capita income differences will be much less because of age-related differences in family size.

nities, as well as risks and uncertainties. At some level of income these other goods surely become more important than money income. Are we preoccupied with money incomes because we think we know how to redistribute them, whereas we don't know how to redistribute power, prestige, and "meaningful" work? Is this perhaps a form of "commodity fetishism," in which we transform the indexes of economic calculation into measures of welfare and even worth? If so, this would be an ironic ideological triumph of capitalism over its critics.

How Much Less Inequality?

Those who infer economic injustice from income inequality are rarely willing to tell us how much inequality would be consistent with justice. "Less" is not an adequate answer.[4] Where is the limit? Many advocates of greater income equality have argued that the maximum inequality compatible with justice is the minimum inequality that will preserve incentives to work, risk, innovate, and perform competently and conscientiously. It is not obvious why this should be so. But in many areas of economic life, this limit has long since been passed. Incentives don't simply "disappear" at some point. They diminish, at different rates for different people under different circumstances. More importantly, they *change*. People *alter* their activities in response to high marginal tax rates; they don't simply retire.

The best evidence that the incentive criterion is not in fact being used by advocates of income redistribution is their widespread indifference to the readily demonstrable effects of high marginal tax rates, explicit on high incomes and implicit in current welfare programs. Imagine a situation in which acceptance of an $8,000-per-year job entails a loss of $6,000 in cash and in-kind transfers such as Medicaid benefits and food stamps, plus payment of $2,000 in income and Social Security taxes and the acceptance of job-associated costs. That amounts to a 100 percent *marginal* tax on earnings. The fact that our income redistribution system has created marginal tax rates of this magnitude and allowed them to persist is fairly

---

4. For a recent instance of this answer and a representative example of the reasoning that accompanies it, see Robert Lekachman, "Capitalism or Democracy," in Robert A. Goldwin and William A. Schambra, eds., *How Capitalistic Is the Constitution?* (1982), pp. 127–47, and especially p. 146.

good evidence that the preservation of work incentives is not an important criterion for those advocating further redistribution.[5]

The Criterion of Need

Equality (or less inequality) in the distribution of income does not seem, then, to be a workable criterion of economic justice. What about the criterion of *need*?

If we define need in terms of what is required to sustain life on an adequate level, we run into two problems. Most simply, the criterion of need is unrealistic in poor economies and irrelevant, at least for most of those who talk about economic justice, in affluent ones.

For the vast majority of the people who have ever lived or are living now, poverty is the consequence of low productivity, not of unequal distribution. No redistribution of income within the country would satisfy the "needs" of all the people currently living in Kampuchea, Bangladesh, or Ethiopia. There is simply not enough to distribute.[6]

At the other end of the income scale, people who speak of "needs" in Canada, Sweden, or the United States clearly do not have in mind anything even remotely close to subsistence incomes. "Need" in these countries is culturally defined. An American family today "needs," if it is to maintain a decent, socially acceptable level of living, enough income to secure housing, clothing, food, furniture, recreation, and medical services in a quantity and of a quality that *could not* have been provided to more than a small minority as recently as fifty years ago. By today's standards, then, a majority of Americans did not have enough income to meet their "needs" at a time when our incomes were the highest in the world and the object of widespread admiration and envy.[7]

5. An illuminating discussion of this issue, along with a presentation of the basic data, may be found in Edgar K. Browning, "How Much More Equality Can We Afford?" *The Public Interest* (Spring 1976), pp. 90–110.

6. Per capita gross national product in 1978 has been estimated by the World Bank at $120 in Ethiopia, $90 in Bangladesh, and less in Kampuchea. These data must be interpreted with great caution, since a much smaller fraction of production enters GNP calculations in poor than in wealthy countries. Data were taken from *Poverty and Human Development* (1980), p. 68.

7. The disposable personal income (roughly income after taxes) of Americans per capita in 1929, in dollars of current (1982) purchasing power, was about $3,765. That's considerably

The fact is that, in wealthy countries, "need" is continuously redefined to embrace whatever becomes widely available as a result of increased production. "Need" defined in absolute or physiological terms is accepted as a standard for economic justice only with reference to very poor countries, where low productivity makes the standard impossible to meet. In wealthy countries, "need" is relative. But as soon as we allow "need" to be determined by prevailing incomes, we have actually abandoned the criterion of need for the criterion of equality. And we are back to the question, When does inequality become injustice?

The notion that "need" or subsistence is more a sociological than a biological fact has a long and respectable lineage. Adam Smith, David Ricardo, and Karl Marx all defined subsistence at least partly in sociological terms;[8] the propensity to view poverty as a relative matter is therefore not simply the product of some modern rage to reduce income inequalities. However, neither Smith, Ricardo, nor Marx had any pressing reason to wonder about the ultimate implications of defining poverty in terms of *relative* deprivation. If it is the social significance of differences that matters, and if, as a great deal of evidence strongly suggests, the elimination of some differences increases the social significance of those that remain, then the pursuit of a just pattern of income distribution based on need could be the costly pursuit of a mirage. It might even be no more nor less than the sanctification of envy.

The Criterion of Merit

What about the criterion of merit or desert? This criterion has always figured prominently in formal discussions of justice.[9] It is therefore somewhat surprising to discover how rarely it is invoked in contemporary

---

less than half of current disposable income per capita, despite the fact that far more services now than then are financed through taxation and hence no longer have to be purchased out of disposable income.

8. Adam Smith, *The Wealth of Nations*, book V, chapter II, article IV, discussing taxes upon consumable commodities; David Ricardo, *On the Principles of Political Economy and Taxation*, chapter V (see pp. 96–97, 100–101 in the Sraffa edition [1951]); Karl Marx, *Wage-Labour and Capital*, chapter VI.

9. J. R. Lucas offers a useful overview in *op. cit.*, chapter 8; see especially the long footnote on pp. 164–65.

ecclesiastical statements on economic justice. Is that because theology, or at least the kind of theology dominant in contemporary economic discussions, has no place for the criterion of merit? If all that we possess, including our intelligence, aptitudes, and attitudes, is the gift of God, then claims or merit or special desert would indeed seem to be ruled out.

I believe that this is in fact the explanation for the puzzling absence of the merit criterion from so many theological discussions of justice. But that absence makes the discussions thoroughly unrealistic. All of us, including the most egalitarian theological ethicist, do in fact regard merit as relevant to the distribution of economic goods. We do not regard the parable of the employer who gave the same wage to all his employees,[10] regardless of how long they had worked, as normative for the employment relationship. Those who have borne the burden and heat of the day *deserve* more than those who started work just before quitting time. The employer may, if he wishes, pay the late arrivals as much as he is obligated to pay those who worked all day. But that would be a matter of benevolence, not justice. And it would surely be unjust for him to strike an average and pay five hours of wages to those who worked eight hours and to those who worked but two. Those who worked eight hours have a claim in justice to receive a reward proportioned to their merit, a merit acquired by their efforts. *In some contexts* it may be relevant to point out that they did nothing to earn their ability and willingness to work long hours at hard labor, or that they wouldn't have had the opportunity to work at all if they hadn't just happened to be standing in the hiring hall when the employer walked in. But no one will claim that these facts diminish their deserts in the case at hand or that it would therefore be perfectly just for the employer to pay them for fewer hours than they actually worked.

A theology of economic justice that neglects merit or desert is simply not addressed to the world of social decisions. What we deserve at the hands of God is not the same as what we deserve from one another.[11] To suppose that

---

10. Matthew 20:1–16.

11. This criticism applies also to some of the core arguments advanced by John Rawls in his influential *A Theory of Justice* (1971). J. R. Lucas puts the problem concisely: "Rawls yearns for a theodicy. To be morally acceptable, a distribution must be justified completely." *Op. cit.*, p. 191. Robert Nozick has pointed out that Rawls' argument finally does not take individual persons seriously. *Anarchy, State and Utopia* (1974), p. 228.

we can settle the one question by answering the other is to abandon the question of economic justice altogether.

Perhaps this is not always recognized in theological statements on economic justice because those statements are so frequently formulated as antitheses to a system which seems to exaggerate the role of merit or desert. Defenders of capitalism often claim that capitalism distributes economic goods justly because it distributes them on the basis of merit. Those who don't accept this claim and who believe that the distribution which occurs under capitalism is unjust may have responded by rejecting the merit criterion when they should have been criticizing its application.

Differing Grounds for Entitlement

There is an important difference between earning something and having a right to it. Neglect of this distinction generates confusion on the subject of merit as a criterion of economic justice. A teenager given the keys to the family car for the evening has a right to use it. The teenager would be unjustly deprived of a right if someone else—an older brother, perhaps— saw the car on a theater parking lot and appropriated it for his own use. This does not imply, however, that the teenager deserved the right to use the car that evening, or that he would have been treated unjustly if the keys had been denied. If he had been promised the use of the car in return for washing and waxing it, then he would indeed have earned its use, and failure to grant the use would have been unjust.

Defenders of capitalism sometimes seem to be assuming that all entitlements are earned entitlements and can therefore be credited to merit. This position cannot be defended without stretching the concept of earning past the point when it loses its ordinary meaning. People are sometimes lucky. They may well be entitled to what came to them as a result of luck, but they cannot properly say they earned it or that it has accrued to them as a result of their merit. Defenders of capitalism do their cause a disservice, I believe, when in their eagerness to establish the moral legitimacy of capitalism they undertake to argue that people deserve, as a consequence of their merit, whatever they receive in a competitive capitalist economy.

It is both interesting and of some theological significance to note the great difficulty that many of us have in accepting as ours what we aren't certain we have earned. Are we consequently tempted to fabricate merit for ourselves so that we may claim to deserve that to which we are merely entitled? It is not enough to possess; we want to possess in good conscience, which too often means that we want to deserve whatever we rightfully possess. Adam and Eve, it seems to me, did something very similar to this when the serpent raised its guileful questions.

The Function of Rules

The mishandling of the merit criterion, both by defenders and by religious critics of capitalism, points to what I believe is the gravest flaw in contemporary theological discussions of economic justice. That flaw is the general failure to perceive the role and importance of *rules*.

Since the position for which I am now going to contend strikes many religious people as fundamentally immoral, let me begin indirectly, with a question based on an everyday dilemma.

After the bus has pulled away from the designated transit zone, should the driver stop the bus and open the door for someone running to catch it?

Some passengers will pull the stop signal and call out to the driver when they see a tardy passenger running to catch the bus. If the driver ignores their signals and drives on, they may comment disapprovingly: "A *mean* driver this morning." If he does stop, open the door, and wait for the running passenger, he will, of course, earn the gratitude of the beneficiary; but he may also be the recipient of approving comments from other passengers: "Someone who likes people more than schedules."

My purpose in recounting this familiar scene is a simple one. Here is a politically uncharged illustration of the function that rules play in a society and of the common ethical confusion that results from ignoring that function.

We begin by noticing that the driver who stops in such a situation is not necessarily helping people more than the one who does not. He certainly helps this one passenger—assuming that the driver's action doesn't cause an accident! But in addition to increasing the probability of an accident, the decision to stop delays all the other passengers on the bus. If the next bus will be along in 15 minutes, there are 25 other passengers, and the driver's action delays them all by 30 seconds, some might argue that the driver's action produces a net social benefit of 2½ minutes.

But this is an unconvincing claim. We can't compare different people's minutes in this manner. The 30-second delay, multiplied by the number of times the driver acts in this way, could cause a dozen passengers to miss their transfer connections. Those dozen people might consequently be late for important meetings, so that eventually many hours of other people's time is lost in the process of saving 30 seconds for each of a handful of late-running bus passengers.

The Rights of Unknown Persons

The argument still involves illegitimate comparisons, however. A minute of one person's time is *not* the moral equivalent of another person's minute.[12] The principal reason for rejecting such an equation is not that people in fact value time differently, although that is certainly true, but rather that punctual people have a right not to be delayed by tardy people, and the bus driver has an obligation to respect that right. The man who gets up late does not have a right to delay the people who arrived at their bus stop on time. He ought to pay the cost of his tardiness, and it is unfair of him to avoid that cost by shifting all or a part of it to others.

Suppose, however, that he overslept because he had been up most of the night tending a sick child, and now must catch this bus in order to keep a counselling appointment with a distraught alcoholic who's contemplating suicide. Would we want to say in such a case that he, rather than the punctual passengers, *ought* to bear the cost of his oversleeping? Doesn't he deserve commendation rather than blame? Moreover, it isn't he but rather the suicidal alcoholic who will bear the cost of his being late.

All of this is quite irrelevant, however. *The bus driver has no way of know-*

12. Economists generally insist that they have no basis for making "interpersonal utility comparisons"; they rarely recognize that judgements about the relative efficiency of alternative resource allocations require either the making of such judgements or prior decisions on who possesses what property rights. What it all comes to is that judgements about efficiency in multi-person transactions presuppose judgements about the justice of people's exercising certain powers. For a concise presentation of the central issue, see John Egger, "Comment: Efficiency Is Not a Substitute for Ethics," in Mario J. Rizzo, ed., *Time, Uncertainty, and Disequilibrium* (1979), pp. 117–25.

ing why his passengers are punctual or late, whether they're embarked on important errands or simply taking a trip for the fun of it. The driver's moral obligation is to provide safe transportation and stay on schedule; the passengers must assess their own individual circumstances and decide whether or not to be at the bus stop by the scheduled time. Adherence to these rules will sometimes produce results inferior to what an omniscient driver could achieve; but bus drivers are not omniscient.

Moreover, a driver who elects to disobey the rules is behaving unjustly. He is violating the rules of the game and benefiting some at the expense of others in an essentially capricious way. The passengers who applaud his behavior when he stops in the middle of the street fail to consider the harm he may be inflicting on others. They may also be quite wrong in assuming that he was motivated by kindness; he could well be trying to curry favor, secure praise for himself at the expense of others.[13]

Rule-Coordinated Social Interaction

Thinking through this trivial example helps us see why it will often be more ethical, more socially responsible, and even more humane to "go by the rules" than to violate the rules in order to serve the known interests of particular people. We have been conditioned to believe that it is morally wrong to adhere to rules in circumstances where we believe our doing so will harm particular people. We are not used to thinking about the broader consequences for others, or the long-term consequences for the system in which we're participating. Not only do bus drivers make punctual passengers late when they choose to violate the rules; they also begin to change the relative costs and benefits of adhering to the rules, which means that the rules start to break down. We would probably be less sanguine about this consequence if we more fully appreciated the extent of our dependence upon rule-coordinated social cooperation.

What we loosely call "the economy" is essentially a system of social cooperation overwhelmingly dependent for its functioning upon rule-

13. Most of the contemporary literature advocating "corporate social responsibility" totally overlooks this point. Examples could be multiplied endlessly. Christopher Stone offers an excellent critical survey of the discussion about business social responsibility in *Where the Law Ends: The Social Control of Corporate Behavior* (1975).

coordinated behavior. If all the farmers in the United States, for example, decided to devote their time and other resources to producing what was specifically wanted by the most needy or otherwise most worthy people they knew, millions of people who are now well fed would soon starve to death. The production decisions of American farmers are in fact made for the most part according to a simple rule: choose the available option from which you expect the largest net revenue. Those who believe that production for profit is morally inferior to production for use have apparently never thought through the consequences of what they're recommending. They are ignoring the incredible complexity of the system of social cooperation by means of which we are fed, clothed, housed, warmed, healed, transported, comforted, entertained, challenged, inspired, educated, and generally served.[14]

We must accept and honor rule-coordinated behavior not only in order to maintain our level of wealth. Justice also demands it. A large society cannot be a just society unless most of its duties and benefits are allocated in accordance with established and accepted rules. This truth is in no way confined to the so-called economic system. A college professor teaching a class of 500 students must, if she wants to be just, clarify the rules in advance and then apply them impartially. If a student confronts her with circumstances that the rules had not contemplated and so do not cover, she must search for a response that can be generalized. She must not allow some students to take advantage of other students by securing unique advantages. Each of the 500 students, if pressed, could probably find an explanation, unrelated to what the student actually knew, for missing one or more items on the last test. It is fundamentally unfair to give extra credit exclusively to those students whose obsession with grades or personal belligerence prompts them to ask for it. If the same privilege is extended to every student in the class through a general announcement, it might seem at first that justice would be salvaged. But now the question arises as to

14. The most serious single error committed by non-economists in their proposals for reform of the economic system is their neglect of *information problems*. I have often wished that I could persuade everyone interested in social justice to begin with a careful reading of the classic essay by F. A. Hayek, "The Use of Knowledge in Society," originally published in the *American Economic Review* (September 1945), pp. 519–30, and frequently reprinted since. It is included in Hayek's 1948 collection of essays, *Individualism and Economic Order*.

whether the teacher can in fact adequately hear and evaluate the explanations of 500 students. Justice in large societies requires not only that general rules binding on all be promulgated, but also that they be applied in a non-arbitrary manner. The more likely outcomes of such an attempt to apply personal criteria in a large-society situation are capricious decisions and poorly-used time.

Knowledge and Justice

What would we say about a judge who discovered that the defendant coming before him on a drunk-driving charge was his next-door neighbor and nonetheless decided to hear and dispose of the case? Justice requires that the judge disqualify himself and turn the case over to someone else. The reason is that he knows the defendant *too well*. The judge is consequently in a position to know far more about the special circumstances of this defendant than he can know in other cases brought before him. To know all is, in a very important sense, to forgive all. It is therefore the responsibility of a judge *not to know too much* about a particular defendant, so that he can save the lives of many unknown persons by applying impartially the rule against drunk driving.

A judge in a small village might be able to act simultaneously as a just judge *and* a just neighbor. Justice will sometimes demand that we go beyond impersonal criteria in allocating burdens and benefits. We are properly horrified by David's famous painting of Lucius Junius Brutus and his two sons whom he had ordered executed for treason; a father owes more than that to the members of his own family. And it is possible to supply something more than impersonal justice in a small society where people know one another well. The size of the society is the crucial issue, however.

It is hard to see, for example, how a law against loitering could be a just law in a city of any size. Its application would inevitably leave too much discretion to police officers who *could not know enough* to enforce the law fairly, and who would therefore necessarily enforce it unfairly. It is conceivable, for the same reason, that the personal discretion which has to be exercised in the enforcement of any anti-loitering ordinance could be exercised fairly in a small village. The essential point remains. Justice itself demands that we use impersonal criteria to allocate burdens and benefits in a large society, where inescapable limitations on our knowledge make it impossible to take personal considerations into account in any consistent way.

Justice, Expectations, and Promises

It seems to me that our reflections on economic justice would be far more satisfactory if we recognized the connection between justice and the keeping of promises. I have increasingly come to think of justice as basically *the fulfillment of legitimate expectations*.[15] This definition is faithful to our most fundamental moral perceptions, I believe, while illuminating a wide range of issues. Injustice is done, I suggest, when someone's legitimate expectations are not fulfilled because others broke their promises.

Sometimes promises are made explicitly by one person to another. The breaking of such promises, other than for reasons beyond the control of the promisor, is an injustice whenever the promisee's well-being is thereby lessened.

More often, however, our promises are implicit, part of the unarticulated compacts that we have with our families, our neighbors, members of our church, associates at work, plus millions of people whom we will never even meet. I commit an injustice when I fail to provide family members, friends, or associates with the assistance, support, or other cooperation that my previous actions have legitimately led them to expect. We won't always agree completely on which expectations are legitimate, because we will inevitably disagree to some extent about what has been implicitly promised. But we always promise more than what we spell out formally, because explicit promises entail prior commitment or tacit assent to a vast network of "background" agreements.[16]

In this approach to the question of justice, laws can be thought of as promises. They bind everyone within their jurisdiction to behave or refrain from behaving in specific ways, and thereby they create legitimate expectations. An unjust law would be a law that repudiated prior prom-

15. This is the tradition first spelled out by David Hume in *A Treatise of Human Nature*, book III, part II, sections I–VI. I do not think my argument here is vulnerable to the criticisms put forward by J. R. Lucas, *op. cit.*, in pp. 208–15, a chapter he entitles *"Pacta Sunt Servanda."*

16. Michael Polanyi, *Personal Knowledge: Towards a Post-Critical Philosophy* (1964; Harper Torchbook edition), especially part II.

ises; because of the resulting inconsistency of promises, the expectations that such a law might create would be less legitimate than the expectations created by a law whose justice was undisputed.

Customs and traditions are also promises. Moreover, every society is grounded in some kind of moral consensus, and the basic principles of that consensus are the most fundamental promises that the members of the society make to one another. Because these principles are not fully articulated, they can become mutually inconsistent in the course of social evolution. This most commonly happens, I think, when new possibilities for behavior lead to situations in which basic principles start to yield conflicting promises. The development of such situations threatens the stability of a society, because it removes, at least temporarily, the common ground which must exist if disagreements about justice are to be resolved. At such moments in a society's history, it is especially difficult but also especially important for the members of the society to refrain from caricaturing the positions they are rejecting. The ultimate bond of any society is its members' commitment to their common humanity; so long as that can be preserved, we are not compelled to say "thy blood or mine" and to settle our disagreements about justice by the naked criterion of force. When we impute immoral motives to our opponents, we are in effect declaring war on them by expelling them from the community of moral discourse.[17]

Now it seems clear that if we make promises or otherwise create expectations that we cannot subsequently fulfill, we inflict harm on others. It is not true that they are neither better nor worse off as a result of our promising but not delivering; they are worse off. People build upon their expectations, and when those expectations turn out to be illusory, the structures erected on them collapse. This is a psychological and an economic truth. In both the realm of feeling and the realm of action, we make investments on the basis of our expectations. And we sustain a loss when those expectations turn out to have been overly optimistic. Not every unfulfilled expectation constitutes an injustice, of course. Some expectations are bound to prove mistaken in a world characterized by uncertainty. Injustice is done only to people whose expectations are disappointed by the failure of others to fulfill promises they were capable of keeping.

17. The controversy over abortion laws in the United States provides the most distressing example.

Promises and the Size of the Society

A satisfactory theory of economic justice must recognize not only the importance of honoring commitments, but also the crucial relationship between the size of the society and the kinds of promises that can be made and fulfilled within it. The members of a nuclear family can conscientiously promise to assign tasks among themselves on the basis of ability and to distribute benefits on the basis of need. In larger societies, such a promise is impossible. If it is made, it is made in ignorance. There is simply no way for even one hundred people, much less 225 million, to acquire the knowledge that would be required in order to assign tasks on the basis of ability and benefits on the basis of need. We don't have to raise the question of whether people would be *willing* to make and keep such promises to one another. Incentive is a necessary but not a sufficient condition. Information is also necessary. This point is important because religious discussions of economic justice tend to focus on the incentive issue and to overlook the problem of information. They thereby hold out the false hope that a "change of heart" would enable us to get rid of capitalism, or at least of certain features of capitalism that they find morally objectionable.

The Nature of "Capitalism"

Let me say at this point what I mean by *capitalism*. I think of it as a social system in which individuals are free to choose what they will supply and demand, offer and bid, subject only to general rules known in advance. These rules will be both legal rules, externally enforced, and moral rules that are internally enforced. I call capitalism a social system because it is the social rules that determine whether the society will be capitalist, socialist, or something in between. Capitalism, in short, is a system of individual freedom under law, where law does not mean "legislation" but rather the whole body of established rules, agreements, and conventions by which the members of a society acknowledge themselves to be bound.[18]

The engine of the system is the individual's perception and pursuit

---

18. The conception of "freedom under law" that I am assuming here was thoughtfully spelled out by Bruno Leoni in *Freedom and the Law* (1961).

of net advantage. Collective behavior is not excluded, but it must be the product of the voluntary choices of individuals. The pursuit of one's net advantage is not a synonym for greed, selfishness, or materialism. All purposeful human action is self-interested, in the crucial sense that it aims at goals accepted by the individual, using means evaluated by the individual. Greed or selfishness, by contrast, is a matter of claiming for the self more than is due. I would want to describe greed or selfishness in terms of a failure to fulfill obligations, and hence as injustice. But the point here is that greed is about as common under capitalism as it is under any other kind of political system, but no *more* common.

Capitalism is thus by definition an impersonal system. It is not altogether an impersonal system, because the individuals within it do participate in families and small, face-to-face associations, where they can know other persons well enough to be concerned with and to care for their unique qualities. But the distinguishing characteristic of capitalism is the impersonal nature of the social interactions that make it up. It can be described paradoxically as a social system in which people do not care about most of those for whom they care. The farmer who feeds me does not even know I exist, and while he wishes me no ill, he does not and cannot care *about* me in any subjective sense. Nonetheless, he cares *for* me, and very effectively, in an objective sense.

We are all dependent, throughout our lives, for our actual survival as well as our many comforts, upon the assistance and cooperation of millions of people whom we will never know and who do not know us. They help us to fulfill our aims in life not because they know or care what happens to us, but because this enables them to fulfill their own aims most effectively. They are *motivated* by their own interests, whatever these may be. They are *guided* by the rules of the society and their perception of the expected net advantages from alternative decisions. These net advantages, or structures of expected costs and benefits, are created by the similarly motivated and guided efforts of everyone else in the society.

The Necessity of "Commodity" Production
Marx was thus correct. He saw more clearly than most of his procapitalist contemporaries that capitalism was a system based on commodity pro-

duction. It had replaced (by supplementing, I would argue, more than by displacing) a system based on relations of personal dependence. Thereby, as Marx and Engels observed in the first part of *The Communist Manifesto,* capitalism had achieved productive wonders. Their mistake, and the mistake of so many who followed them, was in supposing that capitalism could be replaced in turn by a system of production based on "socialist relations," a system retaining the productive powers of capitalism while assigning tasks on the basis of ability and distributing the product according to need.

The Roots of Resistance

I suspect that the deepest root of this belief, a belief remarkably immune to either theory or evidence, is the conviction that an impersonal social system is morally unacceptable. I maintain that this is a tragically mistaken prejudice. Impersonal does not mean inhumane, as we sometimes carelessly assume. Nonetheless, our model for the good society seems to be the family, where production is from each according to ability and distribution is to each according to need and merit (though we tend to underestimate the actual importance of the merit criterion in thinking about family distribution decisions).

The religious heritage of Western thought pushes in the same direction. The Old Testament's criticism of economic behavior often presupposes a society small enough and sufficiently close-knit for its members to care *about* as well as *for* one another. A more prominent feature of this literature, in my judgement, is its emphasis on impartial administration of the rules; but this feature has rarely been noticed by those who turn to the Old Testament for passages with which to support their concern for economic justice. The New Testament emphasis upon love as the fulfillment of all law has further reinforced our inclination to suppose that impersonal relations are somehow morally deficient relations.

A False Option

Our basic mistake may be the belief that we must choose between personal, face-to-face societies and impersonal societies. If we accept as fully legitimate the impersonal, rule-coordinated societies in which we participate, we are not repudiating or depreciating in any way marriage, the family, intimacy, I-thou relationships, the unique value of the individual, or the power and significance of personal caring and sacrifice. If we were in fact compelled to repudiate all of this in order to enjoy the benefits that only large and hence impersonal societies can provide, we would be foolish to opt for those benefits. In the long run that choice would deprive us of the advantages of both worlds, because the moral values essential to the successful operation of a rule-coordinated society can only be nurtured in personal societies.

But we are not *forced* to choose. We are tempted to choose, it is true, and from both directions. The expanding wealth of opportunities that the impersonal society lays before us makes us progressively less dependent (or so we believe) on particular other persons. As we enlarge our individual freedom and power, we simultaneously declare our continual independence. We view commitments as entanglements and we work toward fuller emancipation. That kind of freedom is really perpetual mobility, and I doubt that it is ultimately compatible with the institutions and virtues of personal community.

My primary concern in this paper, however, is the temptation coming from the other direction, a temptation whose appeal might be in large part a function of the anxiety that many of us feel about the decline of personal community in our own lives. Many of the "best people" in our society, including theologians, denominational leaders, and deeply religious people, sincerely believe that economic justice requires the destruction of rule-coordinated societies. Moreover, they are committed to the belief that they may legitimately use the coercive power of state legislation to accomplish this goal. They seem determined to do so, with little thought about what justice might actually entail and often the most superficial attention to what occurs in the democratic legislative process.

False Promises and Injustice

Legislation that aims at the achievement of economic justice cannot succeed in this purpose unless the promises that it offers are genuine, realistic, and not in themselves unjust. Legislators often hold out promises of benefits, for vote-gathering purposes, when they have no intention of enacting the enabling legislation which would impose the requisite costs on the public.[19] For very similar reasons legislators will sometimes refuse to consider the consequences of what they are doing; it is not in their interest to recognize, much less to admit, that a bill which offers electoral gains to those who support it cannot in fact achieve its stated purposes. Legislation of this kind is unjust legislation because it deliberately creates expectations that will not be fulfilled.

Particularly common and troubling is the tendency of democratically-controlled legislatures to defend special-interest legislation on the grounds that it secures economic justice for its beneficiaries, while ignoring the injustices that this legislation will impose on others. The most familiar and to my mind most disturbing contemporary example is the arbitrary expropriation, through legislated rent controls, of people who have invested in residential rental property.

Those who draft the "social concern" statements of church bodies too often endorse this kind of legislated injustice, apparently because they can think of no way to measure economic justice except by looking at the pattern of outcomes. They are not deterred by their inability to provide a coherent, applicable, and defensible definition of a just pattern of outcomes. Meanwhile they ignore or repudiate in their official pronouncements some of the most basic principles of justice that they themselves use in their everyday, "real world" activity. The fundamental dependence of justice in a large society upon adherence to general rules is almost totally overlooked.

What do religious pronouncements about economic justice really accomplish? What interests do they serve? Those are the pressing questions with which I find myself left. But they would be questions for some other study.

---

19. Neither the theoretical analyses nor the abundant empirical evidence put forward by public choice theorists in recent years seems to have influenced church pronouncements on political issues.

CHAPTER 10

The U.S. Catholic Bishops and the
Pursuit of Justice

IF VALUES could always be clearly distinguished from facts and ends from means, debates over economic policy would be more productive and less rancorous.

The recently published *First Draft of the U.S. Bishops' Pastoral Letter on Catholic Social Teaching and the U.S. Economy* claims to be concerned primarily with values and ends. The fundamental issue in economic policy, according to the *Letter*, is the goals we ought to be pursuing and the moral objectives that ought to guide our choices. Throughout the *Letter*, the language and tone are those of the prophet or preacher, calling people to a reexamination of values, a new and compassionate vision, a lively sense of moral responsibility, a commitment to economic justice, a conversion of heart. Specific policies to implement the moral objectives advocated in the *Letter* are treated as a secondary issue that can be worked out later through reflection and dialogue. The first and hardest task is to determine the direction in which we ought to move.

Thirty years ago, in an influential essay entitled "The Methodology of Positive Economics," Milton Friedman ventured the judgment

that currently in the Western world, and especially in the United States, differences about economic policy among disinterested citizens derive predominantly from different predictions about the economic conse-

Reprinted from *Cato Institute Policy Analysis* 50 (5 March 1985): 1–21, by permission of the publisher.

quences of taking actions—differences that in principle can be eliminated by the progress of positive [i.e., scientific] economics—rather
than from fundamental differences in basic values, differences about
which men can ultimately only fight.[1]

In Friedman's view, our hardest task is to agree on the specific policies
most likely to promote our common objectives. Agreement on goals is
much less of a problem, since we don't really disagree in any fundamental
way on our basic values.

If past experience in similar situations is any indication at all, the debate that the bishops have invited in response to their proposals (No. 22)*
is going to founder on this issue. Defenders of the *Letter* will insist that
the fundamental question is a moral one; critics will insist that it is the
bishops' understanding of economics. The debate will turn rancorous as
implications of indifference to suffering and injustice are exchanged for
charges of culpable ignorance, each side maintaining that the other is the
victim of an obsolete ideology.

This inability to agree on what it is we are disagreeing about reflects
the fact that our notions of how economic systems function are bound
up with our conceptions of the goals they ought to serve. The bishops
urge their objectives in passionate language because they believe that the
American economic system is capable of performing in accord with their
prescriptions—once the citizens of the United States commit themselves
to a biblical (and humane) vision of economic life. This critique will argue
that the bishops' moral analysis is misguided because economic systems
cannot operate in the way that the bishops suppose they do.

Do Social Systems Have Goals?

A crucial question at the outset is whether social systems—and an economic system is certainly a social system—can appropriately be said to

---

* All citations of the *Letter* will be by section number. The *Letter* contains 333 sections,
usually of one paragraph.

1. Milton Friedman, "The Methodology of Positive Economics," in *Essays in Positive
Economics* (Chicago: University of Chicago Press, 1953), p. 5.

have goals or objectives. Individuals can entertain goals and pursue them; individuals can also form organizations, such as trade unions, corporations, or governments, in order to pursue specific goals; we can then say that these organizations "have" goals or objectives. But care must be taken at this point to avoid drawing erroneous inferences from the assertion that an organization "has" a goal.

Consider an organization with a clearly and narrowly defined goal, such as the Society for the Prevention of Cruelty to Animals. Insofar as the SPCA is effectively advancing its goal, it will be through providing appropriate inducements to individual persons to behave in particular ways. Should members complain that the SPCA is failing to achieve its objectives, they will be claiming in effect that individual persons are not being induced to behave appropriately. Moreover, it will often be difficult for the critics to determine exactly where and how the inducements are failing. The reason is that an organization is a social system, and social systems pursue "their" goals in a highly indirect way. Many of the activities that contribute to the eventual achievement of the SPCA's objectives will seem trivial or even unrelated to the organization's objectives. (The purchase of a postage meter might be an example.) In such a situation, moral appeals ("We must give priority in our thinking to the suffering of animals") are likely to be irrelevant. They can even be counterproductive if, by stirring up resentment and anxiety within the organization, they interfere with objective inquiry into its functioning.

The social systems that produce wealth and poverty are vastly more complex than any special-purpose organization. To see what this implies, assume for a moment that every American citizen read the bishops' *Letter,* experienced the conversion of heart for which it calls, and gave enthusiastic consent to its proposal to reduce the unemployment rate from above 7 to below 4 percent. How would we proceed? Because the actual unemployment rate is the outcome of a social system rather than anyone's direct goal, it cannot be reduced in the way that we reduce a thermostat setting or the height of a kitchen shelf. To bring down the unemployment rate, we would have to induce millions of people to begin behaving differently. But we don't even know who these people are or exactly how we want them to behave. Each particular instance of unemployment counted in the sample data of the Bureau of Labor Statistics is the result of someone's decision to take employment-seeking action during the survey week, but without finding and accepting a job. It is therefore the product of a vast constellation of employment offers and perceived opportunities, which are themselves the ever-shifting product of complex and constantly changing circumstances. To reduce the unemployment rate, we must somehow alter these circumstances so that they yield the different pattern of choices that we ultimately desire.

Choice and Moral Concerns

The unemployment that so distresses the bishops is the product of human choices, but it is at the same time no *one* person's choice. No one *intends* unemployment, though unemployment is indeed the product of human intentions. If the unemployment of specific persons were in fact intended, in the sense of being consciously aimed at by someone else, then "the effects of joblessness on human dignity," which the *Letter* describes, would seem to confer "moral unacceptability" upon *all* unemployment—not merely upon the amount in excess of 4 percent (No. 163).

The bishops appear to be unclear in their own minds about the role of choices and intentions in an economic system. The *Letter* is unwilling to grant that the choices of unemployed or poor people contribute in any significant way to their status. At the same time, however, the bishops want to insist that current poverty and unemployment are the result of "individual and group selfishness," "the sins of indifference and greed," embedded in institutions as well as human hearts (No. 85). This comes close to the exact reverse of the argument being made here.

The truth is that people do choose whether or not to enter the labor force and whether or not to accept particular employment offers. As a consequence, better employment prospects may actually raise the unemployment rate by increasing the percentage of the population looking for employment. In 1953, when the unemployment rate averaged 2.9 percent, 57.1 percent of the civilian population over 16 years of age was employed. The September 1984 unemployment rate of 7.4 percent, which the bishops find morally unacceptable, was accompanied by a significantly higher *employment* rate than the economy had experienced in 1953: 59.5 percent of the over-16 civilian noninstitutional population was employed in September 1984. There are several explanations for this, but they all turn upon the improvement between 1953 and 1984 in the variety and quality of the choices confronting most prospective labor force participants.

The *Letter* ignores all this, and the explanation isn't hard to find. The bishops want poverty and unemployment to be moral problems for those who are wealthy and powerful *and* they want to avoid "blaming the victim" through any suggestion that poor or unemployed people are responsible for their own condition. Throughout the *Letter,* the poor, the unemployed, and the "marginalized" are presented as persons compelled by forces beyond their control. The suggestion that motivation contributes to poverty is rejected as "insulting to the poor" (No. 193); links between suffering and unemployment "discredit" claims that any significant number are unemployed voluntarily (No. 164); the "marginalized" are described as those who have "no voice and no choice," a phrase quoted, interestingly, from a paper dealing with justice for the child, who is, of course, the paradigm case of the helpless victim (No. 93).

It ought to be possible to talk about the choices that "marginalized" people make without implying that they have *good* choices, that they are solely or even primarily responsible for their plight, or that nothing should be done by the government to help them. If this is indeed only a first draft, then we can still hope that the *Letter* will eventually incorporate something from the best book on these problems to appear in the United States in many years: *How We Live: An Economic Perspective on Americans from Birth to Death* by Victor R. Fuchs.[2] We cannot hope for this with a great deal of confidence, however. Fuchs employs "the economic perspective," which sees social reality as the product of constrained choices, and the bishops reject this approach to the issues. We have here a prime example of how moral concerns can distort social analysis.

Distortion, of course, is in the eye of the beholder. Couldn't it be claimed with equal justification that the economist's perspective on social systems also distorts reality? It certainly can be claimed, and the claim

2. Cambridge, Mass.: Harvard University Press, 1983. This book was widely and favorably reviewed during the time the bishops were gathering evidence, and its omission from the list of authorities cited is surprising. My own review may be found in *This World* (Winter 1984): 151–53.

must be admitted (as Fuchs does) to contain some truth. But a partial perspective can still be a valuable perspective. Economic theory presupposes that people choose in response to changing costs and benefits and that their choices affect in turn the costs and benefits that people confront. While this is not the only legitimate perspective from which to view social phenomena, it has shown itself to be a powerfully illuminating one that cannot simply be ignored by anyone who wants to understand economic systems. Yet this is precisely what the bishops have done. The clinching evidence is the fact that, in an essay of more than fifty thousand words directed toward a transformation of the U.S. economy, no attention whatsoever is paid to relative prices. This is a startling omission.

The Neglect of Information Problems

The principal virtue that most economists find in the so-called market system is its effective management of information problems. A modern economy is an extraordinarily complex system in which innumerable decisions have to be continuously coordinated if food, clothing, shelter, heat, light, transportation, medical care, and a multitude of other goods are to be regularly and dependably made available to those who want them on terms that they are willing and able to meet. It is neither an accident nor a fact of nature that the quantity of milk New Yorkers want to consume each day, for example, consistently makes its way from distant dairy farms to waiting tumblers, cereal bowls, and coffee cups. On the contrary, it is the product of an enormous system of social cooperation that is continuously coordinated and adjusted through the information that relative prices supply.

These information problems would still exist in essentially unchanged form in a nation of saints. The human deficiency that relative prices overcome is not so much selfishness as ignorance. A higher relative price attached to a particular good is first of all *evidence*—evidence that the good has become more scarce. In the absence of such concrete and readily available evidence regarding the relative scarcities of countless inputs and outputs, modern economic life simply could not go on.[3]

3. The classic discussion is F. A. Hayek, "The Use of Knowledge in Society," *American Economic Review* (September 1945): 519–30. Reprinted in idem, *Individualism and Economic Order* (Chicago: University of Chicago Press, 1948) and in many anthologies.

In a section of their *Letter* entitled "The Responsibilities and Rights of Diverse Economic Agents and Institutions," the bishops make the following true and important assertion:

> But simply proclaiming that poverty should be eliminated, unemployment abolished, discrimination ended, and education and leisure made available to all is not enough. We must also reflect more concretely on who is actually responsible for bringing about the necessary changes. Our society is highly complex and so is the apportionment of rights and responsibilities for shaping economic life. (No. 107)

Unfortunately the bishops have not reflected concretely enough to see that the responsibilities for shaping economic life, whether to preserve the status quo or to effect substantial changes, are apportioned with the indispensable assistance of relative prices.

And so the *Letter* talks about the responsible management of economic resources by business and financial institutions without once recognizing the role that relative prices play in promoting good (or poor) stewardship. The use of land and other natural resources "must be governed by the need to preserve the fertility of farmland and the integrity of the environment," the bishops say. Owners, managers, and financiers are urged to be accountable to their employees and their local communities in making investment decisions, and the Second Vatican Council is quoted in support of the position that good stewardship requires people to use their lawful possessions as resources for the benefit of others (No. 119). But the bishops do not see that relative prices reflecting relative scarcities, both current and prospective, are essential information for those who want to manage resources responsibly rather than arbitrarily. The "lively sense of moral responsibility" that the *Letter* commends (No. 122) is simply not enough. The pursuit of profit—an activity always viewed with suspicion when mentioned in the *Letter*—is also required, because pursuing profit means paying attention to relative prices. And relative prices are ordinarily the best available social indicators of what good stewardship requires concretely.

The bishops' defense of private property probably provides the most revealing evidence of their failure to understand the role of relative prices.

Private ownership of property, they say, has value for many reasons. Four are then given. It provides incentives for diligence, allows parents to contribute to the welfare of their children, protects political liberty, and opens space for the exercise of creativity and initiatives (No. 120). Economists will point to a glaring omission from this list: clearly defined and readily exchangeable property rights generate relative prices that offer information on the prospective net advantage of alternative decisions, thereby providing an essential part of the society's system of coordination.

The *Letter* subscribes implicitly to two positions with respect to economic justice that are difficult to reconcile. One is that justice is a matter of intentions. The other is that justice is measured by results. The difficulty here is the one already encountered: in an economic system, results are not intended. Or, to put it another way, the results that emerge are not the results that were intended by the people who produced them.

This point was first made famous—some would say infamous—by Adam Smith in *The Wealth of Nations*. In the realm of economic activity, people promote the public interest not by aiming at it directly but by aiming at their own private interest. It is not from the benevolence of the butcher, brewer, or baker, Smith says, but from their self-love, their regard to their own advantage, that we expect our dinner.[4] Smith's point is missed, however, if we suppose he was contrasting benevolence with selfishness and regard for the public interest with attention to selfish interests. He was not.

Smith had a high regard for benevolence, as his *Theory of Moral Sentiments* abundantly demonstrates. But he knew that benevolence was a virtue too vague and uncertain to guide and coordinate the cooperative activities of a society that depended extensively upon the division of labor. Benevolence doesn't tell people what they ought to do if they want to promote the common good; but people must know *exactly* what to do if the economic system is to function. Moreover, benevolence cannot be depended upon in the way that a complex social system requires. Benevolence doesn't make people punctual and punctilious. Even a beggar, Smith shrewdly observes, does not rely upon benevolence to satisfy his daily wants, but only in order to obtain the means with which to satisfy those

---

4. *The Wealth of Nations,* book 1, chapter 2.

wants.[5] A complex social system such as a modern economy requires conscientious attention to tedious details, discipline rather than spontaneity, and people who play their parts when, where, and how the system requires.

Under appropriate but common circumstances, people's pursuit of their own advantage produces this kind of responsible behavior. Does it, however, necessarily produce *just* results?

The Definition of Justice

That all depends on what we mean by just results. "The fundamental demand of justice," the *Letter* asserts, "is that all persons be enabled to participate in the common good of society" (No. 97). Participation is a prominent theme in the *Letter*, but the statements about participation raise as many questions as they answer. On what terms must people be able to participate? Must they be enabled to do what they want to do, what they enjoy doing, what they are good at, what benefits others, or what contributes to the common good? Who is to decide, and by what criteria? Must people be enabled to do what *they* think contributes to the common good? The possibilities for rationalization are frightening. Should people who do what they want to do be guaranteed an income from their chosen activity? How large an income?

The fundamental demand of justice allegedly "also has implications for how economic benefits are distributed." What are those implications? The *Letter* mentions six factors that "demand attention" in determining whether "the share received by a person or group is a just one":

1. "the basic moral equality of all human beings";
2. "the different needs of different persons";
3. "the level of effort, sacrifice and risk that people have undertaken";
4. "the relative scarcity or abundance of the goods to be distributed";
5. "the different talents and skills of the recipients";
6. "the overall human welfare of all persons in society considered individually and collectively" (No. 97).

5. Ibid.

In what is surely the outstanding understatement of the entire *Letter,* the bishops admit that these "criteria of distributive justice cannot be reduced to a simple arithmetic formula." It is doubtful that they can even be reconciled. Since the bishops give no hint as to who should make these extraordinarily complex determinations and thereby assign each person and group [*sic*] their rightful share, they are offering a recipe for either chaos or tyranny. And all this without even mentioning an operative criterion of major importance in the system they are criticizing: whether what the person or group is producing is something that the potential consumers value.

Despite the central emphasis of the *Letter* upon justice, its authors have not reflected concretely enough to supply any coherent sketch of what they are aiming at. It is clear enough that they consider current inequalities of income and wealth, within the United States but especially in the world, morally unacceptable. But that isn't the issue.[6] The important questions are why these inequalities exist and what can and should be done to change them. If the bishops provide any guidance at all on these questions, it is toward solutions that have already been tried and found wanting.

They urge increased foreign aid, for example, which they say "gets an increasingly bad press in the United States" (No. 307). They nowhere point out that foreign aid has also been severely criticized, from the left as well as the right, for the harm that it often does to the cause of economic development, especially development in directions that might raise the living standards of the poorest people in so-called Third World countries. Aid from governments goes largely *to* governments. The *Letter* gen-

---

6. The *extent* of these inequalities is very much an issue, however. "The top 5 percent of American families own almost 43 percent of the net wealth in the nation," the *Letter* asserts (No. 204), thereby providing data that will no doubt be widely quoted to support the bishops' overall stance. An attached footnote reveals that the survey used in this calculation of net wealth excludes "the value of durable goods, automobiles, and the value of small businesses and private practices. The value of homes and the liability of home mortgages are also excluded." Not mentioned is the exclusion also of human capital. In short, the survey upon which the *Letter* relies to show how unequally wealth is distributed in the United States does not count those assets in which the bulk of most Americans' wealth resides, and which collectively far outweigh the value of the assets counted. One's wealth is realistically the net (capitalized) value of all those matters in which a lending institution is interested when it asks for a financial statement. By that test, the present writer is wealthy; by the bishops' test, he is poor. But the bishops' measure is almost devoid of significance.

erally assumes, contrary to an abundance of readily available evidence, that government officials in poor countries will use foreign aid in just and constructive ways. The premise that runs throughout the section on the United States and the world economy (Nos. 270–319) is that "transnational corporations" pursue profits and are therefore likely to do harm when they enter Third World countries unless they are restrained by international agencies and national governments, which pursue the common good. (See especially Nos. 281, 299, 311). This is sheer prejudice. Greed, corruption, poor stewardship, and economic irresponsibility are generally under much more effective control in multinational corporations, as a result of ordinary competitive pressures, than they are in many national governments and even some United Nations agencies.

Within the United States, the *Letter* recommends more generous welfare benefits offered to more people and with fewer conditions such as work requirements. The impression given repeatedly by the sections on welfare reform (Nos. 218–240) is that the bishops are standing resolutely in the year 1964, urging that we begin the War on Poverty. Has no one called their attention to the abundance of data now available on the actual effects over the last twenty years of the various policies that the bishops recommend as if for the first time? Fuchs would be of great help here, as would the excellent collection of studies edited by Robert H. Haveman for the University of Wisconsin's Institute for Research on Poverty, *A Decade of Federal Antipoverty Programs: Achievements, Failures, and Lessons.*[7] One wonders what would remain of the bishops' proposals if each member of the committee sat down and read Charles Murray's *Losing Ground: American Social Policy, 1950–1980.*[8]

The Justice of Social Systems

The problem runs deeper, however, than the bishops' inability to provide defensible suggestions for alleviating poverty. It goes back to their failure to provide a coherent statement of what they mean by economic justice. The reason for this failure is that they are looking in the wrong direction.

7. Orlando, Fla.: Academic Press, 1977.
8. New York: Basic Books, 1984.

The justice or injustice of a social system will not be found in the pattern of outcomes it yields—its end-states—but in the procedures through which those outcomes emerge. This is simply the only kind of justice of which social systems are capable.

The argument is easier to illustrate than to demonstrate. Suppose we accepted the bishops' end-state approach and made the pattern of income distribution among specific persons and groups the target of a national policy for economic justice. The entire economy would now have to be planned and controlled in minute detail, because only in this way could we prevent anyone from rising above or falling below our income targets. Since the bishops have no intention of endorsing "a highly centralized form of economic planning, much less a totalitarian one" (No. 261), this cannot be what they want.

A less ambitious policy to make incomes more equal in the name of justice would allow people to choose for themselves how they want to allocate the resources under their control, and then use taxes and transfers to redistribute the (highly unequal) incomes that would result. This is much less ambitious because the attainable outcomes would be severely constrained by people's responses to the expected taxes and transfers. A society of saints *might* be willing to take their cues for the coordination of economic activity from pre-tax-and-transfer signals—though even this is doubtful if the saints have differing visions of saintliness that they want to pursue.[9] In any event, we are not dealing with a society of saints, and we would have to expect participants in the economic system to be guided in their decisions by the information provided by relative prices *after* taxes and transfers. The bishops apparently do not see how severely that would limit the ability of any national policy to redistribute income, because there is no evidence that they have recognized the extent to which it *already* constrains redistributive programs in the United States and elsewhere.

The best way to avoid recognizing constraints on redistributive programs is to assume a world divided exclusively into the rich and the poor, with "luxuries" consumed exclusively by the rich, and the poor consuming

9. Since tax-and-transfer policies are sometimes designed specifically to influence allocation decisions, as in the case of pollution charges, one cannot lay down a general moral principle that decision makers should look only at pre-tax-and-transfer prices.

nothing but "necessities." Given this picture of the world, it is relatively easy to accept as meaningful the assertion that "the needs of the poor take priority over the desires of the rich" (No. 106, quoting Pope John Paul II). The next step is the deduction that "government economic policies must ensure that the poor have their basic needs met before less basic desires of others are satisfied." [10] This is perilously close to pure demagoguery. Is the government supposed to call a halt to all skiing (surely a luxury) until everyone in the society is receiving a sound education (deemed a necessity by the bishops)? If it doesn't mean something like this, what *does* it mean to assert that "the needs of the poor take priority over the desires of the rich"? And if it doesn't really mean anything, why is such a statement made?

Numerous passages in the *Letter* that call for taxing the wealthy to provide benefits for the poor would require in practice that each person in the economy be subjected to a unique set of tax-and-transfer rules. How else could national policy possibly promote the bishops' notion of distributive justice, with its fine adjustment of individual (and group!) incomes to unique individual (and group!) circumstances? But such a tax-and-transfer policy, tailored to the peculiar circumstances of each individual, would be tantamount to the minutely detailed system of central planning and control that the bishops explicitly repudiate. If the bishops don't see this contradiction in what they are proposing, it must be because they are assuming that poor people consume nothing but necessities and that the luxuries of the rich can be unambiguously identified. The moment we begin to think concretely about all this, however, we discover how extensively the rich and the poor overlap in many of their choices and activities.

We cannot have it both ways. Either we replace the existing economic system with a minutely detailed central plan or we resign ourselves to the limited possibilities for redistributing income that *general rules* provide.[11]

10. This statement was made recently by a prominent Catholic bishop while testifying in support of legislation to require owners of certain low-rent apartments to continue making them available for rent. The arbitrary nature of such a law is less likely to be seen by someone who divides the world into the neat categories of luxury-consuming rich and necessity-consuming poor. Taken seriously, the bishops' assertion endorses detailed government control over each citizen's spending decisions. Reported in *Seattle Post-Intelligencer*, December 12, 1984, p. E-9.

11. A useful task in conjunction with the preparation of any revised draft of the *Letter* would be a study of the specific practices that gave rise to complaints of injustice in the Old Testament, especially in the writings of the prophets. The prophets usually seem

Since the former option is presumably out of the question, the bishops will have to accept, *as consistent with justice,* a multiplicity of "holes in the social safety net" and tax "loopholes." Some people will consequently receive from the economic system less than the bishops (and many others) think they deserve, and others will receive much more. (This will be the end of the matter only if government is the *exclusive* redistributor of income in the society, which it surely is not; the family is still the principal redistributor of income.) The bishops' criteria for income distribution, even if they could be made consistent, would be useful only to someone who was omniscient, and they could be enforced only by someone who combined omniscience with omnipotence. Economic systems have come into existence, however, precisely because of limitations on individual knowledge and that most fortunate corollary, limitations on individual power.

The servants of God must not suppose that they can *be* God. While the bishops have no such intention, they do seem to be demanding, in the name of justice from a divine perspective, the abolition of institutions capable of achieving justice from a human perspective. Because the bishops evince almost no understanding of how social systems overcome human limitations, they are willing to use the limitations of functioning social systems as a reason for destroying them. What will they put in the place of the system whose functioning would be suspended if their proposals were actually implemented? The bishops do not answer this question because they do not realize that they have raised it.

"Everyone knows the significance of economic policy, economic organizations and economic relationships," the *Letter* states in its introduction (No. 4). This is unfortunately not the case. But the *Letter* goes on to indicate what it means by "significance": something "that goes beyond purely secular or technical questions to profoundly human, and therefore moral, matters." What the bishops need to discover is the significance of secular or technical questions for the opinions they hold on a wide range of moral matters.

---

to be objecting to *violations of the rules* aimed at taking advantage of relatively defenseless people. It is this, not the mere fact of poverty, that constitutes oppression. See also Leviticus 19:15: "You shall do no injustice in judgment; you shall not be partial to the poor or defer to the great, but in righteousness shall you judge your neighbor" (Revised Standard Version).

Human Limitations and Limited Government

The theme of this critique has been *limitation*. Our judgments about matters of fact are limited by our theoretical perspectives, and our conceptions of appropriate moral objectives are limited by our understandings of how social systems function. More importantly and perhaps more controversially, it has been argued here that government policies directed toward economic justice must be limited to what can be accomplished through general rules. The justice or injustice of the system inheres in the justice or injustice of these rules. National economic policies dealing with employment, poverty, pollution, education, discrimination, trade unions, control of corporations, international trade, foreign aid, or any of the other justice-related issues that the *Letter* mentions *must* be expressed in general rules. This is the only way that government policies can avoid arbitrariness, arbitrariness that will inevitably be unjust through its disruption of legitimate expectations as well as inefficient through its disruption of producer planning.

"Limited government" does not mean government that limits itself; *all* governments limit themselves at some point. Limited government means government limited by rules that citizens know and can count on. It means a government that revises the rules only in accordance with the rules. Many students of government have in recent years begun to see the limitation of government in this sense as the critical problem facing democracies. The processes of democratic government are falling increasingly under the control of special-interest groups, groups that can use their intense interest in single issues to coerce legislatures into an endless series of enactments that sacrifice the public interest.

The bishops are not familiar with this literature or the arguments it makes.[12] They state that *"the process of forming national economic policies should encourage and support the contributions of all the different groups that will be affected by them"* (No. 266, emphasis in original). There is no acknowledgment here and almost none elsewhere in the *Letter* that the groups most strongly affected by government economic policies are, in one sense, the groups *least* qualified to form those policies because their legislative proposals are skewed by their special interests. Contributions

---

12. The standard reference is Mancur Olson, *The Logic of Collective Action* (Cambridge, Mass.: Harvard University Press, 1965). See especially pp. 5–16, 98–102, 141–48.

from such groups need to be discounted, not encouraged and supported. How to do this is one of the vexing issues currently confronting students of the democratic political process.

The problem has been much exacerbated by the growing respectability of the idea that government has an obligation to solve all social problems that arise, an idea that easily turns into the notion that government must alleviate all discontents. In such a climate, every interest becomes a right and every harm from any source an outrage. Rights must be secured and outrages redressed, of course, by government. Thus Leviathan grows.

As inheritors of Roman Catholic social teaching, the bishops speak approvingly of the subsidiarity principle (No. 127). This principle requires government to support institutions that stand between the individual and the nation-state, especially families and voluntary institutions. But a government that takes over the responsibilities of such intermediate institutions or that narrowly constrains their functioning through taxation, subsidy, or regulation is going to undermine them whatever the intentions or the rhetoric of that government. For example, a government that convenes a national conference on family policy has *by that act* weakened the institution of the family.

Now, if all this sounds "anti-government," it just may be. National government needs no one today to defend its powers, least of all in the age of Ronald Reagan when the rhetoric of smaller government covers the reality of ever-larger government. The underlying purpose of these comments, however, is to open the important question of justice on another level. There is much that the bishops say about justice that has not yet been touched upon in this critique. The biblical conception of justice is important to the theologians on whom the bishops rely extensively, and it is important to the present writer, who has sometimes tried to be a theologian as well as an economist.

Radical Religion

Biblical research and theological reflection in recent years have done a great deal to recover the social character of the New Testament message,[13]

13. An excellent introduction is John Howard Yoder, *The Politics of Jesus* (Grand Rapids, Mich.: Eerdmans, 1972).

and the bishops' *Letter* has one of its roots in this work. The central concept in the evangelists' accounts of Jesus' message and ministry was the *kingdom* of God; and a kingdom is surely a *society*. Moreover, Jesus expected a realization of that kingdom, or at least a preliminary, partial realization of it, within the actual and historical society that he was addressing. Those who "believed" in him, who accepted his proclamation, would begin to relate to one another in a radically new way.

They would go two miles with anyone who compelled them to go one, give their overcoats to people who demanded their jackets, offer those who struck them on one side of the face a chance to strike them on the other side, discharge the debts of those who owed them money, forgive people who wronged them as many as five hundred times if necessary, and refuse to resist the infliction of evil except by the disconcerting procedure of doing good in return.

This is an extraordinary social vision, and it is no wonder that historically more effort has been devoted to explaining why Jesus did not really mean what he said than to discovering how his vision might be realized. One strategy has been to push this kingdom and the social relationships it entails "beyond history." In this view, the kingdom of God as announced by Jesus is something that cannot be realized until "the end of time." Meanwhile, Christians are expected only to behave considerately while they wait faithfully. In this fashion the New Testament message has been both moderated and deprived of its social implications.

The concern with justice that is so prominent in the bishops' *Letter* entails a rejection of all such "desocialized" versions of Christianity. That is what was meant above in saying that the *Letter* has one of its roots in recent writings on the social character of the New Testament message. But the *Letter* has other roots, too, which the bishops are much less eager to acknowledge.

The opening paragraph of part 1, "Biblical and Theological Foundations," announces:

The basis for all that the church believes about the moral dimensions of economic life is its vision of the transcendent worth—the sacredness—of human beings. The dignity of the human person, realized in community with others, is the criterion against which all aspects of economic life must be measured. (No. 23)

The *Letter* then goes on to develop this vision "more fully in biblical and theological terms," drawing on such concepts as creation, covenant, and community, and eventually establishing "the primacy of justice."[14] From the concept of justice and its primacy the *Letter* deduces "Ethical Norms for Economic Life," including most prominently a set of basic personal economic rights (No. 79) about which the *Letter* states that "there can be no legitimate disagreement" (No. 87).[15]

All along the way, the meaning of the enunciated norms and principles is clarified by indicating their implications. Wilderness areas are to be preserved (No. 96), comparable worth schemes enacted (No. 101), and affirmative action programs supported—though they must be "judiciously administered" (No. 101). Collective bargaining by trade unions must not be resisted (Nos. 111, 112)—though unions should not use their collective power to press demands that would diminish the rights of other workers (No. 113). The principle of the moral unity of the entire human family even implies somehow the legitimacy of the nation-state, which is recognized "as an instrument of justice in a world made up of different cultures, with different traditions and various ways of structuring their economies" (No. 133).

These details from the *Letter*'s "Biblical and Theological Foundations" have been selected for two purposes. One is to indicate how extensively the bishops' concrete arguments depend on nontheological considerations. At what point, one might well wonder, does the bishops' dependence on debatable social theories and empirical generalizations render the purely

---

14. The "primacy of justice" is supported by quoting Matthew 6: 33: "Seek first the kingdom of God and his justice." But "justice," at least as the term will be understood by most contemporary readers, is a misleading translation of *dikaiosune*. The traditional "righteousness" isn't altogether satisfactory, either, because of the misleading connotations of a purely interior "right-ness" that it has come to have. An early footnote in the *Letter* says that all biblical translations are those of the Revised Standard Version "unless otherwise noted." The reader is not told, however, that in the passage cited the RSV translates *dikaiosune* as "righteousness." The footnote on biblical translations also says, "The other translation used is that of the New American Bible." But the New American Bible translates the passage as follows: "Seek first his kingship over you, his way of holiness." Is this a quibble? Or evidence of a less-than-candid use of authority?

15. One would have to search long outside societies that have been influenced by the European Enlightenment to find the concepts of individual dignity and human rights that the *Letter* invokes. This observation is not intended to disparage those concepts, but only to suggest that a study of their history, evolution, and meaning would find little guidance in the sources or authorities that the bishops invoke.

moral authority of their argument negligible? That is a troublesome question for those who want to respect the teaching authority of the bishops but who also believe that their social analysis is gravely deficient.

The other purpose is more fundamental. It is to suggest that the bishops' concrete recommendations for government economic policy, far from being an application of the concept of justice found in the New Testament, *run directly counter to it.* The first step in the wrong direction is the very idea that the gospel presents any kind of agenda at all for government.

Love and Coercion

What does the institution of government have to do with the radically new relationships that are to characterize the kingdom of God? Governments do not offer matching grants to taxpayers who hold back amounts due; they order immediate payment, and penalties in addition. Governments do not forgive wrongdoers, not even once; they punish them, and if the punishment is suspended, it is only on condition that the wrong never be repeated. Government is fundamentally a coercive institution. The New Testament provides no agenda for government. On the contrary, it suggests to the faithful that they ought to depend very little on government. The deep suspicion of government found in so many of the radical Christian sects and the determination to have as little as possible to do with it are far closer in spirit to the gospel than are the persistent efforts of church officials since Constantine to gain control of government for their own ends.

There are difficult ethical issues here that the present essay is not attempting to settle or dismiss. Theologians from St. Augustine to Reinhold Niebuhr have struggled with the relationship between the kingdom of God and the kingdoms of this world, trying to determine the relevance of force to love in a "fallen world." But if radical sects have tended to abandon this world in their devotion to principle, established churches have too often abandoned principle in their desire for power and influence.

The New Testament advocates a degree of recklessness with regard to consequences that is sometimes hard to reconcile with the calculating perspective of *Homo economicus* and economic theory. But however courageous or faithful such indifference to consequences may be when the risks are borne personally by the decision maker, it is impossible to defend when the reckless actor compels other people to bear the costs of "moral" decisions. Good intentions are certainly not enough when the coercive powers of government are being used to "do good." Those who claim to be speaking on behalf of the poor and the oppressed have an obligation to be competent social analysts when they are proposing policies for government.[16]

The attention paid in the *Letter* to voluntary actions and personal sacrifice is perfunctory in comparison with the attention paid to government policies (Nos. 123–24, for example). This is an appropriate emphasis for those who are determined to redirect the course of social events. Voluntary actions move the world slowly and, from the global perspective, imperceptibly. Those who want to be sure of changing the course of history must gain command of governments and armies. That has been abundantly proved throughout history, but especially in the history of the twentieth century. What are the concrete achievements of even Mother Teresa when laid alongside the differences made to the world by Stalin, Hitler, Mao, or almost any ruler of the most minor state in the United Nations? The contemporary turn to government for the solution of all problems is not some kind of neurosis; it reflects an accurate judgment about where social power is concentrated today. The bishops want to transform institutions and structures; they are therefore wise to focus on gaining control of government policies.

When they do so, however, honesty requires that they give up the authority of the New Testament as support for what they are doing. It is the Enlightenment, not the Gospels, that provides the "theological" framework for the debate that the bishops have initiated.[17] It might be

16. Charles Murray calls attention to a tendency among "those who legislate and administer and write about social policy" that seems to be particularly characteristic of church officials discussing economic issues: they "can tolerate any increase in actual suffering as long as the system in place does not explicitly permit it" (*Losing Ground*, p. 235). From this perspective, verbal goals are more important than actual results.

17. The conflict between Roman Catholic social thought and some of the critical presuppositions of Enlightenment thinking is concealed in the bishops' *Letter* by a highly selective citation of earlier social statements. An important issue that deserved careful examination is the extent to which Catholic social teaching has narrowed its options by refusing to give serious consideration to liberalism (in its historical sense) as a framework for thinking about economic policy. The French Catholic economist Daniel Villey

considerably easier to conduct the debate, with the civility for which the bishops call, if *all* parties stopped claiming that the battle is between God and the devil and admitted frankly that we are contrasting the social visions of such mere mortals as Adam Smith and Karl Marx.[18]

---

discussed this issue 30 years ago in an essay that has not received the attention it deserves: "The Market Economy and Roman Catholic Thought," originally published in 1954 and republished in an English translation in *International Economic Papers* 9 (1959).

18. One reader of this critique worried that the concluding sentence might be read by some as an emotional appeal to anti-Marx prejudices. This is certainly not intended. Smith and Marx present similar and yet contrasting social visions that can richly reward comparative study, and those visions do seem to be at the base of important and conflicting theological-social statements. It would be rather odd if the rules of discourse prohibited any mention of Marx in criticisms of liberation theologians who explicitly endorse Marxism or assert "a sense of admiration and gratitude for a movement that, in less than a century, through its direct action in some areas and through indirect influence in labour movements and other social forces in others, has raised to a human condition the life of at least half of the human race." Jose Miguez Bonino, *Christians and Marxists,* as quoted in *Morality and the Market Place,* by Brian Griffiths (London: Hodder and Stoughton, 1982).

CHAPTER 11

Jewish Economic Ethics in a Pluralist Society

MEIR TAMARI'S BOOK *"With All Your Possessions": Jewish Ethics and Economic Life*[1] originated in his dissatisfaction with the way he was teaching courses in corporate finance at Bar Ilan University, an Orthodox Jewish institution in Israel. Tamari found himself teaching in the same way he would have taught the courses at any secular university, with no attention to the Jewish value system. After considerable discussion and debate with colleagues, Tamari created a special course that would present to students this value system and its practical application to economics. That course eventually led to writing this book (p. xi).

I am not competent to judge how adequately Tamari has presented the Jewish position on the ethics of economic life. My goal in this paper is to use the material which he has provided to raise questions that might be of interest to anyone concerned with ethics and economic life, and especially to Christians who hold this concern. What can be learned through reflection on the ideas presented in this book about the nature and role of ethics in the kind of economic system that exists today in the USA? What can religious ethics contribute to the formation of an adequate ethics for eco-

Reprinted from *Cultural Dynamics* 7, no. 3 (1995): 347–62, © 1995 by Sage Publications, by permission of Sage Publications. First draft was presented at a Liberty Fund conference directed by Walter Block on "Judaic and Christian Perspectives on Freedom" in Boston, Massachusetts, 8–10 May 1993.

1. Meir Tamari, *"With All Your Possessions": Jewish Ethics and Economic Life* (New York: The Free Press, 1987).

nomic life in a pluralist and largely secular society? And what is the proper relationship between religious ethics and public policy in such a society?

The Functions of Legalism

The first issue that must be addressed is the issue of *legalism*. "It's too legalistic." I am certain that will be a common reaction among Christians who read *"With All Your Possessions."* In a generally favorable review, Gerald Brock complained that, at least in some cases, "the analysis appears to be excessively legalistic." [2] *Legalistic* in this context means excessively attached to the words, to the letter of the law, rather than to the idea the law is attempting to express. Christians like to insist, especially if they are Protestant Christians, that the spirit is more important than the letter.

Their authority, when they need one, is 2 Corinthians 3:6, traditionally rendered as "the letter kills but the spirit gives life." Most authorities now agree that this is a mistranslation. It is not the spirit but the Spirit that gives life, the Spirit of God. Paul here is not intending to attack written regulations, much less to endorse the claim that it's right if it *feels* right. The target of his criticism was those who, he claimed, could not understand what was written because it was veiled for them and who needed to have that veil removed by the Spirit of God. The problem with literalism is not attention to the letter but rather absence of the Spirit.

This points to an important difference between ethical rules and legal rules. Ethical rules are for people who "have the spirit" (or Spirit); who want to be or become what the rules support or nurture or express. Legal rules, on the other hand, are for everyone in the society to which the rules apply, including those with no interest in the ethos informing the rules. Literalism is consequently, up to a point, a virtue of legal systems. Because the law of the political order may be enforced through coercion, what it decrees should be clear to those subject to its commands as well as to those responsible for enforcing them. The line between lawful and unlawful behavior needs to be a bright one. That inevitably exalts the letter of the law, occasionally at the expense of its spirit.

2. Gerard Brock, review of *"With All Your Possessions"* by Meir Tamari, *Bulletin of the Association of Christian Economists* 11 (Spring 1988): 9.

When people freely and voluntarily accept that spirit of the regulations, literalism or legalism does not have this function to perform. But literalism can play a quite different role in ethical systems, or at least certain kinds of ethical systems, of which Judaism would seem to be an outstanding example. When the ethical system is concerned with the creation or preservation of a well-defined community, literalism serves to mark off those who do from those who do not belong to the community. Here the individual chooses to be guided precisely by the letter of the law because adherence to the letter expresses obedience to a discipline that establishes or delimits a particular community.

Consider the rule that once required Roman Catholics to abstain from eating meat on Fridays. The spirit of the law lay in the discipline of fasting. Those who much preferred fish to red meat might have been adhering more closely to the spirit if they had eaten a large steak on Friday; but they would thereby have separated themselves from the community. And those who treated themselves to spectacular seafood feasts on Fridays, while certainly offending against the spirit of the law, were nonetheless not excommunicating themselves.

There is, consequently, an essential place for literalism in the administration of legal rules and another but quite different place for literalism in systems of ethical rules. "In halakhah," Tamari writes, "there is no gray area between right and wrong" (p. 134). That is ordinarily a characteristic of law rather than ethics; but it might also be a characteristic of an ethical system that emphasizes the distinctive character of the community. These different functions of literalism need to be kept in mind when we start to ask about the relevance of ethical rules outside the community in which they originally arose.

The Functions of Ethics

Why do we want people to be ethical? If the answer seems too obvious to make the question worth asking, it may be because so many of us subscribe uncritically to one particular conception of ethics. Ethics has to do with rules of conduct, particularly those rules that speak to the goodness or badness, or the rightness or wrongness of actions. When we begin considering the rules for conduct that prevail within religious groups, we quickly notice that some seem to have no relevance outside the community that honors them. A substantial number of the rules that Jews observe would appear, at least to an outsider, to be of this nature.

But are these *ethical* rules? Are not dietary restrictions, for example, something other than ethical rules? Why do we think so? Where is the line between ethical rules and other kinds of rules for conduct, and why do we draw it as we do?

One reason to be ethical, the reason most prominent in the influential ethical system of Aristotle and preserved in the word itself, is concern for the shaping of one's own character. Persons who want to become the fullest possible actualization of all that they are potentially will have to discipline themselves. They will *cultivate* particular excellences and *practice* certain virtues. To do this is to behave ethically, at least in one ancient and important sense.

With this in mind we might want to ask whether *any* of the 613 commandments of Jewish law (p. 11) could properly be classified as *purely* ritual laws rather than ethical laws? The decision to be an observant Jew is a decision, it seems to me, to be a certain kind of person, to have a certain kind of character. To that extent it is an ethical decision and the rules to which one consequently submits cannot be clearly distinguished from ethical rules.

Most of us, on the other hand, have learned to think of ethical rules exclusively as rules governing our behavior toward others, and to see the function of these rules as primarily that of protecting the rights or enhancing the welfare of others. From this perspective, we behave ethically when we give others everything to which they are entitled (justice) plus at least a little bit of that to which we ourselves are entitled (mercy or charity). The opposite of ethical, when thought of in this very common way, is *selfish*. And the dominating concept is that of *rights*.

We do not have to get into the question of whether there are such things as *natural* rights, possessed by all people everywhere and at all times, to agree that most of the rights that people actually claim are the products of particular societies. The specific rights that we in the USA enjoy and that others are obligated to respect are overwhelmingly the product of our history, some of it not very recent (such as the Bill of Rights in the US Constitution), some of it very recent indeed (such as the rights created by a promise given yesterday or a contract signed this morning). Rights are therefore social phenomena, both in the sense that they impose obligations on others and in the sense that they arose in, form a part of and derive much of their meaning from the practices of particular societies. Insofar as ethics has to do with respecting the rights of others, therefore, ethics presupposes a particular society. The ethical rules that govern action in a particular society should therefore never be generalized uncritically. The claim that there are universal ethical rules does not imply that all valid ethical rules are universal.

The Discovery of Commercial Society

Meir Tamari invites the reader in his opening page "to see this book as the presentation of a possible economic system determined by the demands of Jewish morality and faith" (p. 1). A bit later he says his purpose is to show, using legal, historical and religious sources, "how economic activity was traditionally guided and determined by the teachings of Judaism and its religious law" (p. 3). There is a troubling anachronism here.

I doubt that Tamari could find anywhere in the Bible the slightest suggestion that there exists an "economic system" or "economic activity" that can be thought of separately from the social system as a whole or general social activity. *Economic* life as something that can be separated conceptually from the rest of life, and for which special ethical rules can be prescribed, is a phenomenon of the past two centuries, and even at this relatively later date dictionaries have trouble defining satisfactorily the word "economic" and its cognates. Is the economic an *aspect* of action, the economizing aspect? Or is it a *kind* of action, action directed toward the satisfaction of material wants? But what are *material* wants? And does economic activity not serve our wants for a lot of non-material goods as well? Most of the time we are not quite sure what it is that distinguishes the economic order from other sectors or aspects of social life and makes it a particular object of ethical concern.

My contention is that there could not have been any Jewish teachings about economic activity prior to the nineteenth century, for the simple reason that no one recognized the existence of a distinct economic order much before 1800. People did, of course, produce and distribute food, clothing and other valuable goods prior to 1800; they just did not suppose they were doing anything conceptually different from what they did in the rest of their lives. What we now might refer to as "economic" laws in the Torah are so thoroughly blended in with laws that no one today thinks of as "economic" that they can only be distinguished by a thoroughly anachronistic imagination, one that uncritically imposes contemporary categories upon materials to which they are really quite foreign.

The concept of a distinguishable economic order and hence of a distinct ethics of economic life developed in the nineteenth century. It grew out of the discovery and analysis, celebration and excoriation, of what Adam Smith called "commercial society." Here is his description of it:

> When the division of labour has been once thoroughly established, it is but a very small part of a man's wants which the produce of his own labour can supply. He supplies the far greater part of them by exchanging that surplus part of the produce of his own labour, which is over and above his own consumption, for such parts of the produce of other men's labour as he has occasion for. Every man thus lives by exchanging, or becomes in some measure a merchant, and the society itself grows to be what is properly a commercial society.[3]

The category of the economic, as used today, developed in response to the recognition of commercial society and its peculiar features. This is a fact of great importance for any attempt to construct a system of economic ethics, because such an ethics must speak to the realities of commercial society. Commercial society is society in which, as Smith so vividly put it, everyone "becomes in some measure a merchant." Economic ethics, *insofar as it claims a separate domain for itself,* must prescribe the rules of conduct that govern a society characterized by extensive division of labor and its corollary, exchange among people who will for the most part have no personal acquaintance with one another. It is the ethics of an impersonal society, the rules of conduct that apply to transactions among people who characteristically do not know one another's name, may not even know of one another's existence and cannot possibly treat all those with whom they transact as unique persons. Economic ethics will therefore be,

3. Adam Smith, *Wealth of Nations* (Indianapolis, Ind.: Liberty Fund, 1981), book I, chap. iv, para. 1.

at least in part, the rules of conduct governing social transactions that are, in many people's opinion, *inherently unethical*.

The first response of Christian social thinkers to the discovery of commercial society was an endorsement of its discerned regularities as the laws of God, coupled with the argument that respect for the laws of the economic order would lead to social progress as measured by morally significant criteria. Anthony Waterman has ably described this response in his recent (1991) book, *Revolution, Economics, and Religion: Christian Political Economy, 1798–1833*.[4] That optimism faded as the nineteenth century wore on, and Christian social thinkers began to view the economic order as something that needed to be regulated from a higher vantage point. The hostility to the accumulation of wealth, to the pursuit of individual advantage and to commercial activities that had characterized Christian thinking throughout almost all of its history reasserted itself. Christian economic ethics became thereby largely irrelevant to the economic order, which it preferred to condemn rather than understand.

Ethical Regulation of Market Forces in the Jewish Tradition

The anticommercial tradition that has been so strong in Christian social thought never existed in Judaism, according to Tamari. The evidence he presents certainly supports this summary judgment. It is hard to imagine any of the Christian fathers saying so many things that are clearly supportive of commercial activity. In Judaism, the merchant and the entrepreneur play legitimate and desirable roles and are hence entitled to a profit without apology (p. 87).

It was the goal of Jewish sages not to cast suspicion upon commercial activity but "to regulate market forces in accordance with the tenets of justice and mercy" (p. 85). The difficulties and dilemmas inherent in such an effort emerge with particular clarity in chapter 5, "Competition, Prices, and Profits."

The ruling concern, Tamari says, was often the welfare of the average consumer. It was this concern that led the rabbis to prohibit speculation

---

4. A. M. C. Waterman, *Revolution, Economics, and Religion: Christian Political Economy, 1798–1833* (New York: Cambridge University Press, 1991).

in basic goods on the part of dealers and middlemen while allowing it for producers themselves. Dealers and middlemen who bought up stocks in anticipation of future scarcity were simply "cornering the market" in order to profit. The producers, however, were ordinarily under no moral obligation to sell and could legitimately withhold their products to wait for a higher price later. The threat of future shortages supposedly justifies this permission. Farmers who can neither sell their entire crop at a satisfactory price nor store it for future sale will reduce their planting in the next growing period and thereby bring about shortage and hardship for consumers. To maintain a demand sufficient to ensure an adequate future supply, Tamari tells us, the Talmudic sage Rav Huna sent a messenger to the market each Shabbat eve to buy up and destroy all the perishable vegetables that gardeners had been unable to sell (p. 92).

Are such rulings and practices likely to achieve their objective of regulating market forces in accord with the tenets of justice and mercy? Or do they reveal a faulty conception of the way markets function? Are they possibly an attempt to apply concepts appropriate to a personal, face-to-face society to the very different structures of a commercial society? Let us analyze Tamari's presentation of the rabbis' position.

It should be noted first of all that dealers and middlemen who buy up stocks of food do not usually have the power to "corner the market." They typically buy in periods of abundant supply, when producers' prices are correspondingly low. This raises the prices received by producers and relieves the producers of the cost of storage. It also benefits consumers by making the relative abundance of good harvest years available later for consumption in years of poorer harvests.

Looking to our own time for possible applications of these principles, Tamari commends the agricultural price-support operations of governments "in most modern economies" as efforts to even out fluctuations and assure a steady and sufficient supply of food. He does not mention the major flaw in such programs in "most modern economies" which is that, for political reasons, the programs quickly become pure price-support operations that raise prices to the consumer and generate persistent surpluses that must then be disposed of. The stabilizing operations of dealers and middlemen, though condemned by the rabbis, are not subject to this perversion of purpose. In order to profit and survive, dealers and middlemen must actually succeed in smoothing out price and availability fluctuations, and they have no incentive or ability to maintain prices above the level decreed by consumer demand and the costs of producing. Dealers and middlemen would thus appear to be more effective guardians of the average consumer's welfare than the producers themselves, the government or even well-intentioned rabbis.

Unless Rav Huna was a man of enormous means, he was probably having no significant effect on the market when he sent his messengers to buy and destroy unsold perishables on the Shabbat eve. He was merely transferring some of his own wealth to the fortunate merchants whose perishable goods he bought, while persuading himself that he was guarding the community's welfare. But if he did have sufficient means, he was encouraging wasteful production by indicating the existence of a demand for more vegetables than people actually wanted to consume.

Restrictions on Competition

The question of free entry for new competitors is a persistent problem for those who wish to regulate the market to safeguard the community's welfare. A large part of the problem is that existing producers and sellers almost always believe that the market is already adequately supplied. They assume that the current level of prices is no more than what is barely sufficient to cover costs, and that costs are as low as anyone can reasonably expect them to be. From the standpoint of the consumer's welfare, however, these assumptions need to be tested: if new competitors do not appear despite there being no legal restrictions on their entry, then the assumptions pass the standard market test.

An adequate alternative test for someone unwilling to accept the market test is hard to devise. Tamari says that the sages rejected the argument that mere injury to existing firms was sufficient reason to prohibit the entry of new firms. But the rulings he subsequently presents and his own arguments do not consistently bear out that claim:

> In a complex economy, unlimited competition in various forms may easily bring human hardship and suffering despite the economic benefits derived. Often the competition is unequal, as in the case of a chain

store vs. an individual storekeeper, or a corporate employer vis-a-vis an individual worker. It may well be that the market is not large enough to provide all the factors with a viable return on their investment, so that further entrants may cause widespread depression. Competition may also be unfair when an individual has made an investment in time, money, or knowledge in order to perfect a new process, create a specific article, or create commercial goodwill: the entry of new entrepreneurs exploiting the fruits may be robbing the individual of his investment. In all these cases society may be faced with such undesirable consequences as large-scale unemployment, depressed industry, and widespread bankruptcy. (p. 106)

Tamari notes the argument of economic theory that the competitive process will move resources about to correct such situations; but this adjustment often takes a long time and may never actually occur when left to ordinary market forces, he says, so that society ends up paying the human and moral costs. Judaism consequently makes provision for restrictive practices to alleviate the hardships caused by competition.

If Tamari is correct that Jewish law is willing to accept and enforce agreements among sellers to restrict competition, fix prices and limit quantities (p. 107), then Jewish law contains everything necessary for the creation of effective cartels. Sellers can set minimum prices and maximum quantities, keep out new entrants and use the law to police the arrangement. The fact that such agreements "require the approval of a prominent personality (*adam chashuv*), who can serve as an arbitrator between the interests of the members of the trade association and the general welfare," may or may not provide adequate protection for the consumer interest. Once the market test has been abandoned, what information will the "prominent personality" use to mediate among the conflicting interests?

The biblical commandment (Deut. 19:14) against removing a neighbor's landmark has been expanded by rabbinic authorities to include "encroachment on another's livelihood" (p. 108). This expansion would appear to offer unlimited opportunities to those unable or unwilling to compete and almost insuperable difficulties for the religious authorities who must distinguish between legitimate and illegitimate uses of the commandment. Consider some of the circumstances discussed by Tamari. Anti-

Semitism has often reduced the economic opportunities open to Jews. Some religious authorities have held that this warrants restrictions on competition to protect the opportunities that *are* available. But what about the opportunities of those who are thus twice excluded, by Jewish law as well as by anti-Semitism?

The Jewish council of Padua in 1583 cited "severely limited" economic opportunities in town to justify a sweeping exclusion of outside entrepreneurs. But why would outsiders want to enter if opportunities were in fact so severely limited? An impartial observer might be suspicious, especially after noting the additional reason given by the council for its edict: the fear that newcomers might not be "upright and moral." The threat posed by morally unscrupulous outsiders is an argument much employed by sellers eager to convince consumers that restrictions on competition benefit the entire community (p. 114).

Most authorities, according to Tamari, did not allow restrictions on the free movement of rabbinic scholars, in accordance with the belief that "the spiritual welfare of the community demanded the maximum availability of Torah teachers" (p. 117). But here too conflicting considerations emerged. What about the effects of free competition on the livelihood of established scholars? At least some rabbis were willing to prohibit entry "where the livelihood of the resident scholar was endangered." This, Tamari comments, accords with "an accepted principle that ruinous competition, as distinct from lowered profits or reduced earnings, was not to be allowed" (p. 117).

Several rulings mentioned by Tamari suggest that the mere fact of fixed investment can confer a right to be protected against new entrants. Even someone who has acquired an exclusive privilege from the government may be able to enlist the support of religious authorities against others who want to compete for the privilege, by claiming that his privilege is a legitimate property right and thus deserving of protection (pp. 117–19).

Tamari also cites a Paduan ruling of 1580 that prohibited Jews from competing to rent a house already rented to other Jews, when the owner was not a Jew. The avowed purpose of the restriction was to prevent competition from increasing rentals, and it was strengthened by the proviso that for three years no Jew could rent a house from which another Jew had been evicted (p. 111). In Egypt, "a well-established communal enactment"

prohibited any Jew from offering a higher rental for a house or store oc-
cupied by another Jew (p. 120). Whatever the advantages of such buyers'
cartels to the "insiders" that employ them, they also create problems. If
the value of using a store, house or any other resource is greater than the
rent currently being paid for it, an agreement among "insiders" not to bid
up the rent by competing for it will only be effective if "outsiders" do not
want the resource. If they do, the cartel members will lose control of the
resource. If outsiders do not want it, the question remains of how it ought
to be allocated among insiders when competing money bids are not allowed to perform this function. And after all this there remains the sticky
question of how such agreements among members of an ethnic or religious group will be viewed and responded to by the "outsiders."

Workable Criteria for Regulating the Market

Why am I so dubious about all this? Why are there so many question
marks in the margins where Tamari discusses communal restrictions on
competition? It is not because I believe in "unbridled competition." There
is no such thing. Competition is always regulated, confined by some
regulae (rules); and this is particularly true for societies in which the net
benefits of competition are undeniably and overwhelmingly positive. My
doubts almost all grow out of the suspicion that the religious authorities
will rarely have enough knowledge to make the kind of wise, community-
supporting decisions that are expected of them, primarily because the
criteria on which they want to base their decisions are far more ambiguous than they realize. Commercial societies are vastly more complex than
face-to-face societies.

There is little evidence in Tamari's book that either the author or the
authorities he quotes have worried about the relationship between rents
and costs. It is one of the axioms of economic ethics among the virtuous
but unreflective that prices ought to cover "costs plus a reasonable profit."
The problem is that, with the passage of time, profits always turn into
costs. Over time, the source of profits comes to be widely recognized,
competition bids up the price of commanding that source (resource) and
profit turns into a rent—and hence a cost.

What this means in practice is that competition will *usually* be "ruinous"

and that it will *almost always* "encroach on another's livelihood." If that
is so, then *ruin* and *encroachment* cannot be useful criteria for those who
want to "regulate market forces in accordance with the tenets of justice
and mercy." In practice these criteria will be a recipe for stasis, for rulings that block all changes that threaten any established interest—which
is to say *all changes.* This is an untenable position, of course, and no system
of ethics would survive that produced such a result. It has certainly not
been the practical consequence of Jewish economic ethics, whose authorities have proved themselves masters in the art of accommodating change
while remaining faithful to an immense body of binding law. Many of the
rulings show a striking concern for what economists would call an efficient use of resources (e.g., pp. 45, 47).

How have they done it? I do not think that Meir Tamari really tells us.
There seem to be more fundamental criteria informing the decisions he
discusses than the ones he gives us, or some deeper rule at work that he
has not recognized or at least not made explicit in his book.

Interest and Inflation

Many so-called ethical dilemmas of modern economic life are really puzzles for economic analysis. A person who genuinely wants to know what
he or she should do when confronted with one of these dilemmas is far
more likely to obtain satisfactory guidance from a good economist than
from someone who claims a speciality in ethics. What the person caught
in a quandary usually needs is a clearer and more adequate understanding of what is going on: *What has created this situation and what will be the
consequences of responding to it in one way rather than another?* This is the sort
of question that can best be answered by people trained to understand the
mysteries and complexities of commercial societies.

For example, people who experience ethical revulsion at the sight of 18
percent mortgage interest rates can be brought to understand that 18 percent is quite fair and reasonable in a society expecting 12 percent annual
inflation and taxing nominal interest at a marginal rate of 40 percent. That
"unconscionable" 18 percent rate will be a slightly negative real return after taxes have been paid. The ethical difficulty dissolves when we look below appearances to the underlying reality.

But what constitutes underlying reality? Tamari's discussion of halakhic problems regarding interest suggest that the rabbinic authorities have decidedly not been willing to turn the question of what is real and what is illusory over to economists, as the following example illustrates:

Jews are forbidden to take interest from other Jews, and are commanded to extend interest-free loans. But what happens when the price level changes during the period of the loan? How can the lender be compensated for the loss sustained when the value of money declines during the term of the loans? The halakhic ruling, according to Tamari, is that an additional money payment to compensate for the loss of the money's purchasing power would be interest and therefore forbidden. But suppose the two parties agree to lend and repay goods rather than money? This is generally forbidden, Tamari says. And the reason, if I understand it correctly, is that a bushel of wheat returned by the debtor for a bushel of wheat loaned earlier contains interest if the money price of wheat is higher at the time of repayment than at the time of the original loan. Tamari quotes the *Shulchan Arukh,* of the sixteenth century:

> It is not permissible to lend a measure of wheat against a promise to return a similar measure even though no time has been specified for its return. The same applies to all goods except silver coins, which are legal tender and not goods. [The reason for this ruling is the concern that] perhaps their price will rise, and the borrower will thereby be returning more than he borrowed [and this will constitute rabbinic interest, which is halakhically forbidden]. (p. 196; Tamari's inserts)

The passage implies that it is money, or at least legal tender money, that is "real"—which is just the reverse of the economist's way of looking at the matter.

The entire discussion may be found in pages 193–207—generously decorated in the case of my own copy with question marks and puzzled comments. To me the rabbinic authorities seem confused, not about religious law, of course, but about the realities to which they are attempting to apply it. I can readily understand why "history has witnessed a constant battle of wits between the rabbis and the businessmen" (p. 178) in this area; that is what I would predict when the religious authorities are misinterpreting the situation. I found myself cheering for the Chief Rabbi of Israel who argued that the continued rapid inflation in Israel requires a rethinking of some of these basic definitions; and I was quite disappointed to find Tamari unsympathetic to his reasoning. If this were a decision by a lower court in the USA, I would predict reversal on appeal. And if it were a decision by the Supreme Court, I would say the decision was untenable and bound eventually to be modified.

Jewish Law and the Common Law

A striking feature of the system Tamari describes is its similarity to the common law. After describing the nature of the written and the oral law in Judaism, Tamari says,

> ...the machinery whereby the decisions of the oral law in new circumstances become binding law is a relatively slow-moving one, so that at any one period of time it is possible to find conflicting opinions existing side by side. Gradually, through the establishment of a consensus, one or another of these opinions becomes binding. (pp. 12–13)

The rulings of the rabbinic authorities, like the decisions of common-law judges, usually arise out of actual cases in controversy. They bind only the parties to the controversy, but they also create precedents that can be consulted in subsequent proceedings. The law evolves out of a dialogue between novel situations and an authoritative tradition. Perhaps this is the missing element referred to earlier, the explanation for the ability of the Jewish authorities to accommodate change while adhering faithfully to a vast body of authoritative law. Jewish economic ethics has the realism, the down-to-earth character of the common law, as well as its complexities, intricacies, unresolved contradictions and arcane formulations. It is the sort of thing that might have grown over time out of the conflicts and conundrums of an actual community.

This would seem to be an important difference between Jewish and Christian economic ethics. Tamari offers an entire chapter on the economic history of the Jews, a chapter that I found extremely helpful for understanding and appreciating many of the rulings he discusses. Most of the material in the book is presented in a specific social and historical context. While this makes it less logical and orderly than it might otherwise have been, it underlines the distinctive nature of Jewish economic ethics. It is ethics for a functioning community.

Moreover, that community is both religious and political. From the Talmud to the present day, Tamari informs us, halakhic authorities have insisted upon the obligation of the rabbinic courts to oversee matters of trade and commerce independently of the non-Jewish world. Until relatively recent times, non-Jewish political authorities have recognized the autonomous communal authority of the rabbinic courts (pp. 45–46, 55). These courts turned ethical obligations into legal obligations and punished violators. However, the enforcement procedures were those appropriate to a religious community. The sanctions were excommunication and ostracism.

All this is changing. Tamari tells us that secularism and assimilation are depriving the community of its power and increasingly restricting communal autonomy to the spheres of religious activity and social welfare, leaving the regulation of economic activity to secular, non-Jewish society. A predictable consequence has been increasing reliance on individual, voluntary judgment in this area (pp. 77, 79). A further consequence, one might predict, will be the gradual disappearance of anything distinctively Jewish in Jewish economic ethics.

Religious Ethics in a Pluralist Society

What I found most distinctive and instructive about Jewish economic ethics as presented in this book is its willingness to forgo universalistic claims. While Tamari sometimes suggests that others might learn valuable lessons from Jewish rulings and practices, the ethics he presents is clearly an ethics for the economic life of a *Jewish community*. The noun and the adjective are both important.

Many of the rabbinic rulings have no point outside a community of people who know one another personally. Far more of the rulings could never be effectively applied outside a community in which economic transactions take place between people with specific knowledge of one another's circumstances. An example of the first kind would be the ruling that sets a limit, based on the host's financial status, to the number of people who can be invited to a circumcision or a wedding feast. This protects people from the pressure that can arise in a small community to spend beyond their means (p. 58). Another example is the blessing of monopolies that bring benefits to the community by raising prices to outsiders (p. 153). An example of the second kind is the rule that no one should offer to sell at a lower price when a poor person is offering something for sale (p. 101).

In a commercial society, the status of the seller (or the buyer) is irrelevant. Someone who says that it does not *have* to be that way overlooks the fact that a commercial society will not evolve unless it *is* that way. The division of labor is limited by the extent of the market, and it will never be "thoroughly established" in a society that restricts exchange to people familiar with one another's status. Even if someone is willing to argue that we would all be better off today had we limited the extent of the market in this manner, and thereby limited extension of the division of labor with all its consequences, we cannot now go back. An ethical system that assumes we can or should go back has no relationship to reality.

If this argument is correct, Jewish economic ethics as presented by Tamari is for the most part simply irrelevant to the larger society. Its "attempt to regulate market forces in accordance with the tenets of justice and mercy" (p. 85) can only succeed within a community small enough to determine what mercy requires. Mercy is always undeserved. It therefore cannot be dispensed according to the sort of general rules that are so essential to the successful functioning of any commercial society. Mercy is always specific to the situation of the one who receives mercy (as well, I would argue, to the situation of the one who shows it). A state welfare grant is not "mercy" even if the original motivation of the law was compassion and concern for the unfortunate. It is an entitlement, the *right* of those persons who qualify for grants under the criteria established by law. Welfare administrators who gave their clients more than the law specifies when they saw special needs or felt strong sympathies would not be showing mercy but violating their own legal obligations.

This does not mean that ethics is irrelevant to the practices of a commercial society. Quite to the contrary, a commercial society will not function effectively unless most of its participants can be counted on to behave ethically. But the ethical rules appropriate to the transactions of a commercial society will be significantly different from the rules that are generally felt to be binding in small, face-to-face communities. They will be much more general, much more abstract.

Jewish economic ethics as presented by Tamari is ethics for a relatively small community. Moreover, it is *Jewish* ethics, not universal ethics. Some Christians insist that Jewish ethics *is* universal ethics because the ethical portions of the Torah express the will of God for all people. These Christians are able to distinguish, in ways that I cannot, the ethical commands of the Old Testament, which are supposedly binding on all people, from the ritual commands, which allegedly are not binding. I am totally unable to make or defend this distinction.

I would go in the opposite direction and say that Christian social thinkers could profitably use Tamari's book to question their belief that biblical ethics, Old or New Testament, is universal ethics. Christianity, at least in its beginnings, was a Jewish religion in ways that many Christians have long overlooked. One important way in which it was Jewish was in its concern for the "chosen people." Christian ethics, at least in the beginning, was also an ethics for a community, the community of those who believed themselves to be the "new Israel." That changed decisively with Constantine. When Christians gained political power, they attempted to extend the principles of Christian ethics to the entire society. They also abandoned in short order everything that was distinctive about Christian ethics.

Judaism does not claim that God wants everyone to live in the manner of Jews. Neither does Christianity, despite its more universalistic intentions. The commission to "make disciples of all nations" (Matt. 28:19–20) is first of all an exhortation to baptize all nations in the name of the Triune God and only secondly an exhortation to instruct them in the principles of Christian behavior. There is no more reason to expect someone who is not a Christian to live the life of a Christian than there is to expect a non-Jew to live the life of a Jew.

Religious Ethics and the Political Order

All this has direct application to the vexing issue of religion's appropriate role in the political order of a democratic society. The minority status of Jews in European civilization has preserved them from the temptation to legislate their ethics and impose it coercively on others. Christians have not been so well preserved from temptation, and to this day they have not shaken off the arrogant and faithless belief that Christian ethics equals natural law. It is an arrogant belief because it claims that the superior quality of Christian ethics will be apparent to any reasonable person not blinded by perversity, and it is faithless because it abandons the distinctive character of Christian ethics in order to make that claim at all plausible.

Religious arguments should be left behind when we enter the political forum. That does not mean we leave behind religious beliefs or religious formation, which would be impossible. We enter the political forum as people who have been shaped by religious beliefs and practices, including any religious beliefs about the best way to organize and conduct our economic life and any habits acquired in the course of implementing those beliefs. It is only the religious *arguments* that we ought to leave behind.

What then is the relevance of Jewish economic ethics to the formation of public policy in a pluralist and largely secular society? I would say its relevance will be found almost entirely in whatever witness it manages to provide through the characters of those who submit to its commands and the communities they create.

PART 4

Economics and History

CHAPTER 12

Christian Social Thought and the Origination of the Economic Order

PERSPECTIVE IS IMPORTANT to have, but difficult to acquire. A history of Christian thought regarding the economic order may be able to provide us with valuable perspective as we try to come to terms with that order in our own time. But it's hard to gain perspective on such a long and complex history. I began the preparation of this paper far more certain than I am now of what I wanted to say. The investigations undertaken to support my various theses repeatedly revealed how much I had forgotten to consider, how little I really knew about the general topic, and how much of what has been confidently asserted in this area has subsequently proved to be naive and hopelessly uninformed. What started out to be a definitive statement has turned into a mere series of suggestions.

I

"It has been said," Franklin Gamwell tells us at the beginning of his keynote address,

> that the economic order is a distinctively modern moral and political problem. Only with the modern age have economic activities become sufficiently differentiated from kinship associations, on the one hand,

Unpublished typescript of a paper presented to a conference titled "Christianity and the Economic Order," at the Divinity School of the University of Chicago, 9–11 April 1984. Reprinted by permission of Mrs. Juliana Heyne.

and from specifically political associations, on the other, that the economy as such might become a subject of moral deliberation, debate and decision.[1]

That's a puzzling claim, at least upon first consideration. The production of wealth has been a cooperative social task in every society of which we have any knowledge. It would seem to follow, then, that an economic order must have existed in every known society. And if something so important existed, how could it have escaped recognition?

Karl Polanyi has given the clearest answer to that question. Until roughly the end of the eighteenth century, he contended, the economy was thoroughly "embedded" in society.

> Accordingly, before modern times the forms of man's livelihood attracted much less of his conscious attention than did most other parts of his organized existence. In contrast to kinship, magic or etiquette with their powerful keywords, the economy as such remained nameless. There existed, as a rule, no term to designate the concept of economy. Accordingly, as far as one can judge, this concept was absent.[2]

If Polanyi and Gamwell are correct—and I believe they are—my task of providing a historical overview of the ways in which Christian thinkers have understood the relationship between Christianity and the economic order is greatly simplified. Prior to 1800, Christians did not discern an economic order that "might become a subject of moral deliberation, debate and decision."

2

Was the concept of an economic order discovered or invented? Polanyi wanted to claim that it was largely invented, and to lament the invention.

1. Franklin I. Gamwell, "Freedom and the Economic Order: A Foreword to Religious Evaluation," p. 1.

2. Polanyi discusses this issue at length in *The Great Transformation: The Political and Economic Origins of Our Time* (c. 1944) and in several of the essays in *Primitive, Archaic and Modern Economies: Essays of Karl Polanyi* (c. 1968), edited by George Dalton. The quotation is from "Aristotle Discovers the Economy," reprinted in *Primitive, Archaic and Modern Economies* (Doubleday Anchor), p. 85.

The concept of the economic order was invented, according to Polanyi, as a way of making room for the machine.

> In order to allow scope to the use of elaborate, powerful machinery, we transformed human economy into a self-adjusting system of markets, and cast our thoughts and values in the mold of this unique innovation.[3]

We transformed Aristotle's *zoon politikon* into *Homo economicus,* a creature motivated by the fear of hunger and the desire for personal gain. Then we made the rest of society fundamentally dependent upon the exchange-directed system of production and distribution that *Homo economicus* generated and so we surrendered to the determinism of the market.

Polanyi's hostility toward the "market mentality" may have misled him, however.[4] The market system is not as artificial or unnatural as he wanted to make it. The eighteenth-century founders of economic science were describing something that was actually at work; they were discovering the economic order, not inventing it.

There is too much design in the account that Polanyi gives us. There were no "we" who decided that the advantages of machinery could not be obtained without a self-adjusting system of markets, and who consequently cast "our" thoughts and values in the appropriate mold.

3

The discovery of a distinct economic order is closely bound up, as we might expect, with the development of a separate science to explain its working. That science, known as political economy through most of the nineteenth

3. Polanyi, "Our Obsolete Market Mentality," *Primitive, Archaic and Modern Economies,* p. 59. See also *The Great Transformation* (Beacon Paperback, 1957), pp. 57, 68–76.

4. "Only since the market was permitted to grind the human fabric into the featureless uniformity of selenic erosion has man's institutional creativeness been in abeyance." "[L]aissez-faire philosophy, with its corollary of a marketing society, . . . is responsible for the splitting up of man's vital unity." "[I]n a truly democratic society, the problem of industry would resolve itself through the planned intervention of the producers and consumers themselves. Such conscious and responsible action is, indeed, one of the embodiments of freedom in a complex society." The quotations are from "Our Obsolete Market Mentality," pp. 71, 73, and 76–77 respectively.

century and as economics since then, had no name at all before 1800. Like the order it would explain, it was in the process of being discovered.

In the eighteenth century the term "political economy" still had the meaning suggested by its etymology. Economy was the art of managing a household, and *political* economy was the analogous art of providing for all the wants of a state. The "principles" of political economy were the principles that ought to guide a statesman or legislator. Thus the subtitle of Sir James Steuart's 1767 *Inquiry into the Principles of Political Economy* is "An Essay on the Science of Domestic Policy in Free Nations."[5] Similarly, Jean-Jacques Rousseau, in the article on political economy which he wrote for the *Encyclopédie*, defined his subject as the wise and legitimate government of that larger family, the state.[6] Steuart and Rousseau simply take for granted that, as an *oikonomia* must have an *oikonomos*, so must a political economy have a statesman to set it in order. And the principles of political economy are the maxims to be observed by sensible rulers who want "to secure a certain fund of subsistence for all the inhabitants, to obviate every circumstance which may render it precarious."[7]

Adam Smith understood the term political economy in much the same way, as *management* of the society.[8] He dissented forcefully, however, on how much management was required. The first four books of *The Wealth of Nations* attempt to show how wealth is produced without the guidance of an *oikonomos*, and why it is likely to increase more rapidly the less control the statesman tries to exert. At the end of Book IV, before discussing the proper tasks of government, Smith sums up his central thesis:

> All systems either of preference or of restraint, therefore, being thus completely taken away, the obvious and simple system of natural

5. Sir James Steuart, *An Inquiry into the Principles of Political Oeconomy*, edited and with an introduction by Andrew S. Skinner (1966), p. 2.

6. The *Encyclopédie* article was translated and printed with *The Social Contract* and other essays by Rousseau in the Everyman's Library series (1935). See p. 249.

7. Steuart, *op. cit.*, p. 17.

8. Smith defined political economy as "a branch of the science of a statesman or legislator" in his introduction to book IV of *The Wealth of Nations*. All his other uses of the term are consistent with this definition. As Jacob Viner has remarked, given Smith's "dim view of the benefits to be derived from national economic policy, political economy must for him have been nearly synonymous with 'economic poison.'" From Viner's article on Smith in *The International Encyclopedia of the Social Sciences*, (1968–79), vol. 14, p. 328.

liberty establishes itself of its own accord. Every man, as long as he does not violate the laws of justice, is left perfectly free to pursue his own interest his own way, and to bring both his industry and capital into competition with those of any other man, or order of men. The sovereign is completely discharged from a duty, in the attempting to perform which he must always be exposed to innumerable delusions, and for the proper performance of which no human wisdom or knowledge could ever be sufficient; the duty of superintending the industry of private people, and of directing it towards the employments most suitable to the interest of the society.[9]

If Smith deserves to be called the founder of economic science, it is because he provided the first comprehensive explanation of the order that establishes itself in wealth-producing activities in the absence of any "visible hand." Others, of course, had made important contributions before him. Richard Cantillon's *Essay on the Nature of Trade in General*, written around 1730 but not published until 1755, and A. J. R. Turgot's *Reflections on the Formation and Distribution of Riches*, composed in 1766 and published three years later, were exceptionally lucid expositions of the economic order. Both these works present a sort of natural history of national wealth, in which events develop by a logic of their own rather than as a consequence of anyone's design.[10]

Cantillon, Turgot, and Smith certainly described what we would today call an economic order. But was it sufficiently differentiated, in their treatments, from kinship and political associations to become "a subject of moral deliberation, debate and decision"? That is less certain. None of these writers seems to have thought of economic activity as something distinct from other purposive human action.

Even Polanyi, who criticizes Smith in *The Great Transformation*, conceded, in notes distributed to his students in economic history courses at Columbia University, that Smith still belongs with the "societal" writers. He considered economic life to be only an aspect of national life, bound

9. Adam Smith, *An Inquiry into the Nature and Causes of the Wealth of Nations*, book IV, chapter IX. The quotation is on p. 687 of the 1976 Glasgow edition, p. 651 of the 1937 Modern Library edition. The editions will henceforth be referred to as (GE) and (MLE).

10. The detached, purely descriptive tone is particularly striking in Cantillon's *Essay*.

to reflect the health or ill health of national life. All through his writings, Polanyi concludes, Smith's approach is "institutional, historical, and societal." [11]

4

Bernard Mandeville was a key figure in the development of eighteenth-century thought on the workings of society.[12] His *Fable of the Bees,* first published in 1705 as a poem of 400 lines, and subsequently much enlarged, elaborated, and defended in 1714 and 1729 reprintings, was widely read and discussed. Mandeville's scandalous thesis was that private vices led to public benefits. His significance for economics and social science lay in the success with which he expounded the notion that social order can and will emerge without the benefit of any advance design, that economy in the larger society does not require an *oikonomos* to direct it. But he also claimed that it was vice, or selfish and anti-social motives, which supplied the principle of coordination. Despite Adam Smith's careful refutation of Mandeville on this score, the belief that the economic order is held together by the operation of essentially immoral motives survived to shape nineteenth-century conceptions of that order and eventually the reactions of Christian thinkers trying to come to terms with it.

Smith himself never claimed that the economic order was maintained through the operation of *selfish* interests. He speaks of self-love, of one's own advantage, security, gain, and interest; and of the "uniform, constant, and uninterrupted effort of every man to better his condition." [13] None of this can be equated with selfishness, however. Smith's attack on Mandeville in *The Theory of Moral Sentiments* clarifies his own position.

After reviewing Mandeville's "wholly pernicious" argument, to the effect that all actions, including those that seem most generous and self-

---

11. *Primitive, Archaic and Modern Economies,* pp. 127–29.

12. F. A. Hayek, "Dr. Bernard Mandeville," a lecture reprinted in *New Studies in Philosophy, Politics, Economics and the History of Ideas* (1978).

13. Some key passages in *The Wealth of Nations:* book I, chapter II, pp. 26–27 (GE), p. 14 (MLE); book II, chapter III, pp. 341–49 (GE), pp. 324–32 (MLE); book IV, chapter II, pp. 454–56 (GE), pp. 421–23 (MLE).

sacrificing, stem in reality from selfishness and mean motives, Smith writes:

> Whether the most generous and public-spirited actions may not, in some sense, be regarded as proceeding from self-love, I shall not at present examine. The decision of this question is not, I apprehend, of any importance toward establishing the reality of virtue, since self-love may frequently be a virtuous motive of action.[14]

The desire to better our condition, which Smith believes is the dominant motive in social interaction among all classes of people, prompts most of them to pursue "an augmentation of fortune," because this is "the means most vulgar and the most obvious" toward bettering one's condition. This desire leads people to work and to save, which in turn fuels the process of economic growth.[15]

And what are people ultimately after? "[W]hat are the advantages which we propose by that great purpose of human life which we call bettering our condition?" Smith answers: "To be observed, to be attended to, to be taken notice of with sympathy, complacency, and approbation, are all the advantages which we can propose to derive from it."[16]

This often culminates in sheer vanity, which is the desire to be praised for what one knows is not genuinely praiseworthy. But it need not produce that result. The crucial point Smith makes against Mandeville is that the desire for approval can take the form of the love of virtue or the love of true glory, as well as mere vanity. The love of virtue is "the desire of doing what is honorable and noble, of rendering ourselves the proper objects of esteem and approbation." The love of true glory is "the love of well-grounded fame and reputation, the desire of acquiring esteem by what is really estimable."[17] Thus the *Homo economicus* in Adam Smith's system

---

14. Adam Smith, *The Theory of Moral Sentiments*, part VII, section II, chapter IV, pp. 308–9 in the Glasgow edition (1976).

15. This is the theme of book II, chapter III in *The Wealth of Nations*.

16. *The Theory of Moral Sentiments*, part I, section III, chapter II, p. 50. For an elaboration of Smith's thought on this issue, see all of chapter II and chapter III in section III of part I and also chapter I of part IV.

17. *Ibid.*, p. 309.

of moral philosophy, while he adapts means to ends, does not necessarily pursue base or ignoble ends. The desire to better one's condition is common to the virtuous and the vain.

The notion that Adam Smith glorified the pursuit of gain could never be maintained by anyone who had read the companion volume to *The Wealth of Nations*.[18]

5

The publication in 1798 of Malthus' *Essay on Population* was a crucial event, both for the subsequent development of economics and for Christians who would later reflect on the economic order.

In his book on the "Clapham Sect," *Saints in Politics,* Ernest Marshall Howse writes:

> Adam Smith, Ricardo, and Malthus had combined to teach that poverty was inevitable; that the increase of population outstripping the means of subsistence, left an inevitable fringe of society on the borderland of starvation; that there was an iron law of wages, allotting with scientific finality the total sum that could be left for labor; and that all interference with those scientific laws was unwise, and ultimately futile.[19]

But this is not what *Smith* taught; it is the Malthusian vision of the human situation. Ricardo employed Malthus' population theory, along with the law of diminishing returns in agriculture, to construct his model of the economic system. But even Ricardo did not maintain that poverty was inevitable. In his influential essay *On the Principles of Population and Taxation* (1817), Ricardo expresses the hope that the laboring classes will acquire a taste for luxuries and so will limit the size of their families.[20]

---

18. It should not be maintained even by someone who has read only *The Wealth of Nations*. It *is* maintained, unfortunately, in Max Lerner's introduction to the Modern Library edition.

19. Ernest Marshall Howse, *Saints in Politics* (1952), p. 128.

20. *Op. cit.*, chapter V, p. 100 in the Sraffa edition. See also p. 96 and the quotation from Robert Torrens in the footnote.

How did Malthus' gloomy view of the human situation come to be so widely accepted as the central teaching of classical political economy? The undiluted doctrine of the first edition of Malthus' essay did not, in fact, command general acceptance among political economists in Malthus' time, not even in England.[21] It does seem to have convinced Malthus' theological colleagues, however. As Anthony Waterman has shown in a recent article on "The Ideological Alliance of Political Economy and Christian Theology, 1798–1833," a number of Anglican theologian-economists subscribed to Malthus' basic doctrine and turned it into a grim theodicy. Poverty and inequality were God's way of propelling mankind, "despite its brutish inertia, toward the higher possibilities of earthly existence."[22]

Here is the surprising solution to the puzzle of how Christian thinkers in England were able to accept so easily the teachings of the dismal science: they were its principal teachers. The doctrines of the Reverend T. R. Malthus conformed more readily to their natural theology than did the teachings of that optimistic deist, Adam Smith.[23]

Christian social thought at the end of the eighteenth century was profoundly conservative. Order was of God, almost without regard to the nature of the order. Inequalities were not inequities, but rather divinely ordained differences that enabled the social organism to function. The church's traditional hostility toward the desire for gain, we must remember, was part of a static conception of the social order, in which people were expected to be content with the lot assigned to them in this life and to avoid envy or covetousness. Respect for property was part and parcel of respect for government, ecclesiastical authority, and Providence itself. And in the last decade of the eighteenth century, there were the chilling lessons of the French Revolution for anyone inclined to doubt that respect for established institutions was the foundation of social order.[24]

21. It was turned rather quickly into the innocuous proposition that population is limited by the supply of foodstuffs.

22. A. M. C. Waterman, *op. cit., Journal of Ecclesiastical History* (April 1983), p. 238.

23. In addition to the essay cited above, see Waterman, "Malthus as a Theologian: The *First Essay* and the Relation between Political Economy and Christian Theology," in *Malthus Past and Present* (1983), and J. M. Pullen, "Malthus' Theological Ideas and Their Influence on His Principle of Population," *History of Political Economy* (Spring 1981), pp. 39–54.

24. For the effects all this had in delaying the success of Wilberforce and his friends in securing abolition of the slave trade, see Howse, *Saints in Politics*, pp. 28–64, and especially pp. 42–45.

6

Some would have argued in the early nineteenth century that the social theology of Malthus and the clerical political economists was more "natural" than Christian. No such charge would have been made, however, against William Wilberforce, Henry Thornton, and the other members of what subsequently came to be known as the Clapham Sect. This small group of wealthy and powerful individuals were committed Evangelicals and active social reformers. How did they approach the problems of the economic order?[25]

The Clapham "Saints," to use the derisive label applied to them in their time, were certainly less tolerant of whatever social wrongs they saw and much more willing to make personal sacrifices to remedy them. Their long struggle to secure abolition of the slave trade provides ample evidence of their Evangelical piety, their conviction that true religion entailed concern for the problems of this world, and their refusal to substitute pious words for personally costly actions. There is no evidence, however, that they saw the economic order in any way fundamentally different from the way in which it was perceived by Malthus or Thomas Chalmers.

Twentieth-century critics have sometimes faulted the members of Wilberforce's circle for attacking slavery abroad while ignoring "wage slavery" at home.[26] Even Howse, in his sympathetic history of the Clapham Sect, and while defending them against unfair and often uninformed criticism in this area, speaks of their "heartlessness," their indifference toward "civil injustice," even their "cruelty" when it came to the legal rights of wage earners.[27] But there is no heartlessness, cruelty, or injustice in accepting what one genuinely believes cannot be changed, or in opposing policies which have kind intentions but are thought to produce cruel consequences.

The Clapham Saints did *not* believe that the condition of the laborer

---

25. My account depends heavily on Howse, *op. cit.*, especially pp. 116–37.

26. Charles E. Raven, in presenting the historical background to the Christian Socialist movement, writes as follows: "Very characteristic is their great hero William Wilberforce, whose private life was a shining example of consistent and earnest goodness, who had a real belief in freedom and spent years in the struggle for the abolition of slavery, and who never realised that, while he was bringing liberty to negroes in the plantations, the white slaves of industry in mine and factory were being made the victims of a tyranny a thousandfold more cruel." Raven, *Christian Socialism 1848–1854* (1920), p. 12.

27. Howse, *op. cit.*, pp. 117–18, 127–29.

could not be improved, though they certainly entertained expectations more modest in this respect than those that came to be held later in the century. They simply believed that combinations and strikes were far more likely to damage the working classes than to help them, especially in the long run. If they were wrong about this, it was not because they had averted their eyes from the conditions of the laboring classes or refused to consider reasoned arguments to the contrary. Their views in this area were generally consistent with the views of the leading political economists of their day and even of the next generation. (It may be noted in passing that Henry Thornton, in whose house in Clapham the Saints regularly met to map their strategies, was probably the most astute monetary economist of the nineteenth century.[28])

7

According to Polanyi, Malthus played a crucial role in the establishment of an institutionally separate economic sphere in society, by invoking Nature herself to secure "the autonomy of the economic sphere."[29] For those who followed Malthus, the laws of the market were not the mere will of particular social classes or arbitrary governments; they were the very decrees of Providence.

How was the economic order perceived in the first half of the nineteenth century by Christian social thinkers who accepted Smith *but rejected Malthus?* The United States provides an interesting case study.

Neither Malthus nor Ricardo ever acquired in the United States anything like the authority they commanded in Britain.[30] The basic doctrine of Malthus (and the foundation of Ricardo's distribution theory), that the pressure of population on limited agricultural land will keep wages at subsistence, had little to commend it in a country where land was abundant and labor was chronically scarce. The European textbook most widely used in the United States was J. B. Say's *Treatise on Political Economy.*[31] In

28. Henry Thornton, *An Enquiry into the Nature and Effects of the Paper Credit of Great Britain* (1802), reissued in 1939 under the editorship of F. A. Hayek with a long and scholarly introduction by the editor.

29. *Primitive, Archaic and Modern Economies*, p. 131.

30. George Johnson Cady, "The Early American Reaction to the Theory of Malthus," *Journal of Political Economy* 39, no. 5 (October 1931): 601–32.

31. Michael J. L. O'Connor, *Origins of Academic Economics in America* (1944), pp. 120–35.

this work, the topic of population isn't even taken up until the end of the second (of three) books, and then no gloomy conclusions are drawn. Moreover, the editor of the American edition of Say's *Treatise*, Clement C. Biddle, chastises the English translator in his introduction for inserting footnotes that defend Malthus and Ricardo against Say. Biddle informs the American reader that he has "entirely omitted" all notes by the translator that "are in opposition to the well-established elements of the science, and have no other support than the hypothesis of Mr. Ricardo and Mr. Malthus." [32]

A statement by the Rev. John McVickar fairly summarizes the position of most American Christians who discussed the economic order in the first half of the nineteenth century:

> That science and religion eventually teach the same lesson, is a necessary consequence of the unity of truth, but it is seldom that this union is so early and so satisfactorily displayed as in the researches of Political Economy. [33]

The Rev. Francis Wayland, whose *Elements of Political Economy* quickly became and long remained the most widely-used textbook in the United States after its publication in 1837, taught that God had established laws governing the accumulation of wealth. Chief among these was the truth that those who honestly strive to promote their own welfare promote thereby the welfare of the whole society. It is our task "so to construct the arrangements of society, as to give free scope to the laws of Divine Providence." And that means allowing each person to keep all that he has justly acquired by his industry, while compelling the slothful to suffer the consequences of their idleness. [34]

---

32. Jean-Baptiste Say, *A Treatise on Political Economy*, translated from the fourth edition of the French, by C. R. Prinsep; New American edition, containing a translation of the introduction, and additional notes, by Clement C. Biddle (1836). The advertisement by the American editor to the fifth edition contains Biddle's complaint against Prinsep for yielding ground to Malthus and Ricardo, p. ix.

33. The statement is in one of the many footnotes McVickar wrote for *Outlines of Political Economy* (1825), which is basically a reprinting with commentary of J. R. McCulloch's essay on Political Economy in the *Encyclopedia Britannica* (1825), p. 69.

34. Wayland's theological economics are discussed at some length in a forthcoming article titled "Clerical Laissez-Faire," which I originally wrote for a 1982 conference on religion and economics. The book containing the article is to be published by the Fraser Institute of Vancouver, British Columbia.

Henry F. May uses the apt term "clerical laissez-faire" to character-ize the most influential school of political economy in the United States at least up to the Civil War.[35] Christian social thinkers who followed the optimistic Smithian line agreed at least in this respect with those who subscribed to the more dismal Malthus-Ricardo position: the laws of po-litical economy were the laws of God, and they basically ordained non-interference, by government or charitably-inclined private parties, with the consequences that flow from the individual choices of the industrious or the indolent, the frugal or the improvident.

8

Why did so many Christian thinkers in the first half of the nineteenth cen-tury embrace the newly-discovered economic order with such unqualified enthusiasm? Why didn't a social system so dependent for its functioning on the pursuit of gain pose a greater ethical problem of thinkers inherit-ing a long tradition of firm hostility to commerce and *turpe lucrum?* Part of the answer, I believe, is that they saw in the economic order described by the new science of political economy the possibility for a radical trans-formation of the human condition. The newly-discovered economic order offered an opportunity for people—everyone, in principle, and perhaps most people in practice—to better their condition in life.

> Socialists, therefore, by endeavoring to transfer the possessions of in-dividuals to the community at large, strike at the interests of every wage-earner, since they would deprive him of the liberty of disposing of his wages, and thereby of all hope and possibility of increasing his resources and of *bettering his condition in life.* . . .

Neither must it be supposed that the solicitude of the Church is so preoccupied with the spiritual concerns of her children as to neglect their temporal and earthly interests. Her desire is that the poor [lit-erally, the proletarians], for example, should rise above poverty and wretchedness, and *better their condition in life;* and for this she makes a

---

35. Henry F. May, *Protestant Churches and Industrial America* (1949), p. 14.

strong endeavor. By the very fact that she calls men to virtue and forms them to its practice she promotes this in no slight degree. Christian morality, when adequately and completely practiced, leads of itself to temporal prosperity. . . .

. . . [A]ll may justly strive to *better their condition.*

The three quotations above are from *Rerum Novarum,* Pope Leo XIII's 1891 encyclical on the condition of the working classes.[36] They don't prove the thesis; indeed, they are hardly even evidence for it, coming as they do almost a century after the discovery of the economic order. Nonetheless, they do suggest how powerfully the ideal of bettering one's condition may have influenced social theology in the nineteenth century. The encyclical does not argue the point; it takes for granted that wage-earners are eager to improve their condition and that this desire is not only compatible with Christian virtue but almost a sign of its presence. We are a long way from the medieval world in which the desire to better one's condition is *cupiditas.*

9

How shall we account for the growing dissatisfaction with the workings of the economic order that Christian spokesmen begin to express after the middle of the nineteenth century? E. R. Norman has become somewhat notorious for claiming that churchmen's pronouncements on social issues do little more than express the shifting opinions of the intellectual classes to which they belong (or aspire). Norman's summary of this thesis, in the Introduction to his *Church and Society in England 1770–1970,* is worth extended quotation:

It is also clear that the leadership of the Church has been internally divided on a number of issues in each successive generation. Some, often a majority, have readily adopted the progressive idealism common

36. I have added the emphasis in quoting from *The Church Speaks to the Modern World: The Social Teachings of Leo XIII,* edited and with an introduction by Etienne Gilson (Doubleday Image Book, c. 1954), pp. 207, 220, 226.

to liberal opinion within the intelligentsia, of which they were a part. The parochial clergy and the laity have often been less open to shifts of intellectual attitude—they were less immediately related to the sources of ideas in the Universities and in public life. They have been more reflective of conservative values, slower to adapt to the fashions of thought which take hold at the top of the Church. Divisions of opinion within the intelligentsia have always been faithfully reproduced within the Church's leading thinkers. This points to another general conclusion of the present study: that the social attitudes of the Church have derived from the surrounding intellectual and political culture and not, as churchmen themselves always seem to assume, from theological learning. The theologians have always managed to reinterpret their sources in ways which have somehow made their version of Christianity correspond almost exactly to the values of their class and generation. Thus theological scholarship justified the structural social obligations of the eighteenth-century world; then it provided a Christian basis for Political Economy; later collectivist principles were hailed as the most perfect embodiment of the compassion prescribed in the New Testament; and even the contemporary doctrines of "liberation" and "secularization" have been given powerful theological support. Theologians, after all, are intellectuals, and they have a natural interest in representing social changes in terms of ideas. It is not surprising that they should believe that their own social preferences are derived from straight intellectual calculation, rather than, as is the case, from the complicated and mixed world of ideas and moral postures characteristic of the intelligentsia as a whole. This is, no doubt, the way of all truth; it takes on the form and the idealism of the intellectual preoccupations of each generation.[37]

If Norman is correct, an explanation of changing Christian views on the economic order over the past two centuries would have to provide an explanation of the changing intellectual and political culture of the Western world. That task would carry me far beyond my assignment or competence and your patience. But is Norman's thesis correct? I am convinced it is. His detailed account of changing Anglican views on society between 1770 and 1970 offers overwhelming evidence to support his thesis with respect to England. As one who has read extensively in the American literature, I am prepared to defend the thesis with respect to mainline Christianity in this country.[38]

I can understand why the Norman thesis would offend many churchmen. But could matters possibly be other than as Norman describes under what Franklin Gamwell has called the conditions of "modernity"?[39] If "appropriate standards of belief and action are those which the reasoning human individual sets for himself or herself" (Gamwell), how could we expect Christian thinking about the economic order to reflect anything except "the surrounding intellectual and political culture" (Norman)?

Gamwell thinks that two recent discussions of Christian ethics and the economic order disagree with his claim "that religious ethics is not credible in the modern world unless its judgments and proposals are defended by humanistic appeal." Philip Wogaman and Robert Benne, as Gamwell reads them, "finally justify their normative judgments by exclusive and, therefore, heteronomous appeal to characteristic convictions of the Christian faith." [40] I think he misreads them. Wogaman, who claims that ideological thinking is unavoidable in this area, also says:

> But it still makes all the difference whether our ideologies really do conform, on the one hand, to all we consider good and humane and true and, on the other hand, to the facts of the real world.[41]

Benne is even more explicit. He appeals to the general evidence of the social sciences for his factual claims and to the political philosophies of Reinhold Niebuhr and John Rawls for "criteria of judgment." [42]

---

38. The mildly interested reader could examine James Dombrowski, *The Early Days of Christian Socialism in America* (1936); Charles Howard Hopkins, *The Rise of the Social Gospel in American Protestantism, 1865–1915* (1940); and Henry F. May, *Protestant Churches and Industrial America* (1949). Anyone over thirty years of age can consult his memory.

39. Gamwell, *op. cit.*, pp. 1–3.

40. *Ibid.*, p. 2.

41. J. Philip Wogaman, *The Great Economic Debate: An Ethical Analysis* (1977), p. 33.

42. Robert Benne, *The Ethic of Democratic Capitalism: A Moral Reassessment* (1981), pp. viii–ix and the entire first chapter.

One does not, of course, make a "heteronomous appeal to characteristic convictions of the Christian faith" by citing Reinhold Niebuhr in support of an argument, especially since Niebuhr himself often wondered whether there was anything uniquely "Christian" about his social analysis.[43] One can also quote the Bible to support an argument without implying anything more thereby than that the text quoted makes a valid point.

To summarize then: Christian thinkers began to offer theological criticisms of the economic order in the second half of the nineteenth century because that order was coming under attack "from the surrounding intellectual and political culture." The process gathers momentum in England around the middle of the century. In the United States it is delayed for about a generation, partly because the slavery issue had to be resolved first, partly because the problems that the economic order generated were less obvious and probably less severe in this country. I know far less about what was happening in other countries. The 1878 encyclical of Leo XIII attacking socialism, *Quod Apostolici Muneris,* and the highly conservative *Rerum Novarum* of 1891 certainly suggest that the Roman Catholic Church was not in the vanguard of those offering criticisms of the economic order in the last part of the nineteenth century.

10

Although the economic order was discovered in the eighteenth century and clearly recognized at the beginning of the nineteenth century, it did not immediately "become a subject of moral deliberation, debate and decision." We do not engage in moral discussion of forces that we consider inexorable; and inexorableness was, I think, a dominant perceived characteristic of the economic order in the early nineteenth century. This claim must be distinguished from the quite different and erroneous notion that *laissez-faire* reigned unchallenged in the first half of the nineteenth century.

It is easy to exaggerate the extent to which *laissez-faire* thinking on the part of Christians derived from the *laissez-faire* teachings of nineteenth-century political economy. When churchmen later in the century wanted

43. Reinhold Niebuhr, *Leaves from the Notebook of a Tamed Cynic,* reissued with a foreword by Martin E. Marty (c. 1929, 1956, 1980). Pp. 166–67 and 196–97 offer some typically Niebuhrean comments on Niebuhr.

to proclaim a new departure in Christian social thought, they found it convenient to blame the dogmas of the economists for earlier positions they were now repudiating. "We were misled" is an acceptable excuse. Moreover, it removes the necessity of explaining why the pronouncements of Christian social theorists should be correct now when they were wrong earlier. The flaw in this excuse is that secular political economists in the nineteenth century were generally *not* advocates of *laissez-faire*.[44]

In any event, *laissez-faire* is a *policy,* and as such it can be "a subject of moral deliberation, debate and decision." The sense of inexorableness to which I am referring was something else, and was expressed in a variety of ways. I shall illustrate from the writings of Smith, Malthus, and Marx.

Adam Smith expresses it in a passage that is actually critical of the excessive claims made by François Quesnay and the Physiocrats on behalf of *laissez-faire* policy:

> Some speculative physicians seem to have imagined that the health of the human body could be preserved only by a certain precise regimen of diet and exercise, of which every, the smallest, violation necessarily occasioned some degree of disease or disorder proportioned to the degree of the violation. Experience, however, would seem to show, that the human body frequently preserves, to all appearance at least, the most perfect state of health under a vast variety of different regimens; even under some which are generally believed to be very far from being perfectly wholesome. But the healthful state of the human body, it would seem, contains in itself some unknown principle of preservation, capable either of preventing or of correcting, in many respects, the bad effects even of a very faulty regimen. Mr. Quesnai, who was himself a physician, and a very speculative physician, seems to have entertained a notion of the same kind concerning the political body, and to have imagined that it would thrive and prosper only under a certain precise regimen, the exact regimen of perfect liberty and perfect justice. He seems not to have considered that in the political body, the natural effort which every man is continually making to

44. Lionel Robbins, *The Theory of Economic Policy in English Classical Political Economy* (1952). Of course, if *laissez-faire* is redefined to cover any predisposition against adding to the agenda of government, then the classical economists were indeed defenders of *laissez-faire*.

better his own condition, is a principle of preservation capable of preventing and correcting, in many respects, the bad effects of a political economy, in some degree both partial and oppressive. Such a political economy, though it no doubt retards more or less, is not always capable of stopping altogether the natural progress of a nation towards wealth and prosperity, and still less of making it go backwards. If a nation could not prosper without the enjoyment of perfect liberty and perfect justice, there is not in the world a nation which could ever have prospered. In the political body, however, the wisdom of nature has fortunately made ample provision for remedying many of the bad effects of the folly and injustice of man; in the same manner as it has done in the natural body, for remedying those of his sloth and intemperance.[45]

Malthus, who wasn't even an advocate of free trade in grain, much less of *laissez-faire,* expresses what I am calling inexorableness in the first chapter of his *Essay on Population:*

> In entering upon the argument I must premise that I put out of the question, at present, all mere conjectures, that is, all suppositions, the probable realization of which cannot be inferred upon any just philosophical grounds. A writer may tell me that he thinks man will ultimately become an ostrich, I cannot properly contradict him. But before he can expect to bring any reasonable person over to his opinion, he ought to shew that the necks of mankind have been gradually elongating, that the lips have grown harder and more prominent, that the legs and feet are daily altering their shape, and that the hair is beginning to change into stubs of feathers. And till the probability of so wonderful a conversion can be shewn, it is surely lost time and lost eloquence to expatiate on the happiness of man in such a state; to describe his powers, both of running and flying, to paint him in a condition where all narrow luxuries would be contemned, where he would be employed only in collecting the necessaries of life, and where, consequently, each man's share of labour would be light, and his portion of leisure ample.
>
> I think I may fairly make two postulata.

---

45. Smith, *The Wealth of Nations,* book IV, chapter IX, pp. 673–74 (GE), p. 638 (MLE).

First, That food is necessary to the existence of man.

Secondly, That the passion between the sexes is necessary and will remain nearly in its present state.

These two laws, ever since we have had any knowledge of mankind, appear to have been fixed laws of our nature, and, as we have not hitherto seen any alteration in them, we have no right to conclude that they will ever cease to be what they now are, without an immediate act of power in that Being who first arranged the system of the universe, and for the advantage of his creatures, still executes, according to fixed laws, all its various operations.[46]

The strongest expressions of the inexorableness of the economic order are found in the writings of Marx, whom no one ever accused of partiality toward *laissez-faire* (or Malthus!). Here is what he wrote in the Preface to *A Contribution to the Critique of Political Economy:*

In the social production of their life, men enter into definite relations that are indispensable and independent of their will, relations of production which correspond to a definite stage of development of their material productive forces. The sum total of these relations of production constitutes the economic structure of society, the real foundation, on which rises a legal and political superstructure and to which correspond definite forms of social consciousness. The mode of production of material life conditions the social, political and intellectual life process in general. It is not the consciousness of men that determines their being, but, on the contrary, their social being that determines their consciousness. At a certain stage of their development, the material productive forces of society come in conflict with the existing relations of production, or—what is but a legal expression for the same thing—with the property relations within which they have been at work hitherto. From forms of development of the productive forces these relations turn into their fetters. Then begins an epoch of social revolution. With the change of the economic foundation the entire im-

---

46. Thomas Robert Malthus, *An Essay on the Principle of Population,* Norton Critical Edition (1798, 1976), p. 19.

mense superstructure is more or less rapidly transformed. In considering such transformations a distinction should always be made between the material transformation of the economic conditions of production, which can be determined with the precision of natural science, and the legal, political, religious, aesthetic or philosophic—in short, ideological forms in which men become conscious of this conflict and fight it out.[47]

The same idea is forcefully presented in part I of *The German Ideology,* the long essay that Marx and Engels wrote together in 1845–46 in an effort to clarify to themselves their position over against Hegelian philosophy.[48] An even clearer and certainly more concise statement is in a letter written by Marx at the end of 1846 to P. V. Annenkov, who had asked his opinion of Proudhon's new book *The Philosophy of Poverty:*

> What is society, whatever its form may be? The product of men's reciprocal action. Are men free to choose this or that form of society? By no means. Assume a particular state of development in the productive faculties of man and you will get a particular form of commerce and consumption. Assume particular stages of development in production, commerce and consumption and you will have a corresponding social constitution, a corresponding organisation of the family, of orders or of classes, in a word, a corresponding civil society. Assume a particular civil society and you will get particular political conditions which are only the official expression of civil society....
>
> It is superfluous to add that men are not free to choose their productive forces—which are the basis of all their history—for every productive force is an acquired force, the product of former activity. The productive forces are therefore the result of practical human energy; but this energy is itself conditioned by the circumstances in which men find themselves, by the productive forces already acquired, by the social form which exists before they do, which they do not create, which is the product of the preceding generation.... [T]he social history of men is never anything but the history of their individual

47. I have quoted from *The Marx-Engels Reader,* Second Edition, edited by Robert C. Tucker (1978), pp. 4–5.
48. It was not published until 1932.

development, whether they are conscious of it or not. Their material relations are the basis of all their relations. These material relations are only the necessary forms in which their material and individual activity is realised.[49]

Marx and Engels were notoriously contemptuous of those who wanted to make the economic order the "subject of moral deliberation, debate and decision." In *The Communist Manifesto* they summarize their attitude toward such utopian socialists:

> Historical action is to yield to their personal inventive action, historically created conditions of emancipation to fantastic ones, and the gradual, spontaneous class-organisation of the proletariat to the organisation of society specially contrived by these inventors. Future history resolves itself, in their eyes, into the propaganda and the practical carrying out of their social plans.[50]

II

In the end, however, the economic order must be recognized as an invention, an imposition on our way of conceiving the social world. It wasn't a mere fabrication. Something was discovered. But the nineteenth century misunderstood it, and Christian social thought has suffered greatly from that misconception.

There is finally no economic order that can be distinguished from other forms or orders of social interaction. There are no economic goals, economic motives, or economic institutions. Economic action is simply purposive action, action that tries to use means to achieve ends.[51]

Activity aimed at securing food, clothing and lodging was once the basic, essential, and therefore in a sense controlling activity in every human

---

49. *The Marx-Engels Reader*, pp. 136–37.
50. *Ibid.*, pp. 497–98.
51. The definitive discussion of these matters is still the series of articles that Frank Knight published in the 1920s in the *Quarterly Journal of Economics*, which were reprinted as the first three essays in Frank H. Knight, *The Ethics of Competition and Other Essays* (1936).

society.[52] Exactly when that ceased to be true in Western industrialized societies, or when it became more false than true, can be debated. But it certainly happened a long time ago in the United States. When Americans "make a living" today, they are not aiming to produce the material conditions of their existence. The materialist interpretation of history once functioned as a powerful critique of wishful thinking disguised as social philosophy. Today it is largely irrelevant. The new social needs which have been created in the course of history, through the operation of the powerful social forces that Marx and Engels emphasized, have removed us so far from anything that might be defensibly designated "material" that the materialist interpretation of history is today an obstacle to realistic social analysis. To identify "economic" with "material" only compounds confusion.

Since economic action is purposive action, it is necessarily "individualistic"; only individuals can have action-directing purposes. Economic action necessarily aims at "gain"; that's an essential part of the meaning of purposive. So economic action aims at individual gain. But this only explicates the meaning of purposive action. It says nothing about what counts as gain for any particular individual. Fellowship, conviviality, discussion, group process—all these could be the gain at which particular purposive actions might be aiming. Who of us knows exactly what we're aiming at, or what our ultimate goals might be? Ends become means to further ends in the process of living, and the process itself is an important "end," even when we aren't explicitly conscious of that fact. We want to win; but we also want a good game.[53]

Is money perhaps the thread which we're seeking? Does money have some essential link to the economic order that might enable us to differentiate that order, or to separate economic actions from non-economic actions? Money is a medium of exchange. It is a means to more effective

---

52. This is what accounts for the early economists' tendency to assign a superior productivity to agriculture. The Physiocrats made agriculture exclusively productive, and labelled manufacturing and trade "sterile." In modern jargon, they were calling attention to the low *marginal* productivity of non-agricultural production. Cantillon's *Essay* makes all this remarkably clear.

53. A point regularly insisted upon by Knight.

social exchange. It facilitates cooperation. Through the use of money, we can more effectively use the resources under our control to secure from others the cooperation that we need to achieve our purposes. The social institution of money encourages "rationality," the ends-means approach to life, by facilitating the accomplishment of purposes. It extends the planning horizon, by establishing more predictable connections between immediate actions and distant goals. The increasing monetization of social interactions—"everything has a price"—extends the realm of social, as distinct from merely physical or biological, order.[54]

We have been learning, since the eighteenth century, that order will emerge from the interplay of human purposes without the existence of any overarching design. We have been slowly discovering the precise conditions which make such orders more or less satisfactory.[55] We have begun to realize that the vantage points from which we once thought we could control the chaos or cruelty of "unplanned" social orders are themselves subject to the control of social orders that no one controls.[56] Politics has no veto over economics, and economics does not control politics; people simply interact, on the basis of the costs and benefits that they anticipate.

This was first discovered in a sphere where it was most readily apparent: the social production of food, clothing, and lodging. It was most apparent there because this was, by necessity, the sphere of the most consistently "rational" action. Through this accident, the social production and distribution of the basic necessities of life came to be thought of as "the economic order"; the regularities or "laws" governing the production and distribution of these necessities were called "the laws of economics"; and the failings, moral or material, of such unplanned social orders were attributed exclusively to the misconceived economic order.[57] It was sup-

---

54. My attempt at description should not be understood as an unqualified endorsement.

55. Clearly-defined rights (or powers) with few restrictions on the exchange of rights turn out to be significant conditions.

56. Marx and Engels never explained how order would be achieved once "social control of the means of production" had been established. Engels occasionally raised the question—in the preface he wrote to *The Poverty of Philosophy*, for example, where he pithily demonstrates the unworkability of socialism as advocated by Rodbertus—but always walked away without actually answering.

57. "Reflection will reveal," according to Frank Knight, "that it is rather an accident that internal social conflicts take the economic form. This will be clear if one pictures

posed that there were other forms of rational, purposive association that could correct the errors and fill up the deficiencies of the "competitive," "individualistic," "selfish," "materialistic," "amoral" (if not "immoral") economic order.

When Christian social theorists became disillusioned with the idea that the "laws of economics" were the decrees of Providence, they began to substitute the belief that the economic order was perfectly malleable. This is an attractive belief. I do not think, however, that there is anything peculiarly Christian or even religious about it. It isn't even true. It does nonetheless seem to possess an enormous power to stir the soul of intellectuals and to stoke the fires of moral indignation.[58] That is probably enough to guarantee it many more years of vigorous life.

---

the situation which would result if every adult were granted the power to work physical miracles, and could bring about any desired physical result simply by wishing, thus eliminating all problems of production and distribution. Problems of associative life would then arise only in the other two of the three main forms of interest and activity we have recognized, i.e., in play and culture. But without some revolutionary change in human nature, conflicts in these fields would be fully as acute as those to which economic interests give rise, and they would not be essentially different in form. It is probable that the necessity of economic activity and co-operation actually reduces social conflict on the whole. Man is by nature self-assertive and competitive, and is also disposed to gang up in conflicts and contests, whether or not any real advantage is at stake." From Frank H. Knight and Thornton W. Merriam, *The Economic Order and Religion* (1945), p. 99.

58. An excellent example is provided by Knight's collaborator in *The Economic Order and Religion*, Thornton Merriam. See especially his chapter on "Economic Intentions of Christianity," pp. 190–205.

CHAPTER 13

Clerical Laissez-Faire: A Case Study in Theological Ethics

IN A RECENT ESSAY on the evolution of Roman Catholic social thought in the United States, James V. Schall laments his church's failure to take seriously the productive achievements of the American economy. He writes:

[I]n the one country wherein we might expect the most enthusiastic and enterprising efforts to relate productive economy to Christian ideas, namely in the United States, with rare exceptions, we do not find in the literature much attention to the extraordinary historical accomplishment of creating a system whereby the physical toil of man and vast natural energies of the earth could be so interrelated that what Pius XI called "a higher level of prosperity and culture" could be conceivable for all of mankind. Attention has been focused almost invariably upon abuses rather than on the essence of the system itself, what makes it productive for a whole society, what makes it grow, what makes it open to correction. There has been very little original thinking by the American Church about its own system precisely in the context of those values religion constantly announces it stands for—those

Reprinted from *Religion, Economics, and Social Thought*, ed. W. Block and I. Hexham (Vancouver: The Fraser Institute, 1985), 125–52, by permission of The Fraser Institute. First draft presented at a Liberty Fund/Fraser Institute conference on "Religion, Economics, and Social Thought," directed by Walter Block, Paul Heyne, and A. M. C. Waterman in Vancouver, British Columbia, 2–4 August 1982.

of justice, rights, growth, aid to the poor, quality of life, ownership, dignity of work, and widespread distribution.[1]

A similar statement could not be made about Protestant Christianity in America, at least not by anyone familiar with its nineteenth century history. Protestant clergymen played a prominent part in the early teaching of economics in the United States, especially prior to the Civil War, and their doctrines generally lauded the productive as well as the moral virtues of the American economy. The Rev. John McVickar of Columbia University, a contender for the title of first academic economist in the United States,[2] was expressing the general conviction of nineteenth century clerical economists when he attributed the rapid advance of the United States in wealth and civilization largely to her respect for the divinely ordained laws of morality and political economy. These laws called for individual responsibility, private property, and minimal government intervention in the economy.[3] This position acquired almost axiomatic status in the second quarter of the nineteenth century among clerical economists, prompting the historian Henry F. May to speak of "a school of political economy which might well be labeled clerical *laissez-faire*."[4]

What exactly did these theological economists teach? On what were their doctrines based? And what was the fate of these doctrines? Those are the questions to which this paper is addressed.

1. James V. Schall, "Catholicism and the American Experience," *This World* (Winter/ Spring 1982), p. 8.

2. Edwin R. A. Seligman conferred this distinction on McVickar in "Economics in the United States: An Historical Sketch," reprinted in his *Essays in Economics* (1925), p. 137. Michael J. L. O'Connor, in the course of surveying existing literature on the origins of American economics, has shown that McVickar's title is open to challenge. O'Connor, *Origins of Academic Economics in the United States* (1944), pp. 6–18.

3. "That science and religion eventually teach the same lesson, is a necessary consequence of the unity of truth, but it is seldom that this union is so early and so satisfactorily displayed as in the researches of Political Economy." John McVickar, *Outlines of Political Economy: Being a Republication of the Article upon that Subject [by J. R. McCulloch] Contained in the Edinburgh Supplement to the Encyclopedia Britannica, together with Notes Explanatory and Critical, and a Summary of the Science* (1825), p. 69. See also McVickar's notes on pp. 88, 102–3, and 159–60 and his Concluding Remarks on pp. 186–88.

4. Henry F. May, *Protestant Churches and Industrial America* (1949), p. 14.

Francis Wayland, 1796–1865

The most influential member of the school of clerical *laissez-faire* was Francis Wayland, author of *The Elements of Political Economy*, first published in 1837. Michael J. L. O'Connor, in an exhaustive examination of the origins of economic instruction in the United States, says that Wayland's *Elements* "achieved more fully than any other textbook what appear to have been the ideals of the clerical school." [5] It also achieved, in its original version and in the abridged version published for secondary school use, immediate and widespread adoption; it was by far the most popular political economy textbook prior to the Civil War. Even after its sales declined in the 1860s, its influence continued to be exerted through adaptations and imitations. Because of the authority and prestige that Wayland commanded as clergyman, educator, and moral philosopher as well as author and teacher in the field of political economy, I will use him as a paradigm case in exploring the origins, nature, and eventual fate of "clerical *laissez-faire*." [6]

The basic facts of Wayland's life may be quickly sketched. He was born in New York City in 1796 of devout Baptist parents, who had migrated from England in 1793. His father set himself up in business as a currier, became a deacon in his church, received a license as a lay preacher in 1805, and by 1807 had given up his business to become a full-time minister. Francis entered Union College in 1811 as a sophomore, graduated in 1813, and began the study of medicine. About the time he completed his medical studies, Wayland experienced a deep religious renewal and decided to study for the ministry. He entered Andover Seminary in 1816, but left after one year, because of severely straitened circumstances, to accept an appointment as tutor at Union College. In 1821 he was called to the First Baptist Church in Boston and ordained as a minister. In 1826 Wayland accepted an

---

5. O'Connor, *op. cit.*, p. 189.

6. Charles Dunbar, in a centennial review of "Economic Science in America, 1776–1876," mentioned "President Wayland's book" as "the only general treatise of the period which can fairly be said to have survived to our day." Charles Franklin Dunbar, *Economic Essays*, edited by O. M. W. Sprague (1904), p. 12. Joseph Dorfman devotes a chapter to "The School of Wayland" in *The Economic Mind in American Civilization*, Vol. II (1946), pp. 758–71. John Roscoe Turner's 1921 essay on *The Ricardian Rent Theory in Early American Economics* states: "[Wayland's] *Elements of Political Economy* (1837) was, as a text, the best work previous to the Civil War, and probably as popular as any American text on this subject. It survives, and is used as a text in some places to this day." p. 61.

offer to return to Union College as a professor of moral philosophy. Before he had moved his family from Boston, however, he received news of his election as President of Brown University, a Baptist institution. Wayland took up his duties in Providence in 1827. He exerted enormous influence on Brown and on American higher education generally until his resignation in 1855. After a vigorous "retirement" devoted to preaching, teaching, writing, and active work on behalf of a variety of social causes, Wayland died in 1865.[7]

Wayland introduced the study of political economy and took on the duty of teaching it soon after assuming the presidency of Brown University in 1827, at the age of 31. In church-related colleges in the first half of the nineteenth century, it was generally the president's prerogative to teach moral philosophy to the senior class, and political economy was considered a branch of moral philosophy. The only training in the subject required of a teacher or author was the sort of philosophical background that a well-educated clergyman would be assumed to possess.[8]

In the preface to his *Elements of Political Economy*, Wayland wrote:

When the author's attention was first directed to the Science of Political Economy, he was struck with the simplicity of its principles, the extent of its generalizations, and the readiness with which its facts seemed capable of being brought into natural and methodical arrangement.[9]

Moreover:

The principles of Political Economy are so closely analogous to those of Moral Philosophy, that almost every question in the one, may be argued on grounds belonging to the other.[10]

7. See *A Memoir of the Life and Labors of Francis Wayland, D.D., L.L.D.*, assembled and written by his sons Francis Wayland and H. L. Wayland, originally published in two volumes in 1867 and reprinted in a single bound volume by Arno Press in 1972.

8. Gladys Bryson, "The Emergence of the Social Sciences from Moral Philosophy," *International Journal of Ethics* (April 1932), pp. 304–12.

9. Francis Wayland, *The Elements of Political Economy*, p. iii. All page references will be to the 1857 edition (Boston: Gould and Lincoln).

10. *Ibid.*, p. iv.

Tariffs

Wayland nonetheless promised not to intermingle the principles of these two disciplines in his textbook, but rather to argue "economical questions on merely economical grounds." He offered the issue of protective tariffs by way of illustration.

> [I]t is frequently urged, that, if a contract have been made by the government with the manufacturer, that contract is morally binding. This, it will be perceived, is a question of Ethics, and is simply the question, whether men are or are not morally bound to fulfill their contracts. With this question, Political Economy has nothing to do. Its only business is, to decide whether a given contract were or were not *wise*. This is the only question, therefore, treated of in the discussion of this subject in the following work.[11]

As we shall see, Wayland did not consistently fulfill this promise. It may be impossible for anyone to maintain a clear distinction between what is moral and what is wise when discussing the organization of economic life. The separation will be especially difficult to maintain if one believes, as Wayland did, that the science of political economy presents the laws to which God has subjected humanity in its pursuit of wealth.

It may be objected, of course, that Wayland was only making a conventional bow to current piety when he referred to the laws which the sciences discover as the laws of God. The *Memoir* published by his sons two years after his death, however, offers persuasive evidence to the contrary. Wayland's religious faith was deeply and sincerely held, and he continually tested his academic labors for conformity to what he perceived as the will of God. The *Memoir* contains extensive excerpts from Wayland's personal journal, and the following extract is quite representative:

> I have thought of publishing a work on moral philosophy. Direct me, O thou all-wise and pure Spirit. Let me not do it unless it be for thy glory and the good of men. If I shall do it, may it all be true, so far as human knowledge at present extends. Enlighten, guide, and teach me so that I may write something which will show thy justice more clearly

11. *Ibid.*

than heretofore, and the necessity and excellence of the plan of salvation by Christ Jesus, the blessed Redeemer. All which I ask through his merits alone. Amen.[12]

Wayland always thought of himself as a theologian first and only secondarily as a moral philosopher or political economist.

The interesting view which Wayland held on the invariability of divine laws almost certainly affected his conclusions in the area of economics. He presents his position near the beginning of his textbook on moral philosophy:

[A]s all relations, whether moral or physical, are the result of this enactment, an order of sequence once discovered in morals, is just as invariable as an order of sequence in physics.

Such being the fact, it is evident, that the moral laws of God can never be varied by the institutions of man, any more than the physical laws. The results which God has connected with actions, will inevitably occur, all the created power in the universe to the contrary notwithstanding. Nor can the consequences be eluded or averted, any more than the sequences which follow by the laws of gravitation.[13]

We should therefore not expect to find in Wayland much sympathy for the idea that different eras, different nations, or different cultures will have their own distinct laws of political economy. Wayland's position is at the opposite pole from the historical relativism imported into American economics from Germany in the last quarter of the nineteenth century.

Wayland's Political Economy

Wayland apparently learned political economy largely by teaching it. He wrote the following, shortly before his death, in a reminiscence reviewing his experience as a teacher:

12. *Memoir*, Vol. I, p. 380.
13. Francis Wayland, *The Elements of Moral Science*, p. 25. The edition used is the 1854 edition (Boston: Gould and Lincoln).

I endeavored always to understand, for myself, whatever I attempted to teach. By this I mean that I was never satisfied with the text, unless I saw for myself, as well as I was able, that the text was true. Pursuing this course, I was led to observe the principles or general truths on which the treatise was founded. As I considered these, they readily arranged themselves in a natural order of connection and dependence. I do not wish to be understood as asserting that I did this with every text-book before I began to use it in my class. I generally taught these subjects during a single year. Before I had thought through one subject, I was called upon to commence another. Yet, with every year, I made some progress in all. I prepared lectures on particular subjects, and thus fixed in my mind the ideas which I had acquired, for use during the next year. The same process continued year by year, and in this manner, almost before I was aware of it, I had completed an entire course of lectures. In process of time I was thus enabled to teach by lecture all the subjects which I began to teach from text-books.[14]

The textbook he used from 1828, when he began teaching the subject to Brown seniors, until 1837, when he published his own text, was J. B. Say's *Treatise on Political Economy,* translated from the fourth French edition and published in the United States in 1821. Since Wayland rarely cites authorities or indicates a source and since the *Memoir* contains only a few paragraphs on the subject of political economy, we have no way of knowing how many other European economists influenced his thinking. We can be fairly certain, however, that he had read extensively in the work that had influenced Say: Adam Smith's *Inquiry into the Nature and Causes of the Wealth of Nations.* Smith is sometimes cited specifically. What is more conclusive, however, is Wayland's use of Smithian classifications, premises, and analyses as well as what might be called a Smithian "tone" on particular topics.

Wayland's discussion of what governments may do to promote the increase of knowledge, for example, brings immediately to mind the language used by Smith in his section "Of the Expense of the Institutions for the Education of Youth."[15] The causes Wayland lists for differences

14. *Memoir,* Vol. I, p. 233.
15. Wayland, *The Elements of Political Economy,* pp. 128–30; Adam Smith, *An Inquiry into the Nature and Causes of the Wealth of Nations,* Book V, Chapter I, Part III, Article 2d.

in wage rates are Smith's famous five circumstances that explain differ-ences in pecuniary returns.[16] Wayland's extended discussion of money and banks frequently teaches notions that could only have been derived from Adam Smith's fatefully erroneous explanation of the ways in which metal-lic and paper money function in an economy.[17] Wayland's refutation of ar-guments for restrictions on imports reveals the clear influence of Smith's treatment.[18] Though Wayland, unlike Smith, preferred direct to indirect taxes, his analysis shows that he had considered Smith's arguments.[19]

The authority of Adam Smith's ideas must have been increased for Wayland by their embodiment in the "Scottish school" which exercised such powerful influence on American colleges in the late eighteenth and early nineteenth centuries.[20] In his student days at Union College, Wayland studied *The Elements of Criticism* by Lord Kames (Henry Home) and Dugald Stewart's *Elements of the Philosophy of the Human Mind.*[21] When he began teaching at Brown, fifteen years later, he used as texts both these books and also *The Philosophy of Rhetoric* by George Campbell, a member of the fa-mous Aberdeen Philosophical Society.[22] It may also be noted that Wayland greatly admired the Scotch theologian-economist Thomas Chalmers.[23] Chalmers was one of the "heretics" who rejected the "orthodox" position of British classical political economy by asserting the possibility of "general gluts." Wayland's treatment of this topic, under the heading "Stagnation of Business," seems unclear and unsure of itself, a reflection, perhaps, of Chalmers' influence.

Ambivalence was not generally characteristic of Wayland's teachings on the subject of political economy. God had ordained laws governing mo-rality and laws governing the accumulation of wealth, and Wayland did not expect to find contradictions between them. "In political economy as in morals." Wayland insists,

---

16. Wayland, *ibid.*, pp. 311– 13; Smith, *ibid.*, Book I, Chapter X, Part I.

17. Wayland, *ibid.*, pp. 188–288, especially pp. 211–12, 231–32, 259–61, 278–79; Smith, *ibid.*, Book II, Chapter II.

18. Wayland, *ibid.*, pp. 145–51; Smith, *ibid.*, Book IV, Chapter II.

19. Wayland, *ibid.*, pp. 391–97; Smith, *ibid.*, Book V, Chapter II, Part II.

20. Bryson, *op. cit.*, p. 309.

21. *Memoir*, Vol. I, p. 32.

22. *Ibid.*, p. 227.

23. *Ibid.*, Vol. II, pp. 39–40, 289–90.

every benefit is mutual; and we cannot, in the one case, any more than in the other, really do good to ourselves, without doing good to others; nor do good to others, without also doing good to ourselves.[24]

Wayland often pauses to call his reader's attention to the divinely intended harmony in the relations he is describing.

All the forms of industry mutually support, and are supported by, each other;...any jealousy between different classes of producers, or any desire on the one part, to obtain special advantages over the other, are unwise, and, in the end, self-destructive.[25]

Nothing can, therefore, be more unreasonable than the prejudices which sometimes exist between these different classes of laborers, and nothing can be more beautiful, than their harmonious cooperation in every effort to increase production, and thus add to the conveniences and happiness of man.[26]

Trade, especially international trade, is a fulfillment of God's plan for amity:

God intended that men should live together in friendship and harmony. By thus multiplying indefinitely their wants, and creating only in particular localities, the objects by which those wants can be supplied, he intended to make them all necessary to each other; and thus to render it no less the interest, than the duty of everyone, to live in amity with all the rest.[27]

Individuals are thus made dependent upon each other, in order to render harmony, peace, and mutual assistance, their interest as well as their duty....

And, for the same reason, nations are dependent on each other. From this universal dependence, we learn that God intends nations, as well

24. Wayland, *Political Economy*, p. 171.
25. *Ibid.*, p. 46.
26. *Ibid.*, pp. 55–56.
27. *Ibid.*, p. 91.

as individuals, to live in peace, and to conduct themselves towards each other upon the principles of benevolence.[28]

Toward the end of the book, after discussing some common causes of inefficiency, Wayland comments:

We see, in the above remarks, another illustration of the truth, that the benefit of one is the benefit of all, and the injury of one is the injury of all.... [H]e who is honestly promoting his own welfare, is also promoting the welfare of the whole society of which he is a member.[29]

Wayland is so impressed with the mutually beneficial aspects of self-interested behavior that he has trouble recognizing or acknowledging that interests can also conflict. Don't poor harvests in one region cause higher prices and greater prosperity for farmers in other regions? Don't sellers sometimes benefit from the greater scarcity that is caused by the misfortunes of others? Wayland is reluctant to admit this. He appeals to the true but irrelevant argument that sellers benefit from the prosperity of their customers, and applies the label "short sighted, as well as morally thoughtless" to merchants who expect "to grow rich by short crops, civil dissensions, calamity, or war."[30]

Monopoly, from this perspective, is self-defeating. If the agricultural interests of Great Britain had not tried to maintain high prices through the Corn Laws, but had allowed imported grain to lower the price of food, population growth and industrial growth over the most recent fifty years would have more than compensated for the landed proprietors' loss. Wayland concludes a somewhat vague analysis with the observation:

If this be so, it is another illustration of the universal law, that a selfish policy always in the end defeats itself; and reaps its full share of the gratuitous misery which it inflicts upon others.[31]

28. *Ibid.*, pp. 159–60.
29. *Ibid.*, p. 378.
30. *Ibid.*, pp. 176–77.
31. *Ibid.*, pp. 343–44.

Wayland on the Relation Between Economics and Morality

The essential unity that Wayland saw between the laws of political economy and the laws of morality emerges most clearly in his chapter "Of the Laws Which Govern the Application of Labour to Capital."

Section 1 of the chapter explains how the laws on this subject are founded on "the conditions of our being," conditions that Wayland summarizes in seven paragraphs.[32]

1. God has created man with faculties adapted to physical and intellectual labour.
2. God has made labour necessary to the attainment of the means of happiness.
3. We are so constituted that physical and intellectual labour are essential to health. Idiocy or madness is the consequence of intellectual sloth; feebleness, enervation, pain, and disease appear in the absence of physical labour.
4. Labour is pleasant, or at least less painful than idleness. People crave challenges on which to exercise their faculties.
5. God has attached special penalties to idleness, such as ignorance, poverty, cold, hunger, and nakedness.
6. God has assigned rich and abundant rewards to industry.

Wayland's seventh paragraph draws the conclusion: We are required "so to construct the arrangements of society, as to give free scope to the laws of Divine Providence." We must "give to these rewards and penalties their free and their intended operation." We are bound, at the very least, to try these means first if we want to stimulate economic growth, and to avoid other policies "until these have been tried and found ineffectual." Everyone should be "permitted to enjoy, in the most unlimited manner, the advantages of labour," and all should suffer the consequences of their own idleness.

In Section II Wayland explains what is required if each is to enjoy, in the greatest degree, the advantages of his labor.

32. *Ibid.*, pp. 105–8.

It is necessary, provided always he do not violate the rights of his neighbor, 1st, *That he be allowed to gain all that he can;* and, 2d, *That, having gained all that he can, he be allowed to use it as he will.*[33]

The first condition can be achieved by abolishing common property and assigning all property to specific individuals. These individually-held property rights must then be enforced against potential violation either by individuals or by society. Individual violations are held in check through the inculcation of moral and religious principles—the most certain and necessary method of preventing violations—and through equitable laws firmly and faithfully applied. Violations by society, through arbitrary confiscation, unjust legislation, or oppressive taxation, are more destructive than individual violations, because they inflict wrong through an agency that was created for the sole purpose of preventing wrong and thereby they dissolve the society itself. The best preventative is an elevated intellectual and moral character among the people and a constitution which guarantees immunity from public as well as from private oppression.[34]

The second condition is achieved when individuals are allowed to use their labor and their capital as they please, without legislative interference, so long as they respect the rights of others.[35]

In Section III Wayland shows what must be done to make sure that everyone "suffers the inconveniences of idleness." If the dishonest acquisition of property is prevented "by the strict and impartial administration of just and equitable laws," then, in a regime of private property, "the indolent" will be left "to the consequences which God has attached to their conduct.... they must obey the law of their nature, and labour, or else suffer the penalty and starve." [36]

What about charity? Where people are poor because "God has seen fit to take away the power to labour," God has also commanded generosity on the part of those who have wealth to bestow. But no one is entitled to support merely by virtue of being poor, and institutions that provide relief to the indigent without any labor requirement are "injurious."

33. *Ibid.*, p. 108.
34. *Ibid.*, pp. 109–13.
35. *Ibid.*, pp. 113–18.
36. *Ibid.*, p. 119.

Dependency

Poor laws violate "the fundamental law of government, that he who is able to labour, shall enjoy only that for which he has laboured." By removing the fear of want, they reduce the stimulus to labor and the amount of product created. By teaching people to depend on others, they create a perpetual pauper class. This process, once initiated, grows progressively. Eventually it destroys the right of property itself by teaching the indolent that they have a right to be supported and the rich that they have an obligation to provide that support. Poor laws thereby foster class conflict.[37]

In cases where a person has been reduced, by indolence or prodigality, to such poverty that he is in danger of starving, he should be "furnished with work, and be remunerated with the proceeds."[38]

Section IV explains how the accumulation of capital increases the demand for labor and the rate of wages. Section V argues for "universal dissemination of the means of education and the principles of religion" on the grounds that intellectual cultivation and high moral character among a people promote prosperity.[39]

In Section VI Wayland reluctantly takes up "bounties and protecting duties, as a means of increasing production." His reluctance is due to his inability to discover how they can produce this effect; but he knows that popular opinion holds otherwise and so he cannot pass the subject by in silence. After presenting a careful and quite classical criticism of such measures on economic grounds,[40] Wayland raises the moral question: *By what right* does society interfere in this way with the property of the individual, and without offering compensation? He declines to answer, however, on the grounds that this question belongs not to political economy but to moral philosophy; but he clearly thinks that no satisfactory answer can be given to his essentially rhetorical question.[41]

After stating and criticizing, again in an orthodox classical manner, the arguments in favor of legislative stimulus to industry, Wayland raises

37. *Ibid.*, pp. 119–20.
38. *Ibid.*, p. 122.
39. *Ibid.*, pp. 123–32.
40. *Ibid.*, pp. 133–40.
41. *Ibid.*, pp. 140–41.

the Smithian question of whether it is not unjust for a government to abolish a restrictive system upon which people have come to depend. "To this objection," he says,

> I have no desire to make any reply. It is a question of morals and not of political economy. Whatever the government has directly or indirectly pledged itself to do, it is bound to do. But this has nothing to do with the question of the expediency, or inexpediency, of its having, in the first instance, thus bound itself; nor with the question whether it be not expedient to change its system as fast as it may be able to do so, consistently with its moral obligations.[42]

The section and chapter conclude with a brief account of what governments *can* do to promote industry and increase production. They can enact and enforce equitable laws; promote education and learning; manage strictly experimental farms and manufactures; and above all:

> They can do much by confining themselves to their own appropriate duties, and leaving every-thing else alone. The interference of society with the concerns of the individual, even when arising from the most innocent motives, will always tend to crush the spirit of enterprise, and cripple the productive energies of a country. What shall we say, then, when the capital and the labour of a nation are made the sport of party politics; and when the power over them, which a government possesses, is abused, for the base purpose of ministering to schemes of political intrigue?[43]

Wayland was not, strictly speaking, an advocate of *laissez-faire*. As we have just seen, he supported government-sponsored industrial research, and he believed that what economists today call "externalities" justified government efforts to increase and disseminate knowledge.[44] He argues

42. *Ibid.*, p. 151.
43. *Ibid.*, p. 152.
44. *Ibid.*, p. 128. For his views on how government should offer financial assistance to education, see pp. 399–403.

that religious institutions also confer benefits upon the state and upon people who have not contributed to their support; but he refuses to draw the conclusion that this entitles religious institutions to a share of the funds from public taxation.[45] He doubts that public funds ought to be used to finance most internal improvements, such as roads, canals, or railroads; these are better left to individual enterprise, which will undertake them when they are profitable and leave them alone when they are not. There will be exceptions, however, such as works of exceptional magnitude or where the public importance of the work is too great for it to be entrusted to private corporations. Works for the improvement of external commerce, such as the improvement of coasts and harbors, are assigned entirely to government.[46]

The relief of the sick, destitute, and helpless is a religious duty, in Wayland's view, and for that reason ought to be left to voluntary efforts. He recognized, however, that purely voluntary relief would occasionally be inadequate and might in addition strain the resources of the most charitable. So he was willing to allow some provision out of tax revenues "for the relief of those whom old age, or infancy, or sickness, has deprived of the power of providing the means necessary for sustenance." For the sake of these people themselves, as well as for the sake of the economy, relief should be provided in return for labor in the case of all those capable of work.[47]

Wayland's Theological Economics

American economists of this period, unlike their European counterparts, were not much concerned with the Malthusian problem.[48] Wayland was no exception. Near the beginning of his chapter on wages, he takes up the possibility that human beings will reproduce too rapidly for the real wage-rate to be maintained above the subsistence level. This does occur,

---

45. *Ibid.*, pp. 403–4.
46. *Ibid.*, pp. 184–86. 404–5.
47. *Ibid.*, p. 405.
48. George Johnson Cady, "The Early American Reaction to the Theory of Malthus," *Journal of Political Economy* (October 1931), pp. 601–32.

he asserts, and the consequences are "painful to contemplate." But after quoting Adam Smith on the high infant mortality rates in the Scottish Highlands and in military barracks, Wayland abruptly changes direction.

God could scarcely have intended so many to die in infancy from hardship and want. It therefore follows that the normal wage level for industrious, virtuous, and frugal workers will be one "which allows of the rearing of such a number of children as naturally falls to the lot of the human race." Improvidence, indolence, intemperance, and profligacy can interfere with this happy outcome; but in such cases "the correction must come, not from a change in wages, but from a change in habits." [49]

It is at first difficult to reconcile this position with Wayland's explanation of how the supply of labor adjusts itself to the demand, or his account of the relationship between the growth of capital and the growth of population. His conclusion to the latter discussion is especially puzzling:

And hence, there seems no need of any other means to prevent the too rapid increase of population, than to secure a correspondent increase of capital, by which that population may be supported. [50]

The clear implication is that, unless God intended many to perish in infancy, capital can always and everywhere be accumulated at least as fast as the population chooses to expand.

Wayland has an escape from this strong implication, however. God is not responsible for evil that is the consequence of immoral behavior, and the rate of capital accumulation is crucially dependent upon moral considerations. Frugality increases it, prodigality diminishes it, laws of entail diminish it, as do all restrictive laws that "fetter and dispirit industry." Above all, however, war diminishes the rate of capital accumulation:

If the capital which a bountiful Creator has provided for the sustenance of man, be dissipated in wars, his creatures must perish from the want of it. Nor do we need any abstruse theories of population, to

49. Wayland, *Political Economy*, pp. 293–94.
50. *Ibid.*, p. 305.

enable us to ascertain in what manner this excess of population may be prevented. Let nations cultivate the arts of peace.[51]

In a properly ordered society of moral persons, capital accumulation will be adequate for the number of people and "we shall hear no more of the evils of excess of population."[52]

This analysis still leaves room for paupers to blame their plight upon others, albeit immoral others. Wayland closes that door with the claim that almost all crime and pauperism in the community is caused by intemperance, and the further claim that America, which has few beggars, would have none at all if intemperance and vice were eliminated.

Wage Determination

The laws that regulate wage-rates are finally beyond the power of individual capitalists or laborers to affect. The competition that will naturally exist where there are no restrictions on the mobility of capital or labor will "bring wages to their proper level; that is, to all that can be reasonably paid for them." Combinations among capitalists or workers designed to raise or lower wage-rates are "useless," Wayland asserts, because combinations cannot change the laws by which remuneration is governed. Without pausing to defend this *non sequitur,* he hastens to add that combinations are also expensive, because they expose capital and labor to long periods of idleness. And combinations are unjust, because they deprive the capitalist of the right to employ labor and workers of the right to be employed on terms to which the parties have freely agreed. Is this another case where moral philosophy has crowded out economic analysis? The injustice of a particular combination does not guarantee that the combination will be unable to increase the wealth of those who participate in it.

Wayland has the same sort of difficulty when he tries to explain why political economy finds laws regulating interest rates "injurious to the prosperity of a country." His first reason is that such laws violate the right of property. One could make this an "economical" rather than an ethical

51. *Ibid.,* pp. 305–7.
52. *Ibid.,* p. 308.

argument by incorporating into it Wayland's case for the dependence of prosperity on respect for property rights. If this is done, however, the distinction between questions of right and questions of expediency collapses.

The point here is not that Wayland *ought* to have maintained a clear distinction between economic and ethical arguments, but rather that he claimed to be doing so when in fact he was not. The nature of his argument is consequently obscured at important points, and the critical reader is left uncertain about the kind of evidence and arguments that would be required to buttress or to refute his conclusions.

What evidence and arguments are we supposed to consider in evaluating Wayland's claim that labor expended in the creation of a value gives one an exclusive right to the possession of that value? Or his claim that different laborers are "entitled" to dissimilar wages? Or that the liability of *all* property to depreciate in value must be taken into account when estimating the job-destroying effects of machinery? That "the act of creating a value appropriates it to a possessor" and "this right of property is *exclusive*"? That a college graduate is "fairly entitled" to a wage that will compensate him not only for the cost of his education but also for the forgone interest on the amount invested? That the capitalist comes into the market "on equal terms" with the laborer because "each needs the product of the other"? Or that the capitalist "may justly demand" a greater interest the greater his risk?[53]

Incorrect Generalization

At one point in *The Elements of Political Economy* Wayland finds it "worthy of remark" that human ingenuity has done more to increase "the productiveness of labour" in manufacturing and in transportation than in agriculture. A generalization of that kind presupposes the solution of some rather formidable problems of definition as well as measurement. What is the common denominator in terms of which one can meaningfully compare rates of productivity growth when it is the *usefulness* of diverse products that matters? But Wayland is sure that his generalization is correct, sure enough to add these comments:

53. *Ibid.*, pp. 19, 26, 98–99, 154, 297, 301, 320.

It is, doubtless, wisely ordered that it be so. Agricultural labor is the most healthy employment, and is attended by the fewest temptations. It has, therefore, seemed to be the will of the Creator that a large portion of the human race should always be thus employed, and that, whatever effects may result from social improvement, the proportion of men required for tilling the earth should never be essentially diminished.[54]

Francis Wayland apparently misread "the will of the Creator": in the United States today fewer than 3 percent of the workforce are employed in agriculture. The error in this case may be unimportant, but the problem to which it points is not. Those who look for the will of God behind concrete social arrangements thereby incur an added risk of failing to perceive the social arrangements correctly. Those who concern themselves too quickly with the moral implications of social interactions may become less able to see how those interactions are evolving. And an empirical proposition that supports an important theological or moral conviction can become extraordinarily resistant to anything as inconsequential as empirical evidence and argument.

The Reaction Against "Clerical *Laissez-Faire*"

Twenty years after Wayland's death and half a century after publication of his textbook on political economy, many influential thinkers and writers still maintained that economics and religion were and ought to be intimately linked. When the American Economic Association was formed in 1885, Protestant clergymen were prominent among its founders. The dominant figure in the organization of the Association was Richard T. Ely, a young economist who insisted upon the necessity of basing economics upon ethics and who wanted to make applied Christianity the foundation of economic reform. Religious impulses played such an open and major role in the Association's early history that even sympathetic participants believed it might be interfering with the scholarly impartiality essential to a scientific body.[55]

54. *Ibid.,* pp. 47–48.
55. For an excellent and fairly recent survey of these events, see A. W. Coats, "The First Two Decades of the American Economic Association" *(American Economic Review,*

The banner under which they organized, however, was decidedly not one behind which Wayland could have marched. The prospectus which Ely sent out in his call for the organization of the American Economic Association included a four-part platform. The first paragraph read as follows:

> We regard the state as an educational and ethical agency whose positive aid is an indispensable condition of social progress. While we recognize the necessity of individual initiative in industrial life, we hold that the doctrine of *laissez-faire* is unsafe in politics and unsound in morals; and that it suggests an inadequate explanation of the relations between the state and the citizens.[56]

The laws of God, which ordained a minimal role for government in economic life according to Wayland, required a vast extension of state activity according to Ely. How did Ely and his associates justify this remarkable about-face? How did they criticize the theological-ethical arguments that had been advanced by Wayland and his school and which were still being taught in the 1880s by prominent academics? The answer is that they did not attempt to do so.

Conflict

The most prominent exponent of "clerical *laissez-faire*" in the 1880s was probably the Reverend Arthur Latham Perry, professor of history and political economy at Williams College, author of several widely used textbooks in economics, and trusted adviser of government officials.[57] Moreover, Perry attacked Ely by name in his *Principles of Political Economy* for urging that government take a hand in the determination of wages. "The fine old Bentham principle of *laissez-faire*," Perry wrote,

> which most English thinkers for a century past have regarded as established forever in the nature of man and in God's plans of providence

---

September 1960), p. 555–74. Joseph Dorfman probably offers the best general introduction to the period in *The Economic Mind in American Civilization*, Vol. III (1949), pp. 113–212.

56. Ely reproduced the prospectus in his autobiography, *Ground Under Our Feet* (1938), p. 136.

57. Dorfman, *op. cit.*, Vol. III, pp. 56–63; O'Connor, *op. cit.*, pp. 265–66.

and government, is gently tossed by Dr. Ely into the wilds of Australian barbarism.

> There are some propositions that are *certainly* true, and one of them is,
> that no man can write like that, who ever analyzed into their elements
> either Economics or Politics.[58]

Ely was not one to steer clear of conflict. He often responded to his
critics, and he took the lead in the 1880s in attacking the "old school" of
political economy. Moreover, ethical and religious premises consistently
played a large part in the arguments he advanced on behalf of a reconstruction of economics. Nonetheless, he never attempted a systematic critique of the theological-ethical claims of his opponents or tried to show
in what specific ways his own theological-ethical premises were more
adequate. His fundamental contentions were that the "old school" relied
upon an obsolete deductive method, that it employed much too narrow a
conception of economic science, and that it refused to take account of the
results of historical research.[59]

Charles Howard Hopkins, in his history of the Social Gospel in American Protestantism, writes:

> The first advocates of social Christianity subjected the presuppositions
> of classical economic theory to searching criticism. They regarded un-
> restricted competition as an arrogant contradiction of Christian ethics
> and the inhuman treatment accorded the laborer as a violation of fun-
> damental Protestant conceptions of the nature of man.[60]

But condemnations of unrestricted competition or inhuman treatment
of laborers do not constitute a criticism of classical economic theory.

---

58. Arthur Latham Perry, *Principles of Political Economy* (1891), pp. 251–52.

59. See especially Ely's contributions to the 1886 exchanges in *Science* between the
"old" and the "new" sciences of political economy: Ely, "Economics and Ethics," *Science*
(June 11, 1886), pp. 529–33; "The Economic Discussion in *Science*," *ibid*. (July 2, 1886), pp.
3–6 (a rejoinder to Simon Newcomb); and his reply to a negative review by N[icholas]
M[urray] B[utler] of his book *The Labor Movement in America, ibid*. (October 29, 1886),
pp. 388–89. For Ely's comments on Perry, see *Ground Under Our Feet*, pp. 127–28.

60. Charles Howard Hopkins, *The Rise of the Social Gospel in American Protestantism,
1865–1915* (1940), p. 25.

Hopkins refers to an 1866 article by George N. Boardman as "one of the most searching utterances of its kind in this period." [61] It may be unfair to take this compliment too seriously, especially since Henry F. May finds Boardman's essay "generally in support of contemporary economic theories." But the fact remains that Boardman's critique is far from searching; that it does not show a wide acquaintance with the literature it purports to discuss; and that the religious critics of "unrestricted capitalism" in the last part of the nineteenth century did not really address the arguments that had been advanced by Wayland or his successors. Neither the economists like Ely nor the clergymen—Washington Gladden, W. D. P. Bliss, and George Herron are more representative figures than Boardman— take the claims of the "clerical *laissez-faire*" school seriously and respond to them.[62]

Refutation?

These views, of course, have been widely repudiated, both in the 1880s and in our own time. But repudiation is not the same as refutation. Contemporary critics have generally assumed that to refute such views as Wayland's it was enough to describe them. Thus Henry F. May, after quoting Wayland on the divine imperative to labor, says: "From this simple proposition Wayland deduced the whole platform of the New England mercantile interest." A page later he refers to Wayland as one of the "simple dogmatists of the thirties and forties [who] set the tone of American political economy for many years to come." May also speaks of "the pat theories of Francis Wayland," his "all-sufficient optimistic formulae," and his "simple, dogmatic method." [63] Simple dogmatisms, pat theories, and all-sufficient optimistic formulae don't have to be taken seriously, especially if they are in reality a defense of special interests rather than an honest effort toward understanding.

One problem with this approach is that it works equally well when ap-

61. George N. Boardman, "Political Economy and the Christian Ministry," *Bibliotheca Sacra* (January 1866), pp. 73–107; Hopkins, *ibid.*

62. The best survey of this literature with which I am familiar, covering both the social gospel and the "new" political economy, is that of Sidney Fine, *Laissez Faire and the General-Welfare State: A Study of Conflict in American Thought, 1865–1901* (1956), pp. 167–251.

63. May, *op. cit.*, pp. 15, 16, 91, 111, 141.

plied to the simple dogmatisms, pat theories, and all-sufficient optimistic formulae of Richard Ely and the clergymen who responded so enthusiastically to his call for organization of the American Economic Association. Consider the conclusions of John Rutherford Everett, at the end of his sympathetic study of the relation between religion and economics in the work of Ely and two of his prominent collaborators in the founding of the American Economic Association, John Bates Clark and Simon Patten:

> They are to be criticized ... for falling into the easy optimism of the nineteenth century progressivist thought. Although the excuse might be found in their unwitting correlation of moral and material progress, the error is nonetheless grievous.... Certainly any perfectionist doctrine of sanctification has ample historical and contemporary disproof....
>
> Patten's analysis of selfishness as a result of deficit economics is superficial to the point of foolishness....
>
> It certainly looks as though the solution to the economic problem offered by these men is nothing short of "social magic." [64]

Moreover, many of the "empirical" conclusions wielded with such assurance by Ely and his colleagues in the 1880s now seem quite as *a priori* as the deductive theories they condemned. And their confident assumption that they were the "new" and "scientific" school of political economy destined to control the future looks almost pathetic in hindsight; most of them seem to have been completely unaware in the 1880s of the "marginal revolution" taking place at that very time, through which "abstract-deductive" economics would acquire a renewed and more powerful hold on the discipline.

"Clerical School"

It would be unfair to fault May too severely, since his understanding of "clerical *laissez-faire*" and Francis Wayland was derived from the scholarly

---

64. John Rutherford Everett, *Religion in Economics* (1946), pp. 143–44.

work of Joseph Dorfman and Michael J. L. O'Connor. Dorfman's *The Economic Mind in American Civilization* is the indispensable source for anyone interested in American economics in the nineteenth century. O'Connor's investigation of *The Origins of Academic Economics,* May's principal source, is actually an examination of the origins and rise to prominence in the northeastern United States of what O'Connor called the "clerical school." As such it was especially useful to someone like May who was interested in Protestant analyses of economic issues but was not himself an historian of economics. The biases of both authors ought to be kept in mind, however, by anyone using their work.

Dorfman tends to present economic theory as a reflection of the theorists' social circumstances, with the result that arguments are sometimes not so much explained as explained away. This tendency is especially marked in the case of early economists with whose policy positions Dorfman is not in sympathy. That would emphatically include Francis Wayland, whose treatment by Dorfman comes close to cynicism.

In the ten pages he devotes to "The Reverend Francis Wayland: Ideal Textbook Writer," Dorfman tells us that Wayland studied at Union College under "the famous Reverend Eliphalet Nott, who was highly successful in acquiring a fortune for himself, in obtaining funds from the New York legislature for the college, and in teaching students the ways of God and the world." He states that Wayland received at Union "a thorough indoctrination in the Common Sense philosophy." He sketches Wayland's changes in vocational plans in a way that suggests flightiness or instability. He tells us that Wayland "took an active interest in all the movements that a respectable person should" after becoming President of Brown. His account of Wayland's position on slavery is highly misleading and seems designed to discredit Wayland rather than to present his actual views. The same might be said of his sketch of Wayland's position on the wage-fund doctrine. Dorfman seems almost to postulate bad faith and apologetic intent, as in the claim: "As the cry for tariffs and government relief became more insistent with every depression, Wayland became increasingly adept at mollifying the one and denying the other." [65] The reader would never

---

65. *Ibid.,* Vol. II, pp. 758–67. Dorfman's treatment of the slavery issue should be compared with Wayland's *Elements of Moral Science,* pp. 206–16. Dorfman accords John McVickar, the other leading clerical economist of this period, a similar treatment: *Ibid.,* pp. 515–22, 713–20.

suspect, for example, that Francis Wayland taught pacifism in his textbook on moral philosophy, raising *and rejecting* each of the standard arguments by which traditional ethical thought had attempted to exempt national governments from the prohibition against returning evil with evil.[66] Dorfman's *ad hominem* arguments are not only irrelevant but also often unfair and occasionally even false, or at least as false as innuendo can ever be.

Omission

May's principal source, however, was O'Connor's meticulously researched *Origins of Academic Economics in the United States*. Because Wayland's *Elements of Political Economy* was the most important text to emerge from the "clerical school," O'Connor presents its contents in some detail. The account is careful and balanced; but there is no systematic criticism of Wayland's economics. The reason for this omission emerges in the concluding chapter, where O'Connor lays out the lessons he would have the reader draw from his study.

The clerical school of political economy, according to O'Connor, was the social instrument of the northeastern merchant-capitalist elite, valuable to them because it taught an ideology that was useful in countering populist political pressures. These religious economists, in supporting the theory of automatic natural-law control, were in reality endorsing the social power of the merchant-capitalist groups and making it easier for that class to enjoy its privileges with a clear conscience. The clerical economists were rewarded with financial aid for the institutions they headed. Their influence lasted well into the twentieth century because cultural lag is so prominent among academics, and because they are willing to use textbooks for sixty or seventy years. The time has now come, however, to purge this obsolete but lingering ideology from economics courses and textbooks and to create a new economics that will "reflect the current social forces of the country" and enable these social forces "to play as directly as possible upon the introductory courses."[67]

In short, there is little point in criticizing Wayland or other representa-

66. Wayland, *The Elements of Moral Science*, pp. 390–95.
67. O'Connor, *op. cit.*, pp. 277–89.

tives of clerical *laissez-faire* because their economics merely reflected their objective social position. The task now is not to construct an economics that will more adequately explain social reality, but to construct a system of economic education that will "command the faith of the people." O'Connor concludes:

> If cultural lags, economic barriers, and vested minority interests prevent such adjustments, the result may be that popular disillusionment which in a democracy leads to social disintegration.[68]

If what purports to be "pure" economic theory can so easily be dismissed by critics as ideology, what fate awaits an economics that is explicitly theological? O'Connor may be extreme in his willingness to reduce social theory to class-based ideology; but he is probably representative in his reluctance to take seriously any theological-ethical justification or defense of a social system of which he disapproves.

Conclusion

This paper began with James Schall's comment on the church's failure to relate Christian ideas to the productive achievements of capitalism. After examining one major effort to do exactly this, we find ourselves wondering at the end what worthwhile purpose it serves. Does theological economics do anything more than polarize discussion? Those who already approve a particular economic system are generally pleased to read arguments showing that the system is also superior by theological and ethical criteria. Those who disapprove of the system are much less likely even to read a theological-ethical defense of it, and the likelihood is still less that they will read it fairly and sympathetically.

Theological economics or economic theology seems to possess a powerful capacity for turning conjectures into convictions and for making the rejection of favored hypotheses seem like moral cowardice. Significant issues that could be illuminated or even resolved by careful empirical inquiry are instead "settled" on the basis of what fits most comfortably

68. *Ibid.*, p. 289.

into the system. That healthy suspicion of one's own argument which is always difficult to keep alive when one is working toward a thesis seems almost impossible to maintain in theological economics. Even more serious is the tendency of those who practice theological economics to assess the cogency of their opponents' arguments by attacking imputed (and, of course, assumed) motives. It is so tempting and so easy, when we imagine ourselves to be standing on the high ground of theology or morality, to slander our opponents by accusing them of slander—or other hidden and malicious intent.

The fate of George Gilder's *Wealth and Poverty* strikes me as sadly instructive. Here is a popularly-written but nonetheless serious and well-documented attempt to examine some of the relationships between economic behavior and religious beliefs. The book deserves the careful attention of any American who is both concerned for the health of the United States economy and convinced that an adequate economic system must satisfy important ethical criteria. The point is not that Gilder is correct: it is rather that he has raised most of the important questions in a careful and responsible way, citing his evidence and spelling out his reasoning. The sadly instructive fact is that his argument for the moral merits of capitalism has not been taken seriously by the moral critics of capitalism within the churches. The book has hardly been reviewed in the religious press. Where it is mentioned, it is usually caricatured, with some such phrase as "a bible for those who have recently come to make absolute claims for private enterprise." [69]

There is little to be learned from those who make absolute claims about economic systems, and even less to be learned from those who imagine that a caricature constitutes a rebuttal.

---

69. The phrase is from John C. Bennett's lecture on "Reaganethics," reprinted in *Christianity and Crisis* (December 14, 1981), p. 340.

PART 5

On Teaching and Learning

CHAPTER 14

"The Nature of Man": What Are We After?

A UNIVERSITY is a place where all knowledge is divided into equal segments, each offering three hours of credit. These segments are controlled and dispensed by autonomous divisions within the university known as departments. Departments are dominated by scholars, a term used to describe people who have spent long years and arduous effort acquiring a certificate of competence in one or two of these segments and the privilege of requiring students to attend their lectures. Students are people usually between the ages of seventeen and twenty-two for whom the university is said to exist. It is the duty of a typical student at a typical university to apply himself, over a four-year period, to about forty of these segments. At the end of this time, assuming reasonably faithful application, the student is rewarded with a diploma. The scholars are rewarded with prestige, income and long summer vacations. Departments are rewarded with research funds, additional secretaries and larger offices.

The course upon which you have now embarked, "The Nature of Man," is the product of many factors and many people, but chiefly of a widespread dissatisfaction with the state of affairs caricatured in the preceding paragraph. The old ideal of a liberal education has retreated steadily in the twentieth century under the onslaught of specialized sciences, vocational-

Unpublished typescript of an introductory lecture for a Southern Methodist University course, The Nature of Man, September 1968. Reprinted by permission of Mrs. Juliana Heyne.

ism, the democratic belief that everyone is entitled to an education, and the bureaucratic pressures of a highly organized society. The retreat has at times become a rout.

"The Nature of Man" course is part of a counterattack. One of its aims is to make a beginning at the task of unifying knowledge once more, in keeping with the vision enshrined in the very name *university*. Another aim is revealed in the formal title of the course, Liberal Studies 1303 and 1304. Liberal studies are studies which liberate, which free the mind from the shackles that ignorance imposes.

Does all this sound just a bit utopian? Do you begin to suspect that there may be more hope than substance in the course? If *not,* then take another look at that title: "The Nature of Man." The whole of human nature, in just two of those three-credit segments, suitably distilled for freshmen, is a fairly ambitious goal. If dissatisfaction was the seed-bed in which this course sprouted, naive optimism may well have been the sun and rain that brought it to its present stage.

The course-ridden, artificially segmented, and departmentalized system of education which rules the modern university has at least this to commend it: its courses deal for the most part with well-defined, manageable subject areas, and are taught by people trained to competence in that area. But "the nature of man" is not a manageable topic; the subject area cannot even be adequately defined in two semesters; and there is probably no one on this or any other campus who is really competent to teach a course with that title.

Critics of the course have suggested that "The Nature of Man" has not only failed to achieve a unification of knowledge; it has degenerated at times into a hopeless hodgepodge of disconnected truths, half-truths, and trivia. Others have protested that it has not liberated the mind of the student so much as it has substituted new prejudices for old. Are these criticisms valid?

Let us pass that question and instead ask another. Do these criticisms *have* to be valid? Is "The Nature of Man" course an attainable ideal? The answer might depend upon you.

You are beginning a year-long exploration of a vast and bewildering terrain. "The problem of human nature," Hannah Arendt once wrote, seems unanswerable in both its individual psychological sense and its general philosophical sense. It is highly unlikely that we, who can know, determine, and define the natural essences of all things surrounding us, which we are not, should ever be able to do the same for ourselves—this would be like jumping over our own shadows.[1]

But "jumping over our own shadows" is exactly what we shall try to do. We shall try to understand the nature of a being who tries to understand his own nature. It is a "troublesome prospect," in the words of Michael Polanyi; for we shall "have to go on reflecting ever again on our last reflections, in an endless and futile endeavor to comprise completely the works of man."[2]

But if the terrain is bewildering, it has at least been charted by many hands. Man has always been interested in his own nature, and we are the heirs of centuries of investigation and speculation. The wealth of sources, however, may be more of an embarrassment than a blessing. In his *Essay on Man,* Ernst Cassirer writes:

> No former age was ever in such a favorable position with regard to the sources of our knowledge of human nature. Psychology, ethnology, anthropology, and history have amassed an astoundingly rich and constantly increasing body of facts. Our technical instruments for observation and experimentation have been immensely improved, and our analyses have become sharper and more penetrating. We appear, nevertheless, not yet to have found a method for the mastery and organization of this material. When compared with our own abundance the past seems very poor. But our wealth of facts is not necessarily a wealth of thoughts. Unless we succeed in finding a clue of Ariadne to lead us out of this labyrinth, we can have no real insight into the general character of human culture; we shall remain lost in a mass of disconnected and disintegrated data which seem to lack all conceptual unity.[3]

1. Hannah Arendt, *The Human Condition.*
2. Michael Polanyi, *The Study of Man* (London: Routledge and Paul, 1959), 11.
3. Ernst Cassirer, *An Essay on Man,* 40–41.

Do we have such a clue, such a leading thread? Without some principle of organization we shall certainly be guilty on the first count mentioned above, guilty of introducing more confusion than unity into the student's reflections upon human nature. But there is an equal and opposite danger. Every principle of organization is necessarily exclusive. As Robert Oppenheimer observed shortly before his death, "Every science sees its ideas and order with a sharpness and depth that comes from choice, from exclusion, from its special eyes." Why should we choose one pair of eyes rather than another? Is there any single perspective on man that does not conceal more of importance than it manages to reveal? So the second count of the above indictment also hangs over us: we do not want to substitute one set of prejudices for another, but rather to liberate the mind of the student from the shackles of ignorance.

An excellent illustration of our dilemma is provided by a problem which has plagued a large number of the students who have passed this way before you. The nature of man is a question to which religion addressed itself centuries before science came into existence. In the Judaic-Christian tradition, man stands at the pinnacle of God's creation. According to the book of Genesis, God formed man from the dust of the ground, breathed life into him, and thereby called him into being "in the image of God." Here is a view of man's origin, nature, and destiny that has infused and vitalized whole civilizations for thousands of years. And still today it provides for many the most authoritative and definitive introduction to the nature of man. Any theory of man that calls this foundation into question is automatically condemned by some as an assault upon the foundations of belief and an attempt to destroy the essential dignity of man.

When the careful and patient observations of biologists began to provide, in the nineteenth century, a massive accumulation of evidence that all life was linked in a developmental chain, and that man himself had evolved slowly over millions of years from less complex forms of life, many protagonists of religion attacked their work as an impious fraud. A monumental battle erupted between "science" and "religion," a battle that raged undiminished into the twentieth century and continues to reverberate in many quarters today. It is a battle that may even be fought in your own mind as this semester proceeds. And the danger that it raises is the danger of a premature perspective.

The scientific evidence for biological evolution is enormous. The logic and the observations upon which the theory rests conform to the highest standards of scientific method. It would be most inconsistent for anyone living in this culture, so heavily informed by and dependent upon the accomplishments of science, simply to dismiss the theory of evolution out of hand. No one of us can provide you, of course, with a criterion for absolute truth. You will always be free to accept or reject any set of presuppositions. And knowledge of *any* kind does rest ultimately upon presuppositions.

But there is more to the matter than that. Presuppositions provide the foundation for understanding and the integration of knowledge; but they are also capable of blinding us to larger visions, more inclusive perspectives, to ways of viewing the world that might be more adequate because they take new as well as old truths into account.

A liberal education *liberates*. But liberty is often a fearful prospect. Sometimes what men call faith is not so much a confidence born of conviction as it is a shelter behind which to hide. We are trespassing here on a profound and mysterious domain. But is it not true that faith must inform and not conceal? That it must unlock the universe and not spirit it away from view? That the God of Genesis has not really been accepted as the Creator if He has been confined within arbitrary categories of human thought?

Many would reply that this is all beside the point. But here is the crux: in a university *nothing* may be rejected *in advance* as beside the point. All perspectives must be admitted. A university is true to its essence when it is committed to but one principle: That there is more to be seen than has yet been seen. We try to hold truth in the little buckets of our understanding. But it keeps flowing over. A university is committed to that ceaseless overflowing, to the endless task of fashioning new and ever more adequate containers for the comprehension of that which is ultimately beyond comprehension.

But all of this may tend to give the impression that "The Nature of Man" is throughout an impartial quest after truth, without any limiting horizons of its own. That is hardly the case. Important things have been said about the nature of man by philosophers, poets, psychologists, and a host of others all viewing the question from different and sometimes radically different perspectives. In this course they will not all be given an equal opportunity to state their case and convince us of what they have seen. Some additional points of view will be entertained in the second semester; but in the first semester, as you will soon discover, only those will be heard from who call themselves scientists.

Does that mean, however, that we are not engaged in an impartial search for the truth? Is science not committed to the quest for truth, let the chips fall where they may?

"Science is a sacred cow," as Anthony Standen has remarked, and it is difficult to point out its limitations without being accused of intellectual impiety. Yet it needs to be said that particular sciences, while they may well be committed to the search for truth, all operate within their own limiting perspectives. Each has its own way of approaching problems and its own peculiar set of questions to be asked. And scientists in one field are sometimes quite intolerant of the suggestion that other perspectives might have equal validity.

Alfred North Whitehead, who has reflected with extraordinary wisdom and perception upon the role of science in the modern world, once wrote:

> Science has never shaken off the impress of its origin in the historical revolt of the late Renaissance. It has remained predominantly an anti-rationalistic movement, founded upon a naive faith. What reasoning it has wanted, has been borrowed from mathematics.... Science repudiates philosophy. In other words, it has never cared to justify its faith or to explain its meanings; and has remained blandly indifferent to its refutation by Hume.[4]

Whitehead was in no sense anti-scientific. The paragraph immediately succeeding the one just quoted defends the necessity of the scientific revolt against the excessive and suffocating rationalism of the High Middle Ages. Against the power of abstract reason science erected the criterion of empiricism, of careful observation and the repeatable experiment. The fruits of its revolt are all about us, in such diverse and comfortable forms as

4. Alfred North Whitehead, *Science and the Modern World*, 17.

antibiotics, central air-conditioning, and the jet airplane. But empiricism always presupposes some very particular way of looking at things. It takes a lot for granted.

It may be correct to say that the criterion of truth in science is observation. In order to be able to apply this criterion widely, however, science strives to divide phenomena into separable parts: to dissect, reduce, simplify. Make no mistake about it; knowledge has been acquired in this fashion, knowledge that is power, the power to predict and control. But this kind of knowledge has no claim to be the *final* truth. And in the study of man, are we willing to assert that the power to predict and control is identical with the knowledge of man's nature? Can science even explain to us why it is that man engages in science?

The anthropologist Loren Eiseley used to search for the secret of life in autumn strolls through the fields. He once wrote:

> It is really a matter, I suppose, of the kind of questions one asks oneself. Some day we may be able to say with assurance, "We came from such and such a protein particle, possessing the powers of organizing in a manner leading under certain circumstances to that complex entity known as the cell, and from the cell by various steps onward, to multiple cell formation." I mean we may be able to say all this with great surety and elaboration of detail, but it is not the answer to the grasshopper's leg, brown and black and saw-toothed here in my hand, nor to this field, nor to the subtle essences of memory, delight, and wistfulness moving among the thin wires of my brain.[5]

It is a matter of the kind of questions one asks. And there are many questions that science has no interest in asking. But that does not always stop it from proposing answers. So once again we must be on guard against the temptation of a premature perspective.

One of the authors whom you will be reading late in the semester speaks of the scientist as someone "under tremendous temptation to practice the art of caricature," especially when man is the object of his study:

---

5. Loren Eiseley, *The Immense Journey* (New York: Random House, 1957), 207.

Like anyone else, the scientist prefers victory to defeat. He wants to work with facts that can be controlled, with determinants that can be determined, with outcomes that can be predicted and measured. He wants to arrive at general concepts and general relationships, searching out the lawfulness beneath the multitude of surface events. In consequence of this bias, the scientist is inevitably disposed to deal selectively with human nature.[6]

The philosopher Paul Weiss has aptly summarized the dangers:

We must be on guard against the error of unwarranted subtraction.... The attempt to show that men are subject to the same laws that govern other beings, combined with the claim that the scope of natural science is universal and its mastery complete, has inclined modern thinkers to subtract from men their characteristic life, desires, hopes, feelings, values, and mind. As a result they have viewed men as little more than inanimate physical things. Having sacrificed man at the altar of an arbitrary theory, such a view can hardly shed light on human needs, goals, concerns. A philosophy which speaks of the human as though it were dead or subhuman can but provide an excuse for ignoring the problems of men.[7]

Those who were responsible for designing this course are aware of these dangers. But that is no guarantee that we have always avoided them, much less that the perspectives urged in this course as an aid to the understanding of man are adequate. Reflect for a moment upon the theme chosen for the first semester, adaptation. It is certainly a useful theme, for it offers an approach to the phenomenon of man that opens up new avenues of understanding and brings novel insights into high relief. But while it reveals it also distorts. Consider the contrasting opinion of Lecomte du Noüy:

Whereas adaptation blindly tries to attain an equilibrium which will bring about its end, evolution can only continue through unstable

6. Robert W. White, *Lives in Progress*, 23–24.
7. Paul Weiss, *Nature and Man*, xv–xvi.

systems or organisms. It only progresses from instability to instability and would perish if it only encountered perfectly adapted, stable systems.[8]

But enough has been said on the subject. Our aim has not been to uproot your faith, but to encourage an attitude without which this course must necessarily fail. If knowledge is to be unified or brought together into a coherent and meaningful whole, we must acquire perspective. But every perspective is a potential tyranny. When a discipline comes to maturity, Paul Weiss has warned, "it begins almost at once to become traditional and soon or late itself presents an obstacle in the way of truth.... The chains of today were forged by free men yesterday."[9]

The attitude which we are urging is a mixture: a passion for integration, order, coherence, without which the course can become trivial and meaningless, but conjoined with an openness of mind and temperament that might best be described as continual amazement.

Whitehead has said it far better:

There remains the final reflection, how shallow, puny, and imperfect are efforts to sound the depths in the nature of things. In philosophical discussion, the merest hint of dogmatic certainty as to finality of statement is an exhibition of folly.[10]

8. Pierre Lecomte du Noüy, *Human Destiny* (New York: Longmans, Green and Co., 1947), 70.

9. Weiss, *Nature and Man*, xi.

10. Alfred North Whitehead, x.

CHAPTER 15

Researchers and Degree Purchasers

I'VE BEEN TEACHING for slightly more than twenty years at a state-owned, taxpayer-supported university. The vast majority of the students with whom I talk believe that the primary function of our university is to teach undergraduates. I'll give long odds that most of the taxpayers in the state, those who pay our salaries and maintain the pleasant facilities in which we work, hold the same belief.

They're quite wrong, of course. Almost all of the faculty appointments in the university are made on the basis of research potential, not teaching potential. Tenure and promotion are granted on the basis of contributions to research in the discipline where the faculty appointment is held. A very few faculty members are appointed specifically to be teachers—I'm one of those few at the University of Washington—but good teaching, even excellent teaching, will not by itself gain anyone tenure at my university. In today's circumstances, with so many more candidates than positions, universities can afford to make satisfactory teaching a necessary condition for tenure. But even the very best teaching is not a sufficient condition.

Why do so many people think that universities such as mine and yours are primarily educational institutions rather than what they are in fact, research institutions? Inattentiveness is part of the answer. Faculty and administrators have no great interest in correcting the public misapprehension; what they don't know can't hurt us. Moreover, since most of us

Unpublished typescript of remarks for presentation at the University of Manitoba at Winnipeg under the sponsorship of the Faculty of Arts Teaching Committee, 7 February 1997. Reprinted by permission of Mrs. Juliana Heyne.

believe that the best undergraduate education occurs in a research context, we don't find anything dishonest about claiming to be effective schools of education while always aiming at becoming more effective schools of research. But does the best education for intelligent undergraduates in fact take place at institutions dedicated primarily to research? Would it perhaps be desirable to separate undergraduate education from faculty research?

While I was in the process of preparing this talk, I decided to pull down from my shelves *The Aims of Education and Other Essays* by Alfred North Whitehead, a book that I first read years ago and have re-read several times since. I wanted inspiration for my task, and no one inspires me as well as Whitehead. As I read I was surprised to discover that every major idea I wanted to examine with you today had originated in one or another of Whitehead's essays. So I decided to be honest and use quotations from Whitehead as the text for my talk. Here is the first one, speaking to the issue I have just raised.

The universities are schools of education, and schools of research. But the primary reason for their existence is not to be found either in the mere knowledge conveyed to the students or in the mere opportunities for research afforded to the members of the faculty.

Both these functions could be performed at a cheaper rate, apart from these very expensive institutions. Books are cheap, and the system of apprenticeship is well understood. So far as the mere imparting of information is concerned, no university has had any reason for existence since the popularisation of printing in the fifteenth century. Yet the chief impetus to the foundation of universities came after that date, and in more recent times has even increased.

The justification for a university is that it preserves the connection between knowledge and the zest of life, by uniting the young and the old in the imaginative consideration of learning. The university imparts information, but it imparts it imaginatively. At least, this is the function which it should perform for society. A university which fails in this respect has no reason for existence.[1]

---

1. Alfred North Whitehead, "Universities and Their Functions," in *The Aims of Education and Other Essays* (New York: The Free Press, c. 1929, renewed c. 1957, Free Press paperback edition 1967), pp. 92–93. Page numbers in this chapter refer to this edition.

"[U]niting the young and the old in the imaginative consideration of learning." We aren't exactly doing that. But before complaining, I want to take a look at the undergraduate students who come to our universities.

I teach the history of economic thought once a year to undergraduates, and at some point in the course I always assign the section in Adam Smith's *Wealth of Nations* that he titled "Of the Expence of the Institutions for the Education of Youth." Three-quarters of it talks about universities and colleges. My students love it. It generates the most lively discussion of the term. They come to class with Volume II of *The Wealth of Nations* under their arms ready to launch an attack on their university and most of its faculty in the name of Adam Smith.

They find Smith witty and wonderful as he argues that faculty members have no incentive to teach well because their salaries do not depend in any way on how well they teach. They positively exult in Smith's claim that wherever teachers do execute their duties in a tolerably effective way, students *never* neglect their own obligations. But I always have to point out to them—I've never had any students notice it on their own—that Smith's proposals for educational reform at the college and university level call for abolishing the "privileges of graduates." This means that schools will not issue transcripts that employers can use as screening devices, which in turn implies that a college degree, as distinct from a college *education,* will have no value on the job market. "How many of you," I ask, "would be here today if successful performance in this class did not lead to a degree that you thought would help you land a job you want?" I get more sheepish grins in response to that question than professions of interest in learning.

I have not seen any empirical studies. I haven't looked for any, because no amount of data collected by others could offset the testimony of my own experience, which says that the vast majority of those who enroll in our universities today have done so to purchase a degree. And so teaching in our modern universities takes place primarily between researchers and degree purchasers.

That raises the possibility of an interesting contract, one to which we would never explicitly consent but into which we are already implicitly sliding: The faculty will give the students high grades and little work if the students will give the faculty decent teaching evaluations and otherwise leave them alone to pursue their research.

Aside from the morality of such a bargain, we have to be concerned about the third party, the taxpayers who support all this. I do not believe that most taxpayers understand or appreciate the value to society of an institution that exists primarily to encourage research. Medical research they understand and will fund if pressed. But not research in the humanities. Attitudes toward the social sciences and natural sciences fall somewhere in between, but mostly toward the humanities end of the continuum. I infer this from the glee with which most people greet the topics of research projects when enterprising newspaper or television commentators decide to publish a list of dissertation titles. Universities are luxuries that wealthy societies ought to support because it is good to maintain places where people are paid to push speculation as far as it can be made to go in every direction. But our democratic societies will not long support universities, I predict, if the word gets out that they are not educating students but merely granting them a meaningless certification.

Thus my argument for better teaching of undergraduates becomes an argument for the maintenance of research universities. But before proceeding let me insert another quotation from Whitehead.

It must not be supposed that the output of a university in the form of original ideas is solely to be measured by printed papers and books labeled with the names of their authors....In every faculty you will find that some of the more brilliant teachers are not among those who publish. Their originality requires for its expression direct intercourse with their pupils in the form of lectures, or of personal discussion. Such men exercise an immense influence; and yet, after the generation of their pupils has passed way, they sleep among the innumerable unthanked benefactors of humanity. Fortunately, one of them is immortal—Socrates.

Thus it would be the greatest mistake to estimate the value of each member of the faculty by the printed work signed with his name. There is at the present day some tendency to fall into this error; and an emphatic protest is necessary against an attitude on the part of authorities which is damaging to efficiency and unjust to unselfish zeal.

But when all such allowances have been made, one good test for the general efficiency of a faculty is that as a whole it shall be producing in published form its quota of contributions of thought. Such a quota is to be estimated in weight of thought, and not in number of words.[2]

Let's return now to Whitehead's bold claim: "The justification for a university is that it preserves the connection between knowledge and the zest of life, by uniting the young and the old in the imaginative consideration of learning." How can that possibly occur in an institution where the students have no interest in the faculty's research and the faculty have little interest in sharing it with them? There is no hope, of course, if we are satisfied with the present situation and have given up all expectation of ever doing better.

> The fading of ideals is sad evidence of the defeat of human endeavor. In the schools of antiquity philosophers aspired to impart wisdom, in modern colleges our humbler aim is to teach subjects.... I am not maintaining that in the practice of education the ancient were more successful than ourselves.... My point is that, at the dawn of our European civilization, men started with the full ideals which should inspire education, and that gradually our ideals have sunk to square with our practice.
> But when ideals have sunk to the level of practice, the result is stagnation.[3]

As an incurable idealist, I believe we can avoid stagnation and disaster. How? Whitehead suggests a way:

> The only avenue towards wisdom is by freedom in the presence of knowledge. But the only avenue towards knowledge is by discipline in the acquirement of ordered fact. Freedom and discipline are the two essentials of education.... I call the first period of freedom the "stage of Romance," the intermediate period of discipline I call the "stage of Precision," and the final period of freedom is the "stage of Generalisation."[4]

2. *Ibid.*, pp. 98–99.
3. "The Rhythmic Claims of Freedom and Discipline," p. 29.
4. *Ibid.*, pp. 30–31.

I think we are failing above all at the stage of Romance. Our students for the most part have no interest in what we are doing because we have not tried hard enough to arouse their interest in our basic disciplines. Here is Whitehead stating what seems to me an obvious truth about education that elementary and secondary teachers cannot afford to deny but which we have blatantly disregarded at the level of tertiary education.

> There can be no mental development without interest. Interest is the *sine qua non* for attention and apprehension. You may endeavor to excite interest by means of birch rods, or you may coax it by the incitement of pleasurable activity. But without interest there will be no progress.[5]

We have all sat in faculty rooms or clubs and complained about the students who would rather watch television than read John Locke or whatever it is that they neglected last night. But why in the world should we expect them to find Locke's *Second Treatise* more interesting than *Spin City* with its Canadian lead actor? Is it *natural* for 18-year-olds to wonder how the coercion of some by others, or what we call government, can be justified, and to open Locke in pursuit of an answer to that question? It is quite unnatural.

I teach introductory microeconomics, which has a miserable reputation among most of those who have encountered it or only heard about it from others. When people at parties find out that I teach the principles of economics, they often grin and say, "I had that once. I don't remember a thing about it." Or "I had that once and I hated it." I think I know why. It's because it is usually taught by people who have completely neglected the stage of Romance. Whitehead once more:

> The first procedure of the mind in a new environment is a somewhat discursive activity amid a welter of ideas and experience. It is a process of discovery, a process of becoming used to curious thoughts, of shaping questions, of seeking for answers, of devising new experiences, of noticing what happens as the result of new ventures.... Now

5. *Ibid.*, p. 31.

undoubtedly this stage of development requires help, and even discipline. The environment within which the mind is working must be carefully selected.

...In no part of education can you do without discipline or can you do without freedom; but in the stage of romance the emphasis must always be on freedom.... [A] block in the assimilation of ideas inevitably arises when a discipline of precision is imposed before a stage of romance has run its course in the growing mind. There is no comprehension apart from romance.[6]

A romantic course in introductory microeconomics is possible, necessary, and *not really all that hard to construct*. But that construction will not occur, will not even begin in the absence of a conviction that freedom in an introductory course is more important than discipline. I'm picking on economists because these are the people with whose habits I'm most familiar; but I know that what I'm describing occurs in other academic disciplines. We construct introductions to our fields on the assumption that everyone in the class will go on to acquire a Ph.D. in the subject. So there's no need to arouse their interest in the subject, to give them a reason for studying it beyond the necessity of passing our examinations, to persuade them that knowledge of this subject can provide the *zest of life*. We have no time to waste on such entertainments. The students must begin learning. They must at once begin mastering those techniques that will be required in the next course. We ruthlessly ignore the fact that, as Whitehead regularly insisted, enjoyment is the natural mode by which living organisms are excited toward suitable self-development. We prefer to rely on noncorporal forms of the birch rod.

I am absolutely convinced that the first course in economics and, I suspect, in every other academic discipline, should be directed almost exclusively toward raising interesting questions and suggesting ways in which the discipline can be used to generate interesting responses. I don't know how many times I have cut off exciting discussions with the excuse, "We have to move on." Even I, who know better, cannot always resist this urge to move along toward *my* goal, to turn the students to what I am inter-

6. *Ibid.*, pp. 32–33.

ested in no matter how effectively that stifles a growing interest on their part. There *is* such a thing as "off the track," and "off the track" is not always as interesting to the better students as it is to those whose limitations of experience or intellect have drawn them off onto a stale route. That is why some discipline is required even at the stage of romance. A good introductory course is not just a bull session. But we don't need to be told that, because we only err in the direction of bull sessions when we have not prepared for the class. *Good* preparation for an introductory class requires constantly asking, What will arouse their interest, fire their curiosity, set them to wondering, stimulate that satisfying "I begin to see"? What should come next?

But when this stage of romance has been properly guided another craving grows. The freshness of inexperience has worn off; there is general knowledge of the groundwork of fact and theory: and, above all, there has been plenty of independent browsing amid first-hand experiences, involving adventures of thought and of action. The enlightenment which comes from precise knowledge can now be understood. It corresponds to the obvious requirements of common sense, and deals with familiar material. Now is the time for pushing on, for knowing the subject exactly, and for retaining in the memory its salient features. This is the stage of precision. This stage is the sole stage of learning in the traditional scheme of education, either at school or university.[7]

It is an essential stage. But it will not succeed if it is not preceded by the stage of romance. Whitehead continues:

During the stage of precision, romance is the background.... The organism will not absorb the fruits of the task unless its powers of apprehension are kept fresh by romance.

...To speak the truth, except in the rare case of genius in the teacher, I do not think that it is possible to take a whole class very far along the road of precision without some dulling of the interest. It is

7. *Ibid.*, pp. 33–34.

the unfortunate dilemma that initiative and training are both necessary, and that training is apt to kill initiative.

But this admission is not to condone a brutal ignorance of methods
of mitigating this untoward fact.[8]

One method of mitigation is to know exactly what you want to accomplish and to aim at it directly and quickly.

A certain ruthless definiteness is essential in education. I am sure
that one secret of a successful teacher is that he has formulated quite
clearly in his mind what the pupil has got to know in precise fashion.
He will then cease from half-hearted attempts to worry his pupils with
memorising a lot of irrelevant stuff of inferior importance. The secret
of success is pace, and the secret of pace is concentration. But, in respect to precise knowledge, the watchword is pace, pace, pace. Get
your knowledge quickly, and then use it. If you can use it, you will
retain it.[9]

No one can make *Intermediate* Microeconomic Theory as interesting as
Introduction to Microeconomics. There will be unavoidable boring stages
in the process of education. But we should not celebrate that fact or suppose that our genuine dedication to the pedagogical task is proved by our
willingness to force our students through tedious experiences.

What is worse, we no longer insist that our students actually master
the material appropriate to the stage of discipline. We seem to be *too* disciplined at the first stage, when freedom and romance should dominate, and
far too *slack* at the stage of discipline and precision. I suspect this growing tendency to let students escape without actually having mastered the
materials is one consequence of the unholy bargain I mentioned earlier.
We don't want to be seen as ogres. We don't want to set definite standards
when no one else seems to be doing so. What difference does it make
after all whether they learn this or not? It's their problem if they come
to the next course and aren't adequately prepared. But what this means

8. *Ibid.*, pp. 34–35.
9. *Ibid.*, p. 36.

is that at the next stage our students will not be able to enjoy the freedom and the satisfaction that comes from the application of material they
have mastered. Our failure to be thorough at the stage of discipline and
precision almost guarantees failure at what Whitehead calls the stage of
generalization.

But before moving on to that I want to emphasize once again what
Whitehead says about definiteness, halfheartedness, and pace. Simple
truths. All teachers should scratch them on their desktops, wooden or
computer. Know what you want to teach. Teach it forcefully. Move along.
"The watchword is pace, pace, pace." Think about it.

> We have now come to the third stage of the rhythmic cycle, the
> stage of generalisation. There is here a reaction towards romance.
> Something definite is now known; aptitudes have been acquired; and
> general rules and laws are clearly apprehended both in their formula-
> tion and their detailed exemplification. The pupil now wants to use
> his new weapons. He is an effective individual, and it is effects that he
> wants to produce. He relapses into the discursive adventures of the
> romantic stage, with the advantage that his mind is now a disciplined
> regiment instead of a rabble. In this sense, education should begin in
> research and end in research. After all, the whole affair is merely a
> preparation for battling with the immediate experiences of life, a prep-
> aration by which to qualify each immediate moment with relevant
> ideas and appropriate actions. An education which does not begin by
> evoking initiative and end by encouraging it must be wrong. For its
> whole aim is the production of active wisdom.[10]

I won't presume to add anything to that. But I do want to discuss one
more supremely important issue before opening the floor to your comments. And again Whitehead supplies my text. Consider these remarks
from the title essay of *The Aims of Education:*

> And I may say in passing that no educational system is possible unless
> every question directly asked of a pupil at any examination is either

10. *Ibid.*, pp. 36–37.

framed or modified by the actual teacher of that pupil in that subject. The external assessor may report on the curriculum or on the performance of the pupils, but never should be allowed to ask the pupil a question which has not been strictly supervised by the actual teacher, or at least inspired by a long conference with him. There are a few exceptions to this rule, but they are exceptions, and could easily be allowed for under the general rule.[11]

A growing frustration in my country with the ineffectiveness of our schools has generated a demand for standard examinations. Whitehead warns against them. He knew about the danger of teaching to the examination and how incompatible this was with any philosophy of education that aimed to impart wisdom, or arouse the zest of life, or unite the young and the old in the imaginative consideration of learning. Here are some of his further comments on the general subject:

> The best procedure will depend on several factors, none of which can be neglected, namely, the genius of the teacher, the intellectual type of the pupils, their prospects in life, the opportunities offered by the immediate surroundings of the school, and allied factors of this sort. It is for this reason that the uniform external examination is so deadly.... [S]uch examinations have their use in testing slackness.... [But i]t kills the best part of culture. When you analyse in the light of experience the central task of education, you find that its successful accomplishment depends on a delicate adjustment of many variable factors. The reason is that we are dealing with human minds, and not with dead matter. The evocation of curiosity, of judgment, of the power of mastering a complicated tangle of circumstances, the use of theory in giving foresight in special cases—all these powers are not to be imparted by a set rule embodied in one schedule of examination subjects.[12]

External examinations do have their use, he admits, in preventing slackness. But the slackness against which he warns is not the slackness

---

11. "The Aims of Education," p. 5.
12. *Ibid.*

of the student, nor even the slackness of the teacher, but *the slackness of the school*. Consider the following:

> Primarily it is the schools and not the scholars which should be inspected. Each school should grant its own leaving certificates, based on its own curriculum. The standards of these schools should be sampled and corrected. But the first requisite for educational reform is the school as a unit, with its approved curriculum based on its own needs, and evolved by its own staff. If we fail to secure that, we simply fall from one formalism into another, from one dung-hill of inert ideas into another.
>
> ...When I say that the school is the educational unit, I mean exactly what I say, no larger unit, no smaller unit. Each school must have the claim to be considered in relation to its special circumstances. The classifying of schools for some purposes is necessary. But no absolutely rigid curriculum, not modified by its own staff, should be permissible. Exactly the same principles apply, with the proper modifications, to universities and to technical colleges.[13]

As an active participant in efforts to improve the elementary and secondary schools of my own city, I have often been challenged to define a good school. I have learned to say that a good school is any school controlled by professionals who work collegially to further a shared vision. I don't want parents or taxpayers or school boards or students to be in charge of schools, although they are certainly entitled to a *veto* at some stage. Parents exercise a veto, for example, when they decline to enroll their children. But I want professionals in charge. The professionals, however, must behave collegially. That means they must know and care what others in their school are doing and be willing to correct what is wrong and to support what is strong in their colleagues' behavior. This will require courage. It will also require a shared vision.

When this conception of a good school is applied to colleges and universities, it carries an implication that faculty members at my university vehemently reject. I experienced that vehemence once when I suggested

13. *Ibid.*, pp. 13–14.

at a meeting of the university's general education committee that effective undergraduate education was being throttled by the power that the disciplines exercised over it. Because every student must choose to major in one of the disciplines, fulfillment of the requirements for a major tends to dominate the design of each student's curriculum. But those requirements are increasingly controlled by the assumption that the student majoring in a subject intends to continue with post-graduate work and acquire at least a master's degree and preferably a Ph.D. in the subject. In this way undergraduate education at our universities is becoming pre-professional education for students who lack both the interest and the ability to become professionals.

The standard defense of the major is that colleges and universities ought not to graduate dilettantes. Students must master at least one subject. But most students are not doing anything of the sort, because the faculties of the various disciplines are for the most part unwilling to do more than lay down *formal* requirements. They are not willing to invest the time, thought, and trouble to design, implement, monitor, and enforce realistic and coherent requirements. They rarely teach the courses they require. They know only rumors about what goes on in them. And when they see undeniable evidence that the requirements are not producing the desired results, they basically do not care. They are not rewarded for caring. The research projects that interest them are so distant from undergraduate education that they would not know what to do if they did start to care.

The problem is a difficult one. Because faculty receive appointments and gain promotion for accomplishments in their disciplines, they are politically as well as intellectually attached to these disciplines. They see the power of their departments as their first and perhaps only line of defense against a sinister administration. I have never understood why administrators are presumed to have interests in opposition to those of the faculty. The general interests of the faculty, it seems to me, are completely shared by the typical university administration. Of course, insofar as the central administration is held responsible for the welfare of the institution as a whole, it will and should question projects that strengthen some departments or divisions by weakening others or by destroying functions that are central to the success of the university though of marginal importance to the faculty in individual disciplines.

One such function is undergraduate education. I do not think it can be revived and therefore I do not think it will survive within the current institutional structure of our research universities. And since I fear that taxpayers, legislators, and philanthropists will not continue to support research universities that do not teach undergraduates, I predict years of famine not far ahead for those who now occupy or hope to occupy research positions within our major universities.

I have been extremely fortunate in being allowed to spend most of my life working within research universities despite my eccentric credentials and idiosyncratic interests. The tolerance of these institutions for eccentricity and idiosyncrasy is a major reason why I love them and, more importantly, a principal source of the benefits they generate for societies that can afford them, as ours surely can.

No one designed the modern research university. It just evolved. And that is a major reason for its successes. Most major social institutions are like economic systems: they cannot be designed or centrally planned. They must evolve if they are to be successful. Social institutions evolve as members of the relevant society pursue their own interests and thereby produce novel situations to which others respond in the pursuit of their own interests, thereby generating further novelty, and so on. This evolutionary process produces complex institutions marvelously adapted to the needs of those who participate in them. But the process can also lead its participants merrily along the road to suicide, because such processes are characteristically blind to the larger context.

I don't expect universities to change in any ways that are not consistent with the interests of those who comprise them, and that means principally their faculties. What I hope for is an enlargement of interests, perhaps set in motion by the recognition that our present course, for all its past success, portends tragedy for the institutions that have served most of us so well. If we can enlarge our interests, think at least a little more grandly of our vocations, we may come to raise and discuss the question: *What do we really want?*

Whitehead has written:

The ultimate motive power, alike in science, in morality, and in religion, is the sense of value, the sense of importance. It takes the various forms of wonder, of curiosity, of reverence, or worship, of tumultuous desire for merging personality in something beyond itself. This sense of value imposes on life incredible labours, and apart from it life sinks back into the passivity of its lower types. The most penetrating exhibition of this force is the sense of beauty, the aesthetic sense of realised perfection.[14]

The question now is whether our universities still harbor that force, that motive power, in sufficient strength to preserve themselves.

14. "The Rhythmic Claims of Freedom and Discipline," p. 40.

PART 6

Teaching Economics

CHAPTER 16

Economics Is a Way of Thinking

WHAT DO ECONOMISTS know that is both true and important? Not nearly as much as we sometimes pretend. Every profession harbors an inability to appreciate the limitations of its perspective and a tendency to exaggerate its own significance in the larger scheme of things. Since this essay comes from the pen (word processor, actually) of a devout economist, it will probably exaggerate the power and social value of economists' knowledge. But the critics of economics have lately enjoyed a substantial amount of public exposure in this part of the world. If you want a sample, see "A Consumers' Guide to Recent Critiques of Economics" in *Agenda,* the new Australian policy journal.[1] A resounding defense of economics can therefore do no harm.

The Heart of the Matter

Why pay heed to economists? What do they know that is worth listening to? The answer differs, of course, among economists. Some know a lot about the form and functions of gross domestic product, labor force data, reserve banks, taxation and expenditure policies of governments, financial institutions and the markets in which they operate, and what economists usually call *macroeconomics*. Some know a lot about the history of economic systems. Most know a great deal of statistics and mathematics. But I shall emphasize what I think is most valuable in everything that

Reprinted from *Economic Alert* 6 (July 1995), by permission of Enterprise New Zealand Trust.

1. *Agenda* 2, no. 2 (1995): 233–40.

economists know, or that at least the good economists know, with "good economist" circularly defined as one who not only knows it but believes strongly in its applicability and importance. A good economist knows how to employ *the economic way of thinking.*

Is it presumptuous to speak about *the* economic way of thinking? Aren't there several economic ways of thinking? There are surely many ways to think about economic life, at least once we've decided exactly what we mean by "economic life" (which turns out *not* to be all that easy). But there is a particular perspective on human actions and interactions that regularly emerges when economists analyze the world that many economists recognize as uniquely *the* economic way of thinking. This article will try to explain and illustrate that way of thinking, with teachers of introductory economics especially in mind.

I like to summarize the economic way of thinking in a short sentence that states its basic assumption: *All social phenomena emerge from the choices of individuals in response to expected benefits and costs to themselves.*

Economizing Actions

It took me many years of practicing with this way of thinking to realize that it actually has two aspects, both expressed in the statement that it offers a particular perspective on human *actions and interactions.* One aspect of the economic way of thinking focuses on human actions. The other—the more difficult, more useful, and more neglected aspect, I shall subsequently argue—focuses on human interactions.

The former, which I shall call the action aspect, picks up the notion that economics is about economizing. To economize means to allocate available resources in a way that extracts from those resources the most of whatever the economizer wants. Scarcity makes economizing necessary. Anyone with access to unlimited resources does not need to economize. Keep in mind, however, that *time* is one of those scarce resources—except perhaps, when we are bored and time hangs heavy on our hands. The scarcity of time compels even those to economize who have more money than they know how to spend because they must ordinarily combine their scarce time with the resources their money can purchase in order to obtain what they want. A week in the Islands of the Aegean leaves less time, unfortunately, for lounging on the Left Bank in Paris, no matter how huge your monetary income.

Because scarcity makes economizing unavoidable, everybody does it. We don't always do it consciously. And sometimes we do it badly, even by our own standards: we allocate our resources in a way that we subsequently come to regret. Most often that occurs because we lacked some relevant information when we made our allocation decision. But information is also a scarce good. If all the relevant information were one of the resources constantly available to us, we would never make mistakes. In the real world, however, we have to sacrifice other goods to acquire additional information. We have to use time and energy that could be employed in some other way to investigate, for example, the characteristics and prices of the various television sets available for purchase. At some point we decide that the results of further investigation probably won't justify the time and trouble it will take. We stop searching for further information, and we act. But we may turn out to have been wrong. One more telephone call, we learn too late, would have revealed a better deal than the one on which we finally closed.

Marginal Decisions

Economic theory has a pair of bright lights to shine on the economizing process: the concept of the margin and the concept of opportunity cost. Even very young students can learn to interpret their own actions in terms of marginal decisions and opportunity costs, often with a sense of gleeful discovery.

Economizing means making trade-offs. We would like to have more of one thing, but we give it up in order to obtain more of something else. The marginal concept highlights two important but easily overlooked facets of this process. One is that trade-offs don't have to be all or nothing affairs.

This is important because additional amounts of almost everything become less valuable to us as we acquire more. Water provides a good example. People like to claim that water is "a necessity of life," and then to draw from this simple "truth" a lot of unwarranted conclusions, such as a city "needs" a specific amount of water and that those who supply water must keep its price very low. The amount of water that people "need," however, will depend on how much they have grown accustomed to using, and that will depend heavily on how much they have had to pay for it. When water is inexpensive, homeowners maintain large lawns and farmers grow rice in desert areas. When water becomes more expensive, homeowners install water-saving devices in their showers and toilets, set their washing machines at lower water levels, and wash their cars less frequently and without letting the hose run the whole time they're doing it. Farmers shift from crops like rice to crops that don't require artificial irrigation.

Housing is another alleged "necessity" that turns out not to be quite what it originally seemed when we look at it through marginal spectacles. The real question is what quality and quantity of housing do people "need." Once again this will prove to depend largely on what people have grown accustomed to, which will depend in turn on their accustomed income and the price they must pay for housing. Families "need" fewer bedrooms when housing costs more, and fewer bathrooms when the cost of installing plumbing goes up substantially. The sensible economizer, whether a householder or a business decision maker, makes trade-offs by comparing the expected benefits of obtaining an additional or marginal amount with the benefits expected to be lost from giving up (trading off) a small amount of something else. "All or nothing" is the slogan of those who either aren't thinking carefully or are deliberately trying to stampede others into giving them something they want.

The other aspect of the marginal concept worth nothing is the emphasis it places on the *variety* of margins or edges along which we can usually decide. When the cost of an option goes up, there are many more ways to react than we initially suppose. What would residents do, for example, if the councils of Auckland or Wellington decided to attack their traffic congestion problems by charging motorists for driving on crowded streets during busy times of the day; perhaps through an automated system of monitoring accompanied by monthly bills? Some few would choose to pay the tolls and drive just as much as before. Most motorists in these cities, however, would search for and discover a variety of margins along which they could adjust their behavior. They would eliminate those single-passenger trips for which they could find good substitutes, such as car pools, walking, consolidation of errands, buses, even the telephone, which is indeed a substitute for a car trip on some margins. We all like to insist that "we are left with no choice" when someone proposes a change in circumstances that is not immediately to our advantage; and we aren't always lying when we do so. We may just not yet have had sufficient incentive to search for good alternatives.

Opportunity Costs

Marginal thinking directs our attention to incremental benefits and incremental costs and to the variety of directions in which choice can be exercised. The concept of opportunity cost focuses our attention on the ultimately subjective character of all costs. The cost of any action—and only actions, not things, can have genuine costs—is the value of the opportunity that will have to be given up if that action is taken. If the price of seeing a particular movie is $10, the cost of seeing the movie to the individual who is thinking about it will be the value—the subjective value, of course—of what he or she would otherwise have been able to obtain with those $10.

If an action does not require the sacrifice of any valuable opportunity, then it costs nothing to take that action. The relevant point for checking on cost is always *at the margin,* at that position in time and space where the decision maker currently stands. Should you fly or should you drive your own car when you want to travel from Christchurch to Dunedin. Which costs less? You will want to ask about the value of the time you give up when you drive as well as the value of the money you give up when you decide to fly. In calculating the money cost of driving, you do not want to include any costs that are not actually the consequences of this decision. Licensing and insurance costs and a substantial portion of your depreciation costs are not costs of driving your car but costs of owning it. So unless you are going to buy a car specifically to make this trip, you do not want to include the costs of owning as part of the opportunity costs of driving from Christchurch to Dunedin. The only costs relevant to your decision will be the value of the opportunities you give up to follow the course decided upon.

Restaurant patrons who eat food they don't want because they have already paid for it; householders who refuse to sell a piece of furniture that is only cluttering up their storage space because the best price they can get is so much less than they (foolishly) paid for it; and business firms that consult their research and development costs in determining the best price to set for new products are all paying attention to past expenses, none of which are relevant to current decisions, because they do not represent the value of opportunities that will be forgone.

Will be forgone! Opportunity costs, the only costs relevant to decisions, in addition to being costs of actions and subjective costs to some particular person or persons, always lie in the future. Teachers of introductory economics can do a great deal to clarify their own and their students' thinking about costs just by keeping in the foreground these three interrelated aspects of costs.

Interactions: Coordinating the Actions of Economizers

The economizing process is so central to the economic way of thinking that many economists have mistakenly concluded that there is nothing more to it. They seem to suppose that interactions among diverse individuals can also be analyzed and understood as an economizing process, in disregard of the fact that economizing presupposes a unified point of view, which implies a single person in command. If the core problem for economic *actions* is scarcity, the core problem for economic *interactions* is a multiplicity of diverse and incommensurable projects. The solution to the scarcity problem is economizing; the solution to the problem of diverse projects is coordination.

Our economizing actions occur in societies characterized by extensive specialization. Specialization is a necessary condition for the increases in production that have so increased "the wealth of nations" in recent centuries. But specialization without coordination is the road to chaos, not to wealth. How is it possible for millions of people to pursue the particular projects in which they are interested, on the basis of their own resources and capabilities, in substantial ignorance and disregard of the interests, resources, and capabilities of almost all of the people upon whose cooperation their own projects depend for success? I specialize in writing about economics, which would bring me quickly to the verge of starvation were it not for the cooperation I regularly receive from editors, printers, paper manufacturers, postal employees, bookstores, teachers, and students, not to mention all the farmers, manufacturers, and service workers whose efforts made it possible for editors, printers, paper manufacturers, and all the others to do for me the things I needed done. How do all these activities get coordinated?

That is the "miracle of the market." One of the economist's most important tasks is to demythologize this miracle by enabling people to see how and why it occurs. We do that by teaching the process of supply and demand, and by teaching it as a process of continuous, ongoing interaction among suppliers and demanders. This is *not* an economizing process. Each supplier economizes and each demander economizes, but their interactions cannot appropriately be viewed as an economizing process in which there is something to be maximized, such as wealth or utility. It is an *exchange* process, and as such it has no maximand. That's one very good reason for economists to suppress their inclination to pass judgment on market processes, usually by labelling them less or more efficient, and to be content with the sufficiently challenging and important task of explaining how markets work.

Markets and Prices

Successful explanations will focus on changing relative prices, because prices provide both the information and the incentives without which coordination could not occur. When demanders want more than suppliers have made available, competition among demanders tends to raise the price, which simultaneously induces demanders to get along with less and suppliers to provide more. Competition among suppliers tends to lower the price when suppliers want to offer more than demanders are willing to purchase. How quickly and smoothly this will occur is going to depend upon, among other things, the clarity with which relevant property rights are defined and enforced.

When governments try to "fix" prices or otherwise to constrain the terms upon which demanders and suppliers may exchange, both sides will search for other margins along which to further their goals. Rent controls, for example, don't prevent rents from rising in a situation where there is excess demand; the most they do is prevent the monetary component of the cost of renting from rising. When tenants want more space than owners are willing to make available at legal prices, owners *and tenants* find alternative ways of negotiating the arrangements they prefer. One acquires proficiency in the art of economic thinking largely by learning to recognize the ingenious ways in which market participants overcome obstacles to mutually advantageous exchanges, obstacles created not only by government but also by ignorance and uncertainty. The great variety of techniques that sellers employ in order to practice price discrimination among their customers provides an endless supply of examples that always fascinate my students.

Explanations, Not Solutions

Skilled practitioners of this art do not so much solve social problems as solve puzzles and mysteries. Social problems don't have "solutions," or at least none that can properly be imposed by economists. The subsidies and protections that New Zealand governments once doled out so generously to both agricultural and manufacturing interests had consequences. The economic way of thinking enables one to discern these consequences more clearly and to predict the consequences of alternative policies. Doing so will often clarify the origin of the subsidies and protections, at least for anyone who believes that democratic legislators pay attention to the interests that are paying attention to them. But the economic way of thinking provides no formula for deciding whether the benefits that a policy confers upon one set of people are greater or less than the costs it imposes upon some other set, even when it enables us to assign fairly accurate monetary measures to these costs and benefits.

There are two principal reasons. One is that the value of money itself varies from one person to another, so that while money measures can and do provide a useful way of comparing the costs to some with the benefits to others, they cannot provide an *ultimate* resolution when interests conflict.

The other principal reason is that some very real costs and benefits slip through the net of the market. Recall the basic assumption of economic theory. All social phenomena emerge from the choices of individuals in response to expected benefits and costs *to themselves*. When the costs or benefits of actions spill over on to others in such a fashion that the actors do not take them into account in making their decisions, economizing actions are leaving out potentially important data. Economists refer to such spillovers as externalities, and some go on to point to them as evidence of *market failure*. The latter is a mistake, another instance of economists' regrettable inclination to pass premature judgment rather than stick to what they do best: explain and predict. The phenomena of externalities offer economists a rich arena in which to practice profitably the economic way of thinking, and there is no good reason for them to declare the whole area off limits to their art by posting the label *market failure*. Externalities, like all other social phenomena, emerge from interactions that are the product of individuals' choices, and the economic way of thinking has a great deal to say about their origins and consequences as well as about the probable consequences of changes in the rules of the game that would produce quite different results.

The economic way of thinking remains useful even when we reach what some people think of as the outer boundaries of the market and where the border of government begins. Government measures and institutions are also social phenomena, and as such they are proper grist to the mill of all economists with a courageous faith in the basic assumption.

Learning by Doing

I have found it extremely difficult to discuss such a large topic as the economic way of thinking in such a short space. It ordinarily takes me an entire school term to introduce the economic way of thinking to my students so that it becomes an enduring component of their own thinking. A short piece such as this had to rely on a lot of vague generalities. We teach and learn the economic way of thinking, however, through a multitude of specific applications. That is certainly how I learned it and how I now try to teach it. And as Adam Smith once suggested, there is no better way to learn a subject than by being required to teach it term after term. So go to it, all you teachers of economics. You learn by doing.

CHAPTER 17

Teaching Introductory Economics

WHEN PEOPLE who have taken introductory economics courses at the college or university level in the United States are asked what they remember about the course, most of them answer that they remember little except that it was boring.

The baleful influence of these benumbing courses has now extended itself to eastern Europe and the former Soviet Union. When Marxian political economy was purged from the curriculum, American-style economics quickly moved in to fill its place. Much of the world, it would seem, is coming to the conclusion that the content of a standard American introductory economics textbook should be part of the knowledge possessed by an educated citizen in any "capitalist" country. The process has even corrupted the secondary schools, where economics teachers are increasingly expected to anticipate the material their students will encounter in college or university, regardless of whether the students have any intention of taking a higher-level economics course or even pursuing a tertiary education.

Australians who have encountered introductory economics at the university level tend more often to look back favorably on their first course, because so many of them enroll initially with the intention of completing a degree in the discipline. By the time they come to reflect on their overall education, they have been socialized to the ways of the economics

From *Agenda* 2, no. 2 (1995): 149–58 (http://agenda.anu.edu.au), reprinted with the kind permission of the journal's editors and its publisher, The Australian National University College of Business and Economics.

profession and consequently recall the first course as a challenging but essential first step toward a satisfying career. But conversations with both teaching economists and their former students in New Zealand, Canada, and the United Kingdom persuade me that extensive dissatisfaction with the first course is by no means confined in the English-speaking world to the United States.

The Problem with Introductory Economics

The problem with the introductory course can be summarized quickly. Its content has evolved on the assumption that everyone enrolling in a first course in economics will eventually go on to earn a specialized degree in the subject, while the degree program itself has been structured on the assumption that everyone who earns a baccalaureate degree in economics will continue to the doctorate. Thus the beginning student is required to learn concepts and techniques that will be almost wholly useless to anyone who doesn't plan to earn a PhD in economics. How did such an absurd situation come about and why does it persist, especially in view of the fact that so many college and university economics teachers essentially agree with this analysis?

However it came about, the situation persists basically because academia, despite all its radical *talk*, is one of the most unrelentingly conservative institutions in society. Colleges and universities derive most of their funding not from customers or clients but from taxpayers and philanthropists who rarely have any clear understanding of what goes on in the ivory towers they support. Undergraduate students, even when given an opportunity to influence the curricula to which they will be subjected, are not altogether sure whether they want education or certification, and insofar as they prefer the latter they are for the most part willing to go along with whatever leads to the coveted degree at a tolerable cost. Because the typical academic institution has no genuine owner and hence no residual claimant, no one in a position to effect constructive changes has the appropriate incentives. Higher-level administrators, who are supposed to have a global perspective, don't want to risk the faculty outrage they would surely encounter if they tried to force changes on departments that have grown comfortable with the status quo.

In economics, the status quo in the introductory course adequately serves the interests of those with the power to control the course's content: teachers, departmental chairpersons or curriculum committees, textbook authors, and textbook publishers. None of this is the product of a conspiracy. We are caught in a kind of prisoners' dilemma, where almost everyone prefers an outcome that is, unfortunately, in no one's interest to bring about. Teachers present what appears in the textbooks, the textbooks offer what the teachers expect, and the teachers expect what has been in the textbooks for as long as they can remember. Paul Samuelson summarized the situation concisely in 1946 when he was trying to predict the lasting impact of Keynes's *General Theory* upon thinking in the economics profession: "Finally, and perhaps most important from the long-run standpoint," he observed, "the Keynesian analysis has begun to filter down into the elementary textbooks; and, as everybody knows, once an idea gets into these, however bad it may be, it becomes practically immortal." [1]

Perhaps the best example of a bad idea that has achieved immortality—or possibly an idea that was once good but has grown bad by living too long—is what passes in the textbooks for the theory of the competitive firm. Generations of beginning economics students have dutifully practiced their arithmetic skills by calculating average fixed, average variable, average total, and marginal costs from an arbitrarily constructed schedule of costs and quantities, have plotted these values on a graph, and have learned to say that in the long run under perfectly competitive conditions price will be equal to marginal cost and to average total cost at the latter's lowest point. The unfamiliarity of the terms and the abstract character of the argument make it difficult for most students to comprehend. The instructor consequently can occupy a great deal of class time with explanations and clarifications that take no time to prepare. And the ease with which examination questions can be drawn from this material compels all students interested in a good grade to attend faithfully upon the entire performance. None of it, however, finds any subsequent application. The whole system seems to be contrived, as Adam Smith long ago observed about the practices of colleges and universities in general, "not for the

---

1. P. Samuelson, "Lord Keynes and the General Theory," *Econometrica* 14, no. 3 (1946): 189.

benefit of the students, but for the interest, or more properly speaking, for the ease of the masters." [2]

Individual instructors have very limited power to change the situation. Not only will they have to devise substitute material for whatever standard textbook material they choose to omit. They also risk the criticism of colleagues and even some of their own students for failing to teach material that turns out to be presupposed in the next theory course. Those who are trying to prepare their students for standardized exams have very little freedom to improvise, because the standardized exams sample heavily the examinees' acquaintance with technical concepts and definitions. Maverick teachers may even acquire a reputation for not teaching a "rigorous" course, in a culture where "rigor" is the most highly-respected virtue and can best be demonstrated by teaching all the conventional theoretical concepts.

So persistence of the situation despite its widely recognized absurdities should not surprise or puzzle us. The difficult question is how we might change it. To answer that question, we must first think about what we want to accomplish. What ought to be the goal in an introductory economics course?

What Should Introductory Economics Aim to Achieve?

Except for students who know when they enroll that they want to specialize in economics, the goal should *not* be to prepare the students for the next theory course. Most of the general students who enroll in the first course will never take a more advanced theory course in economics. Perhaps a larger proportion *would* go on to take "intermediate theory" if the first course conveyed more understanding and made less of an attempt to "cover" everything. That word "cover" may say more than the teachers who use it intend to say. *To cover* means *to conceal;* our goal should be to *discover* or *uncover,* not to cover. Most of the students, general or professional, who do choose to take our intermediate theory courses would probably be better prepared for them if their introductory course discovered or uncovered the usefulness of a few basic concepts than if it tried

2. A. Smith, *An Inquiry into the Nature and Causes of the Wealth of Nations* (Indianapolis: Liberty Fund, 1981), 764.

to anticipate a lot of subsequent technicalities. We should teach the first course in economics as if it is the last course students will ever take in the subject.

Our goal should be to provide students with a few tools that they can use to think more clearly and correctly about the complex interactions that make up a *commercial society*. This was Adam Smith's term for a society in which everyone lives by exchanging and everyone is consequently a merchant.[3] The term is much more helpful and descriptive than "capitalism." It focuses attention on what most needs explanation: the processes of exchange that must accompany the division of labor that has made us wealthy beyond the dreams of anyone living two centuries or even one century ago. The citizens of a democracy ought to understand how a commercial society (or a market economy) works, because such knowledge is a powerful antidote to many of the absurd policy proposals that special interests and thoughtless people press upon their governments.

Scarcity and Exchange

The standard introductory economics course does too little by way of teaching students how markets work. It attempts, and fails for the most part even in this limited task, to teach students how academic economists work. One reason is that professional economists have become hung up on the concept of *scarcity*. Most of them, if asked for the fundamental problem with which economics deals, will unhesitatingly answer "scarcity." That's not so much wrong as misleading. It's true that if there were no scarcity, we would not have to economize. And so we would probably never have extended the division of labor and would never have developed commercial societies. But the genuinely useful light that economics sheds does not fall on the economizing process; it illuminates the process of *exchange*. Just about everyone knows how to economize, and does so effectively. What people do not know and what economics can explain for them is how millions of economizing people, each one pursuing his or her own interest, manage to cooperate effectively despite the fact they are all substantially ignorant of what others want or can do. The fundamental problem of economics is not so much

3. Ibid., 37.

scarcity as a multitude of interdependent projects that somehow have to be coordinated.

Here is a little exercise with which I often introduced economic theory to my students when I was still captive to the scarcity obsession. A student is taking four courses in the current term and he wants to maximize his average grade across the four courses. He has a limited amount of time to study for final exams. He knows exactly by how much additional study will improve his final grade in each of the four courses. The table presents the grades he can count on receiving if he spends the hours indicated on each subject. How many hours should the student spend studying each subject if he has twelve hours to study? How many hours should he spend on each subject if he has only six hours to study?

Hours spent studying	Grade expected in			
	Chemistry	Economics	History	Maths
0	60	40	76	84
1	75	60	81	88
2	80	70	85	91
3	83	75	88	93
4	85	78	90	94
5	86	80	91	94

I used to ask those questions and let the students play around with the numbers for a while before triumphantly demonstrating that with twelve hours to study, three should be devoted to Chemistry, four to Economics, three to History, and two to Mathematics, because only with this allocation are the gains from the last hour studying each subject equal. For the same reason, with only six hours to study, the student should devote two to Chemistry, three to Economics, one to History, and none at all to Mathematics. I thought that I was capturing my students' interest at the outset of the course by illustrating the applicability of economic theory to all of life. In fact I was suggesting its essential irrelevance.

Students trying to figure out how long to study for their various courses don't know in advance what grades their study will secure for them. They are not constrained to studying in increments of whole hours. They are not single-mindedly interested in maximizing their grade-point average. And they obtain no valuable assistance whatsoever in situations like this from knowing the marginal conditions for an optimum. What my exercise demonstrated was that economists have tools that can make simple matters more complicated than they are and complicated matters more simple than they are.

But even if people know how to economize in their private lives without any help from economic theory, do they understand the implications of scarcity for the government sector? Shouldn't economists continue to emphasize the importance of scarcity to citizens who behave as if the public purse has no bottom? It is certainly appropriate for economists to insist, in season and out, that government-funded projects also have opportunity costs and to call constant attention to the realities of what must be sacrificed to obtain desired goods. The question is how this can be done most effectively. It will not be by drawing production-possibility curves and extracting marginal rates of transformation, because that radically misstates the problem. Except in a dictatorship, no *one* economizes for society as a whole or for the government sector. In a democracy, public policies emerge from interactions—exchanges!—among optimizing parties: citizens, elected and appointed officials, and interest groups of many kinds. When the marginal benefits and the marginal costs accrue to different parties, an optimizing model just doesn't fit.

None of this is intended to be a criticism of marginal analysis, but only of its use to illuminate "problems" that it doesn't actually illuminate. Most of these will be economizing or optimizing problems that have been drastically oversimplified so that we can "solve" them, or that postulate an omniscient dictator, or that people typically manage for themselves quite handily without any formal calculations. Nor am I rejecting *all* presentations of the logic of optimizing. I spend a lot of time in my introductory courses dealing with the concepts of marginal cost and marginal revenue and the formal logic of net-revenue maximization. But I don't do so with the intention of helping business decision makers decide how much to produce or what prices to set, because the bare logic of optimization really doesn't provide much help with such decisions. I want to use the logic of net-revenue maximization to explain or illuminate the enormous variety of pricing policies that we regularly observe. My objective is to explain market processes, interpersonal transactions, patterns of exchange—which is, I maintain, what introductory economics is mostly good for. It's good for explaining how markets work, which most people do not understand. It is far less useful or illuminating when it tries to explain how individuals optimize.

In *The Wealth of Nations,* Adam Smith was basically trying to explain how markets work. In order to provide a coherent and persuasive account, he was compelled to explain the formation of relative prices for both final goods and resources, because these prices provide the information and the incentives that coordinate the division of labor. Unfortunately, his theory of "natural" prices contained serious ambiguities and inconsistencies that his classical successors never quite managed to correct satisfactorily. When the science of economics became an academic discipline in the last quarter of the nineteenth century, the professors finally clarified and straightened out the confused and incoherent "classical" theory by developing a general equilibrium theory in which everything determines everything else on the basis of interactions among optimizing resource owners. This system has proved so attractive, so aesthetically satisfying, that many students of economic theory since the neoclassical reformulation never make it back to the issue of how markets work, the issue that inspired the question of relative prices in the first place. That's why so much of elementary economic theory focuses on the optimization process rather than the process of exchange. As the drunk said when asked why he was searching for his keys under the street lamp despite the fact that he had lost them somewhere else, "The light is better here." Many professional economists would rather shine a sharp clear light on nothing at all than wander in partial darkness.

Rigor vs. Plausible Stories

As mentioned earlier, the dominant culture in the economics profession values rigor above all other virtues. The emphasis on rigor, besides encouraging us to emphasize optimization over exchange, also prompts us to treat exchange in an overly formal and mechanistic manner. Supply and demand makes up the core of useful economic theory. But if it is to be

useful to students in a beginning economics course, supply and demand
must be taught as a process rather than as a pair of simultaneous equations. While graphs can be useful aids in teaching supply and demand,
they are not useful when they drive out all consideration of actual social
transactions. Students don't learn how markets work by learning how to
solve simultaneous equations or to manipulate graph lines.

This implies that teachers of introductory economics must leave behind their lust for rigor when they enter the classroom and must learn to be
comfortable with approximations, with uncertainty, and with what is coming to be my favorite phrase: *plausible stories*. We economists are too quick
with the definitive answer, which is usually some variation on "misallocation of resources." Price controls, agricultural marketing orders, protective
tariffs, cartels, restrictive licensing, and a wide variety of government "in-
terferences" always lead for us to a *misallocation of resources*. This summary
judgment is less instructive and less likely to be incorporated into a typical
student's understanding than is a plausible story indicating some of the major effects that will probably follow from this or that event.

Take the case of price controls. Should the government impose tempo-
rary price controls after a natural disaster, such as a hurricane? It's easy to
shift an upward-sloping supply curve to the left along a downward-sloping
demand curve and to demonstrate that the quantity demanded will exceed
the quantity supplied if the price is not allowed to rise. Typical beginning
students, however, will be much less impressed by a gap between the demand curve and the supply curve than by the thought of merchants or landlords profiteering at the expense of poor families. When we tell them that
price controls allow scarce goods to be used for purposes less valuable than
they would be used for if prices were allowed to rise, they are not likely to be
much distressed at the prospect. We have to become concrete and specific.

Ask the students what particular goods are likely to be in very short
supply right after a hurricane. Write their suggestions on the board and
add some crucial ones that they are not likely to think of. Then take several
of them in succession. Electric service will probably have been disrupted
by the hurricane. How will that affect the demand for ice? How elastic will
the supply curve be in response to the increased demand? If the price is not
allowed to rise, how will the ice be rationed among those who are clamor-
ing for it? Is this likely to be a fair allocation? Why is it likely to produce

a situation where some obtain more ice than they really have any use for while others go without altogether? Why is the supply likely to be more elastic in the longer run than in the very short run? What role does a rising price play in bringing more ice into an area suffering from extensive electrical outages and how does it play that role? How does a rising price encourage people to economize on ice and thus make more available to others? What are some of the substitutes for ice that people will begin using as ice becomes more expensive? How does a rising price encourage those who can economize most conveniently or at the lowest cost to do so?

Plywood provides an excellent case study on which students can exercise their imaginations in dialogue with one another and the instructor. Rising plywood prices provide immediate and effective signals to suppliers, not only of wood products but also of transportation services, to alter their behavior quickly and in ways that will relieve the misery of people in the disaster area. Rising prices also tell potential users of plywood that, at least for now, they should postpone less valuable and urgent projects—in order to save money, from their perspective, but with the benefit to others of freeing plywood for the mitigation and repair of hurricane damage.

I'm learning not to say "That's wrong," but to substitute the challenge "Tell us a plausible story about that." My own "answers" are increasingly presented not as the verdict of science or logic or theory but as a story recommended by its plausibility. Of course, I draw on economic theory to devise and recognize plausible stories. A story will not be plausible if it is inconsistent with the basic assumption of economic theory, which is that all social phenomena emerge from the choices individuals make in response to expected benefits and costs to themselves. While this assumption gives me no clear answer to any actual question, it does alert me to what I should be looking for. What are the relevant benefits and costs? What actions by which individuals could cause the perceived value of these benefits and costs to change (often through changes in their money prices)? What substitutes are available to demanders and to suppliers? Economic theory also reminds me that it is marginal values that matter and that there are many margins on which individuals can pursue the projects that interest them.

My teaching has been significantly altered in recent years by taking to heart Ronald Coase's trenchant indictment of "blackboard economics."

We are doing blackboard economics whenever we demonstrate, usually with the aid of a blackboard graph, the non-optimal character of a situation and the Pareto superiority of some alternative arrangement, all without paying any attention to what arrangements real people can actually make and the costs of doing so.[4] Standing at the blackboard seems to confer upon many economists, at least in their own imaginations, such divine attributes as omniscience, impartial benevolence, and omnipotence. They suppose that they are whispering in the ear of a benevolent and all-powerful despot, to employ James Buchanan's telling complaint about this way of doing economics.[5] When we accept the obligation to tell plausible stories, we stop overpowering our students with blackboard proofs that have genuine policy implications only under the wholly unrealistic assumptions that we are holding at the back of our minds.

The Art of Economics

When we shift to the telling of plausible stories, we also begin to recover the lost *art* of economics. As David Colander[6] has reminded those who like to use the positive-normative distinction, the original classification made by John Neville Keynes and quoted by Milton Friedman in his influential 1953 essay on "The Methodology of Positive Economics" was a *three*-part one: positive economics, normative economics, and the art of economics. Policy differences among economists are rarely rooted in disagreements either about positive economics or about normative ideals, but in uncertainty about what additional considerations need to be taken into account and how best to do so. Resolving these questions is the task of the art of economics, an art which is indispensable for anyone who wants to apply economics to real-world issues.

It is an art that will always leave some important questions unanswered, if for no other reason than that we can never be sure when we act or recommend action that we have taken everything relevant into con-

---

4. R. Coase, *The Firm, the Market, and the Law* (Chicago: University of Chicago Press, 1988), 28–29.

5. J. Buchanan, *What Should Economists Do?* (Indianapolis: Liberty Fund, 1979), 145.

6. D. Colander, "The Lost Art of Economics," *Journal of Economic Perspectives* 6, no. 3 (1992): 191–94.

sideration. One of the unfair ways in which we economists bully our students is by responding to their objections with, "We're abstracting from that." Once we recognize that the art of economics plays an indispensable role in any application of economics, and that this art includes the act of deciding what to take into account and what to leave out of account, we confront the obligation to justify any challenged abstraction. Whether we may abstract from a particular ethical, social, or political consideration in recommending a policy becomes a question for discussion as soon as the abstraction is challenged. We can ask the challenger to construct a plausible story indicating the relevance of the omitted consideration, and we can construct our own plausible story to suggest its irrelevance. But we may not settle the matter by fiat, as we can legitimately do in a piece of "pure" rather than applied analysis.

These examples have all been taken from microeconomics; but the teachers of introductory macroeconomics have been no less guilty of teaching familiar techniques rather than illuminating ones. My colleague Charles Nelson has suggested in conversation that introductory macroeconomics is still obsessed with the Great Depression more than half a century after it ended because our legacy of macroeconomic tools contains so many concepts devised to explain equilibrium at less than full employment. It would be hard to find a better example of searching where the light is good instead of where illumination is required. Nonetheless, introductory macroeconomics teachers who fail to lay solid foundations for subsequent IS-LM analysis will work under the nagging fear that they are not doing their proper job and that they are courting departmental censure. Their job, as conventionally misunderstood, is not to educate the citizens of a democracy, but to begin preparing students for careers as professional economists.

The Dominance of Academic Departments

Perhaps we won't be able to free our introductory courses from such disabling presuppositions until undergraduate education itself has been liberated from the dominance of academic departments. Departments at leading universities are oriented to their disciplines, which is probably inevitable so long as teaching staff are rewarded primarily for pushing out the frontiers of knowledge in regions controlled by those disciplines. But is it either necessary or desirable that research-oriented disciplines control the content and delivery of undergraduate education? We cannot realistically expect academicians who are narrowly focused on their research interests to reflect thoughtfully on the requirements of a liberal education, or even to care a great deal about general undergraduate education.

An alternative might be semi-autonomous undergraduate colleges within the research universities. It is not certain that such colleges could in the long run escape capture by the research culture of the disciplines while also maintaining high intellectual standards. But the risk might be worth taking. In the long run, as John Maynard Keynes observed in another context, we are all dead.

CHAPTER 18

Teaching Economics by Telling Stories

I'VE BEEN TEACHING introductory economics for over 35 years and I think I've finally figured out how it ought to be done. That doesn't mean I now do it right. It's very hard to teach introductory economics effectively, and I often blow it. But I think I know what I want to do and what I ought to be doing.

What Should We Teach?

If I'm going to persuade you, however, we'll first have to establish a measure of agreement on why we want students to learn economics in the first place. What is it we hope they will take away from our classes?

Adam Smith began his inquiry into the nature and causes of the wealth of nations by asserting that almost all increases in productivity and hence in wealth could be attributed to the division of labor. Now the division of labor, or specialization, must obviously go hand-in-hand with exchange. Not quite so obviously, the division of labor will extend itself only if exchange can occur *at low cost*. You won't specialize in the making of left-handed scissors unless you expect to find, without too much trouble, people who want these scissors badly enough to give you in return enough

Unpublished typescript, provenance unknown. Reprinted by permission of Mrs. Juliana Heyne.

of what you want to justify your efforts. What this all comes to is that the growth of national wealth presupposes the evolution of an effective, low-cost system to facilitate the quick exchange of innumerable goods, services, and resources among millions of people who don't even know one another.

Economics, as I understand it and try to teach it, is the discipline that takes as its primary task the explanation of such systems. It explains how people manage to advance the projects in which they are interested by furthering the projects of millions of other people whom they usually don't even know. Economics, in other words, explains the working of markets.

Why Should We Teach It?

Why is it important that students learn how markets work? It's not so that they can personally participate more effectively in the market system. I hate to admit this, but I don't believe that a knowledge of economics is of much help to somebody who wants to get rich. It doesn't *hurt,* and it may even convey a *slight* advantage. But the advantage is *very* slight. You get rich by knowing something that other people don't know, or by working hard, or by choosing your parents carefully, or just by being lucky. You don't get rich by studying economics.

The reason we should want everyone to have a basic understanding of economics, or of how markets work, is *political.* In a democracy, ignorance and misunderstanding on the part of the public lead to pressure on government to do all sorts of things that interfere with the effective operation of markets. A high level of economic understanding among the members of a society provides protection against many of the foolish things that governments are inclined to do in response to social problems and popular pressure.

That's the *political* reason for putting economics into the high school curriculum. Is there an *individual* reason for learning it if it won't make the student rich (except for the fact that somebody made it a requirement for graduation and graduation tends to increase lifetime incomes)? I think there is. *It clears up puzzles.* It explains important and interesting mysteries. People with any sort of intellectual life, or just with a healthy human curiosity about the world in which they live, cannot be comfortable participating in a social system that they don't understand.

Moreover, social systems that impinge on us daily in important ways seem threatening when we don't know how they work. They generate alienation and anxiety. So the best reason for anyone to learn economics is that a knowledge of how markets work *empowers the knower.* Economic understanding is a powerful antidote to the sense of impotence that comes from supposing that "they" must be in control because "we" are not. And if enough people learn good economics because it's interesting and empowering, they will generate better government economic policy as a spillover benefit.

How to Make It Boring

Unfortunately, as I said at the outset, it is extremely difficult to impart that understanding. If we can rely on the reports from those who have taken courses in economics, most courses are not interesting at all. They are hopelessly boring. They don't empower anyone; they put everyone to sleep. Why is that? How can a subject that deals with such important problems and processes be so boring?

The root of the difficulty, I have come to believe, is the fact that *economics provides no clear and definitive answers to any significant social questions.* I'll say that again, because it's true, important, and probably a bit surprising coming from someone who makes a good living by teaching economics and even enjoys it: *Economics provides no clear and definitive answers to any significant social questions.* It provides insight, understanding, a wider comprehension, sometimes even a good bit of wisdom. But it does *not* provide a clear and definitive answer to any important social question.

Most of the economists I know would not be very happy with that statement. They believe that economics is a worthwhile discipline capable of making important contributions to public policy. I believe that, too. I merely deny that economics can provide *clear and definitive solutions* to any controversial social problem.

Economics teachers who, despite this fact, insist upon teaching "clear and definitive" answers will end up either *teaching arid definitions,* whether verbal or mathematical, or *trumpeting dogmatisms*. And either one quickly becomes tiresome and tedious.

Here are some illustrations of arid definitions: "There are three factors of production: land, labor, and capital"; "In the long run, under conditions of perfect competition, price will be equal to average total cost of production"; "The balanced budget multiplier is equal to the investment multiplier minus one." For additional examples, consult almost any of the questions that appear on high school Advanced Placement exams in economics. The distinguishing characteristics of this material are that it's difficult to learn, it bores students, and it does not clarify, much less settle, any important social issue.

Here is a good example of what I call a "trumpeted dogmatism": "Free trade makes everyone better off." I call that a *dogmatism* not because I'm opposed to free trade (I'm the most uncompromising advocate of free trade that I know), but because the statement is both false and unilluminating. If it were true that free trade makes *everyone* better off, then people would not spend vast amounts of time and money seeking to impose restrictions on free trade. But people do oppose free trade, and very few of them are completely deluded in their belief that free trade will, at least in the short run, make them personally worse off.

Some statements of this sort, while not strictly true, are nonetheless illuminating, because they are useful first steps along the pathway to improved understanding. "Free trade makes everyone better off" is *not* helpful in this way. It arouses every instinct of resistance, especially among thoughtful students, who have learned that True/False statements containing the word "everyone" are *invariably* false. We should begin with the truth on this issue: that all persons who engage in voluntary trade *expect it to make them better off*. That's a thoroughly defensible statement. And it's a statement that establishes an important beachhead for subsequent assaults on the myths of protectionism. But notice that it does not by itself demonstrate that the North American Free Trade Agreement is good for the United States or that our government should not impose restrictions on imports from Japan. In order to reach agreement on such important social and political questions, we have to go beyond arid definitions and sweeping dogmatisms to something much more difficult: *the telling of plausible stories*.

We teach economics effectively, which is to say that we teach our students how markets work, when we help them trace out the probable consequences of selected market actions and market interventions. I'll present two extended examples to show you concretely what I have in mind.

Stories About Mobile Home Parks

The first example deals with *mobile home parks*. I start off with a story. Stories are not the same as fictions. Stories are narratives: they recount a series of events, which may be true or fictitious. I prefer true stories, but I also use fictitious ones at times. The one that follows is true. It's simplified, as all stories have to be, but it recounts events that have actually occurred. Here it is:

> As the demand to live in mobile homes has increased in Seattle and other West Coast cities, largely in response to very high real estate prices, the demand for mobile home *sites* has also increased. But many of these cities, responding to pressure from neighbors who think that mobile home parks lower property values, have refused to allow the opening of new mobile home parks at a rate adequate to keep up with the demand. Meanwhile, many owners of existing mobile home parks in urban areas are converting their parks to other, more profitable uses. The predictable result is high and rising rental rates for the sites available to owners of mobile homes. This situation has led one angry mobile home owner to write to a local newspaper: "If you want to make money real fast, buy a mobile home park. You can raise the rent to your heart's content, because the tenants usually can't afford to move."

I usually present this story to my students through an overhead projector. After they have had a chance to read it, we talk about it briefly to be sure we all understand what's going on. Then I ask them to write a paragraph that will explain to the aggrieved mobile home owner *why he is wrong:* why people cannot in fact expect to make money real fast by purchasing a mobile home park and raising the rents. Notice that the letter writer has told a story. When I ask my students to explain in writing why he is wrong, I'm actually asking them to explain *why his story is not plausible.*

I usually ask them to compare notes when they have finished. Sometimes I collect the answers *before* we discuss them, sometimes *afterward*. Sometimes I'll postpone the discussion to the next class period, after I've had a chance to read their "counter-stories" and to prepare stories of my own that take off from or amplify or present more plausible alternatives to the stories they have composed.

But it's all stories. The stories I like, and to which I will want to introduce my students in the course of this exercise, tell about politicians kowtowing to the NIMBY sentiment and discriminating against people who would like to move to the city in favor of people who are already there; about people who want to live in mobile homes but can't find sites and who start to bid up the rental rate on sites; about owners of mobile home parks who realize they can get more than they're currently charging; about park owners who do *not* raise rents, either because they're nice guys or because they're not astute price searchers, who consequently confront long queues of aspiring renters, and who begin discriminating against potential renters on other criteria, such as pet ownership, age, size of deposit, race, and so on; about more astute price searchers who recognize in the below-market rents an opportunity for profit and consequently offer the owner a price beyond what he ever thought his park was worth, which he accepts—after which rents *do* go up; about the way in which people looking for a good deal bid up the prices of assets that are good deals, so that you can't buy a good deal unless you know something that almost nobody else knows.

At some point in this festival of stories I raise a new question: What will happen if the city council responds to letters such as this one by legislating ceilings on what owners of mobile-home parks can charge for a site? I may ask them to write an answer; I may ask them to form groups and list probable consequences of such rent controls. What will emerge are stories, which we can examine together for their plausibility. A lot of students will tell stories about the unavailability of sites for people moving into the area. Some will talk about owners who convert their mobile-home parks to other uses when they are denied an opportunity to profit by raising rents. A few exceptionally astute students may talk about mobile home owners who rent or sell their home to someone else at premium prices, because the home has a legal entitlement to a below-market rental rate.

I will be sure that they hear stories about kind and gentle park owners who delayed raising their rents and hence got socked by the city council's rent freeze, and who now sit and fume about the fact that those who were quickest to take advantage of the shortage are also those who managed to escape the freeze, proving again that no good deed ever goes unpunished; about the follow-up measures that the city council finds itself compelled to adopt: prohibitions on conversion of mobile-home parks to other uses, a commission to hear and arbitrate increasingly bitter and complex disputes between landlords and tenants, and so on.

Almost every major concept in economic theory can find illustration in the stories that emerge from reflection on the implausible tale told by the aggrieved letter writer. At no point do I attempt to draw a clear and definitive conclusion. I do not, however, object to students who draw their own conclusions about the arbitrary and unfair nature of all this, or who notice—as they can hardly help doing—that when legislators make special rules for favored groups, they produce a lot of consequences that no one had anticipated and that few would want.

Stories About Prescription Drugs

So much for my first example. For the second I have chosen an important and controversial public policy issue at this time: government controls on prescription drug prices.

I have learned to begin concretely. Here is one approach. Distribute to the students or display on an overhead projector the following information:

> The Swedish pharmaceutical company ABAstra is charging $58 for a daily dose of Foscavir, or more than $21,000 for one year's supply. Foscavir is a new drug that can prevent an AIDS-related blindness caused by cytomeglovirus retinitis, a disease that affects about 30% of people with AIDS. The cost of manufacturing a daily dose of Foscavir is less than $1. Why is ABAstra able to charge such a high price? List as many relevant factors as you can think of.

I like to add the following warning:

Note: "Greed" is not part of a correct answer. Since none of you knows the people who made the decision to set the price so high, you cannot know anything about their motives. More importantly, greed does not *enable* anyone to set a high price. Lots of greedy people have gone bankrupt because they could not manage to charge prices high enough even to cover their costs.

It's a very good idea on this project to divide the students into manageable-sized groups and ask them to prepare a report listing the principal factors that enable the pharmaceutical company to charge a price so far above its actual production costs.

The first lesson to be taught is that when we run across a situation we don't like—"outrageous exploitation of sick people," for example—we should start by asking *how the situation came about and why it persists.* What's actually going on here? That's an extremely important lesson: for the dinner table, the conference room, the legislative hall, and the faculty lounge as well as the economics classroom. We all have a tendency, especially when we're filled with indignation, to begin with the conclusions and subsequently to choose the facts that will enable us to reach our preestablished results. That does little to promote understanding; it merely hardens opinions already held. It does not lead to learning. And it fosters debate rather than discussion. Doesn't it make far more sense to ask why, if the situation is as intolerable as it seems to be, it continues to exist? Social phenomena are not facts of nature, like mountains. They emerge from the choices individuals make in response to the situations they encounter, situations that are in turn largely created by the choices other people make. If we want to change society, we must first understand it. The first step toward understanding how markets work, and the beginning, I would say, of all social understanding, is the recognition that social phenomena are the product of particular choices in response to particular incentives. Incentives matter! To fix any social problem, we must alter the incentives. To do that, we must first discover what they are.

A primary objective of this specific exercise is getting students to see that the persistence of prices that are far above marginal costs requires explanation. We would not expect to find anyone consistently selling for

$5.80 a chocolate chip cookie that cost only 10¢ to produce. We would want to know why anyone would be willing to pay that much for a mere cookie, however delicious, and why other people haven't recognized the opportunity in this situation for huge profits and started to make a competitive cookie whose introduction would bring the price down. The goal is to *tell a plausible story*.

The story about Foscavir that I prefer marshals four explanatory factors. Given time and a few appropriate hints, your students should be able to come up with a similar list. (Always be generous; find what you're looking for in what your students say or write, if you can possibly do so.)

1. There are no good substitutes for Foscavir for people afflicted with CMV retinitis.
2. Insurance pays most or all of the price.
3. ABAstra must have a patent on the drug or some other way of preventing anyone else from producing it.
4. ABAstra can "justify" its high price and thereby reduce the likelihood of political retaliation by talking about the extremely high cost of developing and testing new drugs and the huge risks involved.

A case study such as this one will give the imaginative and flexible teacher many opportunities to move back and forth between specific applications and the two basic concepts in economics, demand and supply. The first two factors listed above make the demand for Foscavir quite inelastic at low prices. The third factor keeps competition from pushing the price down toward marginal cost. The fourth factor introduces important considerations of politics and even ethics, which should never be dismissed as irrelevant or inappropriate to an economic analysis. We want to understand how markets work, and they do not work in isolation from political and ethical forces.

When members of the class have achieved rough agreement on why the situation exists, only then are they ready to begin thinking about *what ought to be done*. The teacher's task at this stage is not to approve or reject any particular proposal but to ask, *What will happen if we adopt this or that proposal?* and to assist the students as they attempt to predict the consequences. Predictions in economics should always be offered humbly, and so should criticisms of predictions. Rather than say to our students, "That won't happen!" we should ask "Is that likely to occur?" The stories we tell can never be more plausible than the assumptions we're making, and the prediction of social phenomena requires the employment of so many assumptions that we can't possibly check on the plausibility of all of them. So humility is always in order.

Someone in the class is bound to suggest price controls, for example. "That will create shortages" is a poor rejoinder. "What will happen if we do?" is the appropriate response. Then together teacher and students can begin predicting the consequences of price controls. How will price controls affect the quantity demanded? How will they affect the quantity supplied? And how will they affect the development of *new* drugs in the long run? The last question is the crucial one. For if demand won't allow pharmaceutical companies to make anything but losses on unsuccessful drugs, while competition won't allow them to make anything more than a small profit on most of their drugs, and the law won't allow extraordinary profits on a few successful drugs, what will provide the incentive for research?

After constructing and evaluating stories that tell how people are likely to respond to various suggested proposals for reform, you could shift gears radically. *How should we finance research?* Maybe it's not something we can legitimately expect the private sector to do. You could point out that there are substantial positive externalities associated with pure research and that this creates an argument for at least *some* government funding. So ask your students to assume that *all* drug research is going to be funded by the national government, and to figure out how Congress might go about deciding in such circumstances how much money to allocate *in total* to drug research.

This can be an excellent exercise for driving home the concept of opportunity cost. The cost of more funds for drug research, which means more resources devoted to drug research, is fewer funds and fewer resources for other projects that we also value. After the students have encountered some of the principal difficulties, learning along the way that members of Congress don't invariably vote for what even they believe is in the nation's interest if something else is in the interest of their district, ask them to take the next step. Explain how Congress could go about deciding how much of that total to allocate to various diseases. I would expect the subsequent discussion to reveal, among other things, some of the differences between market demand and political demand, or between a demand curve and lobbying pressure. Then ask how the sum allocated to research on a particular disease should be allocated among the various research programs that different groups of scientists want to pursue. The students will come to appreciate through the ensuing discussion that it isn't necessarily selfish to pursue the projects in which one is personally interested, but that neither can people—not even scientists—be given a blank check to pursue their own interests.

When your students have discovered for themselves how difficult it would be for the political process to allocate research funds in a defensible way, you might ask them to evaluate the following proposal:

> Those who want to do research must raise their own funds. The total amount allocated to drug research and development will then be the total amount that interested people can raise. And the funds will naturally go to the diseases and particular research projects that these people choose.

I have tried this. The discussion that results is most interesting and instructive, especially because of the many contrary-to-fact presuppositions that students employ, such as that scientists will have to engage in fund raising, which they aren't very good at (or for which we would say they have no comparative advantage), or that research will only be done on the diseases to which rich people are prone. It usually takes a good while and a bit of prodding for them to discover that this is in fact a description of the entrepreneurial system that we currently use to finance most drug research. You want them to begin reflecting on the role of the entrepreneur in an uncertain world and the way in which the possibility of profit and residual claimancy in an enterprise system places the power to allocate resources in the hands of people with an incentive to assemble and apply the best possible information and the most effective resources.

Only after such an extensive inquiry would you be in a position to ask what would happen if the government imposed price controls on prescription drugs. Price controls would undermine the information and incentive mechanisms of the entrepreneurial system and force the question of funding almost entirely into the political arena, where acceptable criteria for resource allocation cannot be expected to function.

Dialectical Science

How long might it take in a high school economics class to examine in this way the question of prescription drug prices? I don't know. Not less than a week. Perhaps not less than two weeks. Done carefully, it might take three weeks. And that prompts the obvious objection: "I don't have time to spend three weeks on the single issue of prescription drug prices." And of course you don't. But that's not what I'm recommending. I'm recommending that you use the issue of prescription drug prices to teach your students how market systems work. You certainly have three weeks for that.

You can't rush through an economics course and be successful, because economics must be taught dialectically and dialogue takes time. It takes time to find out what the problem is, more time to discover that "the problem" is really several problems, still more time to discern the main outlines of the situation in which the problems arise, additional time to explore possible causes and probable effects. It takes time to set the stage for the telling of plausible stories and more time to spell out those stories and to consider counter-stories. If you don't have that much time, you don't have the time to teach economics effectively.

I am not talking now about mere formal or technical economic theory. That can be taught by absolutely anyone with a graduate degree in economics, a standard textbook, and enough indifference to whining students to flunk everyone who refuses to read the textbook and master the theory. Formal or technical theory can be learned by any students with SAT scores high enough to get into college and an instructor who insists that they learn it. But a mastery of the formalities is not the same as really understanding how markets work. I have known dozens of economics students, many of them graduate students, whose command of technical theory would earn them an A grade in an economics course, who were incapable of seeing how this theory illuminated the working of actual economic systems.

I have even begun to suspect that a thorough knowledge of the formal theory is in some instances a *barrier* to the kind of understanding toward which we ought to be working. The theory, you see, is clear-cut, definitive, and yields precise answers—because it operates exclusively with precise concepts. Those who invest long years in its study develop a fondness for its clarity and—a favorite word—its *rigor*. Unfortunately, they also often develop a distaste for any economic analysis that lacks the precision and rigor of abstract theory. They don't want to apply their nice clean concepts to the messy world of real market transactions because that will not yield the clear and definitive result so craved by economists who yearn to be scientists.

I think storytelling is a legitimate form of science. But if those who guard the citadel of Science decide that it's not, then I will let them have their Science and I'll stick to storytelling. For it is through the telling and hearing and critical consideration of stories that people come to understand how market systems work.

CHAPTER 19

Between Sterility and Dogmatism

THIS PAPER WILL TRY to describe an approach to the teaching of economics that might improve our chances of avoiding both sterility and dogmatism.[1] In the course of arguing for the approach, I want to present and defend the heretical claim that economics has a great deal to say about the morality of the market.

Scylla and Charybdis

The sterility with which I am concerned comes from refusing to draw a conclusion until we think we have provided a complete statement of the conditions that must be met for the conclusion to follow rigorously. Economists who behave in this antiseptic fashion give the impression to students that their discipline has nothing of real importance to say about social issues. The opposite danger is dogmatism, which appears when we present conclusions without adequate supporting evidence and argumentation—without just what it takes to produce sterility.

Reprinted from *Journal of Private Enterprise* (Fall 1986): 14–19, by permission of the publisher.
1. The approach is hardly novel. F. A. Hayek is its most eminent contemporary practitioner, but Adam Smith was working this way in the eighteenth century. I presented an earlier version of these recommendations in March 1986 to students and faculty at Whitman College in Walla Walla, Washington. They might not even recognize the present version, but their questions and comments made a significant contribution to my reformulation of the argument.

If this account is roughly correct, there may be no channel through which to steer between the rock of dogmatism and the whirlpool of sterility. In that case we would be in urgent need of an alternative route. Sterility and dogmatism, in case they don't stand self-condemned, are serious impediments to the generation and maintenance of student interest. Interest is essential to learning, because people learn nothing in which they have not first become interested. Threats such as low grades can sometimes stir interest—they induced me to learn the multiplication tables. But threats are far less effective and reliable in nurturing interest than is the belief that valuable insight or understanding lies ahead.

The core of my recommendation is simply that economics be taught with far more attention to social *processes*. We spend too much time, I believe, on the formal relationships among static variables. We neglect the more interesting and significant issues: What processes created and now maintain these relationships? What subsequent processes can we anticipate as a result of these relationships or the introduction of new factors?

Formal Analysis

Suppose you're teaching the orthodox "theory of the firm" (or what we oddly call "the theory of the firm" even when the actors are not firms but net-revenue-maximizing black boxes). You show your students when and why marginal revenue lies below demand for a particular seller, and what will happen when marginal revenue and marginal cost are less than price. You derive and display the familiar triangle between the demand curve and the marginal cost curve that results from the seller's decision to restrict sales to the quantity at which marginal revenue equals marginal cost. What do you do next?

What can be extracted from this set of formal relationships among static variables: demand, price, marginal cost, marginal revenue, quantity? Can we demonstrate waste, inefficiency, non-optimality?

Many of us try. We go through contortions that numb the minds of our students in a largely vain effort to derive some significant conclusion from the analysis without violating our canons of scientific procedure. We would like to demonstrate—rigorously, of course—that an expansion of output to reduce the size of the triangle is a Pareto-superior move. But we need to make some assumptions in order to get to this conclusion, assumptions that are very hard even to state clearly. Zero transaction costs is a favorite. What is there about zero transaction costs or perfect information that makes economists think it will justify policy conclusions? Why don't we allow zero transportation costs to perform a similar function in our analysis? One can defend any policy conclusion at all if allowed to abstract from everything that would defeat the policy. I believe I could "solve" all the social problems of the world if allowed to assume zero transaction costs. Is it not the case that distinctively *social* problems are always the result of positive transaction costs, and would disappear if transaction costs were zero?[2] What in the world are we doing when we introduce such assumptions in order to draw conclusions? The truth of transaction costs is that they exist, in a multitude of surprising and unexpected forms. They are part of the processes of social interaction. There are all sorts of very real and important costs associated with social transactions that we had tended to overlook before Ronald Coase, or Frank Knight before him, taught us to see why the social world so often fails to meet our expectations.[3]

Substantive Analysis

The beginning of substantive as distinct from purely formal economic analysis is dissatisfaction. We begin by observing an unsatisfactory state of affairs, or what we suspect to be an unsatisfactory state of affairs, or what someone else says is an unsatisfactory state of affairs. Our formal analysis, with cost curves and demand curves, is a preliminary exercise, an aid to thinking that acquires meaning only when it is put to work on some real,

2. If all members of every society had "perfect information," including correct information about what everyone else wanted and how much each would sacrifice to obtain (or avoid losing) what was valued, what kind of *social* problems could possibly arise? There would be no wars, for example, because with the outcome of any conflict known in advance, the parties would simply settle on the terms that conflict would impose. The price system on which economists lavish so much study (properly, in my view) would be unnecessary in a world of perfect information costlessly acquired by all.

3. The classic reference is to R. H. Coase, "The problem of social cost," *Journal of Law and Economics* (October 1960). Knight's discussion of methods for meeting uncertainty was a much earlier exploration of these themes. Frank H. Knight, *Risk, Uncertainty and Profit* (New York: Harper and Row, 1965; originally published in 1921), especially part III.

or at least recognizable, social transactions: the marketing of airline tickets, for example, or of restaurant meals, prescription drugs, hardcover and paper-cover books, new textbooks and used textbooks, bachelor's degrees, foreign automobiles, crude petroleum, long-distance telephone service, or any other price-cost relationship troubling enough to prompt the question: Is this what we want?

Our tools are put to interesting and important uses when we employ them to construct plausible accounts of social processes in response to some kind of dissatisfaction with an observed state of affairs. These accounts can look backward or forward in time. We can try to explain how the observed situation came about; or we can try to predict what will happen if some new factor is introduced, such as a change in the law. This, I submit, is the knowledge we're after whenever we are trying to evaluate a situation.

Criticism and Inquiry

Suppose, for example, that a student complains about the difference between what the bookstore pays when it buys back used books and what it charges when it resells them. Does the student have a legitimate complaint? We are regularly told that economic analysis cannot answer such questions; but that is a half-truth at best. If economic analysis cannot tell us what *ought to be*, it can often tell us a good bit of how matters might have *come to be*. What is the social process through which the gap between buying price and selling price is established and maintained? That is basically what we must know in order to judge whether or not the bookstore is behaving in an unfair or otherwise unacceptable way. And that is precisely the sort of knowledge economics can help us acquire. It is true that no finite account of the process can be guaranteed in advance to settle the question of fairness to any particular person's satisfaction. But that implies no more than that any inquiry might have to be extended. In what direction? In whatever direction the continuing questions of the dissatisfied inquirer may point us.

A situation cannot be judged satisfactory or unsatisfactory, of course, until it has been compared with alternatives. Economics provides the same kind of assistance here. If our indignant student judges the bookstore's used-textbook practices unacceptable, the question of an alternative system immediately arises. "What changes would he recommend?" When the recommendation for reform is presented, economic analysis can attempt to anticipate its consequences. Once again the consequences will be a *process,* and not simply a clearly-defined state of affairs at some future date. The proposed reform can then be evaluated in the light of the flow of consequences anticipated from its introduction. There is again no guarantee that the asserted consequences will convince any particular person that the proposed reform is either desirable or unacceptable. Anyone may want to push the inquiry further. While refusing to decide is in practice itself a decision, in principle economic analysis can continue indefinitely.

Positive-Normative or Simple-Complex?

The claim that economic analysis can never settle normative questions is demonstrably false, since it often does exactly that. It is quite true that economic analysis *by itself* can never settle normative questions, but economic analysis never exists "by itself." The knowledge anyone acquires through economic analysis always exists in conjunction with a lot of other knowledge, beliefs, values, assumptions, working principles, and matters taken for granted. Economic analysis presents *arguments,* and no argument, not even the most respectably rigorous one, will necessarily convince anyone, much less everyone. That's just as true, however, of so-called positive economics as it is of normative economics.[4]

Certain kinds of questions are indeed easier to answer than others. Clearly-formulated questions, simple questions, and questions resting upon a broad or deep consensus are easier to answer than carelessly-formulated questions, complex questions, or questions that beg questions. The gulf that so many economists believe they see between positive and normative questions reflects, I think, a misinterpretation. The questions we call "positive" are the ones on which we think we know how to achieve agreement: the clear, simple questions that arise within a well-understood and accepted framework of thought. We label a question "normative" not because it is

---

4. Donald N. McCloskey has done much to make this position more acceptable, or at least familiar, in the economics profession. See especially McCloskey, "The Rhetoric of Economics," *Journal of Economic Literature* (June 1983).

categorically different from "positive" questions but because we don't (yet) know exactly how to go about agreeing upon an acceptable answer.

More Misleading Distinctions

Perhaps economists pay so little attention to processes and so much attention to static outcomes at well-defined points in time and space because we find it so much harder to pose questions we can answer definitively when we inquire about processes. That is probably also why we disavow any knowledge of equity but claim expertise on efficiency. We may know less about efficiency than we suppose, however, and more than we realize about equity. Every measure of efficiency is a ratio of values; there is no such thing as technological or objective efficiency. It follows that every measure of efficiency presupposes the appropriateness of particular evaluations, which means, to make a long story short, that every measure of efficiency presupposes the acceptability of some set of entitlements or property rights. Who has the right to value, or to have their valuations counted? An authoritative statement about efficiency rests upon an implicit judgment about equity.

The means-ends distinction is another device we commonly use to confine the questions we ask within manageable bounds. That dichotomy, too, tends to steer us away from the study of social processes into the examination of static conditions: the formal conditions entailing the most effective allocation of given means for the achievement of given ends. In reality, however, neither means nor ends are ever given. We have no ends, but only provisional goals which are going to be means toward the achievement of further goals if we reach them; and those further goals will also be provisional and also really means. We don't know what we're after, even though we are highly purposive creatures. We largely find out what we want in the *process* of trying to get it. And one thing we want is to discover more about the means at our disposal. Our goals change as we approach them. There are no "final goods," no benefits at the end to be totted up and compared with all the costs in some grand benefit-cost analysis, because benefits often turn into costs and costs into benefits before we get to the end—except that there is no end, unless it's death, whereupon it's too late for benefit-cost analysis to serve any purpose. The means-ends dichotomy is a useful simplification. When invoked as a dogma, however, it distorts our perceptions and obscures the important truth that purposive behavior, especially among a society of cooperating persons, is a process and not a problem in pure logic.[5]

I do not want to be misunderstood. I am *prescribing*, not *proscribing*. Economists should and will continue to engage in static analysis, because it stimulates their interest, advances their careers, and also sharpens the tools we use to analyze social processes. My concern is that the prestige and satisfactions of static analysis not deter economists, especially teachers of economic principles, from also using their tools to construct plausible accounts of social processes in response to problematic situations.

Moral Judgments and Social Processes

I want to conclude with the altogether heretical argument that we are seriously underestimating the power of our analytical tool kit and the relevance of our discipline to public policy when we contend that economics has nothing to say about justice or other ethical issues. By making this self-denying claim, we surrender the right to discuss the morality of the market to those who don't understand how markets work. If economics is practiced exclusively in the formal-static mode, it will indeed have little to say about justice, because justice in large societies characterized by market interactions is far more a matter of process than of outcomes or states. Whether a situation is or is not unjust will depend on the processes that produced it. There is no such thing as an unjust *pattern* of income distribution; or, if there is, I have yet to encounter a clear and coherent explanation of how it could be recognized. There are, however, unjust *actions* that distribute income in particular ways. When economists discuss the social processes through which income is allocated, they are, whether they wish to or not, illuminating the morality of those processes.

---

5. No one has argued more cogently for the position taken in the two preceding paragraphs than Frank Knight. See especially the first two essays in Frank H. Knight, *The Ethics of Competition and Other Essays* (Chicago: University of Chicago Press, 1976). One of Knight's most distinguished students, James Buchanan, maintains that Knight himself failed fully to appreciate the limitations that his own arguments place upon the conception of economic activity as essentially maximizing activity.

It is not the outcome but the process itself that enables us to approve or condemn the functioning of the market in particular cases. Outcomes such as poverty, unemployment, or inequality are only relevant as clues or guides to inquiry. I am not merely arguing that this is how we *ought* to assess the morality of the market; I am contending that this is *in fact* how we do it, even when we describe what we are doing quite differently. I am thus making an empirical claim, a claim that can be tested by examining the processes of moral reflection and moral discourse in which we regularly engage. Someone who asserts, for example, that great wealth amid grinding poverty is an unjust *state* is, I believe, putting forward the hypothesis that any such combinations that we observe will be found to have emerged from unjust processes.

To Be Continued

But what constitutes an unjust process? While that isn't an easy question to answer, neither is it the altogether empty question that so many economists seem to suppose. What processes do we in fact condemn as unjust? What do our actual processes of moral reflection and moral discourse reveal? There is no ultimate answer, of course. There never is, at least not to any human question. Those who practice economics as a humane science, rather than a branch of human engineering, must learn how to be content with less than ultimate answers and with suggestions that are merely plausible.

PART 7

Economic Method

CHAPTER 20

Ethics on *The Road to Serfdom* and Beyond

FRIEDRICH HAYEK began *The Road to Serfdom* with a confession and a promise.

The original preface opens with the following admission:

> When a professional student of social affairs writes a political book, his first duty is plainly to say so. This is a political book. I do not wish to disguise this by describing it, as I might perhaps have done, by the more elegant and ambitious name of an essay in social philosophy. But, whatever the name, the essential point remains that all I shall have to say is derived from certain ultimate values.[1]

That is the confession. The promise follows immediately:

> I hope I have adequately discharged in the book itself a second and no less important duty: to make it clear beyond doubt what these ultimate values are on which the whole argument depends. (Ibid.)

I have deliberately chosen the word *confession* to describe Hayek's discharge of his "first duty." His language strongly suggests that, in his own

Unpublished typescript, provenance unknown, reprinted by permission of Mrs. Juliana Heyne.

1. Friedrich Hayek, *The Road to Serfdom* (Chicago: University of Chicago Press, 1972), xvii. Citations are to the edition with a new, 1976 preface by the author.

judgment, a "professional student of social affairs" violates a rule of the guild when he writes a "political book." That is because political books, unlike scientific books dealing with social affairs, depend upon the author's values. When Hayek informs the reader that "all I shall have to say" is derived from "certain ultimate values," he is confessing to a lapse: he has left the realm of science. He has also, in part, abandoned the realm of reasoned argument. As the word "ultimate" indicates, his values, indispensable though they are for such a book, cannot and therefore will not be defended or argued for. Because they are ultimate, there is nothing beyond or beneath to which one might point to make a rational or empirical case for them.

That explains the author's duty to make clear to the reader "beyond doubt" what the ultimate values are on which the entire argument depends. Clarity and candor are all that can be demanded from the social scientist who introduces value judgments into his work. Hayek intends to satisfy that demand by making his value judgments unmistakably clear.

As it turns out, he does not fulfill his promise. Two readings of the book in its 50th anniversary year, including one reading with just this question in mind, have not enabled me to discover "the ultimate values... on which the whole argument depends." Readers will gain frequent insight into Hayek's values and ideals while reading *The Road to Serfdom*, but Hayek has certainly not made it "clear beyond doubt" what the *ultimate* values are.

He passes up a chance to do so in the first paragraph of Chapter I when he refers to "some of our most cherished ideals" without indicating what they are, and he passes up another chance in the next paragraph when he mentions "the values for which we are now fighting [World War II]" without stating them. He seems to place a high value on that "individualism" which grew out of Christianity and ancient classical philosophy, was first fully developed during the Renaissance, and subsequently grew into what we call "Western civilization" but he does not identify this individualism as one of his ultimate values. He complains that " '[f]reedom' and 'liberty' are now words so worn with use and abuse that one must hesitate to employ them to express the ideals for which they stood" during the post-Renaissance development of Western civilization. He suggests that the word "tolerance" might still preserve the full meaning of the principle which was in the ascendant during this period, but he does not pause to clarify or elaborate the concept, and he does not say that it is one of his ultimate values.

Hayek speculates that the "marvelous growth of science" might be "the greatest result of the unchaining of individual energies... which followed the march of individual liberty from Italy to England and beyond." But the growth of knowledge is also not identified as an ultimate value. One could make a good case that the rule of law, discussed especially in Chapter VI, is the central concept around which the entire argument of *The Road to Serfdom* revolves. But Hayek does not put the rule of law forward as an ultimate value, and for excellent reasons. Its value for him derives from its consequences which must therefore be more ultimate than the rule of law itself.

Every student of Hayek knows how much he valued freedom from the arbitrary power of others, "release from the ties which left the individual no choice but obedience to the orders of a superior to whom he was attached." This, he tells us, was what the word had meant "to the great apostles of freedom." The connotations of the word "apostles" suggest the high value Hayek assigned to emancipation of individuals from the arbitrary power of others. But if this is the ultimate value upon which everything else depends, why did he not say so at this point? An extended discussion of freedom or liberty, defined as emancipation from the will of others, does not appear until Chapter IX. At the end of this chapter Hayek asserts that freedom or liberty can only be had at a price and that "we must be prepared to make severe material sacrifices to preserve our liberty." But if this is one of the ultimate values on which the entire argument depends, it certainly has not been identified as such "beyond doubt."

Hayek comes closest to so identifying it when he quotes Lord Acton, who "*truly* said of liberty" (emphasis added) that it "is not a means to a higher political end. It is itself the highest political end." But the quotation continues:

> It is not for the sake of a good public administration that [liberty] is required, but for the security in the pursuit of the highest objects of civil society, and of private life.

The last part of the quotation seems to make liberty, which is the highest *political* end, a means to the achievement of yet higher ends that are not political. Had Hayek identified this liberty as one of his *ultimate* values, he would not have been vulnerable to George Stigler's argument[2] that wealth does more than the absence of coercion to advance the values that Hayek cherishes.

We know that democracy is not an ultimate value for Hayek. He states clearly that it is a mere means, and he warns against what he calls "[t]he fashionable concentration on democracy as the main value."

What about respect for truth? Is this one of Hayek's ultimate values? He states that "the sense of and respect for truth" is "one of the foundations of all morals," and he warns against the corruption of science that occurs when "science has to serve, not truth, but the interests of a class, a community, or a state." A plausible case can be made from arguments in his later books that respect for truth was indeed one of the deeper values informing Hayek's thought. In Chapter III of *The Constitution of Liberty* Hayek seems to suggest that we fulfill ourselves in the process of learning something new, and that we desire to accumulate additional knowledge because it makes us wiser, even if it also makes us sadder or worse off in all other ways. But that respect for truth is an ultimate value is not "clear beyond doubt" even in later works, much less in *The Road to Serfdom*.

*

Why does Hayek tell the reader that he will state clearly the ultimate values on which his argument depends and then fail to do so? The contradiction points to what I believe is a significant characteristic of Hayek's thought. *He was always troubled by the suspicion that he had no adequate grounds for his own most important convictions.* Hayek craved foundations for his legal, political, and economic philosophy, but he was never able to find any that were capable, in his own judgment, of bearing the weight he wanted to put on them.

In *The Road to Serfdom*, Hayek is a good positivist, as we would expect of one who had reached intellectual maturity in the 1920s and 1930s. He knows that he is making policy recommendations; he believes that policy

---

2. George J. Stigler, "Wealth, and Possibly Liberty," *Journal of Legal Studies*, Volume VII, no. 2 (June 1978): 213–17.

recommendations must rest in part upon value judgments; he knows that he must therefore introduce his value judgments into the argument. But value judgments, he also believes, have no rational foundation. "Surely we have learned," he writes,

> that knowledge cannot create new ethical values.... It is not rational conviction but the acceptance of a creed which is required to justify a particular plan.

In the course of discussing the moral consequences of totalitarian propaganda, he distinguishes between questions about values, which are "questions of opinion," and "questions of fact where human intelligence is involved in a different way." What exactly *is* that difference? He does not say. Is there some other way to exercise human intelligence than the way in which we exercise it to arrive at conclusions about "questions of fact"? Can intelligence be employed to arrive at opinions about "questions of value"? Or are we using some less respectable or less reliable faculty? How can we argue on behalf of our values if neither reason nor facts are relevant to their acceptance? Our *ultimate* values would appear to be especially immune to any kind of rational or empirical test; precisely because they are *ultimate*, they rest on nothing beyond themselves.

This is not a satisfactory position for someone who wants to persuade. And why else write a book, especially a political book? So Hayek simply ignores his positivist principles and argues on behalf of his values and against antithetical values, employing both reason and facts.

Democracy, for example, is not an ultimate value, he insists, despite what many people think. They are thinking *wrongly*. They have failed to see what democracy can and cannot accomplish and how ineffective it is as a means to other goods that they value more highly.

People have placed excessively high value on equality, security, and the "rational" organization of production. Their valuations are misplaced, Hayek tries to show, because they lead to consequences whose negative value exceeds whatever positive value they might have.

The single-minded idealists who have united under the banner of planning will alter their ideals when they come to see that they have adopted a very limited view of society. The socialists who so value "the deliberate organization of the labors of society for a definite social goal" will cease to do so once they have discovered that this presupposes something not available to them, namely, a comprehensive scale of values or a complete ethical code. Those whose moral ideals have led them to support collectivism will adjust their ideals when they learn that the implementation of these ideals will eventually undermine them. Values *can* be criticized and defended, as Hayek shows by doing it.

Consider also some of his remarks about morality in *The Road to Serfdom*. A genuine morality, he maintains, must leave the conscience free and must acknowledge some general rules that the individual is always required to observe. The sense of and the respect for truth is one of the foundations of all morals. Moral principles must be seriously upheld against the expediencies and exigencies of social machinery. Responsibility not to a superior but to one's own conscience is "the very essence of any morals which deserve the name." We must have "moral courage" to defend stoutly the traditional ideals that our enemies attack. These are not the sort of comments one would expect from a thinker who deemed morality entirely a matter of values that have no rational foundation.

Milton Friedman claimed in his well-known essay on "The Methodology of Positive Economics" that most differences about economic policy among disinterested citizens derived from different readings of the facts rather than "from fundamental differences in basic values," and that this was a good thing because the former can, in principle at least, be eliminated by the growth of knowledge, whereas the latter are "differences about which men can ultimately only fight."[3] But that is surely not the case. Even if it is true that men can *ultimately* only fight about *fundamental* differences in *basic* values, value disagreements almost never produce violence among disinterested citizens. They do not reach that ultimate recourse because discussion provides so many better options along the way. If citizens cannot *resolve* fundamental differences in basic values, they also have a hard time *discovering* truly fundamental differences in truly basic values. It is not inability so much as impatience that prevents us from engaging in productive dialogue about conflicting values.

The insistence that there is no "truth" about values usually reflects a

3. Milton Friedman, *Essays in Positive Economics* (Chicago: University of Chicago Press, 1953), 5.

realization that we cannot find an ultimate proof for any value judgment, along with a failure to recognize that we also cannot find an ultimate proof for any other kind of judgment, including the conclusions of science. We do not so much prove as persuade, as Donald McCloskey has been arguing (persuasively) for the last decade or so. Fundamentalists (or foundationalists) lust for sure and certain foundations upon which they can construct knockdown arguments—arguments so powerful, as Robert Nozick once put it, that "they set up reverberations in the brain: if the person refuses to accept the conclusion, he dies. How's that for a powerful argument?" [4] Fortunately or unfortunately, we do not command any arguments with that kind of persuasive power.

It is ironic that Hayek, whose writings over the years demonstrated so effectively that rational arguments and the careful use of evidence can persuade people to alter their ethical positions, apparently never fully persuaded himself that this was the case. In *Rules and Order*, the first volume of his *Law, Legislation and Liberty* trilogy, Hayek repeatedly shows that the fact-value dichotomy is not fatal to rational discussion of ethical questions. He weaves together facts and norms in highly instructive ways, and shows in the course of doing so that David Hume, usually cited by those who claim there is an unbridgeable gulf between "is" and "ought," actually offers valuable instruction on how to go back and forth across that alleged chasm.

The rule of law, arguably the pivotal concept in Hayek's entire legal philosophy, has often been criticized on the grounds that it cannot be stated in an unambiguous way. That did not stop Hayek from employing the concept to formulate highly instructive criticisms of various tendencies in political theory and practice. What economists like to call rigorous arguments, arguments proceeding from clearly-defined postulates through formal logic to precise conclusions, are by no means the only kind of persuasive argument. Most of the published work by Hayek that eventually flowed from *The Road to Serfdom* reveals the power of arguments that persuade not by means of rigorous demonstration, but by highlighting the inadequacy of widely-held opinions and revealing the explanatory potential of novel organizing conceptions.

4. Robert Nozick, *Philosophical Explanations* (Cambridge, Mass.: Harvard University Press, 1981), 4.

That is how he proceeded in *The Road to Serfdom*. His practice was superior to his profession. He never managed to make his ultimate values clear beyond doubt because he in fact had no *ultimate* values, which is to say, no values from which all other values were derived and which could themselves not be strengthened or weakened by arguments and evidence. His *formal* position, taken over uncritically from the intellectual milieu, might even be described as "constructivist rationalism," the term he himself liked to use to describe those who exaggerated the power of the human mind to grasp the world whole and control it. His actual practice rejected the dogmas of constructivist rationalism in favor of a procedure much closer to what his friend Karl Popper called *critical* rationalism.

It is odd that a thinker who had so often demonstrated the folly of trying to construct completely comprehensive systems, capable of answering all questions in advance, nonetheless spent the final years of his career trying to construct an argument that would once and for all compel all socialist thinkers to forswear forever their attachment to central planning, social justice, and all the related mirages of constructivist rationalism. His last book, *The Fatal Conceit*, expresses this—may we say it?—*fatal conceit*. To make matters worse, Hayek ended up constructing the knockdown argument in a form that undermined his own repeated demonstrations in the course of a long career that ethics was a rational enterprise.

The argument first appeared in "The Three Sources of Human Values," the Epilogue appended to *The Political Order of a Free People*, the third volume of *Law, Legislation and Liberty*. Here Hayek argued that there are not two but three kinds of human values: those that are "genetically ordered and therefore innate"; those that are "products of rational thought"; and values that had triumphed in the course of cultural evolution by demonstrating their suitability to the successful organization of social life. Values of this third sort are the values that have made possible the finest achievements of Western civilization, including science, the rule of law, and commercial society with all its miraculous creative and productive powers. While these values are not the product of rational thought, they are not for that reason arbitrary. They are a cultural inheritance, survivors of a competitive struggle, and essential conditions for the successful evolution of our society.

The discovery of this third source of values seemed to provide the foundations for which Hayek had so long been searching. These were the *ultimate* values upon which all his political arguments might be made to depend. There was indeed no way to establish them rationally. But they reigned nonetheless. Those who chose to reject them committed cultural suicide by sawing off the very branch on which they were sitting in order to saw. The knockdown argument lay at hand.

Hayek grew so fond of this argument, unfortunately, that at the end he came to revel in the nonrational and even irrational character of the ethical beliefs that have created Western civilization. In the last chapter of *The Fatal Conceit*, for example, he almost gleefully gives substantial credit to the mystical and religious beliefs of the principal monotheistic religions that he himself does not accept and cannot even understand. And the final appendix to the book—the last word of the last word—announces with great excitement and intense satisfaction Hayek's discovery of a 1909 study by Sir James Frazer arguing that superstitions have often been of immense value. The last paragraph is worth quoting in its entirety.

> Frazer also concluded that "superstition rendered a great service to humanity. It supplied multitudes with a motive, a wrong motive it is true, for right action; and surely it is better for the world that men should be right from wrong motives than that they would do wrong with the best intentions. What concerns society is conduct, not opinion: if only our actions are just and good, it matters not a straw to others whether our opinions are mistaken."

This is surely a strange epitaph to the career of a thinker who did so much to show the enormous damage that mistaken opinions had done in the century spanned by his life.

CHAPTER 21

Measures of Wealth and Assumptions of Right: An Inquiry

Introduction

> There is no more important function of a first course in econom-
> ics than to make the student see that the whole problem of social
> management is a *value* problem; that mechanical or technical ef-
> ficiency is a meaningless combination of words.[1]

It is now almost sixty years since Frank Knight urged this perspective upon teachers of introductory economics, but his advice has not been heeded. To cite just one example: The glossary of a current *Casebook* edited by one of the profession's most experienced and respected specialists in economic education includes the item "technical efficiency" and does *not* define it as "a meaningless combination of words."[2]

The first section of this paper will attempt to demonstrate that Knight was correct, that "technical efficiency" cannot be defined except in a way that completely strips it of significance. Section two will argue that because, as Knight maintained, "the whole problem of social management is

Unpublished typescript of discussion paper prepared for a Liberty Fund conference, "Science, Markets, and Liberty," San Antonio, Texas, 5–8 March 1981. Reprinted by per-mission of Mrs. Juliana Heyne.

1. Frank H. Knight, "The Ethics of Competition," published originally in 1923 in the *Quarterly Journal of Economics,* reprinted in Knight, *The Ethics of Competition and Other Es-says* (Chicago: University of Chicago Press, 1976 Midway Reprint), p. 43.

2. Rendigs Fels, Stephen Buckles, and Walter L. Johnson, *Casebook of Economic Problems and Policies: Practice in Thinking,* 4th ed. (St. Paul: West Publishing Company, 1979), p. 161. The definition offered is: "production by a firm of the most output with given inputs of labor, capital, and natural resources; producing a given amount of output using the least inputs."

a *value* problem," many other familiar concepts of economic theory cannot have the meaning commonly attributed to them. Section three will try to show that economists can coherently formulate and apply a wide range of concepts relating to efficiency and wealth only because they are implicitly using judgments about the rights people ought to have. The fourth and final section of the paper will consider and finally reject the conclusion that might seem to follow from the first three sections, the conclusion that economics is not and cannot be a science. Economics can be scientific, in a very defensible sense of that word, if economists simply recognize what they are doing and give up their claim to possess some wholly impartial perspective.

I

Efficiency refers to the ability to achieve a given objective with a minimum expenditure of resources or, alternatively, the ability to obtain from a given amount of resources a maximum amount of one's objective. Efficiency is thus a ratio of output to input.

The crucial question, however, is how we measure output and input. Economists know that a ratio of mere physical quantities is not sufficient to determine the relative *profitability* of alternative processes. Decision makers who want to maximize net revenue must pay attention to the ratio between dollar values of outputs and inputs. Quite often, however, this concept of efficiency is called economic efficiency and is then contrasted with a purely physical efficiency, usually called technical efficiency. The significance of economic efficiency will often be argued for by showing the irrelevance of mere technical efficiency to any kind of goal-directed behavior.

The fatal slip occurs at this point, for efficiency has no meaning except with reference to goal-directed behavior. From a purely physical or technical point of view, the output of any process will always be equal to the inputs into that process. Technical efficiency is invariably one, at least if we can rely on the laws of the conservation of matter and energy. It follows that there is always a unique, invariant output from "given inputs," so that the notion of "*most* output" simply makes no sense. It *seems* to make sense to economists who use the concept of technical efficiency because they have smuggled in an evaluation: Only selected outputs will be recognized as outputs; the rest will be called "waste." The familiar term "engineering efficiency" acquires its meaning in precisely this way. A machine's efficiency, supposedly measured by the work done or the energy developed relative to the energy supplied, is in fact measured by the *useful* work done or *useful* energy developed relative to the energy supplied. The work or energy is evaluated before it is admitted to the category of output.

The concept of technical efficiency is misleading because it distorts the problem that economists are trying to study. For example, a popular introductory text asserts:

> In economics we generally make the assumption that technical efficiency is being maximized because there is not much else that economists can say about this topic. It is mainly in the hands of managers and engineers.[3]

The technocratic error looms close behind those sentences: the belief that "experts" are in command of costless procedures for achieving optimal arrangements. In reality, managers and engineers search for optimal input combinations until the expected benefits of further search no longer exceed the expected costs.

The same text, one page earlier, had defined "maximum technical efficiency" as a situation in which "resources are not being wasted," and offered this illustration:

> For example, a given amount of labor and capital might produce only 20 bushels of tomatoes if time were wasted or the machine used inappropriately. But if the inputs were fully utilized in the correct manner, 30 bushels might be produced.[4]

The author implicitly asserts in this passage that people producing tomatoes never *want* to use time on the job for conversation rather than single-minded tomato production, and that people who use tomato-picking machines in ways that don't maximize the tomato output have

3. Willis L. Peterson, *Principles of Economics: Micro,* 4th ed. (Homewood, Ill.: Richard D. Irwin, 1980), p. 230.
4. Ibid., p. 229 A similar argument is presented on p. 8.

no *valued* reason for doing so. This is obviously false. There is nothing inherently wasteful, inappropriate, or incorrect about *any* use of labor or capital.

The notion that there is an efficiency which exists independently of any valuations lends support to other misleading ideas. Consider the common belief that society (government officials? voters?) is faced with a tradeoff between efficiency and equity. If equity is valued, however, it will affect either the numerator or the denominator as people estimate the efficiency ratios of alternative processes. If the owner of a firm maintains certain wage differentials on the grounds of equity, despite his belief that net revenue could be increased by reducing those differentials, he is saying that the value imparted to the total outcome by equity exceeds, at the relevant margin, the value imparted by increased monetary income. From whose perspective is it "inefficient" for someone to prefer more equity to a larger money income?

The claim that "society" must choose between efficiency and equity obscures the actual situation, which is that people assign value to processes and their outcomes and that these valuations are often mutually incompatible.

II

The concept of technical efficiency will not be put to rest as long as the concept of objective costs continues to survive. The reformulation of economic theory that occurred in the last quarter of the nineteenth century produced the conclusion that all costs relevant to economizing decisions were the expected value of opportunities that would have to be forgone. Almost a century later, however, many economists continue to employ arguments that implicitly assume the existence of objective costs, costs that can be measured independently of anyone's evaluations of alternatives.

A good example is the concept of "absolute advantage" which most textbooks use to explain comparative advantage. In the typical exposition, "absolute advantage" is rejected as an adequate reason for a nation to produce a good; a nation should import those goods in which it has a comparative disadvantage, even if its "real costs" of production are below those of any other country. This is usually taught with an air of presenting a paradox. There is no paradox, however, because there are no costs that are not the value of foregone opportunities and hence no advantages *except* comparative advantages. The "real costs" whose ultimate irrelevance to trade we triumphantly demonstrate to our students are not costs at all. They are merely physical units of inputs, usually "man-hours" in our examples, which we surreptitiously *assume* to be all of equal value. The existence of a comparative advantage, however, implies that the value of inputs varies as they are used to produce alternative outputs. To assume them equal in value is to assume away the possibility of comparative advantage.

Royall Brandis demonstrated the mythical character of absolute advantage in 1967,[5] but his demonstration seems to have been largely ignored. Perhaps that's just as well. The logic of the opportunity cost perspective, which demonstrates the chimerical character of absolute advantage, will do the same damage, if consistently applied, to much more fundamental concepts in the economist's everyday kit of working tools. The casualties include a disturbing percentage of the supposedly empirical, objective concepts that we regularly use in discussing the performance of economic systems.

"Output restriction" provides a particularly instructive example. Suppose that widget producers establish a cartel and agree to reduce their rate of widget production in order to raise the market price above marginal cost. We commonly refer to this as "output-restriction," and go on to show the "deadweight loss" that the cartel policy generates: the area above the marginal cost curve and below the demand curve between the "competitive" output and the cartel output.[6]

It is true that fewer widgets are produced as a result of the cartel's operation. But is this an "output-restriction"? Outputs are ultimately valued opportunities, not things. The sum of the values produced under the "competitive" and under the cartel arrangement cannot be empirically compared, because the two arrangements produce different distributions of

5. Royall Brandis, "The Myth of Absolute Advantage," *American Economic Review*, March 1967, pp. 169–75.

6. For proof that those who throw stones sometimes live in glass houses, see Paul Heyne, *The Economic Way of Thinking*, 2nd edition (Palo Alto: Science Research Associates, 1976), pp. 106–7, 142–44. The 3rd edition (1980) is more circumspect but still in error. The evidence may be found on pp. 144–47.

different goods among participants in the economic system. There is consequently no way to show empirically that the cartel arrangement results in less *value* than "competition" produces. The cartel arrangement produces fewer widgets, but that is because those who have the *de facto* right to determine widget output and prices believe that the lost widgets will be of less value than whatever it is they expect to gain by their decision.

There is one way in which we might succeed in demonstrating that the competitive situation generates a greater sum of values than the cartel arrangement. This might be done by showing that *every interested person* prefers the competitive situation. But if that were the case, the cartel would not exist. Faced with this fact, we may fall back on the argument that those who prefer the competitive situation could gain enough from its restoration to pay the cartel members a sum sufficient to persuade them to abandon the cartel. The continued existence of the cartel, however, is evidence that consent to its abandonment cannot actually be secured, which means that the prospective gain to any person or group from abandonment of the cartel is in reality less than the prospective cost *to that person or group* of securing its abandonment.

Some economists would reply: "The cartel situation nevertheless entails less total output because it is not Pareto-optimal." And how do they know that? "Because an alternative arrangement exists under which no one would be worse off and some would be better off." Then why isn't the situation changed? "Because positive transaction costs prevent negotiation of the superior arrangement."

That rejoinder amounts to the assertion that people would be better off under different circumstances that no one is able to create. We can all *imagine* a more satisfactory world, of course. We can imagine a low-cost procedure for creating energy by a fusion process and thereby imagine the OPEC cartel out of existence. But we have no more warrant for assuming away transaction costs than we have for assuming away the research costs of discovering an economical fusion process.[7]

Economic theory assumes that what people don't do they don't want to do, given their estimates of the prospective costs and benefits. These

7. The argument of this paragraph is a minor variation on the theme developed by Carl Dahlman in "The Problem of Externality," *Journal of Law and Economics,* April 1979, pp. 141–62.

estimates presuppose a given state of knowledge. More knowledge of the right kind reduces costs, of course; that's why people try to acquire additional knowledge. But until they have acquired it, production possibilities are limited by the knowledge people currently possess. Exchange is production, too, and the possibilities for increasing wealth through exchange are likewise limited by the knowledge people actually do possess. The knowledge they would have if they were, for example, completely familiar with everyone else's true preferences has no significance for any empirical question.

Economic growth is another of the major concepts that economists talk about and even measure with little apparent recognition of their fundamentally subjective nature. The Nobel lecture of W. Arthur Lewis, for example, titled "The Slowing Down of the Engine of Growth," [8] speaks of various percentage growth rates in "more developed countries" and in "less developed countries" almost as if they were data quite as objective as average temperature reports.

Lewis betrays (without admitting) the dubious nature of what he's doing right at the outset, in discussing reasons for the skepticism of many people in 1950 about "the capacity of LDCs to grow rapidly."

> The sun was thought to be too hot for hard work, or the people too spendthrift, the government too corrupt, the fertility rate too high, the religion too other worldly, and so on.[9]

This skepticism turned out to be mistaken, but that's not the point. The point is that what the skeptics were really doubting was the willingness of people in the LDCs to change their preferences and values in ways that would yield a higher annual rate of increase in the monetary value of marketed goods.[10] Empirical measures of economic growth are not, as is so often assumed, measures of increasing wealth.

The much-discussed "decline in productivity" in the United States economy in recent years is another "fact" that presupposes a variety of

---

8. A revised version of the lecture is printed as an article in the *American Economic Review*, September 1980, pp. 555–64.

9. Ibid., p. 555.

10. Ibid.

value judgments. A decline in the ratio of gross national product to compensated working hours is not necessarily a "problem." It might mean, and apparently does in part, that many people are becoming less interested in purchasing money (and the goods that money can buy) with their labor and more interested in making work itself a satisfying experience. If that constitutes a decline in productivity, then productivity is being measured without reference to the human purposes that give to the concept of productivity whatever significance it has.

III

The concept of "voluntary exchange" plays a crucial role in the descriptions, predictions, and explanations of economists. We "know" that specialization and trade increases wealth because people would not voluntarily take actions unless they expected those actions to better their condition. The economist's preferred way of speaking about efficiency, Pareto optimality, also relies upon the distinction between voluntary and coerced transactions. Despite all this, there seem to be no clear and agreed-upon criteria among economists for distinguishing a voluntary exchange from one that is involuntary. When we think carefully about what we mean in saying that a transaction was voluntary, rather than coerced, we discover how extensively economists' descriptions, predictions, or explanations derive their content from assumptions about the rights that people ought to have.[11]

---

11. The central idea in this section of the paper turned out to be much less "original" than I had initially supposed, when I began thinking about it in the course of reflecting on a manuscript by Terry L. Anderson and Peter J. Hill, published as *The Birth of a Transfer Society* (Stanford: Hoover Institution Press, 1980). The concept that informs the argument was clearly stated by John Egger in his comment on a paper by Harold Demsetz, both reprinted in Mario Rizzo, ed., *Time, Uncertainty, and Disequilibrium* (Lexington, Mass.: Lexington Books, 1979). See Demsetz, "Ethics and Efficiency in Property Rights Systems," pp. 97–116, and Egger, "Comment: Efficiency Is Not a Substitute for Ethics,"pp. 117–25. A similar analysis is presented by Mario Rizzo," Uncertainty, Subjectivity, and the Economic Analysis of Law," ibid., pp. 71–89, and by Murray Rothbard in his "Comment: The Myth of Efficiency," ibid., pp. 90–95. An entire issue of the *Journal of Legal Studies*, March 1980, titled "Change in the Common Law: Legal and Economic Perspectives," revolves around the issues discussed here, and several of the authors make the point, from different perspectives, that I am arguing for here. I now suspect that the entire paper may be implicit in the writings of James Buchanan over the years. See especially his unjustly

Suppose an armed robber confronts you with the choice, "Your money or your life." We would say that you are not engaging in a voluntary exchange when you hand him the money in your wallet. We call that coercion, I suggest, because the robber induces you to do what he wants by *threatening to reduce your options.*

Contrast this situation with the one created by a cab driver who won't give you a ride unless you give him your money. If you choose in this case to turn over the contents of your wallet, we would all agree that you are engaging in a voluntary transaction. The difference between the robber and the cab driver is that the cab driver induced you to do what he wanted by *offering to extend your options.*

It follows that we must know who has what options to begin with if we are to be able to distinguish a voluntary from an involuntary transaction. Is someone who induces you to do what he wants by threatening not to give you something you would like to have coercing you? He is not coercing you if what is in his power to bestow or withhold is in fact his and not yours. If the good is by right yours already, then he is coercing you.

We can illustrate by taking the case of an employer who tells an employee who wants to work the eight-to-five shift that he will have to work the graveyard shift instead. If the employee reluctantly agrees, has he been coerced or has he engaged in a voluntary exchange? Someone who maintains that the "job" is the property of the employer will deny that the employee was coerced. But someone who believes that the employee had earlier acquired a right in the job would quite properly deny that the transaction was a voluntary one. We cannot distinguish between voluntary and involuntary exchanges without a prior decision about the initial rights of the parties involved.[12]

---

neglected article, "Positive Economics, Welfare Economics, and Political Economy," *Journal of Law and Economics,* October 1959, pp. 124–38, and his presidential address to the Southern Economic Association, "What Should Economists Do?" *Southern Economic Journal,* January 1964, reprinted in the collection of his essays assembled by H. Geoffrey Brennan and Robert D. Tollison, *What Should Economists Do?* (Indianapolis: Liberty Fund, 1979). Many of us cannot recognize a conclusion until we work it through for ourselves.

12. "Other people's actions place limits on one's available opportunities. Whether this makes one's resulting action non-voluntary depends upon whether those others had the right to act as they did." Robert Nozick, *Anarchy, State, and Utopia* (New York: Basic Books, 1974), p. 262. Consider the opening sentence of a paper by Benjamin Klein, "Transaction Cost Determinants of 'Unfair' Contractual Arrangements," *American Economic*

Moreover, the rights in question are moral rights, not *de facto* rights. The armed robber has the *de facto* right to obtain your money by threatening to take your life. But he has no moral right to do so, and that's what makes his behavior coercion. Or is it coercion because he has no *legal* right to obtain your cooperation by threatening to take your life? Many economists would be extremely unhappy to learn that voluntary exchange can't be recognized except by those who are willing to decide what rights people *ought* to have (moral rights). They might be far more comfortable if the concept of voluntary exchange depended merely upon what rights prevailing law assigned to people (legal rights). In most cases a decision regarding legal rights will in fact be adequate to distinguish voluntary from involuntary transactions. But it will fail in precisely those cases where legal and moral rights diverge. In all such cases the person who wants to know whether an action was voluntary or coerced will be forced to decide whether people *ought to have* the rights that the law assigns them. The alternative is to adopt the position that people ought to have all those rights and only those rights that current law happens to assign them. However, this is itself a judgment about moral rights, and one that few people would be willing to uphold.

Very little of what currently passes as economic description, prediction, or explanation would survive in the absence of shared presuppositions

---

Review, May 1980, p. 356: "Terms such as 'unfair' are foreign to the economic model of voluntary exchange which implies anticipated gains to all transactors." The term "unfair" is implicit, I am arguing, in the concept of "voluntary exchange." The contention of Harold Demsetz that "extortion" is not an economic concept seems to me to require that we simultaneously banish the concept of voluntary as against coerced transactions. See Demsetz, "When Does the Rule of Liability Matter?" *Journal of Legal Studies,* January 1972, especially p. 24, and, by the same author, "Wealth Distribution and the Ownership of Rights," ibid., June 1972, especially pp. 231–32. The question of "extortion" has been usefully examined by, among others, Donald C. Shoup, "Theoretical Efficiency in Pollution Control: Comment," *Western Economic Journal,* September 1971, pp. 310–13; Richard O. Zerbe, "Theoretical Efficiency in Pollution Control: Reply," ibid., pp. 314–17; Harold Demsetz, "Theoretical Efficiency in Pollution Control: Comment on Comments," ibid., December 1971, pp. 444–46; G. A. Mumey, "The Coase Theorem: A Reexamination," *Quarterly Journal of Economics,* November 1971, pp. 718–23; Donald H. Regan, "The Problem of Social Cost Revisited," *Journal of Law and Economics,* October 1972, pp. 427–37; George Daly and J. Fred Giertz, "Externalities, Extortion, and Efficiency," *American Economic Review,* December 1975, pp. 997–1001; David Bromley, "Externalities, Extortion, and Efficiency: Comment," ibid., September 1978, pp. 730–35; and Daly and Giertz, "Externalities, Extortion, and Efficiency: Reply," ibid., pp. 736–38.

regarding the rights that people ought to have. Economists are able to
agree on whether particular actions increase or decrease efficiency, productivity, output, or wealth only insofar as they work within a particular
moral consensus.

This conclusion should not be surprising. Efficiency, productivity, output, and wealth all refer to the values and interests of human beings. These
values and interests do not form a completely harmonious whole. An action that increases the wealth of some will inevitably increase the wealth
of certain others by less than an alternative action would have done, and
in most cases it will actually reduce at least a few people's wealth. Those
who build better mousetraps diminish the wealth of competitors and increase by less than they might have the wealth of those who were hoping for an improved cockroach trap. It follows that economists must have
some way to weigh values and interests before they can assess the relative
contribution of alternative arrangements to overall efficiency, productivity, output, or wealth.

Does monetary or pecuniary wealth provide a common denominator
that will enable us to weigh and thus to compare the otherwise incommensurable values and interests of different people? Wealth measured in
monetary terms is the common denominator used, for example, in the extensive "economic analysis of law" literature associated with the work of
Richard Posner and others.[13] Unfortunately, most of those who advocate
monetary wealth maximization as a norm for assessing alternative social
arrangements omit the qualifying adjective and speak only of wealth maximization. George Stigler, in a provocative essay entitled "Wealth, and Possibly Liberty," equates efficiency with wealth maximization and identifies
changes in wealth with changes in utility. As the rest of the article makes
clear, however, it is monetary wealth and not wealth in the utility sense
that he is talking about. But monetary wealth maximization does not provide a policy norm that is superior, on all counts, to the advancement of
liberty, as Stigler maintains. The cogency of Stigler's essay depends largely
upon the success with which he shifts back and forth between wealth and

13. Richard Posner, *Economic Analysis of Law*, 2nd edition (Boston: Little, Brown and
Company, 1977). See also, by the same author, "Utilitarianism, Economics, and Legal
Theory," *Journal of Legal Studies*, January 1979, pp. 103-40, and "The Value of Wealth:
A Comment on Dworkin and Kronman," ibid., March 1980, pp. 243–52.

monetary wealth as his argument requires, in turn, a criterion relevant to human purposes or a common denominator in terms of which values can be compared by an observer.[14]

Marxists have long complained that conventional economic analysis takes for granted the existing system of property rights. The charge is fundamentally correct. Offers to supply goods and efforts to purchase goods always depend upon people's expectations of what they can and may do under specific contemplated circumstances. What a person may do expresses, in the broadest sense, that person's property rights. In order to predict, explain, or even talk intelligibly about those patterns and instances of social interaction that we call "the economy," we must begin with people's expectations, that is, their property rights.[15]

It is their *de facto* property rights, of course, or people's actual expectations, that generate demand curves and supply curves. Legal rights that exist only as statutory or judicial declarations do not influence action. Similarly, the rights that people believe they ought to have will affect supply and demand schedules only insofar as these people also believe that others will in fact accept the obligations that their claims of right entail. In short, supply curves and demand curves plus the predictions and explanations that they produce can be obtained without any decision regarding the rights people *ought* to have. Economists only have to decide what rights people *do* have in the society being studied.

The contention in this section of the paper is that economists in their professional work have typically gone well beyond what mere agreement on *de facto* rights will allow. They have measured changes in productivity growth rates; they have assessed the relative efficiency of alternative government policies; they have contrasted positive-sum games with zero-sum and negative-sum games; they have articulated such concepts as

14. George J. Stigler, "Wealth, and Possibly Liberty," *Journal of Legal Studies*, June 1978, pp. 213–17.

15. The Coase Theorem is frequently summarized as the assertion that the allocation of resources will not be affected by the assignment of property rights in a world of zero transaction costs. This is an odd way to state it. A rich literature dealing with property rights has grown up over the past twenty years on the soil Coase cultivated, because economists have recognized that transaction costs are important. Why do so many persist in stating the theorem in a way that suggests property rights don't matter, when the obvious contribution of the theorem was in inducing economists to see all the ways in which property rights *do* matter?

"deadweight losses," allocations "off the contract curve," and output combinations "inside the production possibility frontier" and have attempted to illustrate such concepts in experience. It is these extensions of economic analysis that presuppose a moral consensus by assuming what property rights people *ought* to have. Economists who believe that economics should be value-free must therefore give such concepts up.[16]

What would be left? Would an economics deprived of all these concepts still be a science relevant to policy formation?

IV

Anxiety about value judgments in economic science has produced two opposite responses. One is a quest for purity; it aims at eliminating all value judgments from economics in order to create a purely positive science. The other might be called a quest for impurity; it aims at exposing the value judgments that remain even after the purifiers have done their best, in the hope of demolishing the claim that economics can be or is a purely positive science.[17] The anxiety may be a larger problem than the value judgments. A more constructive approach, I shall argue in this final section, is closer attention to what we can and cannot infer from observed behavior, and what we must postulate if we want to offer particular judgments about alternative social institutions.

The best way of making the argument is through examples. I've chosen the issue of rent controls.

The political popularity of legislated controls on residential rents has surged in the United States in recent years, largely as a consequence of actions and misconceptions related to an accelerated rate of decline in the general purchasing power of money. What can economists as economists say about rent controls?

16. Here is as good a place as any to acknowledge a book that I discovered too late for it to influence this paper: A. Allan Schmid, *Property, Power, and Public Choice: An Inquiry into Law and Economics* (New York: Praeger Publishers, 1978). This is a careful, well-informed, and comprehensive examination of most of the issues raised in the present paper. Its "institutionalist" orientation may keep it from having as much impact on "mainstream" theorizing as I think it ought to have.

17. For an excellent historical survey, see T. W. Hutchison, *"Positive" Economics and Policy Objectives* (Cambridge, Mass.: Harvard University Press, 1964).

One common contribution of economists is the prediction that rent controls will prevent residential space from moving to its most highly valued use. This prediction changes no one's mind, because most advocates of rent control *want to prevent* residential space from always moving to its most highly valued use. They believe that elderly people on low, fixed incomes should not have to give up their apartments simply because someone else is willing to pay a higher rent. The advocates of rent control believe that the monetary bids of current tenants should, at least in certain cases, have more weight in social allocation processes than the identical money bids of prospective tenants. "Most highly valued use" as defined by the typical economist does not correspond to "most highly valued use" as defined by the typical advocate of rent controls.

What else might economists contribute to the discussion? They could predict the evolution of key fees; the harassment of tenants by owners who want to terminate tenancies; the disappearance of housing stock from the rental market as owners sell or shift it into other uses; and cases where wealth will be transferred from low-income to high-income people. None of these predictions is a conclusive argument against legislated rent controls, however. Proponents can (and do) respond with proposals to tighten the law and prevent such "abuses."

Still the discussion does not have to end. Economists can ask exactly how the law could be tightened to prevent, for example, a withdrawal of housing stock from the rental market, and then offer predictions about the consequences of such additional legal provisions. None of these predictions will be a conclusive argument, either, because a determined advocate of rent controls will be able to point to additional possibilities or neglected considerations that may overcome the force of the economist's predictions.

Is this not why economists make such extensive use of pseudo-empirical aggregative concepts? Predicting the various consequences of a proposed policy will not be sufficient, in many cases, to establish the consequences relevant to a decision. Economists have long admitted their inability to *evaluate* consequences; but they have insisted upon their ability as "scientists" to *predict* consequences. The difficulty in practice is that the set of predictable consequences potentially relevant to a decision is indefinitely large. As a result, economists frequently cannot even establish "what is" in an adequate way (quite apart from any inability to achieve consensus on their specific predictions, often a considerable difficulty in it-self). The appeal of pseudo-empirical concepts like efficiency or economic growth lies in their supposed summation of the "net effects," a summation that enables economists to "stick to their last" (description and prediction) and still contribute to the discussion and formation of public policy. Few economists seem to be aware of the value judgments that give these con-cepts their content and significance.[18]

Can economists get safely back inside the circle of a purely "positive economics" by abandoning pseudo-empirical aggregates and confining themselves to concrete, well-specified descriptions and predictions? As the opening paragraph of this section suggested, the best answer may be a rejection of the question.

Economists cannot describe *all* the features or predict *all* the conse-quences of any situation. They therefore focus on *significant* facts. Since most economists are opposed to legislated rent controls, the consequences they predict are usually the undesirable ones. Economists are not likely to predict that properly written rent controls will reduce tenant mobil-ity, thereby enabling urban neighbors to become better acquainted and to create safer neighborhoods. Nor are they likely to point out that rent con-trols can reduce congestion in already densely populated cities by restrict-ing in-migration, or that they may contribute to the preservation of older buildings with historic architectural significance. The typical economist will instead predict a decline in the rate of new apartment construction, and will often not even notice that this presumably undesirable effect is the corollary of effects that are desired, at least by some people.

Advocates of a value-free economics seem to suppose that "positive economics" can and should describe all the consequences of a given policy proposal plus all the consequences of alternative policies, and only then allow value judgments to enter into the decision process. This is an im-possible agenda. It is not made any less absurd by invoking the phrase "in principle," the phrase we use so often when we want to argue for the de-sirability of doing something no one currently knows how to do. Econo-mists will not (this is a prediction) be able to spell out all the facts, current

18. A. Allan Schmid, *op. cit.*, especially pp. 24–34, 201–50. I would disagree only with Schmid's conclusion that, when values conflict, we have no rational procedure for resolv-ing the disagreements. See pp. 248–49.

and predicted, relevant to a policy decision in any case where there is substantial public disagreement on the policy. Of course, they can always present *more* of the consequences, working in the dialectical manner illustrated earlier. How long they will continue depends upon the estimated marginal benefits and costs of continuing.

Is there any good reason for refusing to appeal, in this kind of dialogue, to considerations of justice or fairness? That is surely the implicit argument in many predictions, such as the prediction that rent controls will increase the wealth of some tenants at the expense of owners who are less wealthy than themselves. Why not make it explicit? The reluctance or outright refusal of so many economists to appeal explicitly to moral considerations frequently makes their arguments less clear. Does it also make them more purely "economic" or "scientific"?

The belief that it *does* seems to be rooted in two widespread misconceptions. One is the general failure of economists to recognize the extent to which their analyses already make use implicitly of presuppositions regarding justice or fairness. The property rights or expectations that generate supply curves and demand curves are usually assumed by economists to be rights in whose exercise people *ought to be secure*. This is a controversial (and perhaps mistaken) claim which will not be defended here. A defense would run, however, along two lines. One line of defense would point out that prediction and even description becomes impossible in the absence of reasonably stable property rights. The other line of argument would attempt to show how frequently economists use measures of change (in wealth, output, efficiency, etc.) on the assumption that certain people—and not others—have a moral right to control the allocation of particular resources.

The other misconception is the belief that moral argument cannot be rational argument. As Sidney Alexander once observed, "the economist's calendar of philosophy lies open to the year 1936." [19] Economists usually do not question Milton Friedman's assertion that, when a policy disagreement is rooted in ethical rather than factual disagreement, the only

19. For a lucid and cogent refutation (by an economist) of the prejudice that we cannot rationally discuss and resolve normative disagreements, see Sidney S. Alexander, "Human Values and Economists' Values," in Sidney Hook, ed., *Human Values and Economic Policy* (New York: New York University Press, 1967), pp. 101–16. The quotation is from p. 102.

resolution possible is through fighting,[20] as they did not generally question Lionel Robbins' claim twenty years earlier that in all such cases it was a matter of "thy blood or mine." [21] On this issue Robbins, Friedman, and the economists who join them are demonstrably wrong. People do *not* always resort to force when they find the path to policy agreement blocked by disagreement regarding what is just or fair. Instead they frequently turn to moral argument.

"Do you think it's *fair* to change the rules of the game suddenly, thereby confiscating the property of apartment owners?"

"Do you think it's *fair* for landlords to raise their rents even though most of their costs aren't going up at all?"

Answers can be given to these questions. They aren't likely to be definitive answers; but as we saw earlier, definitive assertions are equally hard to produce when we confine ourselves to empirical description and prediction. Moreover, just as the significance of empirical claims often depends upon underlying assumptions about fairness or justice, so people's disagreements regarding fairness or justice often rest upon conflicting empirical claims. An empirical analysis can sometimes resolve an apparent disagreement about justice. It is no less true that attention to moral arguments can sometimes clarify and thereby resolve what seem at first to be empirical disagreements. In fact, it does not even seem possible to separate in any wholly satisfactory way the moral and the empirical aspects of any dialogue concerning public policy.

Economists persist in trying and continue to suppose they can succeed (at least "in principle") because they want to be *scientists*. Interestingly, many people who take stands on policy issues that economists tend to condemn—in favor of rent controls, increases in the minimum wage, usury laws, etc.—are delighted to find themselves the only ones making moral claims on behalf of the policies they support. They know that, in the political arena, the unanswered claim that a particular policy is unjust will almost always defeat a similarly unanswered argument that the alternative is inefficient.

20. Milton Friedman, "The Methodology of Positive Economics," in *Essays in Positive Economics* (Chicago: University of Chicago Press, 1953), p. 5.

21. Lionel Robbins, *An Essay on the Nature and Significance of Economic Science,* 2nd ed. (London: Macmillan, 1935), p. 50.

Surely we would not want it to be otherwise. If the argument of this paper is correct, it *cannot* be otherwise. A defense of efficiency is, in any particular case, a defense of some particular distribution of rights. If we want to argue for efficiency, we have two choices. We can examine the justice of the particular distribution of property rights we are defending. Or we can defend without examination the rights we are presupposing. Either choice is legitimate. Unexamined presuppositions are finally unavoidable at some level, and the search for hidden value judgments can too easily, as Lionel Robbins once suggested, take on the features of a witch hunt.[22]

But there is surely no reason for the economics profession to excommunicate those colleagues who choose to ask about the ethical norms that inform their own analysis or to call explicit attention to the ethical implications of the situations they describe and the consequences they predict.

22. Lionel Robbins, *Politics and Economics* (New York: St. Martin's Press, 1963), p. 6.

CHAPTER 22

The Foundations of Law and Economics: Can the Blind Lead the Blind?

[T]he rules of just conduct which the lawyer studies serve a kind of order of the character of which the lawyer is largely ignorant; . . . this order is studied chiefly by the economist who in turn is similarly ignorant of the character of the rules of conduct on which the order that he studies rests.
—Friedrich A. Hayek[1]

In law as elsewhere, we can know and yet not understand.
—H. L. A. Hart[2]

I. Introduction

When it comes to theorizing, most economists would rather follow David Ricardo than Adam Smith. They crave rigor. A plausible story, consistent with basic theory and supported by substantial evidence, is not as satisfactory as are conclusions established with the binding force of logic.[3] That is why plausible explanations are so often "modeled" before they are presented in the journals. Even when the model is not used and so adds nothing but length to the presentation, a theory is not altogether respectable in economics until it has been presented in rigorous dress.[4]

First published in *Research in Law and Economics* 11 (1988): 53–71. Reprinted by permission of Mrs. Juliana Heyne.

1. Hayek (1973, pp. 4–5).

2. Hart (1983, p. 21). The quotation is the opening sentence of Hart's 1953 inaugural lecture as Professor of Jurisprudence at Oxford.

3. Ricardo had a motive as well as the method and an occasion. He and his friend James Mill wanted the free-trade doctrine to be recognized as a conclusion of *science*, not seen as a disputable opinion. See the instructive essay by T. W. Hutchison on James Mill and Ricardo in Hutchison (1978, pp. 26–57).

4. Richard R. Nelson (1970, p. 127), in commenting on a paper presented to the American Economic Association, once raised in public the question that non-mathematical economists often entertain but fear to ask: "But before proceeding let me remark that while I

This predilection toward rigor has some desirable consequences. For one thing, it discourages *ad hoc* theorizing. A well-modeled argument will more readily reveal the degree of its conformity to the organizing premise of economic theory: that social phenomena are the consequence of self-interested interactions pushing toward equilibrium positions.[5] An explanation that cannot be reconciled with this Grand Model will "make no sense" to economists, and will be sent back to the manufacturer for fundamental repair—or sale in some other territory, such as sociology.

This tyranny of theory often irritates outsiders, and it positively infuriates such dissenting insiders as the American Institutionalists.[6] It also draws an unusual amount of critical attention to the foundations of economic theory. The conclusions of a rigorous argument are no more persuasive, after all, than the premises from which they follow. And so the periodic anxieties of orthodox economists and the ongoing subversive interests of their critics have combined to produce a great deal of foundation-probing in the history of economic theory.[7]

Legal scholars form another group that has been unusually preoccupied with foundation questions.[8] What *is* the law? Is it merely the enforceable dictates of whoever happens to be in power, as positivist theories of law seem to assert? Does it follow then that there is no "right" except might? If we reject this conclusion and maintain that there is reason in the law, what *is* the reason of the law? How do judges decide?

Constitutions, statutes, and precedents can never be sufficient to determine uniquely a particular judicial decision. Every decision is to some

---

found the verbal theorizing clear and provocative I did not find that the mathematical treatment added anything at all, either in terms of sharpening and clarifying concepts or in terms of permitting one to see interesting implications that were not apparent from the verbal discussion. I wonder, therefore, what R. . . .'s purpose was in presenting the mathematics."

5. "The combined assumptions of maximizing behavior, market equilibrium, and stable preferences, used relentlessly and unflinchingly, form the heart of the economic approach," according to the profession's most relentless and unflinching practitioner of that approach, Gary Becker (1976, p. 5). Becker argues that stable preferences must be assumed to keep the approach from degenerating into tautologies.

6. The *Journal of Economic Issues* regularly records their fury. For an example related to the theme of this paper, see Liebhafsky (1976).

7. The achievements and the limitations of such foundation probing, as well as the motivating forces behind it, are probably still best illustrated by Robbins (1935).

8. H. L. A. Hart and Ronald Dworkin have been the most influential foundation-probers in Anglo-American law since World War II. See Hart (1983) and Dworkin (1986).

degree a new decision, an extension of established law to cover a *novel* case, since in the absence of novelty there would be nothing to litigate. Judges are therefore continually creating the law as well as applying it. How can they do this without becoming arbitrary? How can they decide in a way consistent with the "rule of law"?

The difficulties of formulating an adequate answer to that question regularly give rise to the suspicion that no adequate answer exists. Sometimes the suspicion grows into a conviction, as occurred at the height of the American Realist movement in the 1920s and 1930s. But the suspicion is always lurking, constantly nourished by unexpected or sharply divided decisions from high courts and complaints about "judicial legislation" from those who are aggrieved by these decisions. Are judges really deciding on the basis of principles, as they claim? Or are they only expressing, as some critics insist, the particular values to which they happen to subscribe?

One influential attempt to answer the lawyers' question has come in recent years from economics. The so-called economic theory of law has proposed and extensively tested the hypothesis that the evolution of legal rules in common-law countries has been guided by the criterion of efficiency. The logic of the law, even when unrecognized by the judges, is wealth-maximization.[9]

During this same period, however, the concept of efficiency has itself been subjected to searching criticism by scholars working along the borders of law and economics.[10] Many of these critics, among whom the Critical Legal Studies group is most prominent, have concluded that the efficiency concept used in economic theory is "incoherent." As a result, they maintain, much of the work that has been done toward developing an economic theory of law is either tautological or ideological.

Can the blind lead the blind? If economic theory is incoherent, how can

9. The leading name is that of Richard A. Posner, and the definitive explication and application of the theory is in Posner (1986). Much of the supporting work has appeared in the *Journal of Legal Studies,* founded by Posner in 1972 and edited by him until his resignation in 1981 to accept appointment as a Federal Appeals Court judge.

10. For an unusually high-quality selection of articles by legal scholars criticizing the concept of efficiency, along with some defenses of the concept (principally by Posner), see *Journal of Legal Studies* (1980), reprinting a symposium on "Change in the Common Law: Legal and Economic Perspectives"; two issues of the *Hofstra Law Review* (1980), devoted almost entirely to the topic; and Posner's reply to the Hofstra symposium (Posner, 1981b).

it provide foundations for law? This paper accepts the major arguments of the efficiency critics, but concludes nonetheless that economics *can* provide foundations of a sort for law. The allegedly vacuous efficiency concept actually has some foundations, located largely, as it turns out, in law. So the blind do lead the blind, perhaps enabled by this mutual assistance to avoid the ditches into which each would fall without the other's assistance.

II

The most vigorous research programs in recent years within the field of law and economics have been the efficiency approach, identified principally with the name of Richard Posner, and the Critical Legal Studies attack, most ably represented by Duncan Kennedy. The efficiency school has produced a large number of studies assessing the wealth-enhancing effects of legal rules and institutions; the Critical Legal Studies group has concentrated on arguing the "incoherence" of the efficiency concept and hence of much of the law-and-economics output.[11]

The feature of the efficiency concept on which critics fasten is its dependence upon an initial assignment of property rights. The argument can be briefly stated. Every defensible measure of efficiency assesses the value of benefits obtained in relation to the value of benefits forgone. Concepts of technical or objective efficiency simply have no meaning; any meaning they might seem to have will be seen, upon a more careful analysis, to presuppose an *evaluation* of results obtained and alternative results forgone. What counts is the evaluations.

But once this is seen, the question arises, "Whose evaluations count?" Every answer to that question implicitly assigns property rights to some persons and denies them to others. It follows that we cannot use the concept of efficiency without endorsing some set of property rights, from which it then follows that the concept of efficiency cannot be used to resolve disputes over property rights without begging the question. A claim that voluntary exchange within a free market promotes efficiency

11. The seminal study is Kennedy (1976). For further development of the argument, see Kennedy (1981a). The latter paper is directed at the Paretian tradition in economic analysis of law, which, as Kennedy notes, Posner repudiates. A less subtle but considerably briefer analysis widely cited by Critical Legal Studies scholars is Kelman (1979).

or maximizes value has no persuasive force for anyone who denies the legitimacy of the property rights from which that exchange proceeds.[12]

This criticism calls into question considerably more than economists' theory of law. It raises doubts about the objectivity of all economic analysis. Suppose, for example, that economists want to predict or explain the consequences of government price supports in agriculture. How can they even begin without assuming the existing system of property rights? Rational pursuit of self-interest is the fundamental postulate of standard economic analysis; but the postulate cannot generate implications until it is supplemented with specific assumptions about the "rules of the game." Economists who want to predict the effects of agricultural price supports must assume, *inter alia,* that the existing property rights of farmers will be respected, that public servants will carry out the provisions of the law, and that taxpayers will provide the amounts which they are assessed to subsidize the program.

Any or all of these specific assumptions could be substantially false. As a matter of fact, economists also explore the ways in which legislation produces changes in property rights (as parties strive, for example, to capitalize and appropriate the promise of price supports); in the behavior of government agents (legislated programs create client groups among the dispensing officials as well as among the program targets); and in practices of tax avoidance. But the analyses in these cases must again presuppose the rest of the social system and the prevailing rules of the game.

Economic theory takes for granted, far more extensively than economists seem generally to recognize, the normative force of established rights and obligations.[13] Does this undermine the objectivity of the theory?

---

12. This argument is by no means the exclusive property of market-system critics. See Rizzo (1979, 1980a, 1980b) and Rothbard (1979). The question-begging properties of the efficiency concept also form the central theme in Samuels and Schmid (1981) and Samuels (1981).

13. An instructive illustration is provided by the work of Benjamin Klein and his colleagues on the use of contracts to control opportunistic behavior. One study (Klein, 1980) begins with the statement: "Terms such as 'unfair' are foreign to the economic model of voluntary exchange which implies anticipated gains to all transactors." Can this be correct? The concept of an unfair transaction is implicit in the concept of fair transactions, and some baseline of fairness is inevitably assumed in any empirical economic analysis. Can we even recognize a voluntary exchange without implicitly using some notion of fairness? How can the concept of "opportunistic behavior" have any meaning for someone who does not recognize a distinction between fair and unfair? The contracts that Klein discusses as devices for controlling opportunistic behavior will only work

Does it make economic analysis an ideological prop of the established system and a servant of vested interests, rather than an impartial tool for the assessment of conflicting claims? Radical critics have long voiced this complaint, and it would seem that they have a case.

On the other hand, might we not ask whether any of this provides legitimate grounds for *complaint*? It is quite true that economists take the existing system for granted in their work; it would make no sense to do anything else. Karl Marx also assumed the existing nineteenth-century European system of property rights in his efforts to elucidate the laws of motion of the capitalist system.

Marx, however, had no apologetic intent; his goal was to show how capitalism would destroy itself. The thrust of most contemporary economic analysis, on the other hand, is to demonstrate the cooperative features of market interaction: to show how the processes of supply and demand continually move resources toward more highly valued uses, producing economic growth and larger real incomes. And that is precisely the conclusion which the radical critics insist cannot be drawn. The only demonstrable growth that such a system produces is growth in the value of entitlements of those whose initial entitlements enable them to play the game. Economists may be able to predict what will occur; but nothing that occurs can be shown to be more valuable than anything else unless the legitimacy of the controlling valuations is presupposed, which is to say, unless a particular system of property rights is implicitly endorsed.

There are a number of responses that economists can make to this criticism. One is to ignore it completely. For reasons that will gradually become clear, and that are implicit in the quotation from Hart at the beginning of the paper, I consider this a thoroughly legitimate response. That is fortunate, because it is obviously the response most economists have chosen.

Another approach is to go the critics one better and argue that economic theory provides a foundation for the property rights which eco-

---

as long as opportunistic behavior is constrained by fairness! If, for example, the party whose opportunism is to be controlled by the contract subsequently persuades a court to discharge the contract on grounds of unconscionability, opportunism has occurred at a deeper level, and a new kind of contract will have to be devised if further cooperation of the sort in question is to be mutually advantageous *ex ante*. See also Klein, Crawford, and Alchian (1978).

nomic theory necessarily presupposes.[14] Who ought to have which rights depends, in this version of the economic theory of law, upon who values the rights more highly. The law does *and should* assign property rights in disputed cases to the party who would be willing to pay the most to obtain them. That is where they will end up anyway, or, more accurately, where they *would* end up if property rights could be exchanged without significant cost. Since in reality there are costs associated with exchange, and these costs will sometimes prevent the transfer of rights to those who value them most highly, it makes sense for courts, in disputed cases, to place the rights where they ought to be. The "ought" presupposes, of course, that the courts do and should use wealth-maximization as their criterion in rule making.[15]

This line of argument does not have to be as subversive of established rights as it might at first seem. Two qualifying phrases are crucial: *in disputed cases* and *their criterion in rule making.*[16]

No proponent of the economic theory of law contends that all property rights should now be brought before the courts for them to undertake a vast redistribution. If A goes to court and asks for the title to B's house, on the grounds that the house offers a magnificent view which B, a blind bachelor, cannot appreciate at all, while A and his large family collectively value the view at $100,000, A will lose and B will retain his property right. Why? Because A has no basis for his suit! Assuming that B bought the property in a legitimate way (i.e., according to the established legal rules), he has a clear and undisputed title. The fact that A *says* he values the property more than B carries no weight at all. Well-established legal rules specify what A must do to establish a right to B's property: most simply, he must persuade B to transfer the title by offering a price that B will accept. That is how A "proves" his claim that he places a greater value on the house than does B.

14. Posner (1979a, pp. 125–27). For a revised and more complete statement of his views on the economics and ethics of wealth-maximization, see Posner (1981a, especially pp. 48–115).

15. The roots of this argument are in Coase (1960). It has been further developed in a number of articles by Demsetz (1964, 1966, 1967, 1972a, 1972b, 1979, 1982).

16. This is not to say that exponents have always stated these qualifications adequately. The language used by Posner, for example, would seem to justify the criticism that he is urging judges to behave as legislators. If we adopt the interpretation of his argument presented here, the force of these criticisms is greatly diminished. See, for example, Buchanan (1974), reviewing the first edition of *Economic Analysis of Law.*

It is the *rules* which common-law judges apply that allegedly do and should maximize social or aggregate wealth. A case that falls clearly under the rules is not a disputed case. It will not be litigated because no one wants to bear the costs of litigation knowing that he will lose, and by our assumption that the rules governing the case are clear, *he does know* that he will lose. If he is someone who values litigation for its own sake, and who consequently files a case he has no chance to win, the courts will *not* search for a wealth-maximizing rule with which to settle the case. They will apply the (by assumption) clear and well-settled rules that govern such circumstances to dispose of the case quickly.[17]

To understand what the economic theory of law is claiming, you must imagine a disputed case in which the facts are not at issue. Everything therefore depends upon the legal rule that the court applies, but the court does not know what rule it ought to apply. The case must raise questions not previously dealt with, or at least not dealt with in any way that managed to generate a decisive rule. The court is consequently caught between the inconsistent legal claims of plaintiff and defendant, and forced to decide without any rule to determine its decision. In such a situation the court must create a new rule. It is at *this* point that the criterion of efficiency or aggregate wealth-maximization enters to make its impact.

Notice that the new rule, under the ideal circumstances we have described, will violate no one's property rights. If the property right in dispute is assigned to A rather than B, B loses the case but does not lose a property right. He never had it—it was in dispute—and so he cannot "lose" it. All others who might be in B's circumstances likewise do not have anything taken away by the new rule, at least nothing to which they previously had legal title. By our assumptions, there were no legal titles prior to the enunciating of the new legal rule growing out of the case.

What is wrong with the economic theory of law as just stated? For one thing, it completely fails to answer the complaint of those who claim that the concept of efficiency is "incoherent." Assigning property rights on the basis of willingness to pay for them, which is what the wealth-maximization criterion calls for, obviously assigns property rights *at least in part* on the basis

17. What if the rule is clear but the litigant wants to see it changed? Do not lawyers occasionally go to court hoping for a reversal of some long-standing rule? They do, of course, but their arguments in such cases will present *grounds* for reversal. These grounds will be other and more fundamental rules that allegedly conflict with the challenged rule.

of existing property rights. Willingness-to-pay depends partly upon wealth, and one's wealth depends largely upon one's property rights. The argument *assumes* property rights while claiming to justify or settle property rights.[18]

The claim of the critics seems to me logically sound *and almost wholly irrelevant*. Courts do indeed assume established, well-settled rules or property rights in order to conduct their analyses and decide what the rights ought to be in disputed cases. Who would want them to do anything else? The most "radical" court decision, one that stirs widespread cries of outrage (or satisfaction) by upsetting long and firmly established expectations, will depend for its reasoning, impact, and significance upon the vastly greater body of well-settled rules and property rights which it does not touch but wholly assumes.[19] How could it be otherwise?

The Critical Legal Studies group likes to extol "imagination." Legal or economic analyses that presuppose the existing social order are faulted not merely for their "incoherence" (something that turns out, in their analysis, to be unavoidable), but also for their failure to work at the task of imagining an alternative order.[20] It might be that the critics have overestimated the relative difficulty of the two tasks: understanding the existing order and imagining an alternative one. Imagining a new social order is quite easy when one does not have to supply the innumerable details that any actual order would have to display *and reconcile*. Understanding the existing order, by contrast, can be quite difficult, because innumerable actual details are available to contradict any erroneous explanation.

It is decidedly not the case that everyone who assumes the existing order, or who even explicates the cooperative features of the existing order, is necessarily committed to all the features of that order, or opposed to radical change. He *is* likely to be opposed to unrealistic proposals for change, but primarily because he has taken the problem of social order seriously enough to study it and to learn something about what works and what is likely not to work.

18. For a careful statement of the problem, see Michelman (1982).

19. U.S. Appellate Court Judge J. Skelly Wright, praised by Critical Legal Studies scholars for his decision to incorporate municipal housing codes into all landlord-tenant contracts, is much more radical in his *obiter dicta* than in anything else. The judgment and supporting legal reasoning are quite conservative in Wright's celebrated decision *Javins v. First National Realty Corporation*, 428 F.2d 1071 (1970).

20. Kennedy (1976, pp. 1777–78, 1981b, p. 1283), Freeman (1981, pp. 1230–31), Gordon (1981, p. 1056), Frug (1982, pp. 1600–1601).

In the case of a judge, someone whose decisions determine the rights of actual people and not just imagined ones, the argument for assuming existing rules or property rights becomes overwhelming. The mental experiments of an academic writer inflict their costs primarily on uncoerced readers; the experiments of a sitting judge would be coercive and unjust. This can only be denied by someone who has abstracted from the society in which he lives.

Just as the courts, in creating new legal rules, take for granted the existing body of established rules, so economic analysis, in attempting to predict, explain, or prescribe, must take for granted the existing body of established rules. Economic theory merely looks at them from a different perspective and calls them all "property rights." The courts see property rights as something to be clarified and secured; economists view property rights as something to be used. Economists are interested in the supply curves and demand curves that are generated by self-interested action in a particular property-rights setting, and in the consequences to which the interactions of these supply and demand curves will lead.

The foundations of economics are thus in the law, at least insofar as it is the law that clarifies property rights and secures their acceptance. The major qualification is that custom and morality assist the law in its task. The foundations of economics, then, are in the established laws, customs, and morality of the society which the economist is studying.

III

Can economics return the favor and provide foundations for law? In particular, can it help legal scholars dispel what H. L. A. Hart has called:

> the Nightmare view that, in spite of pretensions to the contrary, judges make the law which they apply to litigants and are not impartial, objective declarers of existing law[?][21]

Many legal scholars would prefer to resolve this problem without any help from economics. The logic of economics seems utilitarian, and a good deal of contemporary legal and political philosophy is openly hostile

21. Hart (1983, p. 127).

to utilitarianism. The moral concept with which the law has traditionally been most concerned is *justice;* and that is the moral concept with which utilitarianism experiences the most difficulty.

Economists have not waited for an invitation or a welcome. They have "advanced the hypothesis that the rules, procedures, and institutions of the common or judge-made law...promoted efficiency."[22] This is called the *positive* economic theory of law. A few economists, notably Richard Posner, have gone on to argue a *normative* theory that wealth-maximization is a commendable moral criterion and an appropriate one for judges to use in formulating legal rules.[23]

It is difficult to test the positive economic theory of law without sliding into an evaluation of the normative theory. Moreover, for reasons which will emerge, it seems to me that they largely stand or fall together. So I shall "test" them simultaneously, or perhaps dialectically, if that term has not become too fashionable to retain a meaning.

The "test" will entail a comparison with an alternative positive and normative theory, which I shall call the *fairness theory.* To focus the discussion, keep it within bounds, and not wander too far beyond the limits of my competence, the "test" will be confined to one small but important area of the law, the common law of contracts. Obviously, the word "test" belongs within quotation marks; it would not satisfy George Stigler. On the other hand, it might have some appeal to Ronald Coase.[24] In any event, the results interest me and serve the purpose of this paper.

We begin with a very general question. Why do/should the courts employ the rule of enforcing contracts as they were written by the contracting parties?

One good answer is, "Why not?" It is not obvious that the rule of enforcing contracts as written must bear the burden of proof. But we want to set this answer aside in order to examine two others.

One intuitively plausible reason for the courts to enforce contracts as written is that contracts are promises and it is only fair that promises be honored. This is the *fairness argument.*

The *economic argument* asserts that contracts ought to be enforced as

22. Posner (1979b, p. 289).
23. See especially Posner (1981a, pp. 88–115).
24. Coase (1982).

written because the enforcement of contracts maximizes social wealth, measured by aggregate willingness to pay.

It follows that, under the fairness argument, contracts should be enforced insofar as they express genuine promises. Under the economic argument, contracts should be enforced insofar as doing so will increase social wealth.

Keep in mind that the discussion is about *rules*. The economic argument does not say that judges do or should scrutinize each contract to determine its wealth-enhancing effects, and then enforce only as much of it as will increase aggregate wealth. We are asking about the *rules* the courts follow in contract litigation. The question is whether economics or fairness considerations provide a better explanation or reason for these rules.

Let us consider the rule which says that contracts signed under duress shall *not* be enforced. If Canterbury contracts to pay York $1,000 in return for York's promise not to burn down Canterbury's house, the courts will not hold Canterbury to the contract. Why do/should the courts make this exception to the rule of enforcing contracts?

The economic argument supports contracts and hence contract-enforcement because it supports voluntary exchange as a wealth-maximizing process.[25] A coerced exchange is not a voluntary exchange; therefore it should not be encouraged. People should be discouraged from attempts to substitute involuntary for voluntary exchange. A rule against enforcing contracts signed under duress has this effect.

The fairness argument simply points out that a promise extracted under threat is not a genuine promise and so carries no obligation to perform.

But let us make the case more difficult to see what guidance the two arguments can give. Suppose Canterbury contracts to pay York $1,000 in return for York's promise to repair a puncture in an automobile tire. (Canterbury punctured the tire through his own carelessness.) Should Canterbury be required to pay after York has performed as promised?

Why not? "Because York coerced me," says Canterbury. "I only signed the contract because I was in the desert, had no spare, and would have

---

25. The economic arguments or rationales presented in this section draw heavily upon the writings of Posner. See especially Posner (1986).

missed a speaking engagement and a $2,000 fee if York—the only person around—had not repaired the tire."

Is this coercion? Interestingly, some proponents of the economic analysis of law deny that "coercion" is a concept appropriate to economic analysis.[26] Even "your money or your life," uttered behind a gun, is an invitation to a voluntary exchange, according to this view of the matter. The "victim" is free to choose: to give up the money in exchange for his life, or to reject the exchange and be shot. The "victim" increases his wealth by surrendering his money, if that is what he chooses to do. If he rejects the exchange, that also must be wealth-increasing, at least *ex ante,* which is the only relevant perspective.

The economic argument against encouraging exchange-offers of that sort, and in favor of strongly discouraging them, is that this kind of transfer, while it increases wealth for the two parties involved, is not in the long run wealth-creating for the society as a whole. Deterring such exchanges gives people incentives to seek wealth in ways that contribute more effectively to aggregate *social* wealth.

Let us carry this analysis back to the case of Canterbury, York, and the $1,000 tire repair. The exchange was voluntary. The only question is whether social wealth is likely to be greater or less under a rule that calls for enforcement of such contracts. To answer that, we must ask what incentives such a rule would create. On the positive (wealth-enhancing) side, a rule of enforcement would encourage motorists to take a low-cost precaution (carrying a spare) that could prevent large potential costs. Also on the positive side, it would encourage motorists to carry tire-repair equipment, not only to avoid the risk of paying a $1,000 fee, but also to increase their chances of obtaining such a fee. In fact, tire-repair kits might multiply enormously in response to such an incentive, creating a vastly greater supply of emergency service and eventually competing the fee down to a much lower level. On the other hand, might this not attract *too many* resources into tire repair? Punctures are infrequent; punctures in cases where no spare tire is available to transport the motorist to a repair station are even less frequent. Would not the total cost of acquiring all those

---

26. Demsetz (1972a, p. 24, 1972b, pp. 231–33).

additional repair kits tend to exceed the marginal value to motorists of the extra repair services made available?

Remember, too, that we're talking about legal rules. A legal rule governing this case is going to be a more general rule, covering something like promises made in emergencies to pay monopoly prices that are significantly higher than prices customarily charged. If people expect to be forced to pay such high prices when they find themselves, through some misfortune, in a temporarily "desperate" strait, they may begin taking a wide array of precautions whose aggregate marginal cost will exceed their aggregate marginal value. So the wealth-maximizing rule is likely to be something like: no enforcement of such contracts; or, breach allowed, with "damages" equal to the customary price in the area; or, damages equal to the court-estimated cost of supplying the good. Those are legal rules we actually see applied in cases of this sort. The economic argument "explains" the outcome.

How would the fairness argument handle York's complaints that Canterbury has breached his contract? Contracts signed under coercion are not genuine promises. But did York coerce Canterbury?

It is not coercion and hence not unfair to induce another person to cooperate by threatening to withhold a benefit *if one has a right to withhold the benefit.*[27] This is standard and accepted practice: buyers induce sellers to lower their prices by threatening to withhold their patronage. We do not call that coercion because we assume that buyers have a right to distribute their patronage as they please.

Sometimes, however, this right will be a limited right because of prior commitments. If Canterbury had chosen York's service out of several in the Yellow Pages, phoned to ask York's price, and then requested York to make a road-service call, he would not in fairness have a right, after York arrived, to demand a lower price by threatening to withhold his patronage. Nor would York, in these circumstances, have a right in fairness to insist upon a price higher than the one quoted, after arriving on the scene and discovering that Canterbury would lose $2,000 if the puncture was not repaired at once. The common law rules are clear in such cases: failure

27. Nozick (1974, p. 262); Heyne (1987, p. 323).

to perform as promised, when the promise induced detrimental reliance (York drove all the way out on the basis of Canterbury's promise; Canterbury waited for York on the basis of York's promise, rather than phoning someone else), entitles the promisees to performance or to damages. (Efficiency considerations would yield the same rule.)

We want a case, however, that is not settled so readily by a clear and well-established legal rule. Suppose that there was no prior contract between York and Canterbury. York just happened to be passing by, out on a sightseeing trip, and also just happened to have with him all the equipment required to repair Canterbury's punctured tire. He stopped, discovered Canterbury's plight, and offered to repair the puncture for $1,000. Since Canterbury was carrying no cash, York accepted a written promise to pay within seven days. Once safely back in the city, Canterbury refused to perform (pay the promised $1,000). York sued, alleging breach of contract. What guidance does the fairness criterion provide in this case?

It seems considerably less difficult to *recognize unfairness* than it is to *define fairness*.[28] So let us ask if there was anything recognizably unfair about the contract York induced Canterbury to sign.

The price is certainly extraordinary. What did York do to earn such a huge return for his services? Was it not sheer luck that put him in a position to demand a price so advantageous to the unfortunate Canterbury? It was not *sheer* luck; York had prepared himself for such situations, and that seems to entitle him to *some* advantage. But $1,000 certainly looks excessive. It seems... *unconscionable*.

Unconscionable contracts are not enforceable at common law. But how do we distinguish unconscionable contracts? To claim that a contract is unconscionable if its terms are unfair leaves us with the problem of defining an unfair bargain. The courts are reluctant to rewrite the terms of a contract freely entered into by the parties. But was Canterbury free? Or did he sign under duress? Was he coerced into an involuntary exchange?

The answer is negative if we judge by legal entitlements. York had full legal ownership of his repair services, and an unquestioned right to leave Canterbury in the lurch if his asking price was not met. The com-

---

28. This is an ancient but still much neglected insight. See especially Hayek (1976, pp. 35–48, 162–64).

mon law courts generally do not enforce a Good Samaritan rule, which would confer upon victims of misfortune a legal right to assistance from passersby. Excellent reasons can be given in support of this reluctance to impose duties to assist, reasons grounded both in efficiency considerations and notions of fairness.[29] But reluctance is not the same as blanket refusal. Once York had stopped, discovered Canterbury's desperate situation, and revealed his own ability to help, did he not have some obligation to assist? Would not York himself expect assistance, even from a complete stranger, if he were in a situation where the stranger could provide extremely valuable assistance at low cost to himself? Is not such an expectation especially justified when the assistance does not so much convey an additional benefit as prevent a large loss? Don't we owe something to others simply on the grounds that we are all human beings, members of the same society, fellow motorists, or capable ourselves of being in the same sort of fix? Are we not all much better off, won't we all have greater wealth, if we live in a society where people have an obligation to help each other whenever the help offers an enormous benefit at a trivial cost? Have we not in some sense contracted together, just by living in the same society, to practice elementary decency?[30]

Common law courts would almost certainly refuse to enforce the contract we are discussing. They would invoke the unconscionability rule. This is admittedly a vague rule, which leaves judges with a great deal of discretion. Perhaps it leaves them with too much discretion, so that we would be better off if unconscionability were more precisely defined.[31] But no rule can ever be defined so completely as to obviate any future need for interpretation.

It is a commonplace of conversation that *fairness* or *justice* is impossible to define. We make too much of this commonplace, since, as suggested earlier, *injustice* is regularly and often rather easily recognized. We know more than we fully understand, and far more than we can articulate clearly.[32]

---

29. Landes and Posner (1978, pp. 93–100, 119–27).

30. If it seems to the reader that the efficiency and fairness criteria are getting all mixed up, that is intended.

31. Epstein (1975).

32. Readers who know the work of Michael Polanyi will have noticed that this paper is in part an attempt to apply Polanyi's theory of knowledge. See especially Polanyi (1958).

It probably *is* well-nigh impossible to secure agreement among any substantial number of citizens (or judges) on an acceptable definition of *fairness*. It does not follow from this, however, that we ought to exclude the
concept from legal thinking. It certainly does not follow that we should
substitute efficiency for fairness as the dominant criterion of legal rule
making.[33]

Efficiency and fairness have this in common, that neither one can be
unambiguously defined in a completely defensible way. That is what these
shifting and inconclusive arguments about Canterbury and York were designed to suggest. Efficiency presupposes property rights. An efficient outcome based on an unfair endowment of rights is not necessarily better than
an inefficient outcome derived from a fair assignment of property rights.
But the fundamental rules by means of which the members of a society
assess the fairness of property rights arrangements are not independent
of the effects those rules have on the creation of social wealth, defined as
aggregate willingness to pay. In fact, we can and do assess the relative efficiency of alternative arrangements in order to determine, in hard cases,
what is fair.[34] The plausible assumption that people prefer more wealth to
less will sometimes help us decide what people were intending to do, and
knowledge of intentions is often crucial to determinations of fairness.

This is the important truth that is expressed in both the positive and
normative economic theories of law. Those who reject the economic theory of law on the grounds that justice rather than efficiency is and should
be the criterion of judicial decisions overlook the important assistance
that efficiency considerations can provide in the quest for justice.[35] But advocates of the economic theory of law have invited this response by arguing that efficiency should *take the place* of fairness in legal rule making.
Efficiency and fairness are complements, not substitutes. Each helps to repair the ultimate indeterminacy of the other. We do not have to repudiate

---

The paper has also been influenced by reflection on many of the arguments advanced in
Nelson and Winter (1982).

33. Compare Stigler (1978).

34. The claim here is a bit stronger, I believe, than Michelman's conception of
efficiency as a "tie breaker." Michelman (1978, p. 1047).

35. The change in Richard Epstein's position from the early to the late 1970s reflects,
I believe, a growing recognition of this fact. Compare Epstein (1973) with Epstein (1979).

fairness to obtain help from efficiency; nor must we forgo the assistance that efficiency considerations provide in our groping for fairness.

A continuing problem for those who maintain that common law rules are in effect rules for maximizing social wealth is to explain how such rules could have developed.[36] The reasoning that judges employ reveals no special concern for efficiency. On the contrary, judges seem more interested in devising rules that will yield justice in the case at hand than they are in the incentives these rules will provide in the future.[37] To settle a case by reference to future effects on social wealth rather than to the past actions of the litigants would strike most students of the law as a perversion of justice. How, then, could common law rules have evolved over the years in the direction of efficiency?

Many of the attempts at explanation dismiss as irrelevant the arguments of the judges and the concerns expressed in their decisions. This dubious procedure may be altogether unnecessary. The courts could have developed efficient rules as an unintended by-product of their conscious efforts to develop fair rules. Suppose, for example, that the defendant in the breach of contract case pleads an unforeseen change in circumstances— which is the usual pleading. This amounts to a claim that, had the parties considered the possibility of what actually occurred and written a clause to cover it, the clause would have called for breach. The defendant, in short, claims to have behaved fairly, because in breaching the written contract he was only conforming to the larger, implicit contract in which the written contract is imbedded. The task of the courts in such cases, if they are concerned with fairness between the parties, is to determine the relevant provisions of the unwritten contract. What arrangements would the parties have agreed upon had they considered the possibility of the unforeseen event?

It makes a great deal of sense to assume that the parties would have designed the clause they did not write so as to maximize the positive impact on the *sum* of the two parties' wealth. They would thus have assigned liabilities in the event of these contingencies on the basis of their estimated

36. Posner has himself regularly called attention to this weakness in the positive economic theory of law. See, for example, Posner (1981b, pp. 776–77).

37. Fried (1980).

respective abilities to manage them in wealth-enhancing ways.[38] Legal rules promoting wealth maximization might thus have developed out of judicial efforts to decide, in various classes of cases, what fairness would require. The argument sketched here would apply to the evolution of tort liability rules and rules settling disputed property rights boundaries,[39] as well as to rules for resolving contract disputes.

This explanation for the evolution of efficient common law rules does not have to assume that judges are either dupes or liars. Judges claim to be aiming at fairness, and in fact they are. But through the use of efficiency criteria to decide in uncertain cases what fairness would require, the judges may have been led by an invisible hand to promote a desirable social end that was not part of their conscious intention.

IV

In economics and in law, we always know more than we realize, and far more than we can fully articulate or rigorously prove. Whatever the virtues of rigorous reasoning in these disciplines, it must be used judiciously. Or would it be better to say economically? When we give up our obsession with incontestable arguments, we begin to learn more about what we actually know and about the limitations of that knowledge. And sometimes it even happens that others then begin to listen to us more attentively.

References

Becker, Gary S. (1976) *The Economic Approach to Human Behavior,* Chicago, Ill.: University of Chicago Press.

Buchanan, James. (1974) "Good Economics—Bad Law," *Virginia Law Review,* vol. 60, pp. 483–92.

Coase, Ronald H. (1960) "The Problem of Social Cost," *Journal of Law and Economics,* vol. 3, pp. 1–44.

———. (1982) *How Should Economists Choose?* Washington, D.C.: American Enterprise Institute.

38. Goetz and Scott (1977).
39. The cases discussed by Ronald Coase in "The Problem of Social Cost" read somewhat differently from this perspective. See Coase (1960, pp. 8–15, 19–28).

Demsetz, Harold. (1964) "The Exchange and Enforcement of Property Rights," *Journal of Law and Economics*, vol. 7, pp. 11–26.

———. (1966) "Some Aspects of Property Rights," *Journal of Law and Economics*, vol. 9, pp. 61–70.

———. (1967) "Toward a Theory of Property Rights," *American Economic Review*, vol. 57, pp. 347–59.

———. (1972a) "When Does the Rule of Liability Matter?" *Journal of Legal Studies*, vol. 1, no. 1, pp. 13–28.

———. (1972b) "Wealth Distribution and the Ownership of Rights," *Journal of Legal Studies*, vol. 1, no. 2, pp. 223–32

———. (1979) "Ethics and Efficiency in Property Rights Systems," pp. 97–116 in M. J. Rizzo (ed.), *Time, Uncertainty, and Disequilibrium*, Lexington, Mass.: D. C. Heath and Company.

———. (1982) "Professor Michelman's Unnecessary and Futile Search for the Philosopher's Touchstone," pp. 41–47 in J. Roland Pennock and John W. Chapman (eds.), *Ethics, Economics, and the Law*, Nomos XXIV, New York: New York University Press.

Dworkin, Ronald M. (1986) *Law's Empire*, Cambridge, Mass.: Belknap Press.

Epstein, Richard A. (1973) "A Theory of Strict Liability," *Journal of Legal Studies*, vol. 2, pp. 151–204.

———. (1975) "Unconscionability: A Critical Appraisal," *Journal of Law and Economics*, vol. 18, pp. 293–315.

———. (1979) "Nuisance Law: Corrective Justice and Its Utilitarian Constraints," *Journal of Legal Studies*, vol. 8, pp. 49–102.

Freeman, Alan D. (1981) "Truth and Mystification in Legal Scholarship," *Yale Law Journal*, vol. 90, pp. 1229–37.

Fried, Charles. (1980) "The Laws of Change: The Cunning of Reason in Moral and Legal History," *Journal of Legal Studies*, vol. 9, pp. 335–53.

Frug, Gerald E. (1982) "Cities and Homeowners Associations: A Reply," *University of Pennsylvania Law Review*, vol. 130, pp. 1589–1601.

Goetz, Charles J., and Robert E. Scott. (1977) "Liquidated Damages, Penalties and the Just Compensation Principle: Some Notes on an Enforcement Model and a Theory of Efficient Breach," *Columbia Law Review*, vol. 77, pp. 554–94.

Gordon, Robert W. (1981) "Historicism in Legal Scholarship," *Yale Law Journal*, vol. 90, pp. 1017–56.

Hart, H. L. A. (1983) *Essays in Jurisprudence and Philosophy*, New York: Oxford University Press.

Hayek, Friedrich A. (1973) *Law, Legislation and Liberty:* vol. 1, *Rules and Order*, Chicago, Ill.: University of Chicago Press.

———. (1976) *Law, Legislation and Liberty:* vol. 2, *The Mirage of Social Justice*, Chicago, Ill.: University of Chicago Press.

Heyne, Paul. (1987) *The Economic Way of Thinking*, 5th ed., Chicago, IL: Science Research Associates.

Hutchison, T. W. (1978) *On Revolutions and Progress in Economic Knowledge*, New York: Cambridge University Press.

Javins v. First National Realty Corporation, 428 F.2d 1071 (1970).

Kelman, Mark. (1979) "Choice and Utility," *Wisconsin Law Review*, pp. 769–97.

Kennedy, Duncan. (1976) "Form and Substance in Private Law Adjudication," *Harvard Law Review*, vol. 89, pp. 1685–1778.

———. (1981a) "Cost-Benefit Analysis of Entitlement Problems: A Critique," *Stanford Law Review*, vol. 33, pp. 387–445.

———. (1981b) "Cost-Reduction Theory as Legitimation," *Yale Law Journal*, vol. 90, pp. 1275–83.

Klein, Benjamin (1980). "Transaction Cost Determinants of 'Unfair' Contractual Arrangements," *American Economic Review*, vol. 70, no. 2, pp. 356–62.

Klein, Benjamin, Robert G. Crawford, and Armen A. Alchian. (1978) "Vertical Integration, Appropriable Rents, and the Competitive Contracting Process," *Journal of Law and Economics*, vol. 21, no. 2, pp. 297–326.

Landes, William M., and Richard A. Posner. (1978) "Salvors, Finders, Good Samaritans, and Other Rescuers: An Economic Study of Law and Altruism," *Journal of Legal Studies*, vol. 7, pp. 83–128.

Liebhafsky, H. H. (1976) "Price Theory as Jurisprudence," *Journal of Economic Issues*, vol. 10, no. 1, pp. 23–43.

Michelman, Frank I. (1978) "Norms and Normativity in the Economic Theory of Law," *Minnesota Law Review*, vol. 62, pp. 1015–48.

———. (1982) "Ethics, Economics, and the Law of Property," pp. 3–40 in J. Roland Pennock and John W. Chapman (eds.), *Ethics, Economics, and the Law*, Nomos XXIV, New York: New York University Press.

Nelson, Richard R. (1970) Discussion, *American Economic Review*, vol. 60, no. 2, pp. 127–28.

Nelson, Richard, and Sidney G. Winter. (1982) *An Evolutionary Theory of Economic Change*, Cambridge, Mass.: Harvard University Press.

Nozick, Robert. (1974) *Anarchy, State and Utopia*, New York: Basic Books, Inc.

Polanyi, Michael. (1958) *Personal Knowledge*, Chicago, Ill.: University of Chicago Press.

Posner, Richard A. (1979a) "Utilitarianism, Economics, and Legal Theory," *Journal of Legal Studies*, vol. 8, pp. 103–40.

———. (1979b) "Some Uses and Abuses of Economics in Law," *University of Chicago Law Review*, vol. 46, pp. 281–315.

———. (1981a) *The Economics of Justice*, Cambridge, Mass.: Harvard University Press.

———. (1981b) "A Reply to Some Recent Criticisms of the Efficiency Theory of the Common Law," *Hofstra Law Review*, vol. 9, pp. 775–94.

————. (1986) *Economic Analysis of Law*, 3d ed., Boston: Little, Brown and Company.

Rizzo, Mario J. (1979) "Uncertainty, Subjectivity, and Economic Analysis of Law," pp. 71–89 in M. J. Rizzo (ed.), *Time, Uncertainty, and Disequilibrium*, Lexington, Mass.: D. C. Heath and Company.

————. (1980a) "Law Amid Flux: The Economics of Negligence and Strict Liability in Tort," *Journal of Legal Studies*, vol. 9, pp. 291–318.

————. (1980b) "The Mirage of Efficiency," *Hofstra Law Review*, vol. 8, pp. 641–58.

Robbins, Lionel. (1935) *An Essay on the Nature and Significance of Economic Science*, 2d ed., London: Macmillan and Company, Ltd.

Rothbard, Murray. (1979) "The Myth of Efficiency," pp. 90–95 in M. J. Rizzo (ed.), *Time, Uncertainty, and Disequilibrium*, Lexington, Mass.: D. C. Heath and Company.

Samuels, Warren J. (1981) "Maximization of Wealth as Justice: An Essay on Posnerian Law and Economics as Policy Analysis," *Texas Law Review*, vol. 60, pp. 147–72.

Samuels, Warren J., and A. Allan Schmid, eds. (1981) *Law and Economics: An Institutional Perspective*, Boston, MA: Martinus Nijhoff.

Stigler, George. (1978) "Wealth, and Possibly Liberty," *Journal of Legal Studies*, vol. 7, pp. 213–17.

PART 8

Policy Commentary

CHAPTER 23

What Is the Responsibility of Business Under Democratic Capitalism?

"WHAT IS THE RESPONSIBILITY of business under democratic capitalism?" The topic assigned to me sounds so suspiciously like a sermon title that I've been emboldened to choose a text. Two texts, actually, but both from the scripture according to Adam Smith. The first is quite familiar. The second is less well known.

From Book IV of *The Wealth of Nations*, Chapter 2:

> Every individual is continually exerting himself to find out the most advantageous employment for whatever capital he can command. It is his own advantage, indeed, and not that of the society, which he has in view. But the study of his own advantage naturally, or rather necessarily leads him to prefer that employment which is most advantageous to the society.

And a few paragraphs later Smith writes:

> He generally, indeed, neither intends to promote the public interest, nor knows how much he is promoting it.... [H]e intends only his own

Unpublished typescript of lecture in a series titled The Moral and Ethical Dimensions of Democratic Capitalism, conducted by the Colorado Council on Economic Education and the Graduate School of Business Administration, at the University of Colorado, Boulder, Colorado, 8 December 1982. Reprinted by permission of Mrs. Juliana Heyne.

gain, and he is in this, as in many other cases, led by an invisible hand to promote an end which was no part of his intention. Nor is it always the worse for the society that it was no part of it. By pursuing his own interest he frequently promotes that of the society more effectually than when he really intends to promote it. I have never known much good done by those who affected to trade for the public good. It is an affectation, indeed, not very common among merchants, and very few words need be employed in dissuading them from it.

My second text is also from Book IV, the last chapter (Chapter IX), the second last paragraph:

> All systems either of preference or restraint, therefore, being thus completely taken away, the obvious and simple system of natural liberty establishes itself of its own accord. Every man, as long as he does not violate the laws of justice, is left perfectly free to pursue his own interest his own way, and to bring both his industry and capital into competition with those of any other man, or order of men.

I want to spend the first part of this lecture defending Smith's outrageous claim that people in business promote the public interest most effectively by pursuing their own advantage, or, more precisely, the largest possible net revenue for their own enterprises. It's the social responsibility of business, in short, to maximize profits. I want to defend that claim by showing why it isn't outrageous at all. Some of my arguments have often been made before and won't be strange to most of you. Other arguments may be less familiar and perhaps more controversial.

But the cogency of the entire argument depends ultimately on how we read eleven words in that *second* text: "...as long as he does not violate the laws of justice." That is a very important qualification to every policy argument that Adam Smith ever makes in *The Wealth of Nations*. Smith has been seriously misinterpreted by those who have overlooked the role that justice plays in his system of political economy. I want to show you why the first argument, the case for profit maximization, makes no sense without this qualification. And I hope to persuade you that Adam Smith had a conception of what "the laws of justice" entail that is still deserving of attention today. Indeed, it may deserve especially close attention in an age such as ours, where unexamined and incoherent concepts of justice exercise so much control over public policy.

An economy or economic system is a social system through which people cooperate in using what they have to obtain what they want. This is the function of *all* economic systems: primitive, modern, socialist, capitalist, democratic, oligarchic, coordinated, or confused. Systems differ enormously with respect to whose wants they serve and how effectively they work. But all economies are systems of social interaction, through which people are induced to work, to consume, to save, to invest, to risk: all more or less; and all, of course, in specific, concrete ways.

The primary problem that modern, industrialized economic systems must solve is the problem posed by the scarcity of information. We are inclined to overlook these difficulties and to take their resolution for granted, because we take for granted the remarkable mechanism of social coordination through which we gather and disseminate the knowledge that is essential to the system's functioning. In overlooking the knowledge or information problem, we focus undue attention on a different scarcity, the scarcity of goodwill. We erroneously suppose that goodwill can resolve problems that can in fact be resolved only through the accumulation of additional information. Moreover, many of our proposals for increasing the amount of goodwill in the economy fail completely to attain their objectives, but do manage to subvert the crucial information system.

Modern economies are incredibly complex. Indeed, they are unmanageably complex. But note carefully that something can be unmanageably complex and still work quite satisfactorily. Not everything that works is managed. Some systems can only work, in fact, if they are not managed, for the simple reason that no manager could possibly have command of all the information essential to the system's effective functioning. Our economy is just such a system.

Have you ever pondered the unsettling truth that none of us knows how to produce goods upon which we are dependent for our very survival? In the case of many such goods, *no* one knows how to produce them. That is to say, no *one* knows. The required knowledge is scattered among millions of people. Moreover, it is necessarily scattered in this fashion, because no single mind could possibly grasp and comprehend all the information that must be known if, for example, an antibiotic is to be available for your use when you contract a life-threatening infection. Computers offer no real help in dealing with the kind of information problem to which I'm trying to direct your attention. The required knowledge isn't the kind that can be stored in a computer, and it changes faster than computer programmers could ever hope to record it, because we simply have no timely way of gathering and keeping up-to-date all the detailed bits of information that must be precisely and correctly known if an economy like ours is not to break down in chaos.

This dispersed knowledge becomes available to decision makers, in an appropriately distilled form, primarily through the relative money prices that are generated by the ongoing processes of supply and demand. What people want encounters what people are willing and able to do, and the resulting possibilities are summarized in a vast menu with specific price tags attached to each option.

If that all sounds terribly abstract and even unrealistic, it's because I'm trying to describe everyday occurrences with which we are all familiar, but whose nature and significance we rarely appreciate. We tend to think of prices as costs, which they are, of course, to potential users of a good. But prices are also potential income to suppliers of a good. And in both cases they are signals. Rising prices are signals to users that a good is becoming more scarce and ought therefore to be employed more sparingly. At the same time they indicate to suppliers that more ought to be produced, if possible. Falling prices emit the opposite signals. Moreover, information about changing scarcities is linked in this system with incentives to act appropriately, to alter one's behavior so as to accommodate the new social situation. Rising prices not only tell users they *ought* to be more economical and suppliers that they *ought* to make more available; rising prices at the same time provide financial incentives to do what ought to be done.

That is why, as Adam Smith maintained, people in business who pursue their own advantage thereby promote the public interest. Business decision-makers—let me use the term *executive,* which captures the function in which I'm interested and is also non-sexist—business executives who aim at the maximization of profits are responding to their society's instructions for the allocation of scarce resources. The information is not perfect, whatever "perfect" might mean in this context. But it is far and away the best information available to an executive who wants to be socially responsible. To ignore it or set it aside *in the name of social responsibility* almost always amounts to rejecting the most reliable information available on what social responsibility entails, in favor of a subjective and usually quite arbitrary conception of the public good.

Whatever the *motives* of business executives, the *consequences* of aiming at maximum profit are the maximization of output measured in terms of monetary value. I certainly do not want to claim that a larger dollar value of output is the highest good, or even that it is in all cases better than some particular alternative. But I do want to insist that alternative goals for business executives must bear the burden of proof. Critics of profit-maximization do not seem to realize what a heavy burden that is.

Most of the productive resources in the U.S. economy, apart from human resources, are owned by corporations, and are consequently managed by business executives on behalf of others. The officers of publicly-owned corporations have legal and moral obligations to shareholders that prohibit them from using these resources capriciously. It is the first obligation of corporation officers to do as well as possible for the owners they represent: to be good stewards, in short, of the resources entrusted to their care. It is much harder than we commonly suppose to find circumstances under which "social responsibility" would call for decisions aimed at any other objective than the maximization of profit.

A number of misunderstandings regularly confuse the discussion of this issue. To begin with, in arguing that business executives should aim at profit-maximization, I am actually saying that they should attempt to maximize the present discounted value of the expected stream of net earnings from ownership of the resources under their control. That wordy amplification underlines the point that we are not recommending any kind of shortsighted behavior.

Neither logic nor experience supports the commonly-heard charge that business executives sacrifice long-term results for short-run profits. Where shortsighted behavior is not to anyone's advantage, we shouldn't expect to observe it. The *Wall Street Journal* recently published an article on fire hazards in skyscrapers and laws designed to make such buildings safer. In the course of the article the claim was made that the savings on insurance premiums over a 30-year period would pay for the installation of sprinkler systems, but that such systems were nonetheless only rarely installed because most large office buildings are constructed by speculators who sell them within a few years. The argument is absurd. Developers construct buildings with an eye to their long-run value, regardless of how quickly they intend to sell, because the selling price they can obtain will be the present discounted value of *all* future net income expected from ownership of the building.

Contrary to a widespread belief, corporate managers do not aim at high quarterly profits, to keep shareholders satisfied, at the expense of long-run profitability. Management in this manner would depress current stock prices, which is not the way to please shareholders. Moreover, it would invite and facilitate a hostile takeover, which would clearly not be in management's own best interest.

Whenever we see short-run benefits being pursued in disregard of long-run costs, we may assume with a high degree of confidence that the mis-managed resources cannot be sold. The right to sell a resource is the power to appropriate its long-run value. The right to sell consequently promotes conservation. If you want to examine a social system in which short-run benefits are persistently chosen despite the fact that their long-run costs will be excessive, look at the operation of democratic legislatures. "After me the deluge" is *not* the slogan of business executives in a market economy; it much more closely describes the behavior of legislators who must stand for re-election every two years. It is ironic that so many people believe government intervention in economic life is necessary to secure the interests of future generations, when the preponderance of the evidence suggests so strongly that the effective time horizons of government officials are shorter than the time horizons of private persons managing marketable resources.

We must also not be misled into supposing that profit-maximization is an alternative to such objectives as obeying the law or pursuing humane personnel policies. Business executives will usually find that profit-maximization *requires* law-abiding behavior and diligent attention to the interests of employees. Those who attack the profit-maximization criterion by assuming that its acceptance entails disregard for legality or for people are attacking a straw man.

This is not to say that business firms will always obey the law or that they will never treat their employees inconsiderately. I am in no way attempting to argue that business executives do all things wisely and well. My argument is a quite different one: Business executives ought to use maximum anticipated net revenue, properly discounted, as their decision criterion. When this produces unsatisfactory results, as it sometimes surely will, we should not ask or expect executives to use some other criterion in allocating resources, because we should neither ask nor expect them to behave like benevolent despots.

Isn't that what it finally comes down to? We notice that the economic system turns out a lot of schlock, and so we urge business executives to pay more attention to good taste and high quality. We do not notice that business responds to a wide range of differing tastes and to a market that calls for goods of highly variant quality, and that in asking business executives to ignore the market we are in effect urging them to substitute their own preferences for the preferences of consumers. Is that social responsibility or elitism?

Or we notice that particular corporations are doing business in South Africa, and we urge them to pull out of that racist country even if this entails the loss of some profits. We too seldom ask about the probable consequences of such a pullout. (Who will subsequently take over the abandoned capital resources, for example, and how will this affect the evolving balance of power in South Africa?) But we almost never notice that by pushing such demands we are asking business executives to make foreign policy and to interfere in the domestic affairs of another country. It is true, of course, that doing business in South Africa has effects in that country just as much as *not* doing business has effects. But doing or not doing business for the sake of profits is a very different matter from doing or not doing business with the primary intention of affecting another nation's domestic policies. Against those who would call this an exercise of corporate responsibility I maintain that it is a dangerous and even arrogant assumption of powers that do not belong to business executives and cannot safely be entrusted to them.

We are frequently misled in our consideration of such issues by the erroneous assumption that the choice for business executives is a simple choice between good and evil. This will almost never be the case, however.

The choices that confront business executives are most appropriately seen as choices between alternative benefits and alternative costs accruing to or falling upon different people. When we pay attention to the costs as well as to the benefits of the policies commonly advocated in the name of social responsibility, those policies tend quickly to lose the moral sheen that makes them so attractive to critics of profit-maximization. Consider, for example, a U.S. corporation that operates a factory in Malaysia and subjects employees to workplace hazards that would be illegal in this country. Is that an irresponsible pursuit of profit? Is it an exploitation of Malaysian workers? Or is it the provision of valuable income-earning opportunities to people who would be much worse off if the corporation had to adhere to U.S. safety standards in Malaysia and consequently chose not to operate a factory there? The truth is that people whose life expectancy is low because of desperate poverty do not assign as high a value to occupational safety as do people in the United States, and that employers who adopt the standards of an affluent society in a poor society could easily end up reducing the well-being of people to whom they think they are being "socially responsible."

The good intentions of business executives who would substitute their own notions of social responsibility for the criterion of profitability do not necessarily produce good results. Would it be churlish of me to suggest that the intentions themselves might not always be as good and pure as we are inclined to suppose? Corporate executives who adopt policies being urged upon them by church groups or other self-proclaimed advocates of the public interest, despite the fact that these policies will reduce net revenue for the corporation, will often be applauded for their business statesmanship. What is the value to them of such acclaim? And is it benevolence when people take actions that bring gratifying public approval to themselves at other people's cost? I will applaud the generosity of corporate executives who contribute a portion of their personal incomes and their own time to charitable endeavors; I see no reason to applaud when they contribute the time and money of the shareholders whose resources they're managing.

I would in fact be alarmed by this pseudo-benevolence, this "unbenevolent despotism," if I did not see evidence that it is much more rare in practice than it is in rhetoric. Corporate executives are flattered by the request that they serve as philosopher-kings, and they are eager to proclaim their willingness to serve. I believe we can take comfort from the overwhelming evidence that, in practice, these executives equate socially responsible business decisions with decisions that maximize the market value of their corporation's stock. Departures from this rule are by and large insignificant; corporate charity, which seems to be a contradiction of the profit-maximization criterion, is generally of such modest proportions that it can be justified in terms of public relations.

I want to make one more point before shifting to my second text from Adam Smith. The widespread but confused belief that profit-maximization is a wholly inadequate criterion for socially-responsible business behavior gains much of its appeal from the mistaken assumption that profit-maximizing behavior is selfish behavior.

We are much too quick to impugn people's motives, including even our own motives under certain circumstances. Business executives are human beings, with all the variety of motivation and intention that this entails. People don't do very many things for simple reasons, and they do even less for reasons that are simply selfish. Business executives who focus their attention on the relative costs and benefits of available options are paying attention to the task at hand, not acting selfishly. Their motives at any moment will be infinitely varied, complex, and I dare say unfathomable; but they are no more likely to be selfish or otherwise morally objectionable than are the motives of college professors preparing a lecture, United Way officials planning their campaign, or an architect designing a building. Economy in the use of means for the achievement of worthwhile goals is an important criterion for all the people just mentioned, and it is economy of just this sort that is being practiced by business executives who continuously consult the criterion of profitability. It is a serious mistake to equate concentrated and focused attention on the task at hand with selfishness. That would lead us to call surgeons "selfish" because they totally neglect the personality or family situation of patients while removing their gall bladders.

This confusion is compounded in the case of business executives by the fact that their success is monitored primarily through the comparison of values expressed in monetary terms. We apparently have enormous difficulty in breaking free from the notion that there is something inherently immoral, or at least morally inferior, about making decisions on the basis of relative monetary magnitudes. And we are not deterred by the absurd conclusions to which this prejudice sometimes leads us. If the members of a downtown church in a large city, for example, decide to sell their old building to someone who wants to erect an office tower on the land, they are not necessarily being selfish or greedy or putting monetary values ahead of religious values. Everything depends on what they do with the profit that they make from converting an old building they can no longer afford to maintain into the money that represents its value in alternative uses. A Manhattan pastor who obviously doesn't want to see old church buildings torn down was recently quoted by the *Wall Street Journal* in just such a case: "I don't give a damn what others think," he said. "It's a perversion that property is more important than beauty."

That's an extraordinary statement. Property cannot be more important than beauty for the same reason that beauty can't be more important than property: the categories aren't comparable. What the indignant pastor presumably meant was that the aesthetic values to be realized from preserving old churches are more important than whatever alternative values are promoted through the sale of such property. Whether that's true in any given case surely depends on what must be sacrificed to preserve the old building. The monetary profit to be realized from the sale is not itself that sacrifice. The monetary profit represents command over other resources, resources that could be used in dozens of different ways: to build new churches, support missionaries, feed the hungry, or endow scholarships for promising young church architects.

Profit maximizing, whether by church officers or business executives, is a procedure for behaving economically, for being a good steward. The Greek word for steward, used in the New Testament, is in fact *oikonomos*. If social responsibility entails good stewardship, it calls for economy in the use of available resources. Decisions on the basis of relative money magnitudes are basically good stewardship.

The title of this lecture includes a word that I have barely mentioned: *democratic*. What is the social responsibility of business under *democratic* capitalism? As soon as we begin to take that word into account, a serious gap appears in the argument I've been constructing. The gap was already present in *The Wealth of Nations*.

Adam Smith claimed that the pursuit of private interest by business executives promotes the public interest. But throughout *The Wealth of Nations* he also complains bitterly about the power that merchants and manufacturers exercise in Parliament. He says that they have often obtained "a wretched monopoly against their countrymen" by bamboozling, pressuring, and even intimidating the legislature. Isn't this inconsistent with the claim that the pursuit of private interest will promote the public interest?

What are merchants and manufacturers doing, after all, when they lobby the legislature, except pursuing their own advantage? If a dollar invested in lobbying promises a higher return than a dollar invested in machinery or product development, then profit-maximization calls for investment in lobbying efforts. That's exactly what the merchants and manufacturers of Smith's day were doing, and what business executives still do today. They carry competition into the arena of government, in an attempt to secure laws and regulations that will make their business activities more profitable. In our own time as in the time of Adam Smith, the lobbying efforts of business executives are directed primarily toward the enactment of laws that would restrict their competitors and create preferences for themselves.

Smith obviously disapproved of such efforts and found them subversive of the public good. But how then can he maintain that the pursuit of private interest promotes the public interest? The answer is that the pursuit of private interest for Smith had to be within the bounds of justice. That eleven-word qualification—"as long as he does not violate the laws of justice"—clears Smith of inconsistency, but opens a whole new dimension for our discussion.

Every claim that profit-maximization is socially responsible contains the implicit premise that the actions taken are legal. In a democracy, however, citizens participate in the making of the laws; and business executives are citizens along with everyone else. As a matter of fact, business executives have considerably more influence on legislation than do ordinary citizens. That's not because "corporations have all the money," as populist rhetoric would have it. It's because of the free-rider problem that afflicts the democratic process. And it calls into question the adequacy of the contention that business executives are being socially responsible when they maximize profits within the limits of law. For they have a great deal of power to determine what those limits are going to be.

The Achilles' heel of democratic capitalism is the tendency of the democratic part to destroy the capitalism part. In order to make clear what I mean, I must carefully define my terms. I shall call a political system "democratic" if its laws result from a competition between legislators for citizen votes. That definition isn't as strange as it sounds. Definitions of democratic that refer to "the will of the people" or "the preferences of the majority" are misleading in that they assume what must be proved, namely, that a political system such as the one we have in the United States does in fact produce legislation consistent with what a majority of the voters prefer. The definition I am using has the advantage that it calls attention to the process that actually shapes legislation: the competition among legislators for voter approval.

The basic problem with democracy is that special interests have an enormous advantage in this competition. People know and care about their own interests. But they usually don't pursue them successfully through the political process, because the cost to any one person of exerting influence will typically exceed by a large amount the expected benefit from acting. Each of us is just one voice and one vote. So why bother? Why bear the cost? Since my action will have an insignificant impact, while imposing considerable costs on me in time and money, it is in my interest to behave like a free rider in the political arena: to do nothing and hope that someone else will defend my interests.

The people for whom the expected benefits exceed the costs are people who form part of a relatively small group with a relatively substantial interest. The laws that emerge from operation of democratic processes are consequently laws that cater to an endless succession of narrow, special interests. We are not governed by the will of the majority but by the wills of innumerable minorities. Special preferences and restrictions multiply, and collectively make all of us ultimately worse off. Competition in the political arena subverts competition in the economic arena, and thereby subverts the invisible hand that extracts the public advantage from the pursuit of private advantages.

And what is "capitalism"? Capitalism is a social system within which individuals are free to exchange with one another on the basis of clear and stable "rules of the game." That definition may strike you as even more idiosyncratic than my definition of "democracy." But it directs attention to the essential features of what we actually mean when we talk about capitalist economic systems.

Capitalism is a *social* system, because its defining characteristics are social relationships, relationships among people, not relationships between people and things. (The term "capitalism" was invented by the enemies of the system and is thoroughly misleading.)

Secondly, the definition I have given points up the two conditions that make the system work: voluntary exchange and stable rights, more commonly described as free markets and private property. The trouble with these latter terms—frees markets and private property—is that they divert our attention from the *social* nature of the system. Property rights are rights with respect to other people, and are therefore inescapably social, not private. If I have a so-called "private property right," what I have is the socially acknowledged right to exclude other members of society from making certain uses of my property. And I would rather speak of voluntary exchange than of free markets in order to point out that the freedom people possess under capitalism is again a social phenomenon, dependent upon their ability to persuade other people to cooperate with them.

I don't want to legislate definitions or to get hung up in a purely verbal argument. What is important is that we see how thoroughly dependent a capitalist system is upon *clear and stable rules*. If it helps you see what I'm driving at and how important these rules are, think of them as *clear and stable property rights*.

The freedom that capitalism provides is created by the ability of individuals to manage and dispose of particular resources on the basis of their personal knowledge and interests. That is impossible without clearly defined and stable rights over particular resources. When such a system of rights exists, then social interaction—what the economist calls supply and demand—will establish scarcity-reflecting prices, and the vast, dispersed knowledge that the members of society possess will be effectively coordinated. The productive achievements of capitalism *and* the freedom that it allows individuals are both the result of clearly-defined and stable property rights, or rules of the game.

The big question is: Who decides what the rules will be? The usual answer is: The laws settle the rules. But this only pushes the question one step further back: Who decides what the laws are to be? If the best answer we can give to that question is majority rule, then capitalism is doomed. Majority rule must itself be subject to rules if capitalism is to survive. For majority rule that is not itself subject to a higher rule will inevitably produce special preferences and restraints that will prove incompatible with effective market coordination and individual freedom.

Capitalism requires clear and stable property rights. But clear and stable property rights will not exist except within a political system that is constrained by a constitution. It doesn't have to be the constitution that was ratified in this nation two hundred years ago, although that particular constitution in its original form was a remarkably successful attempt to establish the kind of constitutional rule for which I'm now contending. The necessary condition is that the constitution constrain the pursuit of self-interest within the political arena: that it set rules for changing the rules under which voluntary exchange is going to occur.

But even a constitution isn't enough. Formal constitutions must be interpreted, not only in order to apply them to changing circumstances, but also because no constitution interprets itself. Every formal statement presupposes background statements that fill out its meaning and intent. So every political constitution presupposes antecedent notions of justice out of which it arose and which put flesh on its skeleton. The rules of justice are the ultimate rules that shape the constitutional rules that constrain the legislated rules that finally control the rules of the game within which "capitalist activities" (and all other activities) occur.

In other words, there is finally no substitute for morality. But *what* morality? Don't moralities differ? Who is to decide when moral judgments conflict? I can't answer those questions in a single lecture. But do we have to answer them before we can agree on the issues before us? Personal moralities certainly differ. But what about impersonal moralities, or the morality appropriate to impersonal social systems? Can I induce you to give sympathetic consideration to the proposition that the morality appropriate to large, many-person societies is extraordinarily simple and rarely disputed once we agree what it is that we're talking about?

We're talking about justice in large, impersonal societies. And the only conception of justice that makes any sense in societies larger than a handful of people is the *negative* conception of justice: Avoid *injustice*. Injustice occurs when people are treated unfairly. Unfair treatment in large societies is treatment that is not in accord with the rules: the clear rules that everyone knows in advance and that apply equally to all.

A large society, such as the economic system of the United States, cannot be a just society unless its duties and benefits are allocated in accord with clear and stable rules. Perhaps the force of this claim will be clearer if I apply it not to the economic system but to a large college class. A college professor teaching a class of 500 students (a large society) must, if she wants to be fair, clarify the rules in advance and then apply them impartially. If a student confronts her with circumstances that the rules had not contemplated and so do not cover, she must search for a response that can be generalized. She must not allow some students to take advantage of other students by securing unique advantages. Each of the 500 students, if pressed, could probably find an explanation (unrelated to what the student actually knew) for missing one or more items on the last test. But it is fundamentally unfair to give extra credit to those students whose obsession with grades or personal belligerence prompts them to ask for it. If the same privilege were extended to every student in the class through a general announcement, it might seem at first that justice would be salvaged. But in fact it would not. The problem is that no teacher could adequately hear and evaluate the explanations of 500 students. Justice in large societies requires not only that general rules binding on all be promulgated, but also that they be applied in a non-arbitrary manner. The consequence of any attempt to apply personal criteria in a large-society situation will be capricious and arbitrary decisions. In short, *injustice*. Justice demands that we use impersonal criteria to allocate burdens and benefits in a large society, where inescapable limitations on our knowledge make it impossible to take personal considerations into account in any consistent way. And fairness requires consistency. That is why justice is pictured as blindfolded.

It is therefore the social responsibility of business executives under democratic capitalism to play by the rules, and to participate in the making of those rules in accord with the basic underlying rule of justice: Ask for no special preferences for yourself, and impose no special restraints on others. Legislate for others as you would have them legislate for you. Adam Smith tells us what justice requires when he says that all systems either of preference or restraint are to be completely taken away.

Let me remind you at this point how I defined *capitalism*. It is a social system in which individuals are free to choose what they will supply and demand, offer and bid, subject only to general rules known in advance. These rules will be both legal rules, externally enforced, and moral rules that are internally enforced. Capitalism, in short, is a system of individual freedom under law, where law does not mean just "legislation" but rather the whole body of established rules, agreements, and conventions by which the members of a society acknowledge themselves to be bound.

Capitalism is thus by definition an impersonal system. It is not altogether an impersonal system, because the individuals within it do participate in families and small, face-to-face associations, where they can know other persons well enough to be concerned with and to care for their unique qualities. But the distinguishing characteristic of capitalism is the impersonal nature of the social interactions that make it up. It can be described paradoxically as a social system in which people do not care about most of those for whom they care. The farmer who feeds me does not even know I exist, and while he wishes me no ill, he does not and cannot care *about* me in any subjective sense. Nonetheless, he cares *for* me, and very effectively, in an objective sense.

We are all dependent, throughout our lives, for our actual survival as well as our many comforts, upon the assistance and cooperation of millions of people whom we will never know and who do not know us. They help us to fulfill our aims in life not because they know or care what happens to us, but because this enables them to fulfill their own aims most effectively. They are *motivated* by their own interests, whatever these may be. They are *guided* by the rules of the society and their perception of the expected net advantages from alternative decisions. These net advantages, or structures of expected costs and benefits, are created by the similarly motivated and guided efforts of everyone else in the society.

Marx was thus correct. He saw more clearly than most of his pro-capitalist contemporaries that capitalism was a system based on commodity production. It had replaced (by supplementing more than by displacing) a system based on relations of personal dependence. Thereby, as Marx and Engels observed in the first part of *The Communist Manifesto,* capitalism had achieved productive wonders. Their mistake, and the mistake of so many who followed them, was in supposing that capitalism could be replaced in turn by a system of production based on "socialist relations," a system retaining the productive powers of capitalism while assigning tasks and rewards on the basis of personal criteria, such as criteria of personal need and merit.

I suspect that the deepest root of this belief, a belief remarkably immune to either theory or evidence, is the conviction that an impersonal social system is morally unacceptable. This is a tragically mistaken prejudice. Impersonal does not mean inhumane, as we sometimes carelessly assume. Nonetheless, our only model for the good society seems to be the family, where production is from each according to ability and distribution is to each according to need and merit.

Perhaps our basic mistake is the belief that we must choose between personal, face-to-face societies and impersonal societies. If we accept as fully legitimate the impersonal, rule-coordinated societies in which we participate we are not repudiating or depreciating in any way marriage, the family, intimacy, I-thou relationships, the unique value of the individual, or the power and significance of personal caring and sacrifice. If we were in fact compelled to repudiate all of this in order to enjoy the benefits that only large and hence impersonal societies can provide, we would be foolish to opt for those benefits. In the long run that choice would deprive us of the advantages of both worlds because the moral values essential to the successful operation of a rule-coordinated society can only be nurtured in personal societies.

But we are not *forced* to choose. We are tempted to choose, it is true, and from both directions. The expanding wealth of opportunities that the impersonal society lays before us makes us progressively less dependent (or so we believe) on particular other persons. As we enlarge our individual freedom and power, we simultaneously declare our continual independence. We view commitments as entanglements and we work toward fuller emancipation. That kind of freedom is really perpetual mobility, and I doubt that it is ultimately compatible with the institutions and virtues of personal community.

But we cannot deal effectively with these problems by turning the economic system into a nuclear family. I am not saying it ought not be done. It *cannot* be done. Economic decisions, the day-by-day decisions of business executives, will produce chaos and injustice if they are not guided overwhelmingly by attention to profit maximization, under a regime of clear, stable, and essentially impersonal rules. That is a limited conception of business social responsibility, it is true. It is a thoroughly humane conception, however, because it *is* limited to human possibilities. If we were gods who possessed all knowledge, we might be able to pursue the good society more directly. But we are not gods. It is not irresponsible to admit that fact and to live together in a manner consistent with our common humanity.

CHAPTER 24

The Morality of Labor Unions

A RECENT STATEMENT by the United States Conference of Catholic Bishops on Roman Catholic social teaching includes a short section on the Dignity of Work and the Rights of Workers. "If the dignity of work is to be protected," it asserts, "then the basic rights of workers must be respected—the right to productive work, to decent and fair wages, to organize and join unions, to private property, and to economic initiative." [1] This chapter will wander between economics and ethics to explore a question that the bishops would probably consider outrageous: Why should the right to organize and join unions be one of the basic rights of workers that people interested in social justice are bound to respect?

Economics and Ethics

Economics and ethics is a combination that many economists deem no more possible than oil and water. In what is probably the most influential essay on the methodology of economics ever published, Lionel Robbins insisted that there was no defensible way to mix economics and ethics.

Reprinted from *Morality and Work*, edited by Tibor R. Machan, by permission of the publisher, Hoover Institution Press; © 2000 by the Board of Trustees of the Leland Stanford Junior University.

1. "Sharing Catholic Social Teaching: Challenges and Directions," reflections of the U.S. Catholic Bishops, August 26, 1998.

"Economics," he wrote, "deals with ascertainable facts; ethics with valuations and obligations. The two fields of inquiry are not on the same plane of discourse." Ethics talks about what ought to be, and economics about what is. "Propositions involving the word 'ought' are different in kind," Robbins insisted, "from propositions involving the word 'is.' And it is difficult to see what possible good can be served by not keeping them separate, or failing to recognize their essential difference." [2]

Robbins was writing during the 1930s at the high tide of logical positivism, with its confident presumption that clear distinctions vigorously enforced could sweep away many of the confusions infecting both science and politics as a result of centuries of wishful thinking. By keeping economics completely separate from ethics, the discussion of means distinct from the discussion of ends, we could supposedly do a better job of resolving our differences. "In the rough-and-tumble of political struggle," Robbins wrote,

> differences of opinion may arise either as a result of differences about ends or as a result of differences about the means of attaining ends. Now, as regards the first type of difference, neither Economics nor any other science can provide any solvent. If we disagree about ends it is a case of thy blood or mine—or live and let live, according to the importance of the difference, or the relative strength of our opponents. But if we disagree about means, then scientific analysis can often help us to resolve our differences. [3]

But the relationship between ends and means is not as clear and simple as all that. We each choose some ends while rejecting others in part on the basis of whether we believe ourselves in command of the means for reaching them, and we disagree among ourselves about the value of particular ends in large part because we disagree about whether we have the means to attain them. Robbins says that when we disagree about ultimate ends, it is a matter of "thy blood or mine" if the issue is important to us. But the truth is that we much more often discuss disagreements about ends than

2. Lionel Robbins, *An Essay on the Nature and Significance of Economic Science*, 2d ed., revised and extended (London: Macmillan and Company, Ltd., 1952), pp. 148–49. Robbins's *Essay* was originally published in 1932 and republished in revised form in 1935.
    3. Ibid., p. 150.

we resort to violence. And when we engage in discussion, we rely heavily on facts and reason to make our case, just as scientists do. We point out that this end deserves a greater weight than that one because this one supports some other end of importance to all of us, or that the superior worth of a particular end that we share is largely canceled out by the improbability of our being able to attain it. "It doesn't work that way" is a very common argument in ethical discussions, an argument that is surely as much (or more) in the realm of means as in the realm of ends.

It might be the case that we would have to resort to force to settle the issue if we disagreed about *ultimate* ends. But how often does that occur? It is hard to think of any end, goal, objective, or value that is truly ultimate, that cannot be argued for. The abortion issue probably divides Americans more deeply at the present time than any other issue in the public forum. The division would not be as deep and unresolvable if we did not choose to frame the question in terms of stark alternatives, such as the right to life versus the right to choose. Surely both ends are valuable and worthy of protection. Those who debate the abortion issue are actually divided on the relative weights to be assigned to ends and values that both sides generally share, weights that almost everyone will want to adjust with varying circumstances. We elevate particular values because we believe they serve other values. But whether or not they actually do so is often a question open to analysis and discussion, processes that can be facilitated with information drawn from one or another of the sciences.

Economics and ethics do not in fact inhabit completely separate realms of discourse, and keeping them rigorously apart will not help us to resolve our political differences.

The Economics of Collective Bargaining

Labor unions have served many purposes, but their primary goal, and the one with which we begin, is raising the net compensation of their members. Unions campaign for members by promising to make them "better off" in ways that will presumably impose additional costs on employers. Assuming that employers aren't simply spiteful, they are always willing to make their employees better off if doing so has no cost. But employers aim at increasing net revenue, which is receipts minus wages and other costs, and this sets them at least partially in opposition to their employees, for whom wages are not costs but income. "In union there is strength" has been the constant motto of labor unions, because strength is needed to resist the efforts of employers to enhance profits at the expense of wages.

This model, which depicts employers and employees as engaged in a struggle over division of the product, is implicitly supported in the prelude to the Wagner Act, the original National Labor Relations Act passed by Congress in 1935 to strengthen labor unions:

> The inequality of bargaining power between employees who do not possess full freedom of association or actual liberty of contract, and employers who are organized in the corporate or other forms of ownership association substantially burdens and affects the flow of commerce, and tends to aggravate recurrent business depressions, by depressing wage rates and the purchasing power of wage earners in industry and by preventing the stabilization of competitive wage rates and working conditions within and between industries.

While the "findings and policy" sections of bills must always be taken with a grain of salt, this one does manage to state a presupposition widely held among the general public, that wage rates are determined by the relative bargaining power of employees and employers.

Economic theory offers a more complex perspective. Employers have a demand for labor that reflects the estimated marginal contribution that workers will make to the net revenue of their firms. It is the marginal contribution that determines the demand: the amount of net revenue that a potential worker will add to the firm's net revenue, given everything else, including the number of workers already being employed. The more workers there are already employed, other things being equal, the smaller will be the expected contribution to net revenue of an additional worker. This implies that the lower the cost of obtaining workers, the higher the number employers will want to hire. It also implies that the more workers will be able to secure a higher wage, other things again remaining equal, the fewer will be the number of qualified workers available for hire. Wage rates are determined, in other words, by the interaction of demand and supply.

The implications of the economist's perspective become clearer when we ask what this perspective denies or rules out. To begin with, it denies that employers will want to hire a specific number of employees, the number they "need" to run the operation, regardless of what they must pay to obtain them. It suggests, on the contrary, that the size and nature of the operation will itself depend in part on the cost of obtaining workers. Thus, fast-food outlets, for example, do not *require* any specific number of employees. If a very high wage must be paid to obtain competent personnel, fast-food outlets will be open only at the busiest hours, customers will wait longer for service, and there will be fewer such outlets in operation.

The bargaining-power theory of wage determination tends to assume that the demand for workers is completely inelastic with respect to the cost of hiring. Each employer needs some definite number of employees, a number basically fixed by technology, and will hire that number at a very low wage rate or at a very high wage rate, at least until the wage rate becomes so high that the employer is compelled to shut down the business. Between this shutdown rate and some minimum rate below which workers will prefer to remain unemployed, the relative bargaining power of employers and employees sets the actual wage rate that will be paid. Within this model, labor unions, by increasing the bargaining power of employees, redistribute income from employers to employees.

The economist's model carries different implications. The most important is that the wage rate will be set by the number of workers willing and able to supply their services. If fast-food outlets offer a high wage to unskilled workers, so many will offer to work that the quantity supplied will exceed the quantity demanded and employers will have to ration the available positions. To ration means to allocate according to some kind of discriminatory criteria. The law rules out some kinds of discrimination, but the legal criteria include such usually advantageous (for the employer) discriminatory criteria as education, previous experience, recommendations, personal appearance, and prior acquaintance. The most important potential criterion for discriminating among job applications may be the willingness to work for less. If the employer is interested in increasing net revenue, the last criterion will seem especially advantageous and the high wage rate will fall in response to competition.

This, of course, is the competition that unions try to control or prevent. Employees do not compete against employers but against one another, and it is a primary objective of labor unions to restrict competition between workers with the goal of raising wage rates or keeping them high. A union that can compel employers to hire only union members can restrict competition by making it difficult for potential employees to join the union, either directly or by establishing onerous and time-consuming procedures for acquiring the qualifications for membership. Since 1947 unions have been legally barred from enforcing contracts that require prior union membership as a condition of hiring, a prohibition that makes the unions' task more difficult.

A union that succeeds in negotiating a high wage for its members, a wage at which the quantity of qualified labor supplied significantly exceeds the quantity that employers demand, will thereby create a pool of qualified potential competitors for the jobs of its members. This competition will weaken the union's bargaining position when the time comes to negotiate a new contract because the alternative of "going nonunion" will appear more feasible to the employer.

It follows that the unions able to negotiate the highest wage rates for members will be the unions representing workers with valuable skills that are difficult to acquire. These, however, will be workers who would tend to be well compensated even in the absence of a union. Health care organizations offer high wages to the physicians whom they hire because they could not otherwise obtain the employees they want. Electricians would earn much more than file clerks whether or not electricians were unionized. And file clerks will probably not be able to raise their earnings appreciably by forming a union because any significant improvement in their position will attract a flood of new applicants who will weaken the union's bargaining position.

This is why economists have historically been skeptical about both the claims of supporters that unions have greatly improved the position of workers and the claims of opponents that unions have done grave damage to the economy. The economist's model of wage determination suggests that in the long run unions will not be able greatly to affect relative wage rates or the distribution of income between owners of businesses and their employees.

Testing the Model

"In the long run" is a useful phrase for anyone who wants to generalize without fear of empirical refutation. In economics, the long run sometimes seems to mean a period of time long enough to make the generalization irrefutable. Has the impact of unions on the distribution of income really been as limited as our argument suggests? Were the efforts of the various craft unions associated after the 1880s in the American Federation of Labor (AFL), of the United Mineworkers of America under the legendary John L. Lewis, of the United Automobile Workers and the United Steel Workers beginning in the 1930s, or of the American Federation of State, County, and Municipal Employees in recent years simply much ado about very little?

A brief look at each of the cases mentioned may help to clarify the analysis and indicate some of its limitations. The history of craft unions in the United States, such as the various unions representing workers in the construction trades, seems to confirm the analysis. These unions were able to negotiate high wages for their members early on because their members possessed valuable skills that were relatively difficult to acquire. The unions also developed and deployed a variety of tactics to prevent nonunion workers who did acquire the requisite skills from offering their services in competition with union members. Racial exclusions, enforced by contract, custom, threat, or even legislation, were an important tactic in the North as well as the South. So was mutual support among the craft unions; by prohibiting their members from crossing picket lines erected by other unions, the various craft unions made it more difficult for employers to hire nonunion labor even when it was abundantly available. And until they were made illegal in 1947 by the Labor-Management Relations Act (Taft-Hartley Act), closed shop contracts prevented employers from gradually substituting less expensive employees for union members. The steadily declining percentage of unionized workers over the past two or three decades in trades traditionally dominated by the craft unions of the old AFL would be a predictable consequence of laws banning the closed shop, restricting such mutual support tactics as secondary strikes and boycotts, and suppressing racial and gender discrimination.

The United Mineworkers Union under the formidable John L. Lewis secured dramatic improvements in the wages and working conditions of coal miners between the 1920s and the 1940s, improvements that almost surely would not have occurred in the absence of the union. In this case the exception proves the rule. Lewis openly avowed his intention to eliminate coal mining jobs by raising the cost of hiring coal miners and, thereby, forcing the mine owners to substitute machinery for labor, thus accomplishing simultaneously the twin objectives of reducing the number of people employed in an unhealthful and dangerous occupation while improving the lives of those who remained in that occupation.

Automobile workers and steelworkers were the aristocrats of semi-skilled labor for a number of years after World War II, thanks to the efforts of the United Automobile Workers (UAW) and the United Steel Workers (USW). The founders and leaders of these noncraft unions took full advantage of the favorable environment created for them by the 1935 Wagner Act. This act imposed upon employers a legal duty to bargain collectively and outlawed as unfair labor practices many of the most effective devices that employers had regularly used to resist unionization of their enterprises. Once certified by the National Labor Relations Board as the exclusive bargaining agent for everyone employed by each automobile or steel manufacturer, the UAW and the USW used the strike threat to secure wage rates that were the envy of manufacturing workers elsewhere. They negotiated union shop contracts, under which workers must join the union when they are hired, as a way to make sure that the high wages accrued to their members. By organizing all the firms in the industry, these unions prevented the erosion of their gains through competition from nonunionized domestic firms. Competition from foreign manufacturers was, for a time, effectively controlled by successful lobbying for tariffs and other restrictions on imports. The power of the UAW and the USW diminished, however, and the differential advantages of the workers they represented shrank correspondingly when foreign automobile manufacturers and small, nonunionized steel mills took advantage of high labor costs to undersell the large corporations organized by the UAW and the USW. The once munificent wages of automobile and steel workers have proved to be a major cause of high unemployment rates in areas such as Detroit and Pittsburgh, where very high wages came to be regarded as the norm.

Almost all United States unions, craft and industrial, have suffered severe membership losses over the past twenty years. A marked exception is the American Federation of State, County, and Municipal Employees. The AFSCME has attracted loyal members by bargaining successfully for improved compensation and benefits in a period when other unions were being forced to moderate their demands and were losing members, often through having priced themselves out of the market. The percentage of unionized firms in the building trades, for example, has declined in a striking fashion. This is true even for some regions with strong union traditions, as unionized contractors increasingly found themselves unable to match the job bids of contractors who had shifted to nonunion labor. The AFSCME bargains, however, with employers who generally don't face much competition: state, county, and municipal governments. It is harder to obtain a wage increase from an employer who must recover any higher costs by increasing prices to customers who have good alternatives than it is to obtain a wage increase from an employer who can extract additional revenue from clients who have no option except to pay their taxes. Economic theory predicts that the AFSCME will do less well in the future as "tax revolts" increasingly threaten elected officials, and that it will continue to lobby hard against "contracting out" of government services. The competition that causes employers to hire fewer workers when wage costs rise can and does take many forms. Even governments are not exempt.

Questions of Justice: A First Look

In striving to increase the job compensation of their members, labor unions are certainly intending to alter the distribution of the goods and services produced by the economic system. Just *how* they alter it, however, is a much more complex question than either the friends or the foes of labor unions traditionally assume.

When the United Widget Workers Union increases the labor costs of the Wedgwood Widget Company, Wedgwood acquires an incentive to produce widgets at a somewhat lesser rate and to increase its price by some amount. By how much will depend on the price elasticity of the demand for its widgets, or how responsive its customers are to price increases. If all the widget makers with whom Wedgwood competes are subjected to the same increase in labor costs, and if there are no decent substitutes for widgets, Wedgwood could end up raising the price of its widgets by an amount close to its additional wage cost per widget. If Wedgwood's competitors are nonunion and their labor costs do not increase, or if good substitutes for Wedgwood's widgets are readily available (the best substitute for a Wedgwood widget will be another maker's widget), Wedgwood may have an incentive to reduce output substantially or even to give up widget production altogether. In that case, the increased compensation that the UWWU obtains will benefit only those of its members who continue to work for Wedgwood, and they will obtain their gains partially, perhaps largely, at the expense of those who no longer have jobs with Wedgwood.

Widget consumers will also lose, obtaining fewer widgets and paying a higher price for them. The owners of Wedgwood will take some of the loss because Wedgwood's net revenue will decline. Wedgwood's suppliers will also be somewhat worse off. The town in which Wedgwood is located might find its tax base diminished. Anyone with the slightest understanding of how a market system functions and who takes the time to think the matter through will realize that the UWWU does not simply make its members better off at the expense of Wedgwood's shareholders, who might include, just to highlight the uncertainty and ambiguity of the effects, the workers' own pension fund.

Advocates of increased minimum legal wages often say that they would be perfectly willing to pay more for a burger or a cotton shirt in order to provide a living wage to the workers who produce burgers and cotton shirts. But would they go on purchasing *as many* burgers or cotton shirts as they formerly purchased? Even if they would, would everyone else do the same? A market system is a social system in which it is rarely possible to alter one variable without affecting others. Actions have unintended and unanticipated consequences.

Members of the building trades unions in the United States long enjoyed rates of compensation that were the envy of workers elsewhere. They did not do so, however, at the expense of wealthy capitalists. Their benefits were obtained at the cost of higher housing prices and, hence, less new housing, as well as at the expense of workers excluded either directly or indirectly from participation in the construction industry. When the lobbying efforts of construction unions secured federal legislation that required all contractors working on federally funded projects to pay "prevailing wages," with "prevailing wages" defined as union scale, unionized contractors were protected against competition on government jobs from nonunion contractors. That was, of course, the goal of the unions' lobbying efforts. But the goal was attained partly at the expense of taxpayers and partly at the expense of workers excluded from opportunities for employment on government jobs.

Labor unions succeed in raising the compensation of their members insofar as they can protect the jobs of their members against competition from nonunion workers. If this is correct, why should people interested in social justice be bound to respect the right of workers to organize and join unions? Would people interested in social justice be equally bound to respect the right of grocery store owners to organize and join trade associations, especially if the associations' goal was to raise prices and protect their members against competition from new stores that wanted to enter the industry? What makes the cases so different that our laws actively support the organization of unions while outlawing the organization of trade associations that try to fix prices or restrict entry?

Assuring Competence

If unions did nothing except try to increase the labor costs of employers, we would not find many employers actively supporting unions. We do find such employers because unions perform other functions as well.

The building trades unions have long operated apprenticeship systems that provide employers in their industry with a continuing supply of skilled and certified workers. The unions' claims that those who hire their members are assured of competent employees and that hiring nonunion workers can be risky are not mere propaganda. Of course, an organization that wants employers to hire exclusively from the ranks of its members will have an interest in providing a continuing supply and in monitoring the competence of those whom it provides. Moreover, by operating the training system for its industry, the unions in the building trades made it easier for themselves to reserve these well-compensated jobs for those whom they favored, such as white males exclusively and preferably the sons and nephews of current union members.

There is another question to be raised. Is a more competent worker always to be preferred to a less competent one? We would all want strong assurances of high competence levels on the part of the electricians who are installing new circuit breakers in our home. Would we also be willing to pay union wages to have an electrician attach new plates on our light switches? When greater competence means higher costs, greater competence will not always be preferable. We should not send a boy to do a man's job, as the old saying has it; neither should we send a man to do a boy's job. A system that guarantees competence can easily become a system that forces people to pay for more than they really want or require. A pretended dedication to public safety or consumer protection, by business firms even more than by craft unions, has often functioned as the justification for government-enforced restrictions on competition.

Grievance Systems

The widespread belief that labor unions are responsible for the high wages generally prevailing in wealthy nations largely reflects a failure to understand the market forces that prompt employers to pay workers close to what they are worth, or, to be more precise, to pay them the value of their net contribution to the revenue of the enterprise. If a firm can obtain workers for $10 an hour who each hour add $15 worth of value to the company's product, the firm will ordinarily want to hire more such workers. These differences between workers' value to employers and their cost to employers—closely akin to what Karl Marx dubbed "surplus value"—create an incentive to hire more workers. Increasing productivity thus generates an increased demand for workers that continually pulls wages up toward the value of the workers' output.

The market system does a less effective job of protecting workers against other forms of exploitation, such as arbitrary and unfair treatment by a supervisor. Even in a highly competitive labor market, workers who are disciplined or demoted or discharged because a foreman took a dislike to them will often have to incur substantial costs to find fair treatment with another employer. That is why a good grievance system, operated by the union that represents all the employees in the collective bargaining unit, can be so important. The "inequality of bargaining power" of which the Wagner Act speaks can be a serious problem when employees work under supervisors who are petty tyrants.

Employers, of course, do not want their employees to feel resentful because they believe themselves to have been unfairly treated. Employers naturally prefer high employee morale, a cooperative spirit, and feelings of loyalty toward the employer. A good grievance system can nurture all of these, or at least retard the growth of their opposites. Many employers have expressed a willingness to trade off the reduction in the degree of their control over job conditions that unionization entails in order to obtain the employee grievance system that unionization also brings with it.

Democracy and Labor Unions

But what if the union representatives fail to do an effective job of prosecuting an employee's grievance? An employee might be irritating to a shop steward as well as to a foreman. Or union representatives might be willing to sell out their membership for the sake of some personal advantage. Complaints of unfair treatment directed by union members against their own unions are not unknown. The Labor-Management Reporting and Disclosure Act of 1959, known as the Landrum-Griffin Act, gained considerable support from the belief that unions often exercised a tyranny of their own over those whom they were supposed to protect.

There have certainly been corrupt union officials and even entire unions, or at least union locals, that were riddled with corruption. A union such as the Teamsters, which represents transportation workers (among many others), has the ability to inflict large damages on selected employers at a relatively small cost to itself or its membership. It can do so by interfering with the movement of supplies or finished products at critical times and in ways that appear, on the surface, to be completely legitimate. That ability creates the power to practice extortion, and the power to practice extortion attracts criminals. The Teamsters union, with its long history of corruption, does not so much breed corrupt union officials as attract criminals who find union power an effective means toward personal enrichment.

It would be a mistake to suppose that more democracy, mandated by legislation and monitored by special government overseers, will be an effective cure for this problem. The strategic position that enables corrupt union officials to enrich themselves through extortion also enables honest union officials to secure benefits for their members. Members of the

Teamsters union consequently have been far less dissatisfied with their leadership than members of Congress, crusading journalists, or concerned citizens, and have sometimes voted right back into office officials who were earlier removed by the government for "undemocratic" behavior.

Campaigns for more democratic procedures in labor unions are often supported, it should be noted, by people with a record of opposition to labor unions, and for good reason. Democratic collective bargaining is likely to be as ineffective as democratic foreign policy making, because democratic procedures make strategic ploys more difficult, if not impossible. They tip the hand of the union bargaining team and reveal some of the weaknesses in the union's position, making it harder to bluff and narrowing the space for compromise and accommodation in directions disadvantageous to the union.

When public policy forces union leaders to pay more attention to minority opinion in the union, it also reduces the union's ability to overcome the free rider problem. It will always be in the self-interest of a union member, at least if we conceive self-interest very narrowly, to let others pay the dues and bear the costs of a strike. Loyalty to the union and firm support for its policies are essential parts of a union's strength. That strength begins to dissolve when dissidents obtain the right to refrain from supporting union policies without penalty or to employ union resources to argue for positions opposed by the union leadership. No one wants to take a stand against democracy. But democracy can take many forms, and some are simply not compatible with union strength.

Labor Unions and Inequality

But why should we be interested in union strength? What is it about labor unions that should make those interested in justice eager to enhance the bargaining power of unions?

The reviewer of a recent biography of the late Supreme Court Justice Thurgood Marshall praises Marshall in these words:

> No member of the Supreme Court has ever been more keenly alive to social inequalities. For twenty-four years, in a few notable opinions for the Court, and many impassioned dissents, Marshall consistently

supported organized labor, racial minorities, the advancement of women, the broadening of rights to freedom of expression, and the narrowing of police authority.[4]

Does organized labor belong in that list? Do labor unions reduce social inequalities?

From the 1880s, when the American Federation of Labor was created, to the 1930s, when the rival Congress of Industrial Organizations was created, labor unions in America generally represented the more skilled and better paid workers in the country. Union advocates claimed, of course, that their members were better paid because they were represented by unions. We are closer to the truth when we say they were represented by unions because they were better paid. It would be most correct to say that they were better paid *and* represented by unions because they possessed relatively high skill levels that made it hard for employers to replace them when they went on strike.

It is difficult for a union representing unskilled workers to bargain successfully for higher wages, because such a union cannot make a credible strike threat. Employers can too easily replace workers who go on strike. Even if the union is able to prevent the replacement of strikers and to compel the employer to pay a higher wage, the gain is likely to be a short-term one. With workers available for a wage below the union wage, nonunion firms will be able to chip away at the net revenue of the unionized firm, prohibiting it from charging a higher price to help cover its higher labor costs.

Wage rates in the United States have shown a pattern of increasing inequality over the past two decades, a phenomenon that some commentators have attributed to the decline of union strength. Once again, though, it would seem that an association may have been identified incorrectly with a cause. The industries in which union members tended to be most heavily concentrated have declined as a percentage of the total economy as production has moved increasingly in the direction of services. Some of this decline has undoubtedly been a consequence of the relatively high

4. Randall Kennedy, review of Juan Williams's biography of Thurgood Marshall, *The New Republic*, April 5, 1999, p. 39.

costs that unions have imposed. From 1980 to 1995, membership in the automobile workers union declined by 45 percent and membership in the steelworkers union by 67 percent, not because union members were a smaller percentage of the workforce in unionized plants, but because unionized plants were hiring fewer workers.[5]

The once powerful building trades unions also suffered major membership losses over this period. Membership in the carpenters union fell by 52 percent, membership in the electrical craft union by 35 percent, and membership in the plumbers union by 37 percent. The basic reason was the growth of nonunion contractors.

But isn't this evidence of declining union strength? Not necessarily. We want to distinguish between membership losses due to a decline in union strength and membership losses due to the exercise of union strength, that is, to unions pricing their members' services out of the market.

If union strength declined between 1980 and 1995 because public attitudes and government policy turned against unions during this period, we should expect to see membership declines in unions of government employees. We find on the contrary that membership in the two teachers unions, the National Education Association and the American Federation of Teachers, increased by 28 percent, and membership in the American Federation of State, County, and Municipal Employees rose 8 percent. Combined membership in the letter carriers and postal workers unions fell by 2 percent from 1980 to 1995, but that is inconsequential when compared to the size of the losses in most of the unions that bargain with private employers.

When nonunion contractors take over jobs that were formerly performed by union contractors, does inequality increase? Does the average wage paid by contractors decline? No clear answer can be given. A loss of jobs by members of the International Brotherhood of Electrical Workers to nonunion electricians will *reduce* inequality among electricians. Inequality among airline pilots clearly declines when new airlines, paying pilots half the wage rate that the pilots union has negotiated with the major carriers, expand by taking business away from the major carriers.

---

5. Data on union membership were taken from *Statistical Abstract of the United States*, which reproduces them from the biennial *Report of the AFL-CIO Executive Council*.

Mention of the airline pilots union raises the question in vivid form. If we choose to think of organized airline pilots as regular union members, we would not want to assume automatically that every increase in the wage rate paid to union members diminishes income inequality. The gains achieved for their members by powerful unions that organize highly-skilled workers distribute income from poor to rich insofar as they restrict entry of workers into their trades.

There are unions that have shown a particular concern for employees receiving very low wages and working under especially unpleasant conditions. The United Farmworkers of the late Cesar Chavez come to mind. But such unions are very far from representative of unions generally. There seems to be no good reason to assume that unions play a significant role in reducing income inequality in the United States.

Inequality and Injustice

"Inequality" is not a synonym for "inequity." Whether a particular inequality is also an inequity will depend on our conception of justice. Whereas achieving agreement among people on what constitutes "justice" is a notoriously difficult task, it is much easier to discover a consensus on the meaning of "injustice."

There is no defensible way to attach a specific numerical value to the concept of "a fair wage." However the concept is defined, its monetary value will vary hugely with time and place. The "social activists" who want American apparel firms to pay a fair wage to their employees in manufacturing establishments in underdeveloped countries do not expect them to pay a wage even remotely close to what the average American worker receives. Those activists who believe that the differences they are willing to tolerate reflect differences in living costs are deluding themselves. Wage rates are lower in Indonesia than in the United States because workers in Indonesia are willing to accept less; they are willing to accept less because their alternative opportunities are so much poorer; their alternative opportunities are poorer than the alternative opportunities available to American workers because the marginal productivity of workers in the United States is far higher than the corresponding productivity of Indonesian workers; and the differences in productivity at the relevant margins reflect the much greater productivity of the economic system in the United States.

An American shoe or apparel firm with a factory abroad might easily be capable of paying its foreign employees a wage rate equal to what it pays in the United States. But if it had to do so, it would have no incentive to open a factory there—which would leave its foreign employees worse off. Moreover, an American firm offering ordinary semiskilled operatives seven dollars an hour in Indonesia would find itself flooded with job applicants. How would it choose the tiny percentage of them whom it would want to hire? And how would it justify this transfer of wealth from the shareholders of the firm to a small and arbitrarily selected set of Indonesian workers? Those who are the sole owners of the firms they manage have a right to distribute the wealth of their enterprise pretty much as they choose. But arbitrary decisions on the part of those who manage companies owned by others will not be tolerated long if those decisions reduce the value of the companies. The managers will be violating fiduciary obligations in order to satisfy charitable inclinations that are not truly charitable, because their inclinations are leading them to give away other people's money.

Can we even talk sensibly about a fair wage just within the specific context of the United States at the beginning of the twenty-first century? How would we define it? A wage sufficient to support a family? Such a wage would exclude from employment those whose skills and experience do not make them worth that much to an employer, such as teenagers who don't have families to support. The same wage for everyone? That would not work for reasons too obvious to list. A wage that meets the employee's needs? Consider the implications of a wage policy that allocates three times as much to an employee with seven children and an invalid spouse as to an unmarried employee with spartan tastes. The customary wage? A wage that the employee considers fair? A wage of which the employer is not ashamed? We are getting closer.

Suppose we turn the question around and ask what might be meant by "an unfair wage"? We can begin to make a little progress when we approach the question from this direction. A wage would clearly be unfairly low if it was less than had been agreed upon, or if fraud or deception had played a part in its determination, or if the wage was agreed upon under coercion. In introducing the concept of coercion we raise the troublesome question of whether someone can be coerced by circumstances. Is a worker who has no good alternative opportunities being coerced? Suppose my university is able to hire foreign undergraduate students to perform highly skilled work for no more than the legal minimum wage because American immigration law will only permit them to accept work related to their education and they are in urgent need of income. Is the university coercing them? Is it taking advantage of the fact that they must either work for the university or not work at all? Or is the university making them better off by providing them with an opportunity to work when otherwise they would have no opportunity at all? Or is it both coercing them and making them better off?

We can always find complicating circumstances to raise doubts about simple definitions. I shall nonetheless suggest a simple definition of a fair wage. It is a wage agreed upon by employer and employee under circumstances that are not unfair. And what are unfair circumstances? They are circumstances that violate the generally understood and accepted rules: the laws, conventions, and reigning moral consensus of the society in which we live. If that seems much too vague to be useful, I suggest that any definition that tries to become less vague will prove increasingly ambiguous as efforts are made to render it more specific.

Two Kinds of Justice?

Reinhold Niebuhr introduced an important distinction into ethical discourse in the 1930s that has subsequently been largely forgotten in the moral and religious communities to which he, as a theologian, was primarily addressing himself. In his 1932 book on *Moral Man and Immoral Society*, Niebuhr argued that collectives are less moral than individuals and that reason, religion, and moral suasion are consequently less effective against collectives than they are against individuals. Niebuhr concluded that collectives must consequently be restrained by power if injustice is to be checked, and that conscience and reason, though they may modify struggles between collectives, can never be completely adequate substitutes for power.[6]

---

6. Reinhold Niebuhr, *Moral Man and Immoral Society: A Study in Ethics and Politics* (New York: Charles Scribner's Sons, 1949). Original publication was in 1932.

Niebuhr was basically arguing for two different concepts of justice. Justice in families or in small intentional communities will require that everyone receive what contributes to their full flourishing insofar as the resources of the group will allow it. If available resources are inadequate, they must be shared in a manner that takes into account the specific past and future prospects, needs, and abilities of each member of the group and of the group as a whole. The pursuit of justice in this sense presupposes a degree of knowledge and specific concern that cannot exist except in relatively small groups. A more limited concept of justice must be employed in social relationships outside of small societies in which everyone is capable of knowing and caring for specific others.

Niebuhr did not push his analysis far enough. He was impressed by the lack of any conscience in collectives and the consequent need to erect some kind of checks upon the exercise of group power that would be more effective than mere moral exhortation. He does not seem to have noticed a deeper dimension to the problem, namely, the absence of personal relationships in the collective encounters with which he was largely concerned. Most of the relationships among people who interact in modern, urban societies are almost wholly impersonal. We typically know very little about the people, for example, on whom we depend every day for the food we eat, i.e., those who grow it, transport it, process it, and sell it to us. At most we may know the face and perhaps the first name of the person at the checkout counter in the grocery store. We consequently could not assume responsibility for the well-being of those whose services provide for our own well-being, even if we wanted to. We would not know enough about them. How could we even begin to compare the relative needs of all those people who feed us so that we might be able to share our wealth equitably with them? The very idea is absurd. We cannot be responsible for them.

This unavoidable "irresponsibility" is fully reciprocal. Those who grow, transport, and process our food know nothing about us and, as a result, cannot decide to provide our daily bread because they care about our nutrition. They take their cues not from our needs or wants but from the wholly impersonal signals that monetary prices provide. To put it crudely, they do what they do because they expect it to pay them better than anything else they might do.

What does justice mean in this world of completely impersonal transactions? If we take the most general definition of justice—giving to each their due—how do we decide what each is due? In such a world the Golden Rule is simply irrelevant. Social transactions in a market-coordinated economy cannot be governed by the principle "Do for others what you would like them to do for you." The appropriate rule is what someone has called the Silver Rule: "Do not do to others anything that you would consider unfair if they did it to you."

And what is unfair? Most people will shrug their shoulders hopelessly if asked, "What is fair?" But we know surprisingly well what is *un*fair. It is violating the rules by which we have agreed to be bound in our social relationships.

The concept of distributive justice has almost no relevance in a market economy. The only justice we can hope to secure is procedural justice, which we pursue by correcting perceived injustices. Injustices are committed when people violate the rules, when they fail to accord others due process.

An obvious question immediately arises: Can't the rules themselves be unjust? Indeed they can. But how do we recognize an unjust rule? It would be a rule that violates a deeper rule, which might itself be unjust if it violates a still deeper and more fundamental rule.

Anyone who objects that this entails an infinite regress should note that this is, in fact, how almost everyone thinks about justice whenever they are concerned with actual cases and not merely engaged in academic discussion. We may think and talk like complete relativists when we are asked what justice requires, but we display passion and confident conviction when we discern injustice. Injustice will almost invariably turn out to entail a violation of some right that an individual or group possesses. Where do these rights come from? They are created by the acceptance of obligations, by the explicit and implicit promises that we make to one another, by the "social contract" under which we live.

The Justice of Concerted Action

A fair wage, then, to return to the point where this discussion began, is any wage upon which employer and employee agree so long as no injustice has been done.

Would that include wages determined by collective bargaining? In the nineteenth century, the common law doctrine of conspiracy led the courts to look askance at any concerted action intended to harm another. Those doctrines found statutory expression in the 1890 Sherman Act, which prohibited contracts, combinations, and conspiracies in restraint of trade, and in similar legislative enactments by state governments. After half a century of vacillating on the issue of whether combinations of employees fell under the prohibitions of federal "antitrust law," the Supreme Court finally decided that they did not. The Court said that Congress had clearly shown through the labor legislation passed in the 1930s its intention to exempt labor unions from the Sherman Act's prohibition of contracts, combinations, and conspiracies in restraint of trade. And under the preemption rule whereby federal legislation in an area trumps all state legislation in that same area, the Court's decision authorized labor unions to engage in practices that were *prima facie* illegal when engaged in by business firms.

Some critics of labor unions have proclaimed this an indefensible double standard. Most people haven't thought about it, and those few who have done so generally conclude that the inequality of bargaining power to which the Wagner Act referred justifies the double standard. The economic analysis of collective bargaining presented earlier in this chapter suggests that the best response might be to ignore the issue. Concerted action among employees organized into labor unions can restrict to some extent the competition among employees that works to keep wages down, but it cannot restrict competition effectively enough to prevent labor markets from allocating resources with reasonable efficiency and fairness. In recent years, critics of the Sherman Act have begun calling for its repeal on the grounds that ordinary market competition is sufficient to prevent concerted action by business firms from doing the damage to the economy that advocates of the act have always feared. If this conclusion came to be generally accepted, the alleged double standard would be eliminated by exempting business firms as well as employees from statutory prohibitions of concerted action.

The ordinary laws would still apply, however. That must be added because competition becomes markedly less effective in preventing the acquisition of excessive power when the competitors can employ violence or the threat of it. If business firms can assassinate those who try to compete with them or torch their establishments and hijack their shipments, they will find it much easier to charge very high prices and still obtain large net revenues. Similarly, if workers can employ violence or the threat of violence against those who try to compete with them, they will find it easier to obtain and sustain for longer periods of time wage rates well above the market-clearing level.

The issue is complicated somewhat by disagreement over what constitutes a threat of violence in the case of labor disputes. Is the practice of picketing a struck plant merely the dissemination of information? Or is it a physical barrier to anyone who wants to work for the struck employer? How about *mass* picketing? Jeers and insults directed at those who cross the picket line? What is the difference between a genuine threat and a mere expression of anger?

Principals, Agents, and Power

What are the moral obligations of union leaders? Many of those who believe that justice requires us to respect the right of workers to join unions and bargain collectively with employers also believe that justice requires union leaders to consider the common good or the public interest in setting their goals.

This belief is closely akin to the "social responsibility of business" argument often put forward by moral critics of the economic system. Under this doctrine, corporate executives are supposed to aim not at maximum net revenue for the corporation but at some broader set of objectives that incorporate the public interest or the common good. A currently popular version of this argument is the "stakeholder thesis," which asserts that the shareholders of large corporations are merely one group of stakeholders in the corporation. Other stakeholders include the corporations' employees, suppliers, and customers as well as the communities in which they are located.

Most presentations of the stakeholder thesis confuse the issue by arguing that net revenues will actually be larger if corporate managers do care for the interests of all stakeholders. If this were true, there would be no conflict between the shareholder thesis and the stakeholder thesis. In one sense it is obviously true. The managers of corporations require the goodwill and cooperation of employees, suppliers, and customers, and so will have incentives to pay attention to the interests of these groups in order to maximize the returns to shareholders. Advocates of the stakeholder thesis must want more than this if they are saying anything relevant. So let us assume that they are assigning managers the duty of trading off some amount of shareholder income in order to pay just attention to the interests of other supposed stakeholders.

How much should they trade off? Trivial amounts can be justified as contributions toward the creation of goodwill and thus, in the long run, in the interest of shareholders. But what should be the criteria employed by the managers of large, publicly held corporations when they decide that an enhancement of one group's well-being is worth the reduction of another group's well-being? Doesn't the stakeholder thesis implicitly elevate corporate managers into benevolent despots?

Similar questions must be directed at those who want union leaders to set their goals in terms of something broader and grander than the interests of union members. Union leaders are the agents of the members just as corporate executives are the agents of the shareholders. Union leaders have fiduciary obligations that should prohibit them from sacrificing the interests of their members to their own notions of the greater public good. If either union leaders or corporate executives have the power to act contrary to the interests of their principals, their power ought to be constrained. That is a moral argument. The economic or political argument asserts that their power will be constrained, or taken away, if they begin to behave in the manner that advocates of the social responsibility doctrine want them to behave.

None of this is intended to assert that agents should be unscrupulous or ruthless. They ought to conform their behavior not only to the law but also to the accepted conventions and moral principles applicable to their profession. Agents who go beyond these boundaries will not ordinarily be working in the long-run interest of their principals. But within these boundaries, they should be permitted to make their decisions according to what they believe will most effectively advance the interests of those whom they are paid to represent. Labor union leaders are not employed by the government or the nation at large. Moral condemnations based on the mere fact that they are not acting in the public interest are completely misguided.

Individualism and Labor Unions

The carpenters union in the United States is officially known as the Brotherhood of Carpenters. Whatever the actual level of fraternal feeling is among union members today, there was a time when labor unions did have a great deal in common with such organizations as the Fraternal Order of Eagles and the Benevolent and Protective Order of Elks. Ought we to wish for those days to return?

Markets exercise a powerful centrifugal force in modern society. Adam Smith observed that in "civilized society" each person "stands at all times in need of the cooperation and assistance of great multitudes, while his whole life is scarce sufficient to gain the friendship of a few persons."[7] That presents an interesting dilemma. We cannot begin to produce on our own even the goods we need for survival, much less the goods that create our ordinary comforts. And we don't have enough time in our whole lives to find and make friends of people who would be able to help us produce what we want. Yet we do survive, and survive very well indeed. How do we do it?

Through the marketplace, of course. We earn money at some specialized task and use that money to register our many wants in a way that generates prices that function as information and incentives to people capable of satisfying our wants. The degree of interdependence in a modern economy is astounding, and the smoothness of its coordination is almost miraculous. We obtain "the cooperation and assistance of great multitudes," and we do it easily and quickly, because doing so does not require us to "gain the friendship" of anyone.

That is a mixed blessing. It is possible for all of us to live well, relying on "the cooperation and assistance of great multitudes," without being personally acquainted with any single person in those multitudes. That enables us to be extraordinarily independent despite the extreme degree of our mutual interdependence. We need others, but not any specific others. We therefore don't have to form friendships except with people we like, people like us. We can effectively ignore everyone else. We don't have to get involved in community activities. We don't have to learn the

---

7. Adam Smith, *An Inquiry into the Nature and Causes of the Wealth of Nations*, bk. I, chap. II (Indianapolis, Ind.: Liberty Fund, 1981). Originally published in 1776.

names of our neighbors. If we don't like the neighborhood, we can move, with the eager assistance of the real estate market and its pseudo-friendly personnel. We can live anonymously in a densely populated city.

Adam Smith worried that those who come to live in a great city will find their conduct "observed and attended to by nobody" and will therefore begin to neglect it themselves, with the result that they will abandon themselves "to every sort of low profligacy and vice." But he noted that those who join a small religious sect will emerge from their obscurity, will attract the attention of respectable society, and will thereby develop "regular and orderly" morals.[8] We seem to have lost sight of the civilizing effect of being "observed and attended to" and are extremely quick to abandon any association that starts to monitor our conduct.

Has a growing sense of individualism, fostered by the wealth with independence that the market provides us, contributed to the declining interest of American workers in labor unions? Has union membership shrunk so dramatically in recent decades because more and more Americans want to make it on their own? It would be absurd to suggest that a revival of unionism might counter the emphasis on personal rights to the neglect of personal obligations and the indifference toward community that have bothered a growing number of social commentators in recent years. But raising the issue enables us at least to think about a socializing function that labor unions might perform, or might once have performed, for their members.

In Conclusion

This chapter began with the claim of the Roman Catholic bishops that the right of workers to organize and join labor unions ought to be respected. We might conclude by citing the opinion of Abraham Kuyper, a distinguished and influential Protestant theologian, who believed that unions advanced the cause of justice and that governments should therefore promote unions.[9] Numerous additional examples of similar views could readily be provided. Not only church commissions and ecclesiastical officials

8. Ibid., bk. V, chap. I, pt. III, art. III, §12.
9. Kuyper's social theory is explained and defended by John P. Tiemstra, "Every Square Inch: Kuyperian Social Theory and Economics," in *Religion and Economics: Norma-*

but also many others who believe themselves to be representing the common good assume, without argument, that to support labor unions is to promote justice and morality.

In June 1999, delegates to the annual convention of the American Medical Association meeting in Chicago voted to organize a labor union for physicians, specifically for salaried physicians and medical residents, which together represent about a third of the nation's 620,000 practicing physicians. The AMA also announced its intention to work toward unionization of the 325,000 self-employed doctors in the United States. That will require some legislative assistance. Because self-employed doctors are clearly not employees, any attempts on their part to raise their incomes through concerted action will run afoul of the Sherman Act and its prohibitions of contracts, combinations, or conspiracies in restraint of trade. The chairman of the AMA board of trustees stated that the objective of unionization on the part of physicians would be to make sure that patient care is not sacrificed for the sake of profits.[10]

The only conclusion to be drawn at the end will be brief. We should not assume without reflection and examination of the case at issue that to support labor unions is to promote justice and morality.

---

tive Social Theory, ed. James M. Dean and A. M. C. Waterman (Boston, Mass.: Kluwer Academic Publishers, 1999), pp. 85–98.

10. Information on the AMA convention was taken from a syndicated New York Times article of June 24, 1999.

CHAPTER 25

An Economic Perspective on Illegal Drugs

THINK HOW MANY more muggings there would be if muggees sought the experience as eagerly as muggers do! That's roughly the situation today with the trade in illegal drugs. The law is a weak deterrent because the absence of a self-identified victim drastically lowers the probability of apprehension, conviction and eventual punishment.

Our legislators have responded by adjusting the other factor in the formula for deterrence: severity of punishment. Since twenty lashes if convicted when the probability of conviction is only 5 percent will have about the same deterrent effect as two lashes when the probability of conviction is 50 percent, legislators have increased the penalties to compensate for the ineffectiveness of enforcement. But they have not done so in an even-handed way. Draconian penalties have been legislated only for suppliers, not for demanders.

One can usefully think of the penalty as a kind of tax on a criminal transaction. If the penalty for selling one unit of a drug is a $1,000 fine and the probability of having to pay the fine is 10 percent, then the penalty raises the cost of supplying the drug by $100 per unit. That is how laws imposing severe penalties on sellers, while only slapping the wrist of buyers, manage to deter use. In the jargon of economics, the law will reduce the quantity demanded (by raising the price), without reducing the demand

Originally published in *Forum*, Institute for Economic Research 1, no. 3 (February 1990). Reprinted by permission of Mrs. Juliana Heyne.

itself. However, this approach has had some disturbing consequences that surely weren't intended.

First of all, it's not the objective penalty that increases the cost of supplying drugs, but the subjective weight prospective drug suppliers attach to the penalty. The possibility of ten years in prison will terrify conventional folk but will mean relatively little to someone who "doesn't give a rip." People who think of themselves as invulnerable, who believe in seizing the moment and letting the future take care of itself, will heavily discount the penalties with which the law threatens drug sellers. They will consequently be low-cost suppliers with the competitive advantage that this confers in the business of supplying illegal drugs.

What our laws have done, in conjunction with the processes of competition, is eliminate the profit from the illegal drug trade except for people who display very limited concern for their own future, for other people, or for the laws of the land. These people gradually come to dominate the business. That's what happened between 1919 and 1933 when the United States tried to prohibit the consumption of alcoholic beverages by threatening suppliers without seriously threatening demanders. The demand remaining strong, huge potential profits continued to exist for those who were able to satisfy that demand at a low enough cost. Need I add that low-cost providers of illegal services are generally dangerous people to have in the neighborhood?

I have treated a legal penalty as if it were a tax. In a very important respect, however, it's quite unlike a tax. Suppliers who pay their taxes are entitled to the full protection of the law. That's not the case with suppliers whose costs take the form of criminal penalties. The police and the courts are not available to enforce contracts in business transactions that entail illegal trade. Enforcement of contracts must be entirely private. This implies that people who have special skills in the area of private contract enforcement—those who aren't squeamish about mayhem and murder, for example—will have a comparative advantage in the business of selling illegal drugs. This is another reason for expecting the competitive process to gradually weed out all others and leave the business of supplying illegal drugs concentrated in the hands of persons predisposed toward violence.

We mustn't speak harshly of all drug suppliers. There is one category of "nice guys" which also has a comparative advantage in the business, namely juveniles. The objective risk and hence the cost of doing business in the drug trade is considerably lower for juveniles than it is for adults because the law is so much more lenient in dealing out punishment to juvenile offenders. This is why they are so actively recruited into the business. Another important but unintended effect of current legal policies, then, is strong pressure upon juveniles to enter a business and social world filled with so many threats to their future: an arrest record, addiction, neglect of their education, and early, violent death.

The law sets itself an imposing task when it attempts to reduce the quantity demanded without reducing the demand. (Educational programs attempt to reduce demand, of course. But does anyone still take them seriously?) A strong demand will almost inevitably generate its own supply, and attempts to restrict that supply through threats directed against suppliers will produce powerful criminal gangs to supply drugs to those who want them and who are willing to pay the price. That price won't even be very high if the threats are not credible.

The task would be less imposing in a less free society. It is usually possible to punish more of the guilty by being willing to punish more of the innocent. Local governments are beginning to hold the owners of buildings responsible for the illegal drug transactions that occur on their property, even when the owners have no effective way to prevent the activity, and despite the fact that the law itself sometimes prevents the owner from evicting drug traffickers. The property of law-abiding citizens has been seized, condemned and destroyed—essentially because the owners, with their limited resources, were unable to do what the official representatives of society could not do with far greater resources. This practice probably interferes modestly with the flow of drugs.

If we are willing to impose high enough costs on everyone who enters or brings goods into this country, we can probably reduce somewhat the flow of cocaine from South America. We have already experimented with "intercept" operations that managed to raise slightly the street price of contraband drugs at the cost of long delays for every honest citizen attempting to cross the U.S.-Mexican border. Customs officials have also begun to inflict heavy costs on selected importers by delaying and damaging shipments in their search for smuggled drugs. And we have done a remarkable job of tearing Colombia apart by intervening in that country to prevent its citizens from supplying a commodity for which our citizens are willing to pay. All these measures have their effects: huge violations of liberty and fairness and small reductions in the supply of drugs from outside our borders—reductions that can probably be made up quickly through increased production of wholly domestic methamphetamines.

What is it that prompts us to threaten suppliers with everything short of decapitation while refusing to legislate significant penalties on demanders? Is it because so many voters and politicians are themselves at least occasional users of illegal drugs? Is it because we see users as weak and helpless victims? Or is it because, as a basically liberal society, we are reluctant to punish people for behavior that principally damages themselves?

The last possibility suggests a new direction in which policy might try moving. Suppose we committed ourselves to the position that all adult persons have the legal right to mess up their own lives as long as they do not let the costs spill over onto others? They would be legally entitled to purchase and use marijuana, heroin, cocaine, methamphetamines or alcohol but would have no right to impose the costs of their altered mind states on other people who had not consented to bear those costs. Costs imposed on others without their consent are known in economics as *negative externalities*. The solution to the problem of negative externalities lies in turning the costs fully back upon those whose actions generate them.

What are some of the negative externalities generated by drug use that are clearly illegitimate impositions on others? Criminal behavior is one. Operating a motor vehicle in a drug-impaired state is another. Incompetent performance of tasks for which someone else is paying ought to qualify. And what about using taxpayer-funded medical care services for the treatment of conditions caused by the use of recreational drugs?

Suppose we conditioned bail, probation and parole upon the passing of regular drug tests? (You lose your right to an altered state of consciousness when you commit crimes against other citizens.) Suppose we denied the privilege of operating a motor vehicle to anyone who refused consent to a system for the random drug (including alcohol) testing of motorists? (We would first have to agree that no one has a constitutional right to propel a lethal object through crowds of fellow citizens; it's a privilege to be granted only to those who earn it.) Suppose we allowed all employers to establish their own employment criteria with respect to drug use and to adopt the means they deemed most effective for monitoring these criteria? (Remember that tough criteria will be costly to any employer because they will contract the available pool of eligible employees.) Suppose we declared that those who impair both their health and their ability to earn income with which to pay for medical care through their use of recreational drugs have no right to taxpayer-funded medical care? (If this is too extreme, we could at least ask whether the promise of free rehabilitation programs doesn't tempt some people into risky experiments.)

None of these propositions provides a solution to the drug problem, which has no "solution," in any event, because it is not a single or simple problem. This essay is simply a suggestion for looking at what we are doing in a somewhat different way. Perhaps it offers a middle ground on which those who want to decriminalize drug use and those who want to intensify the war on drugs can meet to converse.

CHAPTER 26

Economics, Ethics, and Ecology

HOW MUCH IS ENOUGH? Are the costs too high to justify the benefits? As chapter 1 points out, we cannot ignore these questions if we want to be responsible guardians of the environment. They are ethical as well as economic questions.

During most of this century, economists who chose to write or talk publicly about ethics risked the contempt of their colleagues. The standard objection to mixing economics and ethics contained two arguments. One was that ethics should not be brought into economics classrooms, textbooks, or journals because economics is a science. As such it is in principle independent of any ethical or value judgments, and the progress and well-being of the science require that it be kept clean and clear of all corrupting admixtures. The objective truths of economic science would be contaminated if they were linked in any way to the arbitrary pronouncements of ethics.

Ethics, according to the orthodox dogma, was entirely arbitrary, a matter of subjective personal preference. That was the second argument. Ethical assertions rest upon value judgments, which, unlike factual judgments, cannot be true or false. Since there is no way to test ethical assertions, economic scientists should not touch them in the course of their professional work.

Originally published as chapter 2 in *Taking the Environment Seriously*, ed. R. E. Meiners and B. Yandle (Lanham, Md.: Rowman and Littlefield, 1993), 25–49; reprinted by permission of Rowman and Littlefield.

Do Economics and Ethics Mix?

This position would appear to be mistaken on both counts. Taking the latter argument first, we do not in practice behave as if our ethical judgments were nothing but subjective preferences that cannot be tested. What we actually do in almost all cases of ethical disagreement, at least when the disagreement is important enough to bother about, is discuss it. We give reasons, predict consequences, suggest principles, point to experience, argue for logical connections, compare alternatives. Economic science can be useful in such a process, especially when our ethical disagreements have to do with the operation of economic systems.

Of course, there is no *ultimate* foundation for ethical or value judgments that everyone is compelled to accept. But there is no ultimate foundation that everyone must accept for any other kind of proposition, either, including the propositions put forward in the name of science. That is the fatal flaw in the other half of economists' traditional argument against mixing economics and ethics. Economic research always employs presuppositions, and some of these presuppositions will almost inevitably have ethical implications. Those who claim to be engaging in value-free economic analysis are simply unaware of all the subtle ways in which values influence economic inquiry.

The result of all this is that economists can now discuss ecology and ethics in public without losing their licenses. A good place to begin is with the concept of *efficiency,* a concept dear to the heart of most economists and usually central to any policy analyses they construct.

The Subjective Nature of Efficiency

The crucial fact about efficiency, although one widely ignored by economists, is that at its core it is fundamentally and inescapably an *evaluative* concept. There is no such thing as *technical* efficiency, an efficiency that is independent of subjective valuations. Efficiency refers to the relationship between ends and means. One process is more efficient than another when it achieves a given end with less means, or uses given means to achieve more ends, or does some of both. From a purely technical point of view, however, every process is exactly as efficient as every other process. The ratio of output or ends to input or means is necessarily unity from a technical point of view, if physics is correct in its claim that matter-energy can be neither created nor destroyed. Even when we do not realize that we are doing it, we always attach value to the ends and the means when we are trying to assess the efficiency of alternative procedures. The engineer who says that one engine is more efficient than another because it does more work with a given amount of fuel really means that it does more *useful* work, work that some party values.

Since the variables in any calculation of efficiency are valuations, not physical quantities, the question immediately arises of *whose valuations are to count*. I like to present my students with a multiple choice question before introducing them to the concept of efficiency: "Which is the most efficient way for a suburbanite to commute to work in the downtown area?" I give them a wide range of options: single-occupant passenger vehicle, car pool, bus, bicycle, on foot, hitchhiking. One option I always include is "In solemn procession, carrying candles and chanting psalms," and another is "Whatever way the commuter chooses." The point I want to dramatize is that, if the values to be served are the values of the individual commuter, the most efficient way to commute has to be the way that each commuter chooses. The commuter assigns values to all the inputs and outputs, including the values that decide whether a variable such as physical effort is an input (pain) or an output (exhilaration), weights them all according to a subjective calculus (which may well contain substantial amounts of concern for other persons), places the result in context ("Is it raining?" "Will I have a chance to jog when I get home tonight?" "Do I have a cold?" "What are the most pressing demands upon my time at the moment?"), and then chooses, almost surely while recognizing that it is not efficient to spend too much time worrying about how to maximize efficiency.

It follows that someone who tells suburbanites they are behaving inefficiently when they commute to work all alone in their cars is mistaken. If it were inefficient, they would not do it. The fact that they choose to do it is irrefutable evidence that, for them, it is efficient. What such critics may mean (assuming they aren't just saying that their own values are different from those of the commuters) is that the suburbanites are paying insufficient attention to the costs that their decisions impose on one another and on noncommuters. Alternatively, the critics might mean that they can imagine a differently organized world in which people would not choose to commute to work each day in single-occupant passenger vehicles. Whatever the critic means, efficiency does not seem to be the relevant concept.

Why Does Efficiency Matter?

According to the conventional understanding of the concept among economists, efficiency is maximized when net value is maximized, which means when the difference between the value of benefits and the value of costs is at a maximum. Inputs or means are the costs; outputs or ends are the benefits. Efficiency so defined is an appropriate goal for social policy because it expands the range of possibilities. It enables us to obtain more of what we want without having to give up anything else that we also want. The opposite of efficiency is *waste,* and our moral intuitions tell us that waste is inherently reprehensible. It deprives us of resources that we could otherwise use for worthy purposes and represents a kind of ingratitude for what we have received. That is why everyone will agree that the first step in balancing the budget—*any* budget, but especially the government budget—is the elimination of waste.

The problem is that when we begin to talk about efficiency from the standpoint of society, we have no common denominator in terms of which we can compare the costs and benefits of different people. If we want to insist that individuals maximize—as many economists insist—then the single individual could be said to maximize utility. When we are talking about more than one person, however, utility fails to provide a workable common denominator, because we have no way to compare one person's utility gain with the utility loss of another.

Economists usually dodge this difficulty by using the *monetary* values of costs and benefits. Thus most economists would say that protective tariffs are almost always inefficient because the increase in monetary wealth they create for those who benefit from the tariffs is characteristically less than the decrease in the monetary wealth of those who lose from the tariffs. Monetary value, or what people are willing to pay, provides a common denominator that allows us to aggregate and compare the benefits and the costs of different people. Sometimes this is expressed by saying that a change is efficient if the benefits to those who gain are sufficient for the gainers to purchase the consent of those who lose and still have something left over for themselves.

All of this depends, however, on the conditions from which we begin. The set of outcomes that is "most efficient" in one social context might be grossly inefficient under a different system of laws, customs, and property rights. The upshot of the matter is that the concept of efficiency is of very limited use when we want to resolve disagreements about the proper use of resources—including disagreements over environmental policy—because such disagreements are typically disagreements over *what the rules of the game ought to be.*

What Are We Arguing About?

The situation is further complicated by the fact that the contending parties often cannot even agree on what the rules are about which they are disagreeing. Consider, for example, recent controversies over the trading of rights to emit harmful substances into the air. Imagine the following dialogue between an efficiency-loving economist and a "typical" environmentalist:

"I understand that you want to reduce electrical utilities' emissions of sulfur dioxide," the economist says to the environmentalist. "What's your goal?"

"Cut those emissions in half," the environmentalist replies.

"All right," says the economist. "Here's what you do. First, assign each utility the legal right to emit, after whatever target date you choose, only 50 percent of the amount of sulfur dioxide being emitted currently. Then allow those rights to be traded. You will thereby achieve your goal at the lowest possible cost. Net value—taking your target as a given—will be maximized. We shall have achieved your environmental goal in the most efficient way."

The economist is predicting in this case that the lowest-cost emissions reducers, the ones with a comparative advantage in emissions reduction, will specialize in producing cleaner air. This will occur because the utilities able to reduce their emissions at very low costs will find it profitable to reduce them by more than 50 percent in order to sell their unused rights to those utilities whose costs of reducing emissions are higher and that will therefore want to purchase rights to continue their higher levels of emissions. Economists proudly refer to such arrangements as "using the market to serve the environment." They are somewhat hurt, as well as puzzled, when environmentalists spurn their offers of assistance and refer contemptuously to tradable emissions rights as "licenses to pollute."

Costs and Moral Wrongs

Economists think of sulfur dioxide (or any other) emissions as costs, costs of achieving the much-desired benefit of usable electricity. The economist sees nothing immoral about the generation of costs in the pursuit of socially desirable goods.

Many environmentalists see it quite differently. They view sulfur dioxide emissions as *wrongs*. In an imperfect world, they will concede, wrongs can never be *completely* eliminated. *But wrongs should never be condoned.* These environmentalists might compare sulfur dioxide emissions to muggings. We could reduce the number of muggings that occur on our city streets to almost any number we chose if we were willing to pay for a sufficient quantity of police officers, but we accept some muggings, because "we can't afford more police officers." (The economist would prefer to say that, at the margin, we have more valuable uses for the police officers; but this is a quibble.) When we decide not to hire more police officers and thereby implicitly to "accept" a certain number of muggings, we do not thereby condone any single mugging! We do not "license" the muggers whose crimes we are in effect unwilling to prevent because the cost of doing so would be too high.

Similarly, we may decide to let electrical utilities put some sulfur dioxide into the air because it would cost too much to stop them completely. But we do not want to *approve* those emissions. We certainly do not want to grant the utilities a *right* to emit sulfur dioxide. If any utility finds itself able to reduce its emissions below the target level, it should do so. It should most emphatically not then be allowed to authorize some other utility to emit the sulfur dioxide that it has stopped emitting by selling a "right to pollute."

The issue we must decide, therefore, is whether the emission of sulfur dioxide by electrical utilities is an immoral or only a costly activity. Let's look at the matter more closely.

Can There Be a Right to Pollute?

One trouble with the argument just given is that the principle behind it cannot be consistently applied. If every action that contributes to what we call air pollution is morally wrong, then it is wrong to breathe, because the everyday act of breathing emits carbon dioxide and so contributes to global warming. I don't know of anyone who thinks that exhaling is a wrongful act.

We can push this argument further. All of us want certain goods whose provision will necessarily entail the burning of fossil fuels and other acts that lower air quality. Is it not mere self-deception or hypocrisy to will the end and refuse to concede that we are willing the means? Is it not better to be clear and explicit about what we are doing? Do we really want to say that it is legally and morally acceptable to turn on your home furnace on a cold day but wrong to contribute to global warming through the burning of fossil fuels?

The fact is that we do concede rights to emit undesirable substances into the atmosphere. My favorite example is the emissions test form I must submit if I want to renew the license on my automobile. It states explicitly that I am legally and, I presume, morally, authorized to emit specific quantities of hydrocarbons and carbon monoxide when driving. While I am not allowed to sell my unused emission rights, I have without question been granted a "right to pollute." I doubt that many motorists think of themselves as engaged in wrongful acts when they exercise such rights.

Open and authorized emission of sulfur dioxide is a *costly* act. Mugging, by contrast, is a *criminal* act. They are not the same. The person who emerges from jail and says, "I have paid for my crime," is employing a misleading metaphor. You are not authorized to commit a crime if you are willing to go to jail for it or to pay the fine established by law. Someone who treats a fine as if it were a mere fee is likely to discover that the "fee" increases exponentially with consumption. On the other hand, if the generation of electricity in the midwestern United States is a socially desirable activity, as it surely is, then sulfur dioxide emissions should be viewed as costs, not as crimes. The owners or managers of a utility should indeed be able to say, "We have a right to emit these quantities of sulfur dioxide."

Incommensurable Goods

This does not settle the issue of tradable emission rights, however. Steven Kelman has made the important point that a law which grants explicit rights to pollute—and the trading of rights will not occur in the absence of explicit, well-defined rights—interferes with consciousness-raising efforts (Kelman 1981). Some environmentalists will argue that the advantages of a system for trading emission rights are more than offset by the negative political consequences of granting that anything less than zero emissions is acceptable.

The economist has no conclusive rejoinder to such an argument, because it exposes a conflict between incommensurable goods. The economist wants to achieve *given* environmental targets at the lowest cost in other goods forgone. "At least everyone favors greater efficiency," says the economist who is looking for a neutral vantage point from which to begin. "Whatever our goals, we all want to achieve them at the lowest cost." Economists are completely baffled by environmentalists who refuse to specify any goals, because their objective is *cleaner* air without any relaxation of the pressure to do *still better*. Efficiency is for them a mixed good insofar as it pushes air pollution issues lower down on the political agenda.

Exclusive concentration on issues of efficiency does not, as it turns out, enable economists to deal constructively with environmental issues while avoiding all normative questions. One might even ask whether the concept of efficiency does any useful work at all. Nobody is actually opposed to efficiency. Moreover, the issue in dispute never turns out to be, "What is efficient?" but rather, "Whose valuations should enter our benefit-cost calculations?" Is there any point at all in asking whether it is more "efficient" to leave a section of national forest standing or to turn it into lumber? We cannot determine which alternative would have the largest net value without first deciding whose valuations we are going to count. That is a decision about who should have which property rights and about the processes through which we are going to arrive at decisions affecting the evolution of the natural environment. It is not a question about efficiency.

My doubts about the usefulness of the efficiency concept are not doubts about the usefulness of economic analysis. They are doubts about the usefulness of a certain kind of economic analysis, one that tries to aggregate different people's benefits and costs in order to compare the totals. The type of economic analysis that I find useful in the examination of environmental issues and other problems of public policy is one that pays at least as much attention to processes as to outcomes, and that tries to predict or explain the consequences of alternative laws and institutions, without ever attempting the kind of quantitative measurement and summing-up required by the economist's standard judgments of efficiency.

Recycling and Dumping: A Case Study

The current debate in our society about recycling as an alternative to solid-waste disposal nicely illustrates both the usefulness and the limitations of economic analysis in disputes over environmental policy. The rising cost of solid-waste disposal in the 1980s prompted many cities to promote recycling programs that would reduce the volume of solid waste. The programs made eminent sense, at least at the outset. Why should city governments pay large sums to bury old newspapers that, if properly collected, could be sold for a profit? Using a mixture of financial incentives, ecological appeals, and threats, a growing number of cities have in the past few years induced their residents to recycle large proportions of the solid waste that formerly had to be trucked to landfills for burial.

When recycling saves money, everyone is happy, from the environmentally insensitive boor who sees no further than his checking account to the environmental activist who with Wordsworth's "high Heaven" totally "rejects the lore of nicely calculated less and more." It is now becoming clear, however, that the rising cost of solid-waste disposal in the 1980s was due to a lack of political imagination. There are plenty of places in the United States to bury, at quite tolerable costs, the solid waste that Americans regularly generate. Clark Wiseman, a visiting fellow at Resources for the Future, has calculated that all the municipal solid waste generated over the course of the next 1,000 years would fit in a square hole 44 miles wide on each side and 120 feet deep. That may seem like a big hole to people living in the eastern United States; but it would scarcely be noticed in many of the western states. The problem is not a scarcity of land for fills but a scarcity of people willing to have landfills in their neighborhood.

To an economist the solution is obvious: pay the surrounding community to accept solid waste, just as we pay people in other areas of life to accept costs for the benefit of others. That is now beginning to be done. Early efforts are already demonstrating that the cost of constructing safe and environmentally sound landfills, of transporting waste to these sites, and of fully compensating people who are adversely affected by the landfill is far less than the cost of many of the recycling programs that federal, state, and local governments have either already instituted or are contemplating.

Many of the initiatives that advocates of recycling are pushing will have very large hidden costs. For example, have those who are eager to ban disposable diapers, because they use up space in landfills, thought about all the costs of the alternative? The effects on our water supply of laundering cloth diapers? The impact on urban air quality of all the diaper trucks that would return to circulation? The discomfort and diaper rash of the babies who are kept so much drier overnight by disposable diapers? The infections that would spread more readily through child-care centers? If the people who want to use disposable diapers are willing to pay the full cost of dumping them in landfills—through, for example, a disposal charge included in the price—why should they be prohibited from exercising their preference for disposable over cloth diapers?

The economist conceives of social problems as the product of systems in which, for some reason, people are either not compelled to bear the full cost of the burdens they impose on others or are unable to collect adequate compensation for the benefits to others that their activities will generate. The economist's first move is therefore to see whether some low cost way can be found to assign the costs and the benefits to those who are responsible for them. If people who want to generate solid waste are not imposing burdens on anyone but themselves and others whom they are compensating appropriately, *there is no problem.*

Most environmentalists don't see matters quite in that way, and some don't see it that way at all. They think of recycling more as a moral duty than as an effort to minimize costs. The process of searching for products sold without elaborate wrapping; of separating junk mail, facial tissues, and newspapers; of sorting cans, bottles, and plastic containers; of putting all these things out at the curb in neat piles each week—this is a ritual of dedication through which we ought to go willingly. It is an educational, consciousness-raising process, that gradually changes the "tastes and preferences" beyond which economists refuse to go, even when those tastes and preferences are increasingly generating environmental problems. Recycling may cost more than it saves in the short run; but in the long run, when values have been transformed, it could well prove to be efficient from even the economist's narrow perspective. In some ways the application of benefit-cost analysis to a household's recycling efforts is akin to using time-and-motion studies to appraise the act of lovemaking.

Pursuing Justice Rather than Efficiency

What would happen if economists abandoned their preoccupation with efficiency and talked openly about *justice*? Since judgments about efficiency presuppose judgments as to who shall have which rights, economists who employ efficiency criteria are implicitly making use of a theory of rights. Does economics have anything useful to say about the rights that people *ought to have*?

One thing economists can say with some confidence is that clear and stable rights promote more effective cooperation than rights which are vague and subject to unpredictable alteration. Given that voluntary exchange increases the value of resources and that clear and stable property rights (and other "rules of the game") facilitate voluntary exchange, economists can construct a strong argument in favor of clear and stable property rights. In doing so, they are also supporting a particular conception of justice, one associated with what has come to be known as "the rule of law."[1]

"Unconstitutional by reason of vagueness" is a sound judicial principle for assessing legislation, because vague laws grant arbitrary power to enforcement authorities. The liberty of the citizen disappears in the presence of arbitrary governmental power. Unclear laws constitute a fundamental violation of the principles of justice for anyone who believes that arbitrary government is the essence of political injustice. It follows that the government is violating the rules of justice when it obscures people's rights and

---

1. A clear exposition of this conception of justice may be found in Leoni, especially Chapter 4.

makes it difficult, if not impossible, for people to know what they may and may not legally do.

It is also violating the rules of justice when it arbitrarily decrees that an activity which had previously been lawful and protected is now illegal. The emphasis here is again on the *arbitrary* nature of the government's actions. An arbitrary action is one dependent solely on the will of the actor, rather than one that is determined or at least constrained by principles laid down and known *in advance*. While *ex post facto* legislation cannot in practice be avoided completely (an absolute prohibition of rules changes that penalize actions already taken would bar *all* new legislation), the avoidance of such legislation is a fundamental tenet in the American legal and political tradition.

A regime of clear and stable property rights, as it turns out, will be supportive of both efficiency and justice. If we pursue justice by establishing the rule of law, efficiency will largely take care of itself. This is, of course, a limited conception of justice: clear and stable property rights and other rules of the game. But it is not nearly so limited as one might at first suppose. It is a conception of justice deeply rooted in the American political tradition and one with extensive and important implications for environmental policy. I want to develop, apply, and defend it briefly. Those three activities—development, application, and defense—are interrelated. Showing the applicability of a theory defends it, and the process of defending the theory against criticism results in its development.

How Do We Begin Talking About Justice?

It may help the reader to realize at the outset how unsympathetic the writer is to all forms of foundationalism. A synonym for foundationalism is fundamentalism, a word familiar to most of us in another context. Religious fundamentalists have historically maintained that there are a few fundamental doctrines upon which all other doctrines can be constructed. If these fundamental doctrines are not affirmed, they maintain, the system collapses.

The same kind of fundamentalism can often be found in the sciences. Scientific fundamentalists also insist upon the acceptance of certain basic dogmas, such as *"the* scientific method," the nature of causation, the non-existence of particular entities, or—to take a dogma from economics—the consistency of preferences. While I have the highest respect for heuristic postulates, I acknowledge no fundamental dogmas. I shall therefore not take the approach of beginning with the foundations. I have never found it to be true in political or moral discourse that we proceed most effectively if we begin with solid foundations. The best place to begin is with the questions that seem most interesting or important, or the ones on which progress seems most likely, or the ones that we need to settle to take the next step. And when we have finished, the whole will often be more than the sum of its parts.

The Importance of Property Rights

I have already suggested that disagreements about environmental policy can usefully be viewed as disagreements about property rights. They are disagreements about the property rights of human beings, it must be added, even if we should finally decide to grant legal rights to natural objects. As Christopher Stone observed in his seminal law review article "Should Trees Have Standing?" (Stone 1974), any legal rights assigned to natural objects would have to be asserted, so far as we can presently ascertain, by human beings acting as "guardians." Moreover, any dispute about the rights of trees, streams, or mountains becomes at some point a dispute about the rights and obligations of human beings. So I think we beg no important question by saying that environmental disagreements are disagreements about the property rights of human beings.

It has long been complained by Marxists and other radical critics of orthodox economics that economists, or at least bourgeois economists, "take property rights for granted." In one sense this is no longer true. The critics have not been keeping up. Bourgeois economists have in fact been diligently examining the origins and evolution of property rights systems and inquiring about the prerequisites and consequences of alternative systems for the past 30 years or so. There is a better response to the radicals' complaint: "Of course! What else should we do? We take existing property rights for granted almost all the time."

You do not upon leaving a restaurant ask whether the cashier is authorized by the owner to collect payment for the meal. You do not then inquire to find out whether the owner's title is in order. Nor do you refuse to pay until you have been assured that the system which validates the owner's legal title is itself valid against the claims of Native Americans. In some situations these might be legitimate questions to ask. But for the most part we simply take generally accepted property rights for granted. In part we do so to avoid wasting our time. But we also take for granted generally accepted property rights because *it would be unfair not to do so.*

We all make decisions, committing ourselves through our actions, on the basis of the rights we *think* we hold. Our opinions about our rights are continually monitored and confirmed for us by the ongoing actions of others in society, who acknowledge through their transactions with us that we do indeed own the resources that we are regularly controlling, allocating, transforming, or distributing. It is unfair for those who have encouraged us in our commitments by going along with our claims to declare suddenly and arbitrarily that we are not entitled to the rights we have long been exercising.

Recognizing Injustices

The key concept is *unfair* or *unjust*. I want to direct your attention not to justice but to *injustice*. When I ask, "What's fair?" you can almost hear the skeptical tone and see the cynical shrug: "Who's to say?" But we are much more ready to give definite answers when we are asked, "What's *unfair*?" There are some very important differences between "striving for justice" and "striving to correct injustices." The former is presumptuous and dangerous, at least insofar as it means anything more than trying to correct injustices. The only defensible way to pursue justice in the political realm, I submit, is to work at eliminating recognized injustices.

Although we cannot begin to say what justice would require for each person in our nation, Americans agree substantially and extensively about what's unfair or unjust. Stated most simply, it is *violating the rules.*

I am here making an empirical claim, one that you should test against your own experience. My claim is that Americans overwhelmingly agree that injustice is done whenever persons are not treated in accordance with the rules that are supposed to apply in the situation. I test this proposition regularly, for example, when students come to me asking for some kind of special treatment. (I teach a lot of very large classes.) I always begin by pointing to the rules: the course syllabus, the university regulations, the other known and accepted rules of the game. And I ask them whether the exception for which they are asking would be within those rules. It would be unfair to grant an exception that violates the rules by, for example, giving this particular student an advantage that cannot be granted to everyone else who is similarly situated. And my students agree. I have regularly found that students arrive at the same conclusion I reach when they are asked to decide whether the granting of their request would be unfair to others.

An interesting book appeared about a decade ago, written by a professor of politics named Jennifer Hochschild, who wondered why the poor in the United States did not give effective political support to the downward redistribution of wealth. The book, titled *What's Fair? American Beliefs About Distributive Justice,* was based on in-depth, open-ended interviews with 28 working adults who had been carefully chosen to represent both high- and low-income white residents of New Haven, Connecticut. Hochschild concluded from her study that Americans fail to support downward redistribution because they are confused, a state in which they are encouraged to remain by corporations and other components of "the hegemonic process." But I was more impressed by the actual reports of her interviews than by her conclusions, which seemed to me to fly frequently in the face of what her respondents had actually said.[2] For the most part they were saying that inequality, even enormous inequality, in the distribution of income was not in itself unfair. It was unfair only if it had been gained by *cheating.* By breaking the rules, in other words.

Does Agreement Make It So?
One could still ask about the significance of the fact (assuming it is a fact) that Americans generally agree on what violates the principle of fairness. Does mere agreement establish the truth of the matter? Was our treatment of women "not unfair" during all those years when almost everyone agreed that a woman's place was in the home? Is the treatment of women

2. Hochschild summarizes her conclusions on pp. 278–83. The "ambivalences" she finds among her interviewees seemed to me largely their refusals to accept her interpretations of social reality.

in Iran today "not unfair" if almost no one in Iran considers it unfair? Was racial slavery "not unfair" in the United States at the time when the Constitution was approved?

My response is that I don't know how we can talk sensibly and usefully about justice and fairness independently of specific cultural contexts. As what I have called "the rules of the game" evolve over time, so do our generally accepted notions of what is unfair or unjust. We can look back and claim that we have made progress with respect to justice, but we always do so from the perspective of our current values, institutions, and practices. We can also compare our culture with other contemporary cultures and make comparative judgments, but we ought always to recognize that we do so within the limitations of our knowledge and experience, and that injustice cannot be eliminated from any society until the institutions that permit it are in place. (I have long found the propensity to condemn other cultures and our own ancestors a pointless exercise at best, and at its worst a technique for justifying self-righteous obtuseness.)

The question about the relativity of standards is an important one, however, because many environmentalists are now objecting precisely to the reigning "rules of the game." Just as we once enslaved Africans and even more recently denied women their basic rights, and did so with a good conscience, so we are now with a good conscience trampling on the rights of nonhuman nature. We cannot appeal to any American consensus, the environmentalists say, to find out whether our treatment of nonhuman nature is unfair, because there is no consensus, and because the closest thing we have to a consensus is woefully inappropriate.

These objections deserve thoughtful attention. But I want to postpone any attempt at discussing them until we have dealt more adequately with the issue of justice and injustice in our dealings with one another.

Promises, Rights, and Injustices

A crucial element in our concept of *social* ethics—our obligations to one another as human beings—is *promise*. Consider what it is we are objecting to when we complain about "unethical behavior" and what we are taking for granted. We are objecting because others have not done what they promised to do, either implicitly or explicitly. They have violated the agreed-upon rules. And that is simply *not fair*. If that is not the foundation of all social ethics in our society, it is certainly the dominant principle. The implications for environmental legislation are extensive.

To begin with, the principle calls into question the command-and-control approach to protecting the environment. The *Annual Report of the Council of Economic Advisors* for 1990 defined command-and-control regulation as "a system of administrative or statutory rules that requires the use of specific control devices on classes of selected pollution sources or applies admission standards to narrowly defined pollution sources" (Economic Report of the President 1990, 189–91). At first glance there would seem to be no ethical objection to such a system. In practice, however, the command-and-control approach will almost inevitably substitute arbitrary decisions for the rule of law. Fairness requires that the rules of the game be laid down in advance and that the rules treat those who are similarly situated in similar ways. This ideal is unlikely to be realized when the regulatory authorities are allowed or even commanded to operate on a case-by-case basis. Command-and-control systems provide no incentive to design a set of generally applicable rules.

Trying to protect the environment by requiring environmental impact statements is another approach that is ethically hard to defend for the same kind of reason. The law mandating the filing of environmental impact statements (EIS) arbitrarily and, therefore, unfairly reduces the property rights of the party that wants to act. It does so by allowing projects to be challenged on the grounds that the EIS is incomplete when, as everyone knows, *all* environmental impact statements are necessarily incomplete. In practice the EIS requirement enables determined parties to hold up projects indefinitely until the project developers agree to pay ransom or decide to abandon their project. It should be added that members of Congress were evading their ethical obligations when they mandated environmental impact statements as a way of satisfying the environmentalist lobby without offending any other specific interests. Bad laws often originate in this way.

Environmental regulations that impose politically intolerable costs are also ethically indefensible because they will not be uniformly enforced. It is unfair to impose costly requirements and then, after some have made substantial investments to meet the requirements, to suspend them for everyone else because it turns out to cost too much. Not only does that create incentives not to cooperate; it also discriminates against those who have been the most cooperative.

Allowing environmental regulations to be shaped by a political process that is dominated by special interests is another ethically indefensible procedure. While this is, of course, the only political process we have, we can at least recognize that environmentalists who object to the political influence of special interests are themselves often special interests, sometimes with no strong regard for the principles of fair play. The Natural Resources Defense Council, *60 Minutes'* Ed Bradley, and the others who orchestrated the national hysteria over Alar showed no concern for the apple growers who had to bear the cost of their publicity-seeking. This was inexcusably unfair behavior that was undertaken to promote the institutional interests of the NRDC and the CBS network.

Finally, there exists a strong ethical case for reviving and applying once again the constitutional prohibitions against uncompensated takings. When we discover that concern for the environment requires a change in property rights, the necessity of paying compensation acts both to avoid injustice and to assure that this really is a public interest requirement, not a special interest action. Rezoning, for example, is an unfair way to "preserve public amenities." If the public interest requires that a particular urban hillside be left as a greenbelt, rather than be developed, the public should not be allowed to secure its amenity at the expense of those who own the land by rezoning the land to prohibit development. Fundamental fairness requires that the public purchase the development rights from the owner.[3]

Observations on Conservatism

It cannot have escaped the notice of even the most sympathetic reader that all these implications of the fairness principle are profoundly conser-

---

3. In some cases where government legislates controls on development, the incentive to develop was originally created by questionable government actions, such as bridges built from the mainland to barrier islands or implicit promises of disaster relief to those who then built in floodplains. To what extent is the government obligated to *continue* a promised subsidy? The ethical problem in removing an unjustified subsidy arises from what lawyers call *detrimental reliance*.

vative, and that my conception of social ethics privileges the status quo. I am not bothered by that. If social justice requires above all else that we honor our promises, then social justice is itself profoundly conservative. Promise-keeping is conservative in that it binds the future to the past. And that is of enormous human importance. When we honor our promises, we help one another to realize in the future the expectations that we have formed on the basis of our past transactions. Promise-keeping facilitates planning, including the formation of those life projects that constitute our individual identity. There is an important sense in which the opposite of *conservative* is *capricious*.

As Edmund Burke observed, a society without the means of some change is without the means of its conservation. What was tolerable yesterday and therefore allowed may become intolerable with the passage of time. This would seem to be especially likely in the case of actions that damage the environment.

It must be noted first of all, therefore, that the principle of fairness does permit extensive revisions in the rules of the game. The constraint it imposes is the constraint of compensation for those who thereby become the victims of broken promises. Those who have incurred substantial unrecoverable costs by investing in good faith reliance on the laws of the land should not be made to bear a heavily disproportionate share of the costs of changes designed to benefit everyone.

"But polluters don't *deserve* compensation," someone responds indignantly, "any more than slave owners deserved compensation after the Civil War."

I would ask in response whether the offer of compensation (prior to 1860, of course) might not have been a better route than civil war toward the abolition of slavery. Be that as it may, it is not at all clear that pollution, when explicitly tolerated by law and custom, is a morally reprehensible act. Moreover, when we reflect on the social changes that have produced the environmental movement and the demand for changes in the rules of the game, the case for compensation grows stronger.

One change has been rising private incomes and a consequent increase in the relative value of such public goods as clean air. When we were much poorer, we placed a positive value on discharges from factory smokestacks because they were signs of prosperity. Insofar as rising incomes have increased the demand for a cleaner environment, increased ability to pay for those improvements accompanies the increased demand for them. So we have the ability to pay the compensation that fairness calls for. We cannot plead poverty.

Another factor lending interest and strength to the environmental movement has been dramatic increases in the impact of human activities on the environment—due partly to rising income levels and consequent increases in consumption, partly to new technology, partly to population increases. The implications here for our obligation to provide compensation are less clear. New technology and increased consumption are associated with greater wealth and hence enhanced ability to pay, but population increases present more ambiguous implications. In general, though, there seems to be a strong case for purchasing the environmental improvements we want by compensating the losers. The temptation, of course, is for the most politically adept and influential—who are frequently also the most wealthy—simply to extort the changes they want from their victims.[4] The necessity of providing compensation helps to counter this temptation.

Duties and Aspirations

The most interesting and challenging stream nurturing the environmental movement in recent years is the one that has been fed by changes in our moral conceptions. We have begun to develop new perceptions of our moral obligations and of the kinds of entities that are deserving of moral consideration. These changes are raising fundamental questions about the adequacy of our inherited moral traditions. How can we address these questions?

We might begin with a useful distinction made by the legal philosopher Lon L. Fuller between the *morality of aspiration* and the *morality of duty* (Fuller 1969, 3–32). The morality of aspiration has to do with the desire for excellence. It is an open-ended pursuit, one whose goals are never fully

---

4. In July 1991 San Francisco passed a law prohibiting owners of service stations from converting the land to other uses if they had earned a "fair return" over the past two years. The newspaper headline reprinting this story from the *San Francisco Chronicle* proclaimed: "Urban Ecology: New San Francisco law protects gas stations." (Rights for gas stations?)

achieved. A person in the service of the morality of aspiration is always striving for more. The driving force is the desire to realize every potential excellence or virtue. Satisfaction with what one has achieved is in itself an offense against the morality of aspiration.

The morality of duty imposes much more limited demands. Its goals are clear and attainable. Its prescriptions are predominantly negative: *"Thou shalt not."* The morality of duty is basic. It may not be particularly inspiring, but it is essential to social order, fundamental to all social relations. Its importance is demonstrated by the fact that it is regularly supported by legal sanctions to secure compliance with its demands.

The justice I have been talking about largely expresses the morality of duty. But the environmental movement is fueled by the morality of aspiration. Direct evidence may be seen in the phenomenon referred to earlier: the unwillingness of environmentalists to become specific about the goals that will satisfy them. They want *less* pollution, *cleaner* air, *more* recycling, *less* consumption. Environmentalists' talk about the rights of nature is further evidence that they are serving a morality of aspiration. If nature has rights, where do those rights begin and end? If whales have rights, do other mammals have them, too? Do all animals have rights? And what about other living things, such as plants? What about such nonliving entities as rivers and mountains? It is not my intention to criticize the claim that human beings have duties to the nonhuman world, a claim which I shall subsequently defend. I am only trying to characterize the morality of aspiration and to make the case that the environmental movement is nurtured and informed by a morality of aspiration.

Aspirations and the Morality of Duty

Any good society will contain both a morality (or moralities) of aspiration and a morality of duty. But one component of any defensible morality of aspiration must be commitment to the morality of duty, or what we might call "a passion for justice." Moral aspirations that ignore duty are a proper object of severe criticism. The man who aspires to help all of humanity, for example, but neglects his duties toward his wife and children is not an admirable figure. Does not the environmental movement sometimes slight the morality of duty?

Environmentalists want us all to live more responsibly, to be more attentive and respectful toward nature, toward that which is given to us independently of our own actions. This aspiration is certainly a part of my own morality. But we do not want to forget that the polis, the human community in which we live, has also been given to us independently of our own actions. Responsible persons are not free to improvise without regard for what has been given—including the legitimate expectations of their fellow citizens. In our efforts to express respect for nonhuman nature and to nurture that respect in others, we may not display contempt for the rights of those human beings among whom we live.

Many features of contemporary political conflicts over environmental issues can be usefully viewed as aspects of a struggle between the morality of aspiration and the morality of duty, in which our duties, including our legislated duties, are being raised over time by our aspirations. Two simple examples of how aspirations generate duties and of aspirations that cannot easily become duties may clarify the argument.

Nondiscrimination on the basis of race in hiring or promoting was an aspiration of many before it became a legal obligation for all. The duty was sufficiently clear (notice its negative character) to make it suitable for legal imposition. The contrast with "affirmative action" is instructive. As the controversy over "quotas" and "rigid goals" has shown, we cannot state the goals of affirmative action programs with sufficient clarity and precision to make affirmative action a duty. Significantly, the duty cannot be stated as a prohibition.

Child abuse provides another example. The moral aspiration to assure a safe haven for children has led to a spate of laws and ordinances that have not worked out as well as we had hoped. For one thing, it turns out that what we want from parents is considerably more than not beating their children. We want something positive. We want parental love and concern. But these are more a matter of aspiration than of duty. Moreover, our attempts to marshal the larger community against child abuse has produced laws imposing positive duties on doctors, ministers, social workers, and child-care providers whose effects have been quite mixed. Protecting someone else's children against parental abuse cannot be made a clear, definable duty (and therefore a duty that may appropriately be imposed by law) unless we are willing to deny parents *any* special authority over their children.

Moral aspirations are important! But the moral aspiration to transform moral aspirations into legal duties must be examined with judicious skepticism before we act upon it. To what are we aspiring when we proclaim ourselves dedicated environmentalists?

When an environmental "extremist" says that human beings are not "superior" to animals, or to plants, or to natural objects, I have no immediate argument. Human beings, so far as I can tell, are in fact inferior to elephants, Douglas fir trees, and mountains. I am judging superior and inferior here by the criterion of height. I do so not to be perverse, but to make the point that in much of the debate over these matters the parties are talking past each other. What precisely is the criterion of superiority or inferiority that we have in mind? Is a newborn baby superior to its mother? Not by most of the criteria we could think of. But that does not prevent the child from presenting moral claims upon the mother that overwhelm, in the mother's own judgment, any moral obligations the child might have toward the mother. If we want to bridge the gulf that is widening between many environmentalists and their opponents, we must think more carefully about what exactly we do and do not want to claim.

Forms of Tyranny

Some of the more extravagant statements of environmentalists ought to be seen first of all as responses to the attitude expressed in a sentence such as this: "A tree in the forest that few or no people can see may still exist in the philosophical sense, but a bloody lot of good it does for anyone." Or this:

> By fulfilling our nature and responsibilities as human beings, we *bring* meaning and value into the world.... [U]nseen and unappreciated, the environment is meaningless. It is but an empty frame, in which we and our works are the picture. From that perspective, environmentalism means sacrificing the picture to spare the frame. (Emphasis added.)

The authors of those statements, whose anonymity I shall protect, are saying explicitly what is implicit in the way many of us have learned to behave: There is no meaning or value in the universe except the meaning or value that human beings experience. *But how can we possibly know this?* It is

sheer dogmatic assertion. What's worse, it is self-serving dogmatic assertion, and it smacks of tyranny. It is a license to do as we please.

Statements of this sort remind me of Bishop George Berkeley, the
eighteenth-century British philosopher who was able to deny the existence of a material world by pointing out that all we really know are our
own perceptions. And I wonder why the authors of statements such as the
two above don't go all the way and insist that it is only their own private
seeing and appreciating that allows the world to have meaning and value.
I think I know the answer to that question. It's because other human beings would protest such solipsism, and no one is indifferent to the opinions of other human beings. Why is that? Why do we care so much what
other human beings think or say about us and our opinions? What gives
their opinions so much weight in our calculations when all the rest of nature has no moral significance for us at all?

Jeremy Bentham, no one's candidate for fuzzy-minded idealist of the
year, inserted a disturbing footnote into Chapter XVII of his *Introduction to
the Principles of Morals and Legislation* (Bentham 1948, 310–11):

> Under the Gentoo and Mahometan religions, the interests of the rest of
> the animal creation seem to have met with some attention. Why have
> they not, universally, with as much as those of human creatures, allow-
> ance made for the difference in point of sensibility? Because the laws
> that are have been the work of mutual fear; a sentiment which the less
> rational animals have not had the same means as man has of turning to
> account.... The day has been, I grieve to say in many places it is not yet
> past, in which the greater part of the species, under the denomination
> of slaves, have been treated by the law exactly upon the same footing
> as, in England for example, the inferior races of animals are still.

Bentham suggests that we show respect only to what we have learned
to fear. That may put the matter too harshly. It would be more accurate
to say that we generally learn to show respect only for that which *commands our respect*. The key fact is that respect cannot be "given." It has to
be "earned" or it is not respect; it is only condescension.

This does not imply that we have no obligations in the matter. Our
obligation is to *be attentive*. No person can earn the respect of another
person who is not paying attention. Inattentiveness, of course, is commonly

rooted in a lack of respect, which creates a circular bind. Think of the way we "turn off" someone whom we take to be merely babbling. Adults are often inattentive to children because they assume that the child has nothing important to say. Teachers are inattentive to the questions of students whom they do not take seriously. Members of groups with social power often block out the distinctive characteristics of "inferiors" with whom they interact by assuming that "they" are "all the same," and that this "sameness" does not include the rich inner life that we are aware of in ourselves.

Nature will hardly be able to command the respect of anyone for whom it is an unchallengeable dogma that we human beings bring into the world all value. I have no cure for the disease of inattentiveness, especially since inattentiveness *per se* is not a disease at all but a condition for any sort of effective action and perhaps for sanity itself. How do we learn to ignore that which deserves no attention while remaining alert to everything that merits our attention? A short excerpt from Aldo Leopold's *Sand County Almanac* presents the dilemma (1966, 19–20):

A cardinal, whistling spring to a thaw but later finding himself mistaken, can retrieve his error by resuming his winter silence. A chipmunk, emerging for a sunbath but finding a blizzard, has only to go back to bed. But a migrating goose, staking two hundred miles of black night on the chance of finding a hole in the lake, has no easy chance for retreat. His arrival carries the conviction of a prophet who has burned his bridges.

A March morning is only as drab as he who walks in it without a glance skyward, ear cocked for geese. I once knew an educated lady, banded by Phi Beta Kappa, who told me that she had never heard or seen the geese that twice a year proclaim the revolving seasons to her well-insulated roof. Is education possibly a process of trading awareness for things of lesser worth? The goose who trades his is soon a pile of feathers.

Rights and Duties

I am not now going to argue that nature or even nonhuman animals should have "rights." Those who argue on behalf of rights for whales and trees risk losing everything by claiming too much. They fail to make an effective case for the duties upon which they really want to insist because they have pinned everything on a weak case for rights. They overlook the fact that, while rights entail duties, duties do not entail rights. For example, I acknowledge a moral duty to make charitable contributions of various kinds; but my acceptance of this obligation creates no rights for any potential beneficiary.

Laws that prohibit cruelty to animals are grounded in the belief that human beings owe certain duties to animals, duties to at least do no needless harm and to minimize suffering. I do not know of anyone who wants to remove all such laws from the books, although I know of many people who would vehemently deny that animals have legal rights. Here is a clear case where duties, even legally enforceable duties, exist and flourish in the absence of anything analogous to human rights. Our enforcement of laws against cruelty to animals reflects our widespread belief that animals suffer in a manner with which we can identify. There is no implication of moral equality in the assertion of a duty toward animals.

Do plants suffer? Most of us don't seem to think so, at least not in any way that interferes with our pruning them. Does this imply that we have no duties toward plants? Not necessarily; the ability to suffer is not the only characteristic of nonhuman entities that is capable of generating duties toward them. We might have duties toward nonhuman entities that require allowing them to behave in accordance with what we perceive as their nature. We might have a duty not to dam a free-flowing stream, for example, or a duty to remove an obstruction that was causing a plant to grow in a distorted manner, or a duty to keep a wilderness area uncontaminated by machinery.

But are these *moral* duties? Are they duties *toward the nonhuman entities*? Or are they mere *aesthetic preferences*?

Duties, Preferences, and Other Distinctions

I might have a better notion of how to reply if I were more sure of the difference between the moral and the aesthetic, if I knew the grounds of duty, and if I could always distinguish duties from preferences. (Why do I so dislike the word *mere*?) This is not to say that there are no differences, or that one can be reduced to the other. It is rather a recognition that moral and aesthetic claims often overlap and reinforce one another, perhaps because they have a common ground in the way things fit together, and that we can have strong preferences (aspirations?) toward the fulfillment of our duties. Our duties do not necessarily conflict with our interests, and they will very rarely conflict for those with a strong interest in maintaining their self-respect.

I would particularly want to emphasize the way things fit together, or what we might call *appropriateness*. In *The Theory of Moral Sentiments*, Adam Smith pays a great deal of attention to *propriety*, or appropriateness (Smith 1982). All of Part I, one-sixth of the entire book, is devoted to that topic. We recognize that conduct can be appropriate or inappropriate. By what criteria? I suspect that we often recognize the propriety or impropriety of conduct more easily than we can identify the criteria by which we made the judgment. The concept seems to be closely connected with a sense of *creatureliness*. I am not the creator of all this; I am not even my own creator. While I do have creative capabilities, they are the capabilities of one who is himself a creature. The world is not mine to do with as I please. I may do much of what I please to do; but what I please to do will not be good—not true and right and lovely—if it is not appropriate to the world that has been given to me.

All this may strike the reader as bordering dangerously on the religious. Yet one need not be at all religiously inclined to agree that none of us has created the world in which we live. The implications of this fact will no doubt be perceived differently by religious people, but the underlying claim is quite similar to the one insisted upon by Richard Rorty, a thoroughly nonreligious philosopher, in his emphasis upon the importance of contingency for the understanding of oneself and one's world (Rorty 1989, 5):

> To say that the world is out there, that it is not our creation, is to say, with common sense, that most things in space and time are the effects of causes which do not include human mental states.

In Conclusion

It seems to me that some of the more extreme claims of environmentalists have at least this virtue, that they call our attention to possibilities foreclosed by our attachment to modes of thought that are proving increasingly inadequate. Even their intolerance will have served us well if it reveals to us our own intolerance. "The duty of tolerance," Alfred North Whitehead once said, "is our finite homage to the abundance of inexhaustible novelty which is awaiting the future, and to the complexity of accomplished fact which exceeds our stretch of insight" (Whitehead 1933, 52).

The comprehensive eloquence of that simple and powerful statement summarizes most of what I want to say in conclusion. The morality of aspiration is both essential to a free society and dangerous to it. It is essential insofar as it generates respect for the rights of others; and I do not see how a democratic society can remain free unless such respect deeply informs the great majority of its members. The morality of aspiration is dangerous, however, when it tempts us to employ coercive measures to establish a Kingdom of Righteousness.

We can recognize injustices; but we can never really know what justice requires. Central economic planning was perhaps the most momentous product of the godlike aspiration in this century. A godlike aspiration—the desire to establish a human regime that would be omniscient, omnipotent, and universally benevolent—was the source of the zeal with which Marxist governments pursued the conceit of a centrally planned economy long after its futility should have been obvious. This aspiration was also the source and justification of all the cruelties perpetrated in the course of that long and tragic pursuit. Ardent environmentalists need to discover and acknowledge that the same limitations which made central economic planning impossible will make it impossible to establish a comprehensive system of central environmental planning.

Some of the intransigence of conservatives in the environmental area stems from the fear that environmentalists are eager to legislate all their aspirations, with utter disregard for the costs that this will impose on others. The morality of aspiration will inevitably run ahead of—and *ought to* run ahead of—the morality of duty. It is legitimate to entertain, nurture, and advocate aspirations for which society is not yet ready, aspirations that cannot be considered duties and should not be legislated because the institutional preconditions for their implementation have not yet evolved. But our aspirations should not induce us to neglect or violate our duties. When we take the *whole* environment seriously, we will acknowledge that our primary moral obligations are to respect the persons, the liberties, and the rights of those among whom we live. After all, these are the people upon whose cooperation we must ultimately rely, whether it is to "make a living," to "save the earth," or to see the realization of any other of our larger aspirations.

References

Bentham, Jeremy. 1948. *An Introduction to the Principles of Morals and Legislation.* New York: Hafner Publishing Company.

Economic Report of the President. 1990. *Annual Report of the Council of Economic Advisors.* Washington, D.C.: U.S. Government Printing Office.

Fuller, Lon L. 1969. *The Morality of Law.* New Haven: Yale University Press.

Hochschild, Jennifer L. 1981. *What's Fair? American Beliefs About Distributive Justice.* Cambridge, Mass.: Harvard University Press.

Kelman, Steven. 1981. Economists and the Environmental Muddle. *The Public Interest* 64 (Summer): 106–23.

Leoni, Bruno. 1991. *Freedom and the Law.* Indianapolis: Liberty Fund.

Leopold, Aldo. 1966. *A Sand County Almanac with Essays on Conservation from Round River.* New York: Ballantine Books, Inc.

Rorty, Richard. 1989. *Contingency, Irony, and Solidarity.* Cambridge: Cambridge University Press.

Smith, Adam. 1982. *The Theory of Moral Sentiments.* Indianapolis: Liberty Fund.

Stone, Christopher D. 1974. *Should Trees Have Standing? Towards Legal Rights for Natural Objects.* Los Altos: William Kaufman.

Whitehead, Alfred North. 1933. *Adventures of Ideas.* New York: The Macmillan Company.

Index

The text of this book was set in Monotype Dante,
a digital version of the hot-metal typeface designed by
master printer Giovanni Mardersteig (1892–1977). Characterized by
its even color and classic proportions, Dante was first used by Mardersteig
in 1955 at his Officina Bodoni press for an edition of Giovanni
Boccaccio's classic, *Trattatello in laude di Dante*
(Little Tractate in Praise of Dante).

Printed on paper that is acid-free and meets the
requirements of the American National Standard for
Permanence of Paper for Printed Library
Materials, z39.48–1992. ∞

Book design by Mark McGarry,
Texas Type & Book Works, Inc.,
Dallas, Texas
Typography by Newgen-Austin
Printed and bound by Worzalla Publishing Company,
Stevens Point, Wisconsin